The

www.practicalmba.ca

ISBN: 9798838463364

Published by Brands Fifth Avenue Inc.
Toronto - New York

THE PRACTICAL M.B.A. ON
ECONOMICS

WHAT THEY DO & DON'T TEACH YOU AT BUSINESS SCHOOL

UNLOCK THE KEY TO...
WEALTH – KNOWLEDGE – INSIGHTS

JOSEPH GULESSERIAN

Acknowledgements

Much goes on behind the scenes when putting together a work like this, it is gratifying, intellectually challenging and exhausting.

I want to thank my editor Brian Baker for his professional editing services, including the documentation of footnotes and invaluable feedback. My wife Nyree, who provided solace and a sanctuary for me to be able to create this economics book, and then worked diligently with feedback and rigorous final editing. I owe her much.

My studious and well-read friend John Piekos, for his encouragement and feedback on excerpts I sent him. Other notable mentions include my friends Phil Summerfield and Loyd Miller for their vibrant intellects. And of course, Gregory Mannarino, the Robin Hood of Wall Street, who taught me much.

My father, who has passed into time but left me much, my mother who is still my cheerleader and has forgiven me for the indiscretions of my youth.

And finally, the many mentors that saw in me what I did not, of which time has taken into its tragic hands, but I carry each day the treasure of the knowledge they left behind.

Contents

Prologue

In a world affected by rapid economic change and the fast-paced business environment it has created, written by an actual front-line participant, The Practical MBA on Economics presents readers with an alternative view of practical economics.

With decades of business experience, Gulesserian bridges the gap between real world economics and that of academia.

Initially, the book lists the types of competitive businesses, putting them in the context of money and income mechanisms. From this list, the author discusses a variety of symptoms, focusing in particular on the root causes of inflation, unemployment, economic recessions and their cures.

A detailed account of economic theory and history including, Adam Smith, Ricardo, Keynes, The Great Depression, Breton Woods and the economic crises and tumultuous events that have marked the last half century.

This all sets the scene for the final three chapters of the book. Here, together with several interesting slants and predictions, the author concludes by describing the pressing economic issues of our time.

With a no holds barred approach, the author then courageously tackles controversial issues, such as modern political thought and the world economic order. Thus, urging the reader to choose between the natural harmonics of Adam Smith's invisible hand or a planned economic dystopia—The Four Seasons versus The Sorcerer's Apprentice, Vivaldi or Dukas? I know who I would choose!

As a revision of standard economic history and theory, this book provides readers with an excellent foundation for the study of practical economics.

Introduction

Originally, I was going to create this MBA series for entrepreneurs, and the initial title was going to be *The MBA for Entrepreneurs*. It then occurred to me that I wanted to cast a wider net and include everyone who has a curiosity about commerce, and in particular, economics.

This book puts the dots together, gives not only a strong foundation, also delves into some advanced topics, insights and perspectives that will help one's career, right up to the C suite, while having a better understanding of how we got here, the world we live in and what might lie ahead.

During the writing of the book, I was torn as to what level I should introduce the academics of the topics and how I could integrate some of my personal experiences without crowding out the objectivity of ideas. I also wanted to reconcile with the breakneck speed at which recent developments and changes are occurring in an unprecedented world economy, where governments and universities can't keep up. People are always looking for answers—how can I provide them in a meaningful way? How can I give readers insightful and useful knowledge in return for the time that they are sacrificing to study this book? How can readers feel more learned, solid, and equipped with intellectually captivating perspectives that they can use in their business, career, and personal lives for financial and intrinsic gain?

My hope is that the readers walk away with new insights, the practical use of new ideas, and a more dexterous and intuitive, and perhaps unorthodox view of our economies, that is not convoluted by the financial mainstream media who rarely get anything correct. I thought about my formal education and tried to reconcile it with my business background and realized that time and business experience had gifted me with an incredible learning curve that I wanted to share. As an entrepreneur, I spent 30 years at the edge of the diving board, with no safety net, looking at the horizon, and then down at sharks in the bottom of the pool waiting for their next meal. These are the two choices I have lived with all my life.

Simply put, it is my goal to make the reader feel full, reconciling with the global economy around us, and the tempestuous yet exciting times we live in during the advent of the dawning of a new Industrial Revolution.

With this in mind, I went through many of my coveted MBA books on economics where I received a classical education from a Scottish university that was deep in academic rigour and immersed in the hands of Adam Smith. After rereading my economics books, many of the concepts were quite abstract, and for sure would lose the reader, but the foundations are timeless, and they just needed to be reconsidered in an understandable way against the backdrop of today's dynamic world economy of easy money and its social ramifications. But still, there were some gaps missing and I needed to find a way of putting the puzzle together.

In my classical education I learned about John Maynard Keynes, but not his life, I learned about Bretton Woods, but not why Nixon took the U.S. dollar off the gold standard. I learned about Adam Smith, but not Richard Cantillon's 19th century works on money supply and inflation. I learned about GATT, WTO, commercial diplomacy, and David Ricardo's compelling case for free trade and comparative advantage, but not how we sold our inflation and imported unemployment from China. I was taught about production, but not why a nation's loss of manufacturing diminishes inventiveness, which is a symptom of a declining power. I was schooled in monetary theory and money expansion, but not versed as to why, since the Romans, fiat money always returns to its intrinsic value, which is zero. When I was getting my MBA, the only cure for fiat money was still a gold backing, but that has now been taken away, as governments can no longer live within their means, and rely on money printing and taxation to addict and then oppress. When I went to school, the world had not yet created a hard digital currency like Bitcoin to separate state from money.

I was taught about recessions, but not the economic policies of FDR that deepened and prolonged the Great Depression. I was not schooled on the difference between CPI inflation and effective (real) inflation. I was schooled about interest rates and inflation, but not their tragic history. No one warned me that the Central Banks, which started out as relatively docile creatures in the early 20th century, would eventually turn into an insatiable monster that would orchestrate economic distortions and become the politico that would create a further wealth divide. In my studies, I was not schooled on why we have never had a natural recovery from an economic downturn since 1921, when Harding was president. No one endowed me with the knowledge in my graduate degree as to why the United States, Canada, and Europe since 2008 are still in the Intensive Care Unit, dependent on easy money like a helpless child. But my brilliant economics professor Keith Lumsden, at a dinner party in Toronto in 2012, warned me about a pending tsunami that is not far off in the horizon. I was educated in expanding and contracting economies, but not schooled in the history of booms, busts, and manias.

Yes, I was educated in stock valuations, but not how Wall Street banks and the Feds were manipulating price discovery, through derivatives and SPACs. I was never schooled on the moral hazard, but somehow knew in the back of my mind that these bailouts are ruining the fruitions of capitalism. I was not taught about the great divide that easy money is exasperating. I was trained in bonds yet did not know that the next economic collapse will come in the bond market that will make 2008 look like Bambi in the woods. When I went to business school, it wasn't apparent that semiconductor chips would be replacing oil as the lubrication of the world economy, while they might be the real barometer of inflation in certain categories. I was educated on the sovereign debt default of Latin American and Asian contagion countries, but no mention was made of a major economy in the West suffering the same catastrophic collapse.

We are at the dawn of yet another Industrial Revolution that includes technologies, such as artificial intelligence (AI), autonomous vehicles, the internet of things, and the metaverse that are merging with humans' physical lives—it is already here with voice-activated assistants, facial ID recognition, digital healthcare sensors, and decentralized finance in the way of Bitcoin. We live in a tenuous, yet most technologically transitionary time that comparatively rivals the time of Edison, Tesla, the Wright brothers, and Henry Ford. There are always victims in the brutality of progress, as was the case of the Luddites during the British Industrial Revolution.

The victim this time is a fragmented attention span, a difficult to explain trance, or hypnotic-like obedience to groupthink, where we are seduced by the riveting technology created, only to be strangled and enslaved by its tentacles, as we gasp at the last vestige of truth. From social media, where our hard drives are reformatted by the day, to all our communication and information technology, we walk like zombies, aimlessly with our phone in hand, out of touch with ourselves, so connected yet so alone, and waste the most precious thing we have: time. Because we need time to discover ourselves and to explore our insatiable human curiosity in an age of unprecedented possibilities, in this miracle called the "human voyage."

A friend of mine, Emmanuel, once said to me, "With all this hip tech clatter around, it has resulted in a youth generation that knows a little about everything, but not a lot about one thing." Regardless of trendy ideas cultishly ingrained into the youth, complements of intellectually unbalanced subjective learning, impressed upon them by their professorial high priests, I posit that there can never be a sustained wealth redistribution without first redistributing knowledge, skills, insights, drive, and discipline. But with knowledge we gain hope, we gain confidence, since knowledge liberates us, because as Oliver Wendell Holmes said, "Man's mind, stretched to a new idea, never goes back to its original dimension," and this is what I humbly propose to the reader. It is this I hope to deliver.

Writing a book can be exciting, because it puts the writer in a meditative state to look at things in a very focused and precise way—all writers, dreamers, poets, artists, scientists, creators, and entrepreneurs live in a bubble until they can produce works with what they hope are worthy for the world to consider.

Economics is a complex matrix that incorporates human

ingenuity, tragedy, industriousness, societal organization, inventiveness, emotion, cooperation, and barbarity—it is a platform to display our innate competitiveness in the fight over scarce resources, rational behaviour, production, and distribution, while coming to understand the denial of the collective beast within.

It is this enigma we study. It is this story I present to you!

Joseph Gulesserian

Employ your time
in improving yourself
by other men's writings,
so that you shall gain
easily what others have
labored hard for.

–*Socrates*

1

Economic Ideas at a Glance

In economics there are two separate areas of study, namely macroeconomics and microeconomics. As the name suggests, macroeconomics addresses the larger picture, which includes the state of the economy, such as unemployment, inflation, taxation, monetary policy, money velocity, GDP, government spending other people's money, better known as fiscal policy, liquidity, the Central Bank, equity and other asset price valuations, money supply, the business cycle, trade inflows and outflows.

Microeconomics, on the other hand, deals with detailed profitability of economic output, productivity, marginal cost of labour integrated with machine fixed costs, quality and quantity of the labour force, the deployment of industrial robots, variable costs and fixed costs integrated into total costs, marginal diminishing returns, and price elasticity. All this is done with a view to determine resource allocation.

Often concepts of microeconomics are misaligned with classical industrial age manufacturing, but this is no longer the case since we can now look at output of productivity in call centres, working on site versus remote, or even output of innovation.

Microeconomics is essential in determining cost behaviour in commerce, and its ethos really is built around profit maximisation, and is intertwined with accounting and finance.

Because of the more complex quantitative nature of microeconomics, which might leave the reader in a matrix of the quantitative abyss, I have not included it in this edition.

It is interesting how as a civilization the things that affect us most, such as our own economic well-being within a state and the state's economic competitiveness within the global paradigm, are the least understood. We go about our daily lives paying little attention to this, even though we are indelibly emersed in this, and by not doing so one will eventually pay a financial price for such apathy.

With intellectual curiosity and energy, which we are all gifted with from our childhood, we together discover the building blocks of both the glory and tragedy economics delivers, so without any further ado, the story begins.

THE ORGANISATION OF INDUSTRIES

The Competitive Environment

Many people either work in or own companies, without perhaps having a formal framework as to the competitive dynamics of their industry. Having this knowledge is imperative to understanding competitive dynamics, of one's firm and career.

There are four types of competitive environments that affect a business. This is important in understanding strategic competition but is especially vital in marketing, as it relates to differentiation and understanding the competitive theatre of different market-places. They are as follows.

Monopoly

This is the most intuitive one to understand, and it lends to conjectures of greedy, villainous participants in the marketplace or lack thereof. In a monopoly environment there are substantial, if not insurmountable, barriers to entry.

Google, which owns YouTube, has a monopoly on search engines and video uploading. This includes control of algorithms and de-platforming peoples' YouTube channels that do not agree with their ideological bent. Another good example is Twitter, which has the monopoly on instant mass communication with a contingency of digital minions in tow. It seems the Web 2.0 has turned into a jury of public opinion, a town hall, if you will, where on occasion, we are all participative digital minions deliberating the events of our times, while in denial of the digital cages we can no longer escape from.

Never in modern free markets have such monopolies driven by political agendas with shifting rules of conduct have been allowed to stay intact.

In the late 19th century and beginning of the 20th century, U.S. Steel was formed by J.P. Morgan, who bought Carnegie Steel, which provided the steel to create skyscraper buildings to help America create its magic moment, and was then combined with Federal Steel and National Steel to form U.S. Steel, which was the more notorious recipient of The Sherman Antitrust Act. This law was passed in 1890 and was designed to break up anticompetitive monopolies across state lines, but allowed natural monopolies to exist. The Sherman Act was employed in 1902 to break up the U.S. Steel, but the government lost the case. However, in 1902 the full weight of the legal remedy fell on John D. Rockefeller and his Standard Oil, which eventually had to break up into Chevron and Exxon.

Neither of these organizations had the might of today's tech giants—try starting up your own video uploading or search engine business and you would be hard pressed to find venture capitalist backing for such a heroic proposition.

This does not mean that monopolies do not create public good, since they often do. For example, consider how Henry Ford reduced the cost of cars, increased wages, created the modern assembly line, put cars in the hands of the working man, single-handedly invented industrial engineering, and created competition against the railroads. Incidentally, Ford was chief engineer of Thomas Edison's Edison Illuminating Company of Detroit from 1893 to 1899.

Or consider when Bill Gates gifted the world with standardized operating system software, resulting in both domestic and global efficiencies of IT, since fragmented operating systems would create a more heterogenous outcome while expending scarce resource on training workers on a host of operating systems. Then let us consider YouTube (censorship not withstanding) and how it changed the fabric of how we get our entertainment, news, commercials, documentaries, explanation videos, music, and how we can now look at our visual history with the click of a mouse or remote control.

Then, if we get creative, intellectually rebellious at the expense of being virulently in contempt, could we not argue a case that government has a monopoly on taxation and oppression? Better still, how do we access the monopolies that the untouchable civil service unions command at the expense of the industrious and the public purse, while diminishing consumer welfare, and not acting in the public good? In fact, this is the case in Canada where 500,000 government employees got raises during the pandemic.[1] This is on top of the of the fact that in April of 2020, most civil servants were sent home and continued to receive their full pay—this is in exchange for votes, of course. Many could be seen having leisurely days on the golf course and elsewhere. In fact, the federal civil service also grew from 300,450 workers in March 2020 to 319,690 workers in March 2021. In the private sector in Canada in February 2020, before the pandemic hit, there were 19.1 million Canadians working, and the unemployment rate stood at 5.6 percent. By May 2020, the number of people working had dropped to 16.4 million and the unemployment rate stood at a pandemic high of 13.7 percent. The mantra during the pandemic was "we are all in this together", which certainly was not the case for the civil service.

Not to be outdone, the mostly idle Canadian members of Parliament and senators who often cowered during the virus have seen their pay increase by $6,900 over two pay bumps, while Prime Minister Justin Trudeau has seen an increase of $13,800. Do they reduce consumer and public choice with marginally diminishing returns on taxation? In many respects, Google, Facebook, Twitter, and other noted members of the Silicon Valley Cartel are a monopoly, but they also act as a public utility, meaning there are trade-offs from the necessity of having such bedfellows.

---

1   Brian Lilley, "As Many Lost Jobs and Hours, Government Workers Got Raises," Toronto Sun, January 24, 2022, https://torontosun.com/opinion/columnists/lilley-as-many-lost-jobs-and-hours-government-workers-got-raises

Perfect Competition

I was about to bring out graphs going over marginal cost meeting average total cost, but that would be academic gibberish, and would not help you in your true goal after reading this book, which is to take over the world and make it in your own image. The important thing to remember about an industry in perfect competition is that there are, for practical purposes, little or no barriers to entry. Building on this, perfect competition is when the marketplace decides that there is no room for differentiation for your service or product, and the only factor within the determination of purchase is price, since in the eyes of the marketplace may it be consumer or B2B, all offerings are considered homogenous (the same). Another prerequisite of perfect competition is that moving in and out of the industry has little friction costs. What is also important to consider in this type of industry organisation is that having equity in a brand name is nearly impossible for practical purposes, since there is no room for differentiation of product or service, as only price is the determinant of purchase. In many ways perfect competition is often referred to as hyper-competition. Here are a couple of examples that might bring this to light.

> 1. An importer of plastic caps for water or shampoo bottles can bring the product from an Asian manufacturer, where, assuming the product meets quality requirements, all other plastic caps made in the region can be perceived the same. Subsequently, the importer can only compete on price, since other importers are willing to sell near cost, resulting in hyper-corroded margins.

> 2. A circuit board or battery importer for computers where, let's say, 15 different importers bring in computer parts from the same recognized aftermarket manufacturer that costs less than an original equipment manufacturer (OEM) part. Again, price is the only battleground to settle accounts of this blood sport and, if competition becomes

unbearable, one could import different parts to gain temporary advantage.

Building on the prior examples, desktop IBM PC clones were in this category, meaning if you saw one PC clone you saw them all—that is until solid state drives (SSDs) were introduced. What many small companies did in the past was buy local computer parts from importers who stocked parts. This was certainly the case when I worked in L.A., and entrepreneurs would assemble and sell desktop computers on a made-to-order basis. Distributors of parts were careful, as to levels of inventory, since prices could suddenly drop overnight due to gluts in supply or a new generation of chips or circuit boards coming out, because parts themselves were in perfect competition. It was a cat and mouse game where one did not want to get caught holding the bag, since $500,000 in parts inventory could lose 50 percent of its value overnight, based on obsolescence and drops in price if the technology leapfrogged.

Eventually, international participants such as Dell, Lenovo, and the likes flexed their economies of scope and scale to drive out small players by pricing below the cost structure of smaller players. Hence, large competitors built brand equity, which included service, tech support, and warranty, which shifted the desktop industry into an oligopoly category. This, of course, drove out all the small players.

A final example of perfect competition is possibly having your imported wares sold at Dollar Tree. If you sell a wooden spoon at $0.53 to retail at $1, your competitor might come in at $0.50 to give the retailer a higher margin for essentially the same goods, and then you might lower your price to $0.47, and so on, until you or your competitor reach your cost of goods.

When your brand or service comes under immense price competition, you will probably colloquially refer to it as being in a commodity business, or interchangeably you will come across the term "cutthroat competition". Thus, at a visceral level, you have defined the practical meaning of perfect competition.

Monopolistic Competition

Monopolistic competition is when many market actors use a combination of price and differentiation in the marketplace. In this theatre, price is not the only determinant of the marketplace, since the entrant can command a premium and there are opportunities for perceived or real differentiation. In a monopolistic environment you can have few or many competitors, and the customer sees the service or product as heterogenous, which allows a better opportunity to build brand equity. Another characteristic is that there are barriers to entry that may be a combination of stand-alone or technological brand preference and financial barriers to entry, and competitors cannot enter or exit businesses without financial repercussions. Other attributes of monopolistic competition are both economies of scope and scale. For those not familiar with economies of scope it means using common parts for different finished goods, which was historically developed in the auto industry, where Buick and Chevrolet would use common parts. This was later adopted by other industries from smart phones to laptops.

Some good examples are the fashion industry, where clothing and shoes are not perceived to be all the same. Simply put, a designer labels holds weight in the eyes of both the channel and consumer.

As a side note, a marketing person needs to have a deep understanding of the ritual as to why and how women buy shoes to understand the intrinsic motivation and reward system of the female psyche and incorporate it into their own brand in so many categories from cosmetics to shoes, to fashion. Unfortunately, only the bravest of males will ever explore this opportunity to understand the female consumer!

In the monopolistic environment, there may be substitutes but not exact substitutes, and the clever person who understands this plays on emotions. Some real-world examples include: Is a phone case just a phone case, and do you want one to match your attire?

Is a laptop just a laptop? Is a silverware set just a silverware set? Is a suit just a suit, or is it worth paying more for Armani, and how do you monetize how it makes you look and feel? Is wine, wine? Is a book a book? Are all shaving creams the same? Can your no-name shaving cream give you the nostalgic moment of Barbasol in that time when you watched your dad use it while he was still in the world? By using your father's shave cream brand, are you still holding the connection to your dad, and is this the reason you subconsciously buy this brand? Are all homes perceived as the same, or do location, build, quality, and features matter? Are all shampoos the same? Are all Amazon stores the same?

You can now see why you would want to ensure your firm is in a monopolistic competitive environment, where differentiation is financially rewarded, and you can build brands and associated profit sanctuaries, that is until the imitation or emotional got-to-have-it gap is closed by competitors, which could then push you into Perfect Competition, and you would then have to perpetually innovate and leapfrog so that you do not get stuck in a commodity business.

Oligopoly

Barriers to entry in an oligopoly environment are substantial, making it cost prohibitive due to economic outlay, products can be perceived to be unique, the number of competitors is few, competitors are large with substantial economies of scale and scope as a prerequisite to be in this marketplace. Good examples would include oil companies, the auto industry, cell phone manufacturers such as Apple and Samsung, as well as Netflix. Some would argue that Netflix is a monopoly because of its dominant market position, but it does have competitors such as Amazon Prime, YouTube Premium, Crave and Apple TV. One could argue that Google, Facebook, Twitter, and Amazon fall in the category of oligopoly because they have competitors like Rumble, BitChute, Parlor, Vimeo, and other alt-tech sites.

The Semiconductor Industry

A classic example of an oligopoly in physical product categories are computer processing chips, which require enormous outlay of $25 billion plus to open a new plant, cutting-edge engineering, and manufacturing processes, with a highly trained team. All this leads to substantial barriers to entry.

Once upon a time Intel could command premium prices over AMD, since they used to run cooler semiconductor chips. However, this is no longer the case, since Apple has switched suppliers, from Intel to contract manufacturer Taiwan Semiconductor Manufacturing Company because Intel has lagged technologically behind the competition as a result of investing in stock buybacks rather than investing in cutting-edge plants and processes. This led to Taiwan Semiconductor becoming the go-to supplier for many technology companies. Under the moral hazard dilemma, which rewards bad actors for cavalier behaviour, the U.S. government has given Intel grants as part of its strategic industry initiative to ensure they remain the market leader and reclaim their technological edge.

There are other substantial players including Micron Technology, Texas Instruments, Samsung, and Nvidia Corp. At the time of this writing there are substantial shortages and competition over chips that will be discussed in Chapter 5 and Chapter 16. For a firm to thrive in the semiconductor industry, they must leapfrog over each other through technology, economies of scale, advanced engineering and production efficiencies, with the endgame being that competitors vie to get a premium on their brand of chips.

Eventually, when all chip makers have a zero-sum technology advantage, where there are no perceived technological advantages, the industry goes into perfect competition within an oligopoly setting—that is until the next generation debuts, which results in a temporary premium by technologically leapfrogging on a temporary basis, and then slips back into perfect competition. This will occur unless one company can bring down long-term average costs through higher volume, and put competitors out of business through price, as is the case with Taiwan Semiconductor.

Another industry that is in oligopoly are internet service providers (ISP), who, unlike the early days of the internet in the 1990s, need massive economies of scale and tech support as there are substantial barriers to entry for an ISP. For example, you need quite a large technological infrastructure to provide high-speed internet to homes and businesses. You also have to consider the outlay in capital for equipment as well as tech support, then of course to build and maintain market share, you would need a substantial promotional budget.

Today's industry giants Verizon, Xfinity, AT&T, and other big players bundle ISP services with wireless, television, and landlines, often with two to three year contracts. These contracts create switching costs between competitors, encouraging people to stay with them. Small competitors are also not able to offer the emerging 5G technologies in wireless. When added all together, a small entrant does not have the economies of scale or the offerings of scope to make a feasible business.

In summary, both the semiconductor and ISP businesses are in oligopoly competition because they have few competitors, substantial barriers to entries in terms of capital, technological, and human resources outlay, while at the same time they can differentiate through branding. However, within the oligopoly setting, there is off and on perfect competition as competitors try and leapfrog each other through broader offering and technological advances.

Money is not an invention of the state. It is not the product of a legislative act. Even the sanction of political authority is not necessary for its existence. Certain commodities came to be money quite naturally, as the result of economic relationships that were independent of the power of the state.[1]

–*Carl Menger*

Monetary Theory and The Central Bank

Central banks have a checkered record of prescribing the correct prescription. This was evidenced in the Great Depression when they mistook deflation for inflation. Once divorced from a hard money standard, it had carte blanche to print money without accountability, as was the case in 2008. The question becomes, who owns the money? How is it created? Who has the moral right to create it, and what is it really backed by?

We are inundated with the term "monetary policy" in the news, and to make it simple, we could just say that monetary policy in the U.S. involves the setting of interest rates by the Federal Reserve System (the Fed) and be done with it. However, interest rates have more complicated ramifications, since they can lead to creating too much or too little oxygen for the economy, and a sudden increase or decrease in interest rates can acutely affect asset prices including stocks, bonds, and the housing market. There are other major Central Banks including the European Central Bank (ECB), the Bank of England, the Chinese Central Bank, the Bank of Japan, the Bank of Canada, all of which might differ from U.S. monetary policy (although this is not necessarily the case) by increasing or lowering their interest rates depending on how their economies are doing.

The second function of monetary policy is the money supply. Today we see ourselves in this position, because since the Great Recession of 2008, the patient has never left the ICU, and we are addicted to the contradictions of easy money passing off as a recovery.

It is here where our story begins.

Central banks have monetary tools at their disposal that can expand the money supply by purchasing debt that the market will not necessarily buy in the way of bonds, with the outcome of creating liquidity. This was referred to in 2009 as "quantitative easing," which is an opaque term for printing money out of thin air to lend and create liquidity, while exacerbating higher government sovereign debt—meaning this is how governments for the most part finance deficits. Since the Great Depression, Keynesianism (more on

1   Carl Menger, "On the Origin of Money," *The Economic Journal* 2, No. 6 (June 1892): 239-255.

John Maynard Keynes in Chapter 4) has convinced governments, specifically the U.S., Europe, and other parts of the West, that market downturns can be softened by inoculating us from the natural behaviour of the business cycle, by creating fiscal stimulus to soften economic troughs, though this has had mixed results.

However, just like a racy Instagram rumour about a celebrity, there is more to the story. There is a wide array of empirical evidence to show that government usually causes, prolongs and deepens the pain of an economic downturn, while allowing underlying structural issues, namely low monetary policy that creates perpetual structural competitive distortions such as asset price bubbles to continue unabated, leaving behind oceans of unsustainable sovereign debt. The end result is that the stage has been set to bring about even a bigger market collapse into the future.

But before we discuss this further, let me endeavour a primer as to how the component of the monetary system works.

Understanding What Money Is

Money has three purposes: 1) a store of value, 2) a unit of account, and 3) a medium of exchange. There are various mediums of money, from coins, gold bullion, paper currency, bank deposits, which are not legal tender, and now cryptocurrency is entering this space with a narrative as a store of value, divorced from the state.

Historically, gold coins and bullion have been the most acceptable exchange of value, especially in times of economic turmoil. The gold exchange standard was used from 1948 until 1971, when President Nixon took the U.S. dollar off the gold-backed Bretton Woods system, meaning the U.S. dollar went from hard backing of gold (where a fixed amount of gold equalling the amount of cash in circulation was stored in the U.S.) into a fiat money backed by only trust. This allowed the Central Banks to print money out of thin air, ballooning government debt as they lent to the U.S. Treasury with no real chance of getting paid back, except through a Ponzi scheme of rotating bond debt—the Treasury issues new bonds to pay for the maturity of the old ones. Why? Because the government has not taken the fiduciary duty of putting money aside to pay for the maturing debt.

Goldsmiths and Private Money

In 17th century England, modern banking was ushered in via goldsmiths—they were the first bankers that acted as safekeeping houses for gold for merchants who deposited their gold with them. Goldsmiths issued receipts (private bank notes) to the merchants that used these notes to show that they could settle their debts with gold. In practice, these gold certificates were used by merchants to make purchases and could be redeemed for physical gold if presented to the goldsmiths. Gold certificates were more convenient than carrying gold. This can be defined as hard money backing, meaning that the certificates were backed by gold and not merely trust—at least for a while.

The goldsmiths essentially evolved to be private bankers to the wealthy. In practice their notes issued to commercial businesses and the likes were being exchanged as a means of payment, while the gold coins and plates still remained in their vaults. This created a profit opportunity for goldsmiths and by the late 17th century, they were issuing more notes than the gold they had in their vaults, leading the goldsmiths to be pioneers in money creation, as well as lenders on money they simply did not have in the way of hard backing. In essence, goldsmiths were issuing gold certificates as a form of private money, away from state, for commercial exchange settlements in trade. Separately, the state money included the pound sterling, which was a unit of currency as early as 775 AD in Anglo-Saxon England, and the name derived from the Roman era in England, which meant weight. Today, the pound is the oldest fiat money in existence. In 1690 Dr. Nicholas Barbon, an English economist, physician, and financial speculator, explained the creation of goldsmiths' money in his work *A Discourse of Trade*.

The banknote in the 17th century was not the same as money created by a government's printing press. The private money developed by goldsmiths was in its time much like the private currency we see today of cryptocurrency, namely Bitcoin.

Eventually, as business dynamics grew, a more complex banking system developed where bankers started issuing gold backed notes into the economy—firms and consumers used these gold-backed bank notes as both a medium of exchange and unit of account, and it was this dynamic that helped create a more modern monetary system. In fact, Article I, Section 10 of the U.S. Constitution states that only gold and silver are considered legal tender to settle debts. America's founding fathers were men educated in philosophy and government dating back to the Greeks, the Romantics, and John Locke, all of which was incorporated into the U.S. Constitution. They also knew the history of all fiat currencies, which eventually revert to their intrinsic value, which is zero. Our modern monetary system is discussed in Chapter 7.

Eventually, the system evolved so that banks no longer had enough gold to back their notes and they relied on confidence and the promise of liquidity. Hence, the fractional banking environment was born that we have today.

A First Look at Bitcoin

Bitcoin does not have uncapped fiat printing ability and is based on blockchain technology. It has about 18.7 million units in circulation as of mid-2021, with a market cap of over $1 trillion, and a maximum of 21 million units that can be created through Bitcoin miners via the blockchain.

Opponents of Bitcoin say it is nothing more than the medium of exchange for drug dealers, terrorists, and tax evaders. However, this is a weak argument given that by 2020 only a miniscule amount of Bitcoin transactions accounts for this, as the technology is transparent through the blockchain. Further, they are concerned because Bitcoin is private money and cannot be confiscated by government, also, it has scarcity value with a limit of 21 million coins, unlike the U.S. dollar that can be infinitely printed, causing currency debasement. Treasury Secretary Janet Yellen has made exaggerated claims that Bitcoin is used for illicit activities, but this does not coincide with the evidence. *Forbes* states that the majority of cryptocurrencies are not used for criminal activity.[2] Relying on an excerpt from Chainalysis 2021 report, in 2019, criminal activity represented 2.1 percent of all cryptocurrency transaction volume (roughly $21.4 billion worth of transfers). In 2020, the criminal share of all cryptocurrency activity fell to just 0.34 percent ($10.0 billion in transaction volume). With a transparent blockchain, criminals would be ill-advised to use crypto currencies, unless your significant other is willing to talk to you through plexiglass as you appear dressed in orange attire.

However, it is estimated that up to $2 trillion is laundered through financial systems every year, according to a report by Deloitte[3] and the U.S. Treasury estimates that $300 billion a year of drug cartel money is laundered yearly.[4] A silent but tolerated example is laundered money that enters the Canadian real estate market with the result being distorted home prices in Toronto and Vancouver. The U.S. dollar, which is the preferred "store of value" for drug dealers in $100 denominations, substantially helps the U.S. dollar maintain its reserve currency status. Janet Yellen's true agenda is perhaps her concern that Bitcoin is a competitor at some level to the U.S. dollar as a store of value that is out of the reach of the government. And the government historically points at perceived villains in order to leverage their true agenda, which is control.

But the key message of Bitcoin is uncontestable: it separates state from money, is decentralized as part of the Web3, rebels against government issued fiat money, at least as a store of value, and is

2   Hailey Lennon, "The False Narrative of Bitcoin's Role in Illicit Activity," *Forbes*, January 19, 2021, https://www.forbes.com/sites/haileylennon/2021/01/19/the-false-narrative-of-bitcoins-role-in-illicit-activity/?sh=31ab059e3432
3   "Anti-Money Laundering Preparedness Survey Report 2020," Deloitte, https://www2.deloitte.com/content/dam/Deloitte/in/Documents/finance/Forensic/in-forensic-AML-Survey-report-2020-noexp.pdf
4   "The 2021 Crypto Crime Report," Chainalysis, February 16, 2021, https://go.chainalysis.com/rs/503-FAP-074/images/Chainalysis-Crypto-Crime-2021.pdf

gaining traction as a medium of exchange. In addition, it protects against currency inflation in the long run and eliminates the need for banks. Bitcoin has a future and is followed by the price quotes on Yahoo Finance—how it will manifest itself is the only remaining unknown. At this time no Bitcoin ETFs exists in the U.S., but they can buy in through Greyscale on the OTC market, but it often trades below NAV (meaning below its underlying asset). However, in Canada you can buy Bitcoin ETFs via Purpose Investments and 3IQ on the TSE, and it should be noted that both these ETFs hold the underlying asset of Bitcoin and Ethereum that perfectly follow the price of these two cryptos, meaning you are not buying paper derivatives.

We return to a robust deep dive of Bitcoin in Chapter 16.

Fractional Banking: Strategies on How Banks Create Money

One way to get a feel for fractional banking is to consider the following scenario. Let us say that during uncertain economic times, such as during the 2020 COVID-19 pandemic, you go buy gold paper certificates from your local Bank of America or Bank of Nova Scotia as a measure of security. But there is a problem: gold certificates are not backed by physical gold within the banks' vaults. On the contrary, gold certificates are issued by banks based on perceived confidence of the bank and the banking system, so in essence, the consumer is buying paper that is not backed by physical gold, and the bank might only have 10 percent physical gold backing.

Paper gold is unquestionably a mirage of confidence—a folly if you will—in the event of a real meltdown. Hence, in a real meltdown, where fiat money collapsed and the butcher said he will not accept government issued currency, or at least wanted $5 million for a slice of steak (don't laugh, this happened in the Weimer Republic in the 1920s and 30s), but wanted to be paid in gold, and people went to exchange their gold certificates for physical gold, it would result in a run on the gold reserves of the bank. Imagine that you ran a company and sold promissory notes of inventory you do not have in your warehouse to customers, and took money upfront based on a promissory note—I believe this is called fraud!

The total physical gold in the world has a value of about $10 trillion. However, the total paper derivatives market that are traded on Wall Street, the London Stock Exchange and the likes is estimated to be 200 to 250 times the size of physical gold reserves. This means that for every ounce of gold in reserve, there is 250 times the amount of speculative paper being traded. Most analysts in this space believe that J.P. Morgan continues to manipulate the gold market by artificially keeping prices low. In fact, in 2020, J.P. Morgan agreed to a $920 million fine for spoofing the futures market by artificially keeping the price down. (You will not get this information from the mainstream media, but you will on Kitco News or Max Keiser Report, which can be found on YouTube).

Spoofing and derivatives need some explanation here for those who are not familiar with the terms. It entails bad actors, who are known as "spoofers", through algorithmic methods, put in fake orders to sell gold contracts (shorting them) to create fake interest in trading futures, stocks, and other products in financial markets, resulting in an illusion of false demand and supply of the traded assets. The goal of spoofing is to move market prices in a way that financially benefits the trader's pre-existing positions in the market. Hence, if you had short positions on gold, meaning you had bets on gold prices dropping, you would create fake type of "sell" spoofing orders to artificially weaken demand with no intention of executing the orders. The result being that if this causes gold to drop 3 percent, you make a tidy $15 million off your leveraged $500 million position as a Wall Street heavy hitter. If J.P. Morgan, one of the Wall Street super banks did this with $10 billion of gold paper, the same position at 3 percent shift in manipulating gold prices would result in $300 million of profit. When caught, bankers don't go to jail, they pay fines, unlike purse-snatchers that are treated more like real villains.

For those not familiar with derivatives or futures, for the time being, the best explanation is that you can literally purchase

$50,000 dollars of gold, currencies, oil, sliver, equity indexes, commodities, agriculture and the likes, while controlling them with only a 3 percent down payment. The two basic types of derivative vehicles are futures and options, both of which are highly leveraged instruments where huge profits and losses can occur within hours. Don't worry if you aren't familiar with derivatives—it feels a bit overwhelming at first, but you will eventually gain comfort and be liberated with newfound knowledge.

Some MBA graduates might not have a working knowledge of financial derivative instruments unless they are traders. In my case, when I was studying derivatives, I had to ask my professional options trader friend for help but was familiar with it since I used to trade options and futures on the Swiss currency.

The Fractional Banking Multiplier

By regulation, banks hold back about 10 percent of deposits (some as low as 5 percent) in reserves, for immediate liquidity purpose, so if you deposit $100 in your bank account, $10 is held in cash to meet the mandated reserve requirements.

As a side note, as of March 2020, the Federal Reserve requirement was set at 0 percent, because of the COVID-19 pandemic, to help create supposed liquidity, but then this would put banks in a precarious position of suffering from lack of liquidity in a crunch. Then, without adequate reserves, one would naturally ask the question: How would banks fare on a stress test?

It is safe to say that reserve cash is a liability for the banks, since they cannot receive interest on stagnant cash that cannot be deployed. So, in our example, a bank we have named Hope & Change Bank, where at least you get change for your hope, we demonstrate how the 1:10 ratio of cash reserve multiplier works. The answer is brought to light with the fractional banking multiplier effect from deposit creation.

Consider a deposit by Walmart Jack who had $1,000 left over after paying for junk food, beer, cable, an internet subscription, one ounce of cannabis to help self-flagellate his mind under the guise of freedom, and an abundant supply of low-cost goods from Dollar General and Walmart. Of course, many of these products are made in China, the country that helped the West tame inflation, since Clinton naïvely allowed them to join the WTO that for over 20 years increased our standard of living as a result. Unfortunately for Walmart Jack, this came at a cost of hollowing out both his job as well as the North American manufacturing base that has acted as a catalyst for unmatched knowhow, and Western inventiveness, which has shaped and built the world we live in since the British industrial revolution and the Renaissance. Incidentally, economic historians considered the loss of manufacturing the key driver of the fall of the British Empire.

Getting back to Metropolis and fractional banking money multiplier, you will find below the big $1,000 deposit and its multiplier effect that Walmart Jack has made to save for a rainy day. This is how it looks on the banks balance sheets:

Asset		Liabilities	
Cash	$1,000.00	Deposit Reserves Available to lend	$1,000.00 $(100.00) **$900.00**

At this point, under the 10 percent reserve banking rules, the bank could only lend $900, since $100 is held back in reserves to keep within their 1:10 ratio rules. So, Hope & Change Bank now has a balance of $900 to lend out, which it lends out to Jane, who in turn gives the money as a retainer for her divorce attorney. The attorney in turn deposits the money in a bank called Easy Money Bank, and now Easy Money Bank has a $900 deposit, with a 10 percent holdback, and it in return lends out $810 to Johnny Rocket's mother to buy him more video games to further fry his brain cells in the precarious virtual world of video games, where the line between reality and virtual becomes razor thin. What we see now is that the original $1,000 deposit from Walmart Jack has created an extra $1,710 of money creation after two tiers.

In essence, the $1,000 deposit based on a 10 percent reserve will in theory create $10,000 in new fractional banking money. The formula is available online. Also, see footnote for an excellent instructional short video.[5]

How Banks Create Money

Most people have a misguided belief that banks lend money against deposits—after all, how can one lend money they don't have? But this is only part of the story, because the Ponzi scheme gets more interesting as banks increase assets and liabilities, and in practical terms, allowing it to create money they do not have by expanding their balance sheets. Then they leverage these assets created from thin air to create profits through interest earned on lending. Consider that you went to get a mortgage for $1 million on your overpriced home in the Toronto region that was inflated to $2 million due to a combination of insidious factors that include unsustainable low interest rates that distort asset prices, money launderers, dreamers, and speculators.

After the bank has done its due diligence on you that may resemble a senate investigations committee hearing, let's say, it lends you $1,000,000 at 3 percent interest. To keep it simple, the bank will create a journal entry under Accounts Receivable as an Asset and offset this with a Liability for the same amount. Then the interest it makes on the lifetime of the loan augments the bank's profitability and this get backed into an increase in Owners Equity and Assets.

---

5   Jacob Clifford has an excellent four-minute video on fractional banking, which is quite humorous and makes it simple: "How Banks Create Money—Macro Topic 4.4," YouTube, https://www.youtube.com/watch?v=JG5c8nhR3LE

As you make your mortgage payments, the bank's accounts receivable and liability comes down simultaneously, while the interest charged goes into profitability section of their income statement, which in return increases their retained earnings on their balance sheet.

The journal entry for practical purposes looks like this.

How Mortgages are Created from Thin Air

Bank Mortgage Asset		Bank Mortgage Liability	
Mortgage Receivable	$1,000,000	Money Creation Payable	$1,000,000

In time, this loan will be reduced in five years, let's say, to $800,000, hence, concomitantly reducing both the Asset and Liability side of the Balance Sheets to the same amount, while making interest of $140,000 in the same period that increases profitability, which increase their Assets and Equity. Banks love lending on hard assets like real estate, while conveniently joining government in the mantra call of home ownership dream. And just in case real estate goes for a belly flop, the Canadian banks' residential mortgage portfolio is insured by the CMHC, and in the case of the United States, Fannie May, Freddie Mac, and the Central Bank creates a back stop through the purchase of mortgage-backed securities.

In essence, what the bank has done is create money out of thin air by a journal entry, leveraged an asset that was conceived out of fictitious pretenses, and then lent it out for interest, which allows them to increase their mortgage book business and money supply. Basically, when you sign your documents for your mortgage, it is really a promissory note to the bank—the bank then uses this promissory note to create a deposit into your account. To make it more solid, the bank will ask you for a personal guarantee on the promissory note as well as a hold your home as collateral. At the same time, if the bank goes insolvent you do not get a personal guarantee on your deposit from bank directors, and in essence, you are an unsecured creditor.

In the spring of 2020, George Floyd attempted to increase his own money supply by handing out a counterfeit $20 bill. What gets lost is that he was merely imitating the bank by creating money out of thin air, resulting in the police being called to defend the U.S. dollar. The outcome was that a sovereign money creator, namely Mr. George Floyd, who was merely acting as a banker of sorts, was met with an overwhelming rogue police officer, Derek Chauvin, who is now in jail for defending the money supply system. The oxymoron is that Fed Chair Jerome Powell and the congress get applauded for printing their own fiat money to give away in exchange for votes, and inflating asset prices for Wall Street. The moral of this story is this: if you wish to print money in your basement and do an imitation of the fractional banking system or the Fed, consider that men with guns will show up to defend the U.S. dollar.

We now see how the fractional banking system works, of course at a much larger scale, in the real world, fractional banking is in the trillions of dollars and much more complex than presented, especially when we look at overnight repos, LIBOR swaps, and exotic derivatives. At the same time, we must note that the manufacturing of a bank deposit to issue a loan is not legal tender. After taking a look at fractional banking, one might ponder that a bank run is a very real possibility, especially during an exogenous shock on the economy, as we saw during the COVID-19 pandemic, because, if interest rates go to zero, or even negative, which is the case in Europe and Japan, it could easily create a run on banks. Why? Because why would you keep money in a bank that charges you interest? I trust you now have an appreciation of the delicate nature of our banking sector.[6]

6   If you still feel a little bewildered by all of this, there are excellent two- to seven-minute videos on YouTube—just do a search under "How banks create deposits from thin air" or "Fractional Reserve Banking Explained—Fraud Becomes Legal."

Since we are on the subject about manufacturing deposits out of thin air, it brings us to the subject of our next villain or savour, depending on whether you are on the receiving end of their kiss or slap. So, without further ado, I introduce to you the facilitator of asset bubbles, and price discovery distortions—namely the Fed.

A Brief History of Central Banks

When we understand the incremental influence Central Banks have been able to acquire in the economy, we see with more clarity the present. In the case of the United States just after World War I, and much longer in the case of Europe, we gradually see a story of the decline of the free markets, as Central Banks and government fiscal stimulus now have carte blanche in interfering and distorting the natural market mechanisms and fanning the flames of an economic downturn. Central banks often prescribe the wrong medicine in terms of monetary policy, as we start seeing during the Great Depression in Chapter 8. The history of Central Banks gives us clarity of the political economy as our story unfolds.

Central Banks have been positioned in history as the lender of last resort, and unfortunately, with so much fiat money in the system, the Central Banks must keep the printing going, since without a weekly fix of endorphins (money printing), the patient (the economy) would die. When we look at economic history, even France's treasurer under Napoleon, Nicolas François, Count Mollien, was opposed to bailing out industries, and would much rather take the position of letting the natural mechanisms of the free market rinse out economic distortions, such as weak and unsustainable players in the marketplace, so new ones that could create growth and emerge.

Mollien's position went against the tragic current reality of the treasury being stuck with the bailout bill, meaning the public purse. On the other hand, Napoleon wanted to save failing manufacturers as a vehicle to save French jobs. This might sound familiar. To put it less eloquently, the taxpayer will be saddled with debt to create artificial, unsustainable jobs, and firms that will eventually disappear—all of which are diametrically opposed to the tenets of a real free marketplace, which would not tolerate such unnatural distortions in supply, demand, consumer choice, and distorted price formation, all of which hurt the consumer.

Pivoting to the UK, the lender of last resort in the 18th century was already established in what we now know as the Bank of England. There were many British intellectuals at the time who were opposed to increasing the money supply in times of economic contraction (aka recessions), which is a natural outcome of free market mechanisms. Eventually, by the early 1800s, the Bank of England had become the lender of last resort, especially after the publication of Walter Bagehot's influential 1873 book *Lombard Street: A Description of the Money Market*. It was at this time that Central Banks in the UK gained intellectual credibility with theorists. Economic intellects during this period had trepidations about an institute that could simply print the British pound, which was essentially the world reserve currency at the time, backed up by the British Royal Navy, of course. History is steeped with lessons, as we can see from Bagehot's 1848 article "The Currency Monopoly:"

> *It is a great defect of a purely metallic circulation that the quantity of it cannot be readily suited to any sudden demand…. Now as paper money can be supplied in unlimited quantities, however sudden demand may be, it does not appear to us that there is any objection on principle to sudden issues of paper money to meet sudden and large extensions of demand…. [T]his power of issuing notes is one excessively liable to abuse…. It should only be used…in rare and exceptional cases. [emphasis added]*[7]

As we see, some British intellects of the time had vision and seemed to believe in the tenets of good fiduciary governance.

---

7   Walter Bagehot, *The Life and Works of Walter Bagehot*, Volume 8, ed. Emilie Barrington (London: Longmans, Green, and Co., 1915), 182-183.

The Original Role of the United States Fed

The Federal Reserve System (the Fed), a system of 12 regional Federal Reserve Banks, for practical purposes, was formed in the United States in 1913, although they existed in various forms on again and off again in the 1800s. Its premise of existing originally was to create a common currency that would be accepted from coast to coast. Prior to 1913, individual banks issued bank notes after one deposited gold in the bank's vaults, and these notes acted as a currency of sorts, which were usually honoured in local states. This was based on the goldsmith system of classical England.

At the time, only certain banks would cooperate in honouring each other's bank notes, based on trust and fiduciary arrangements. Subsequently, state banks issued their own currency or bank notes that one could use to purchase goods. However, the drawback was that if one travelled across the country to California, a local state bank might not honour an East coast bank note. Hence, the Fed's original mandate was to issue a common national currency that was accepted across the United States, as opposed to regional heterogenous currencies or bank notes that did not have national acceptance.

To resolve this, the Central Bank was formed, where banks would deposit some of their assets with the Federal Reserve Bank, and in turn, it would issue its own notes to individual banks. This is how the U.S. dollar was born as we know it today, and admittedly it served a needed purpose, which was to have a common national currency, backed by gold and or silver in accordance with the U.S. Constitution, which states that gold and silver are the only legal tender.

At the time, the Fed was only allowed to increase the money supply if it had enough gold and commercial paper to support it. Subsequently, as the economy expanded, the Fed would increase the money supply with a hard currency—the U.S. dollar—to facilitate commerce, and when the economy contracted, it could reduce or increase the money supply. This was referred to as "elastic money supply," meaning it could not print money without hard assets backing it.

This all changed, as we shall soon see, but to go there, we must first look at monetary policy.

How Monetary Policy Works: Expanding the Money Supply

The classical role of a Central Bank is to control the banks in such a way as to regulate the monetary policy of the economy. Simply put, monetary policy is the implementation of interest rates, but there are other mechanisms to consider. If interest rates are set low to help expand the economy, assuming there is little inflation, the Central Bank will purchase government bonds and print money against these bonds—in the case of the U.S. Fed, it will produce a deposit into the U.S. Treasury. This is called increasing the money supply, which is concomitant with reducing interest rates, thus, in a classical sense, the economy will expand using monetary stimulus since interest rates are lower for both firms and consumers. With lower interest rates, the cost of borrowing is reduced for both firms and consumers (excluding credit cards that seem to always hover around 24 percent). Consequently, with the cost of borrowing coming down, firms show higher profits for a host of reasons, but mainly because the lower cost of borrowing increases their profits, and this is built into the valuation of equities (stocks). Subsequently, in theory anyway, monetary stimuli foster consumer purchases on big-ticket items, assuming that we are near full employment and consumer confidence is strengthening.

Increasing the money supply has trade-offs in the way of inflation that first started to officially show in the first quarter of 2021, in the 4.1 percent (CPI) range as of February 2022 surpassed 8 percent, but effectively closer to 14 percent, which is well above their 2 percent annual target set by the Fed's CPI index.[8] With too much money chasing too few goods, we are seeing the supply nightmares caused by the Fed and government, which is discussed in

---

8   "Alternate Inflation Charts," Shadow Government Statistics, accessed March 27, 2022, http://www.shadowstats.com/alternate_data/inflation-charts

some detail in Chapter 5. However, when discussing the money supply, the Fed and economists look at two practical measurements, namely:

1. M1 money supply: Often referred to as "narrow money," meaning coins, notes, bank demand deposits, currency, and other forms of current assets that can easily be converted to cash.
2. M2 Money supply: Includes M1 + savings deposits + money market funds + certificates of deposit + other time deposits.

In practice, the U.S. Treasury, which is the government and not to be confused with the Fed, raises money from issuing bonds, and when they mature, they have to be paid back to the holder, which is increasingly the Fed. The Treasury depends on the Fed, because on its own, the U.S. Treasury would not be able to raise enough capital from bond purchasers in the open market. In his book *The Real Crash*, Peter Schiff claims he predicted the 2008 meltdown. He writes that the U.S. Treasury is in such dire circumstances that when the bonds mature, it borrows from the Fed to honour current bond maturities that come due.[9] This is a Ponzi scheme, and at the expense of sounding undiplomatic, it is the same strategy that Bernie Madoff employed when he bilked investors, including banks and sophisticated funds as well as individuals, with a $64.8 billion pyramid scheme. The difference between the U.S. Treasury and Madoff is that the former gets showered with accolades and the later with a 150-year jail sentence.

Since 2016, the Fed has attempted to decrease their balance sheets by unloading treasuries and other instruments on the open market. However, the strategy has worked to the contrary where their balance sheets have expanded from $1 trillion in 2009 during the Great Recession, to $8 trillion in 2021. Simply put, they have

9   Peter Schiff, *The Real Crash: America's Coming Bankruptcy—How to Save Yourself and Your Country* (New York: St. Martin's Press, 2012).

attempted to re-sell bonds it purchased from a practically insolvent U.S. government. Put differently, the U.S. Treasury is issuing more bonds to finance government debt than it could hope to sell on the open market. For the government to be in this position would require a perfect world of natural Treasury Bill liquidity. However, that is not the world we live in today, since, as I mentioned, the primary recent buyer of U.S. treasuries is the Fed, who is not only encouraging reckless deficit lending to an insolvent U.S. government, but is distorting and inflating all asset prices, while stifling price discovery. In defence of the Fed, it has gradually tried to increase interest rates from 2016 back up to 2.38 percent but had to reduce them again in late 2019 because of issues in the repo markets.

The fact of the matter is that world economies have been on life support since 2008, and money expansion will not cure it. At the same time, there is no political capital to undertake the needed fiscal and monetary reforms. In other words, the markets are addicted to easy money, much like hostages experiencing the Stockholm syndrome. There has been no Fed Chairman since Paul Volker, who fought inflation by raising interest rates to 21 percent in 1981, to put an end to these pretentious shenanigans. However, back then the U.S. government debt was at only $994 billion, compared to over $30 trillion today, without including legacy costs. This will be examined in detail in Chapter 15.

Since 2020 we have been experiencing the effects of easy money, and it has had a host of intended and unintended consequences. Artificially low interest rates seem like a great idea until you look under the hood and realize that near zero percent interest rates caused asset price inflation. Simply put, the stock market goes up due to low interest rates, and home prices increase, with the toxic by-product being that if you do not own home and/or equities, collectables, gold, silver and/or Bitcoin—you are on track to a life of economic deprivation of sorts. The story is even more traumatic when we see that younger people cannot afford these inflated assets, with the end consequence being the phenomena of intergenerational poverty.

It is this wealth gap created by monetary policy that both the Fed and the government are causing as they convince anyone who believes the mainstream narrative agenda of deflecting from its toxic consequences. There is a thorough discussion of inflation, and its effects in Chapters 5 and 13.

The Money Multiplier Revisited

Building on our expanded knowledge of monetary policy, banks are offered liquidity through the Fed, with a view of not only increasing the liquidity of banks in order to lend to consumers and small businesses, but also to stimulate demand. This of course is on the assumption that banks are willing to lend to either consumers or small businesses in a contracting, high-risk economy, since they must consider the risks involved in lending against battered household and business balance sheets. So then, if the risk is higher, especially if there is no backstop against a loan default, at the very least, the banks should set a higher interest rate to offset this risk, which technically defeats the easy money policy of the Fed. A good example of this is 24 percent interest on credit card debt in a 2 percent cost of capital environment for credit card companies. This is further elaborated on in Chapter 13, as we reveal the psychosis of new villains that make a grand entrance into the theatre.

The money multiplier is essentially the same idea mathematically as the fractional banking formula, except this time the reason the Fed is providing liquidity to the bank is to stimulate lending to businesses and/or to consumers to help with employment and demand formation.

In theory, this works the same as the fractional banking system, keeping it simple let's say the Feds give a bank $55,000 to Easy Lending Bank, which will lend 90 percent of this deposit from the funding (remember historically it has to hold back 10 percent in reserves) is lent out as a car loan in the sum of $50,000, and then the car dealer deposits the money in another bank, and that bank lends out $45,000 to another consumer for home renovations. Then the consumer purchases brick, stucco, supplies, and the funds received by the brick and stucco company received is deposited in the sum of $45,000 in the Happy Loan Bank, and the Happy Loan Bank in return then lends out $40,500 of this to Happy Jack. Then Happy Jack borrows $40,500 to buy diamonds and clothing for his mistress, without considering that he should have held some of this back to deal with his wife's divorce attorney after she gets the news, leaving Happy Jack unhappy, and the Opulent Retailer Inc. deposits this sum in the bank. (Remember the banks must hold back 10 percent reserves under Fed mandated banking rules.)

In summary, what we see here is the money multiplier in action. But this much is for sure; you now have an understanding that through fractional banking and bond purchasing the Fed has these tools and then some, in their arsenal to increase the money supply.

The last 25 years, we have seen little inflation up until 2020, if we are to believe the official Consumer Price Index (CPI) inflation numbers that some economists say are skewed. Thus, since Alan Greenspan who served as Fed Chair from 1987 to 2006, the Fed has taken more of an expansionary view of the money supply. However, from the 1950s to 1990s, inflation was a real concern that occurred during economic expansion, and the traditional way of tackling inflation was to reduce the money supply by increasing interest rates. The way Central Banks do this is by selling bonds and pulling in cash from the money supply in circulation. Hence, with less money in circulation, interest rates go up, and contract economic activity to fight inflation. But since 1945, the Fed has increased its strength within the political economic theatre with an ever-expanding reservoir of tools, as we shall soon see.

The Art of Printing Money

In 1944, the Bretton Woods Agreement established the gold standard and the system that supported currency, and it acted as a hedge against governments racking up huge deficits, making it difficult, in effect, to bribe voters with their own money. (The Bretton Woods system is discussed in detail in Chapter 7.) Simply put, the gold standard ensured that the government spent within its means. It is true, though, that the U.S. government had $251 billion dollars of debt constituting 112 percent of the GDP in 1945, at the conclusion of World War II, but this debt was for practical purposes owned by American bondholders, not the Central Bank, which did not have the legal mandate to print money without gold backing, and by the late 1950s total government debt came down to 40 percent of GDP—by the early 1970s it became more manageable at 23 percent. The primary reason America was able to bring down debt to GDP in the 1950s was because of unprecedented post-war GDP growth, where they commanded 50 percent of the global GDP, while being the type of industrial powerhouse perhaps never seen in history. It is also interesting to note that the Korean War was not financed through debt either, but by its equally sinister compatriot, namely taxation.

Remember, the treasury did not decrease debt, only as it relates to debt to GDP to create a narrative that economists applaud.

Figure 2.1 charts the U.S. total public debt as a percentage of GDP from 1790 to 2021, and Figure 2.2 charts GDP from 1945 to 2020.

Figure 2.1: Total public debt as a percentage of gross domestic product from 1790 to 2021

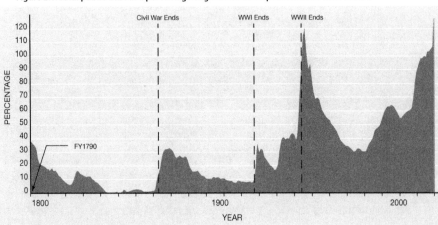

Source: Wall Street Journal The National Debt, Visualized Aug, 2019

Figure 2.2: Gross Domestic Product 1945 to 2020

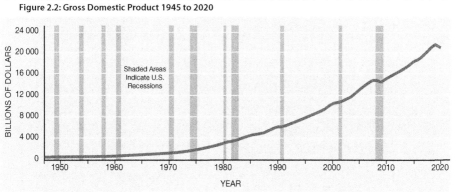

Source: U.S. Bureau of Economic Analysis

It is interesting to note that the last time America was debt-free was in 1835, when President Andrew Jackson paid off the entire national debt—it's the only time in U.S. history that this has been accomplished. This type of miracle and responsible spending was well before the Fed asset purchasing and the introduction of the income tax, which was introduced cunningly during World War I, as a temporary tax to support the war. Most people are unaware of the illegal origins of the income tax, but its origins have allowed this present economic atrocity resulting in large, bloated government that lives off the avails of the industrious, and in slow motion evolves into a kleptocracy, which fairly describes the United States and Canada today.

Before Nixon took America off the Gold Standard in 1971, the U.S. dollar was backed by gold, which means the U.S. dollar was a hard backed currency. This meant the U.S. Central Bank could not print money with such rigour—proof of this is the Vietnam War, which was financed through taxes, and not money printing. Taking the U.S. dollar off the gold standard gave the Central Bank carte blanche to create fiat money that was not based on hard money, but by trust. This gave the Fed the ability to rapidly increase the money supply, resulting in a dollar debt that will easily rise to $33 trillion by the end of 2022.

Tragically, this equates to a debt of nearly $240,000 per U.S. household, and this does not include legacy obligations or state or county debt, which is discussed in some detail in Chapter 15. Simply put, if there was still a gold backing, the U.S. government would not have been in the position to commit an economic genocide against its own people, as well as fund its cavalier direct and proxy wars. With a gold backing, or even a cryptocurrency backing, or the combination of the two, the government fosters financial accountability, and without the illegal actions of money printing by the Fed, these countries would not have the current state of a bloated kleptocracy, inefficient crony capitalism, and a welfare state that is decaying the individual psyche and self-reliance of its citizens, all collectively manifesting itself into the socioeconomic fabric of the nation.

With such a cosmic view, the Fed being in concert with the U.S. Treasury, has been mistakenly credited for staving off recessions and a potential depression, when, in fact, they have planted the seeds of even larger economic catastrophes by not letting what is left of the free market's natural forces to rinse out structural distortions, all of which have been caused by the preceding.

Sadly, it is my thought that the corporatocracy of government, media, and corporations working in tandem to obscure the undeniable fact that government either causes or exacerbates the most pronounced market failures in the first place, where its policies further prolong and worsen recessions, while inadvertently ignoring the systematic macroeconomic distortions it leaves behind. The tragic outcome is that it creates an even more severe economic downturn in the future, while the remedies only deteriorate the state of the patient, namely the economy and the citizens of perhaps a decaying empire, much like the last days of ancient Athens. The Fed and the U.S. Treasury have heroic words and a well rehearsed tapestry of fables to promote wasteful fiscal spending, but when peeled to the core, amounts to fiat money printing as the only cure for the patient. No other therapies need apply! This does not mean government does not have a role in being a force for good, because it does have a role to play by way of infrastructure, roads, rails, airports, clean water, setting the rules for commerce, equitable law, and maintaining a forum for the tenets of fair play. Where it does not have a mandate is exasperating market failures and sitting as a heavy weight on the shoulders of both commerce and its industrious citizens, as it masks failure for achievement. Later, when we analyze the Great Depression, the folly is more empirically and intellectually dissected.

The Moral Hazard

Simply put, the moral hazard dilemma asks the following question: Do we bail out weak performers in the marketplace? Should we ignore the fact that Henry Ford came along with the assembly line and introduced the Model T, and put the horse and buggy business out of its misery? Would it have been a good idea to subsidize horse and buggies, since it did provide substantial employment once upon a time?

It would be reasoned to say that if we clung onto the past as such, our predicament today would be tenuous.

The conservative economic historian Paul Johnson commented that the best advice President Herbert Hoover received in the Great Depression, which he did not heed, was from his Secretary of the Treasury, Andrew Mellon. Mellon had a background in banking, business, philanthropy, and was an industrialist, and counselled the president with the following advice:

> Liquidate labor, liquidate stocks, liquidate the farmers, liquidate real estate.... It will purge the rottenness out of the system. High costs of living and high living will come down.... enterprising people will pick up the wrecks from less competent people.[10]

Mellon went on to say that letting weak firms fail was perfectly fine.

> People will work harder, live a more moral life. Values will be adjusted, and enterprising people will pick up the wrecks from less competent people.[11]

---

10 Herbert Hoover, *The Memoirs of Herbert Hoover: The Great Depression, 1929-1941* (New York: Macmillan, 1952), 30.
11 Ibid.

Mellon was eventually impeached, and such empirically valid advice today would be counter to the Keynesian hypnotics that casts a toxic spell on the political theatre, which is religiously preached in both academic and government circles, where taxpayer money is used to fund artificial consumption, demand, and even price formation, with little regard to the hangover of the patient desperately trying to recover. Because the patient—the economy—has a king-size debt that will have to be managed or dealt with by future generations while emotions will not make it go away. Put simply, the raising of taxes to pay for all this cheap Champagne, the largess of government will suffocate inventiveness and lead to perpetual acute contractions on the GDP, and greatly diminish competition and societal welfare.

Fiscal policy, which is the spending of government resources to stimulate the economy, is the child of John Maynard Keynes where he extensively discusses creating artificial demand and consumption in his book *The General Theory of Employment, Interest and Money*, published in 1936.

So, the moral hazard dilemma is in many ways the ghost of Keynes playing havoc today by empowering government and Central Banks to subsidize firms. Should Berkshire Hathaway, General Motors, Bank of America, or United Airlines know that they can be bailed out? Should they operate without impunity, with the Fed underwriting toxic loans and bond purchases, as certain firms buy back shares to drive up their stock price, giving tidal wave returns on managers with share options while depleting company working capital that drives innovation, which is the kernel of economic growth? Then, after depleting working capital, should these firms have their hands out to the government and or Central Banks? Is this fair play? Should companies in a free market be allowed to offer poor wares that are diametrically against the shifts of the marketplace in the name of artificially induced employment at the expense of taxpayers and an unimaginable accumulated deficit? Should people be encouraged to stay at home and watch Netflix paid for by the government? It goes to say that both firms and households will not act prudently and in a fiduciarily accountable way if they know they are going to get bailed out as a reward for their bad behaviour! Further, this will create a host of unintended consequences in the way of distortions in interest rates, employment, price formation, and demand and supply.

Free markets are not perfect, while admittedly market failure is a by-product of capitalism, which naturally mean reverts into equilibrium when temporary distortions are formed in the macroeconomy, if they are not being perpetuated by outside hands not schooled in the art of commerce. The following questions arise: Should the public purse naïvely finance and perpetuate these distortions and inefficiencies, and allow zombie companies to exist through subsidization, as is the case in many Chinese companies owned by the government? Is there a diminishment of consumer welfare when newer smaller, more nimble and creative firms that define future growth are held back from the gates of innovation and opportunity? Are we destroying the tenets of capitalism by using market failure to create largess bureaucratic government to bail out unsound positions that, in essence, exasperates an economic pullback? Must firms be as unsound as government?

Has capitalism failed us, or have we failed capitalism? To many, the ghost of Adam Smith's invisible hand is a tenet of relic, but eventually reappears with vengeance to greet a new generation a timeless lesson.

In a June 2020 article in the *Wall Street Journal*, Ruchir Sharma eloquently argues the following:

> *The idea of government as the balm for all crises is appealing in the short term, but it ignores the unintended consequences. Without entrepreneurial risk and creative destruction, capitalism does not work. Disruption and regeneration, the heart of the system, grind to a halt. The deadwood never falls from the tree. The green shoots are nipped in the bud.*

As lockdowns began in March of 2020, the Fed promised to start buying debt at a rate twice as fast as in 2008, including corporate bonds for the first time. Gradually, the Fed has loosened the definition of what it will buy. Even after the credit markets had settled down in June of 2020, the Fed ramped up purchases, and it now owns debt issued by, among others, Apple, Walmart, AT&T, Disney, Nike and Berkshire Hathaway.[12]

The moral hazard dilemma, unlike the political will, rewards bad actors while desperately keeping antiquated industries alive at the expense of the public purse and progress. It is a form of B. F. Skinner's behaviour modification psychology of reinforcing certain behaviour.

Innovation and its first cousin disruption is tragic, yet glorious, with no compassion for the static, but it is this enigma that entrepreneurs provide in the economic history of creative destruction as a tool of progress, dating back to the Industrial Revolution, the Luddites and even Mesopotamia.

Quantitative Easing

We first saw the term Quantitative Easing (QE) being used to in the 2008 meltdown, commonly known as the Great Recession. It sounds like it came off the assembly of media communications speak and denotes benevolent relief of some kind, but deserves a better explanation.

There are times when the U.S. government cannot sell enough bonds, or in the case of the Bank of England, gilts (UK bonds), to meet cash obligations when they come due. Meaning, the markets on their own will not buy enough U.S. Treasury bonds to meet these demands. Sometimes, you might hear that Congress is going to increase the debt ceiling—in other words, spend more than they bring in.

---

12 Ruchir Sharma, "The Rescues Ruining Capitalism," *Wall Street Journal*, July 24, 2020.

Then this brings up questions. Could this be more wasteful, addictive and empirically ineffective public spending doing more harm than good? Could this eventually be ruining the tenets of free market capitalism, or what is left of it? Should bad actors such as banks and corporations be bailed out, as was United Airlines, which spent $10 billion between 2014 to 2019 on share buybacks, just to be bailed out in 2020, or should they be allowed to fail for their imprudent allocation of capital?

Consider the example of Intel being bailed out for $50 billion by the Biden administration to upgrade their lagging plants and technology, when they have spent over $60 billion since 2010 on share buybacks, as opposed to modernizing and building new plants. So much so that their once leading semiconductor chips are lagging behind Taiwan Semiconductor Manufacturing Company, which is investing $100 billion in plants, including a $12 billion plant in the United States. The moral hazard of awarding firms for their bad behaviour is ruining capitalism as we know it. Hence, blaming a disfigured form of free markets for the economic woes and the need for governmental market interference is an intellectual abdication of sorts.

This now brings us to 2008, when the capital markets had a meltdown, and the Central Bank went on a bond buying binge starting with the U.S. government. In turn, what the U.S. Treasury did was sell Treasury bills to the Fed, and the Fed printed money out of thin air and deposited it as credit on the Treasury balance sheet and a debit on the Central Bank. Thus, where the U.S. government could not raise $1 trillion in a month, the Fed can and does provide cash to the government, while at the same time it can provide liquidity to the markets, which was sorely missing when the capital markets seized after the Lehman Brothers failed. Hence, by printing money the Fed is increasing its balance sheets.

With an understanding of Quantitative Easing (QE), and what it constitutes, which amounts to printing fiat money without the real backing of gold, we turn our attention to 1971, when President Nixon took the U.S. dollar off the gold standard. It was to be a temporary measure, something like the introduction of income tax during World War I. So, then it might occur to oneself in a moment of inner thinking and a Zen meditative moment during the lockdown of the pandemic, what do I trust more, fiat money, gold, or Bitcoin? Perhaps the answer to that comes when we channel to a time gone by, in a magical moment before World War I, where the Fed, under their charter, could not print money and lend it to government, and for that matter, there was no such thing as income tax to punish people for the fruits of their labour.

Woodrow Wilson was president during the World War I, and armed with political capital, he managed to persuade Congress to amend the law, allowing the Fed to print money and lend it to the government. Thus, the introduction of income tax and money printing was the alcoholic mix government was salivating for—both acts were an affront to Jeffersonian democracy, which incidentally had a disdain for the Bank of England as well as oppressive taxation, which in itself is against the tenets of the U.S. Constitution, as written by the founding fathers. So much for building a nation on philosophies.

Now armed with all this extra fiat money, the Fed can come in and supposedly heal the woes of the economy through monetary policy, in the way of asset purchases, as they administer more heroin to the junky. Instead, what good governance should promote is letting the addict dry out, allowing them to have a sense of self-reliance and promote a policy of macroeconomic equilibrium so they can truly heal the woes of the patient, namely the economy. The problem is that when the collective mind becomes obscured by the seduction of intravenous abuse and dependency masquerading as benevolence, it will welcome what seems like an easy proposition, and tolerate nothing but more of the same in the way of a short-term titillation. In essence, we have bought into the folly that all recessions and other economic pullbacks have to be managed by government. And it is this line of thinking that has tampered and distorted the natural equilibrium and self-healing tenets of the marketplace, with the outcome of perpetually keeping the patient in ICU.

Stepping back into history, during the last decades of the

Roman Republic that evolved into dictatorship, the Roman government provided welfare in the form of wheat and other grains to its people. They tried to take away these perks from the citizenry, but were politically rebuffed, and eventually very few were prepared to fight for the Empire. Eventually Romans refused to fight to defend the Empire when they could stay home and get free food, so Rome hired the Visigoths as mercenaries, who would occasionally turn on the Empire in mid-battle if they were paid more in tribute by the opposing side. Eventually Rome fell at a peril created by its own success, as all empires rot from the inside.

Murray Rothbard, one of the great economic thinkers of the 20th century, who subscribed to the Austrian School of Economics, provides us with the following insights in his book *America's Great Depression*:

> *If government wishes to alleviate, rather than aggravate a depression, its only valid course is laissez-faire—to leave the economy alone. Only if there is no interference, direct or threatened, with prices, wage rates, and business liquidation will the necessary adjustment proceed with smooth dispatch. Any propping up of shaky positions postpones liquidation and aggravates unsound conditions. Propping up wage rates creates mass unemployment, and bolstering prices perpetuates and creates unsold surpluses. Moreover, a drastic cut in the government budget—both in taxes and expenditures—will of itself speed adjustment by changing social choice toward more saving and investment relative to consumption. For government spending, whatever the label attached to it, is solely consumption; any cut in the budget therefore raises the investment–consumption ratio in the economy and allows more rapid validation of originally wasteful and loss-yielding projects. Hence, the proper injunction to government in a depression is cut the budget and leave the economy strictly alone. Currently fashionable economic thought considers such a dictum hopelessly outdated; instead, it has more substantial backing now in economic law than it did during the nineteenth century.*

Laissez-faire was, roughly, the traditional policy in American depressions before 1929. The laissez-faire precedent was set in America's first great depression, 1819, when the federal government's only act was to ease terms of payment for its own land debtors. President Van Buren also set a staunch laissez-faire course, in the Panic of 1837. Subsequent federal governments followed a similar path, the chief sinners being state governments which periodically permitted insolvent banks to continue in operation without paying their obligations! In the 1920-1921 depression, government intervened to a greater extent, but wage rates were permitted to fall, and government expenditures and taxes were reduced. And this depression was over in one year—in what Dr. Benjamin M. Anderson has called "our last natural recovery to full employment."[13]

The underlying concept of Quantitative Easing, where the Fed bails out government and purchases asset classes from bonds, commercial paper, and shares in unsound firms that in the 2008 meltdown, were deemed *too big to fail.* Mentioned earlier, the mandate was that the Central Bank could purchase government bonds and print money accordingly, under very extraordinary circumstances. In other words, a lot of bad actors were bailed out by being rewarded for lack of judgment and competence, which then brings us back to the moral hazard. In 2008, the Fed entered market territory it would not dare in the prior century, and it is this precedent that has put the economy in a conundrum and perpetual spiral to this date. This has resulted in a U.S. deficit at near $10 trillion when Obama took office and will reach $33 trillion by year end 2022. One might then ask what we have tangibly to show for all this spending?

Matters are so perilous, consider that when the U.S. Treasury issues bonds, they often cannot sell enough of in the open market

13   Murray N. Rothbard, *America's Great Depression* (Princeton: D. Van Nostrand, 1963).

to meet cash requirements. To alleviate this, the Fed purchases U.S. Treasury bills, and they magically create cash that they have lent to a government that is on life support, at least since 2008. This can only be described as a Ponzi scheme, as the band keeps playing, we are told to keep a stiff upper lip and carry on! In the 2008 Great Recession, the government laid down the foundations of even a bigger meltdown, which it seems we are now on the cusp of (a deep dive on this in Chapter 11). During the Fed's asset purchasing program, they purchased equity positions in General Motors and acted as a lender of last resort to AIG, Bank of America, hedge funds, and the list goes on. Once firms, government, and households know that acting treacherously and destructively is rewarded, it leads us back to the conundrum of the moral hazard. This has roots going back to Woodrow Wilson, who served as President from 1913 to 1921, where the Fed supplied liquidity for the U.S. Treasury by buy bonds, that gave great impetus for government to grow.

Central Bank Policy

The Central Banks, both in the U.S. and Europe, are now playing a role in the political economy that is, quite frankly, outside of its mandate. In the case of the European Central Bank, it cannot create its own bonds, so it purchases or guarantees European country bonds from some of the most chronic debt-ridden countries. As of the second quarter of 2021, a sampling of the all-star line-up of chronic debtors includes, but is not limited to, Italy at 167 percent of GDP, Greece at 247 percent of GDP, Portugal at 170 percent of GDP, Spain at 195 percent of GDP, and France at 120 percent of GDP. The common thread of this suffocating debt are unsustainable social government programs, and any government that weans the citizenry off these entitlements might have the same fate as King Louis the XVI did at the guillotine. So, it is this trap that governments find themselves after decades of entitlements were exchanged for votes going back to just after World War II.

The conundrum of largess government continues across the pond. Not to be outdone, the United States is at 139 percent of GDP, and Canada, a chronic government addict, is at 120 percent of GDP. All these bad actors are in emotional denial of the complete failures of largess government, subsidized by the fiat money printing of Central Banks, and the eventual reckoning that awaits them. Interestingly enough, Russia, which is the West's go-to villain, even without the relics of Khrushchev in the picture, has a manageable debt of less than 20 percent of GDP. Much of this is because the ruble cannot be printed without the hard backing of gold and or natural resources.

Simply put, if the Fed stopped buying U.S. Treasuries and weaned government off easy money, it would lead to the Treasury not being able to meet its bond repayment obligations. For example, with approximately $32 trillion of bonds in float, when only $200 billion come due in a month, the Treasury could easily honour it. But what would happen if $3 trillion of bonds mature in one month, when the federal Treasury's intake of revenue is $3.8 trillion for the whole year? This is a very real possibility. If this happened, they would have to either borrow more money from the Central Bank or default on U.S. Treasuries. Now with the Central Bank bloating its balance sheets from $1 trillion in 2008 to $8 trillion in 2021, and on its way to $10 trillion in 2022 it would have to print additional fiat money to keep this Ponzi scheme going. Simply put, the band keeps playing while the Titanic is taking on water!

Subsequently, the government would be forced to pull back its litany of ineffective and inefficient social programs posing as benevolence, where the net outcomes inadvertently lead to oppressing the liberation of the human psyche, while collectively weakening the spirit of a civilization. Put differently, without fiat money printing, the government would not be able to buy votes by creating a crisis and then having a financially irresponsible solution that always comes with a diet of oppression and dependency. Also, the loss of these programs would cause civil unrest, which is tantamount to taking away heroin pack from a junkie who prizes their needle marks as a badge of honour, without perhaps considering the tragedy of their addiction.

To avert this, since the U.S. dollar is the world's reserve currency, the Fed could print more fiat money, expanding their balance sheets to $12 trillion and beyond. What would be the likely outcome? Unquestionably, it would lead to an acute weakening of the U.S. dollar, (U.S. dollar index against other currencies can be tracked on Yahoo under DX-Y.NYB) some of which we are seeing today, with the importation of massive inflation (imported goods costing more), as a result of hyper-liquidity, and as of early 2022 this is only the tip of the iceberg. Further, if the Fed stopped its bond purchasing program, the wheels of the capital markets would have a corrosive seizure, much like in 2008, except this would lead to an even more catastrophic outcome with interest rates skyrocketing. Just imagine if interest rates to float U.S. Treasuries had to go to 6 percent, which is closer to the historical mean reversion of interest rates. Just the interest on the bonds would equate to nearly $2 trillion a year, for the government that pulls in approximately $4 trillion a year. One does not need to be a Harvard MBA to figure out that 50 percent of tax revenue would go to just pay the interest on the debt.

But the real threat is, if the debt market explodes, meaning the Fed can no longer control the 10-year Treasury yield through a fancy term called yield curve control, whereas the Central Bank sells short-term bonds and buys long-term bonds to ensure the long-term bond pays higher interest than a short one-year bond. Subsequently, if this happened in the bond market, through a rebellion in the private purchasers of bonds it could be the likely suspect for the next catastrophe, this would come to a meltdown in short order, with spiking interest rates to double digits. In fact, this is the thinking of Gregory Mannarino, who screams this out daily on his YouTube blog. If this played out, which is a very realistic possibility, the cascading tragedy in the world equity markets worth $95 trillion, and being conservative, could lose 50 percent of its value in short order, which would amount to $47.5 trillion. The contagion could spread to the U.S. housing market worth $36.2

trillion, which would lose nearly $10 trillion—banks would be reeling with so many homes underwater, where mortgages are worth more than the homes (remember 2008).

If this makes the reader feel depressed, please accept my apologies for not insisting you have some antacid tablets nearby before you read this section, but we should also consider that the total derivatives markets, which is worth about a quadrillion dollar ($1,000 trillion) could easily lose $300 trillion overnight. In this scenario, what we have is the biggest catastrophe since civilization invented government. After quickly dissecting our denial of debt, we might arrive to the rational moment that all this would make Charles Ponzi look like the leading candidate for the next Bambi movie. This is discussed at some detail in Chapter 15 (The House of Cards).

The mess that we see ourselves in right now has no easy solution, since so much euphoria has flowed into the pleasures of today at the expense of tomorrow. The only question is, who will be around to hammer the final nails in the coffin of Western civilization?

The Central Bank and the Moral Hazard: Some Final Thoughts

The original role of the Central Banks, at least in America, as mentioned earlier, was to unify the U.S. dollar coast to coast, to promote stable interest rates, and reasonably flexible money supply, as its prime function. During the 2020 pandemic meltdown, the Fed extended itself well outside it mandate by buying toxic assets, such as junk bonds, to save ETFs, to save poorly run companies that expended the cash on the balance sheets by way of share repurchases as opposed to directing capital to more productive outcomes. Their role is not to buy mini-bonds, state bonds, encourage a Treasury to move toward $35 trillion of debt—it is not their function to hand out helicopter money through the U.S. government to people, knowing full well that this will be expended.

It is not their role to manipulate the stock market into purchasing equities to artificially inflate asset prices, while the real economy is in contractionary disequilibrium. And it is not the role of the Fed to create monetary polices that will ensure an even bigger meltdown with easy money that does not cure the patient, but merely distort asset prices. Finally, it is not the role of the Fed to print money and saddle the public with spiralling debt that will lead to a combination of higher taxes, less expendable personal income, and more than likely, bouts of inflation, stagflation, and deflation.

Simply put, in its current format, the Fed along with its cohorts on Wall Street and bailed out firms, gives capitalism a bad name, while the government, through fiscal policy, suffocates the free market's natural resiliency, and in tandem this is diametrically opposed to the tenets of the natural marketplace, which is something the West has not had since President Warren G. Harding. Later, in Chapter 8, we visit the history of booms and busts, where we discover the 1921 depression that few people are aware of, caused by many factors including the Spanish flu. It was Harding who quickly and effectively staved off the depression of 1921 by letting the market distortions self correct itself with the last truly laissez-faire approach, by not having government meddle in the mechanisms of the natural economy.

For those not familiar with economic speak, some of these concepts might seem abstract and it might be a good time to espouse some economic ideas and framework. Economics makes for great theatre as we try to make sense of the villains disguised as the virtuous, and the virtuous depicted in a lesser light.

The price decline is a result
of having to pay debts.
That drains income from
the circular flow between
production and consumption—
that is, between what people
are paid when they go to work,
and the things that they buy.[1]

–Michael Hudson

Some Macroeconomic Tools

Circular Flow of Income

The idea of circular flow of income was first introduced by the Irish-French economist Richard Cantillon, in the 18th century, and was then developed by various economists (this is discussed further in Chapter 5). In 1933, Frank Hyneman Knight, an economist who helped form the Chicago School of Economics, and whose most notable student was Milton Friedman, was the first to visualize it. The circular flow of income is a foundational concept in macroeconomics.

Understanding the key fundamentals of the circular flow of income starts by understanding the interlinking relationship between households, governments, and firms. For example, in modern economies, government expenditure on programs in what we call fiscal spending, at least theoretically, helps to stimulate, or lubricate facets of the economy. When the government pays out social security money, retailers depend on this to drive revenue and profits, so much so that they have calendars marked with the exact dates when the social security checks will be sent out. Of course, government spending is much more involved in the way of building infrastructure, Medicare, military, and a host of programs in the interest of the public good. From this point of view, government does create demand, but also inefficiencies.

Households are the second primary area of the circular flow of income. For example, if households are not indebted, which certainly is not the case today, they are in the position to stimulate an economy through expenditures of money they have saved up or personal disposable income. Unfortunately, distortions occur when households are enticed to spend beyond their means by borrowing, and at 24 percent interest rates (that credit card companies have a cost of interest at less than 3 percent) for credit cards it puts the household under incredible pressure. Further, one of the reasons people end up financially challenged throughout

1 Michael Hudson, *Super Imperialism: The Economic Strategy of American Empire* (New York: Holt, Rinehart, and Winston, 1972).

their lives is because they spend without attaining appreciating countervailing assets such as gold, investment property, non-central digital assets, namely Bitcoin, and equities. This being said, in a perfect economy, it is consumers driving primary demand, not the government.

The third major component of our circular flow are firms, and regardless of some of their actions that has been considered here including share buybacks, it is imperative to understand that companies create natural jobs, not the government. Any government job created is at the expense of the taxpayer, better known as the public purse. It is imperative that firms and households alike, operate in the low tax environment that will create more natural opportunities in the way of jobs and wealth. Households and the government are customers in the circular flow of income, while firms, at least theoretically, invest in lucrative projects in the interest of creating wealth.

As a side note, firms not only pay corporate taxes (although they employ accountants to avert not paying as much as possible), but pay a portion of their employees' unemployment, Social Security, and insurance costs. For example, in the United States the current tax rate for Social Security is 6.2 percent for the employer and 6.2 percent for the employee, or 12.4 percent total. The current rate for Medicare is 1.45 percent for the employer and 1.45 percent for the employee, or 2.9 percent total. Hence, corporations not only pay taxes, but pay toward Social Security on behalf of the employees, at the same time, while creating employment, they alleviate pressure on government unemployment rate. Much of this is lost when firms are vilified under the "pay their fair share" myth!

As a peripheral offshoot of the three core components of the circular flow of income, namely the government, households, and firms, we also discover other facets that include exports, imports, taxation, purchases, government purchases, social transfers, financial sector in the way of capital markets, demand, and supply.

Figure 3.1 gives a robust visual explanation of how the puzzle fits.

Figure 3.1: The Circular Flow Model

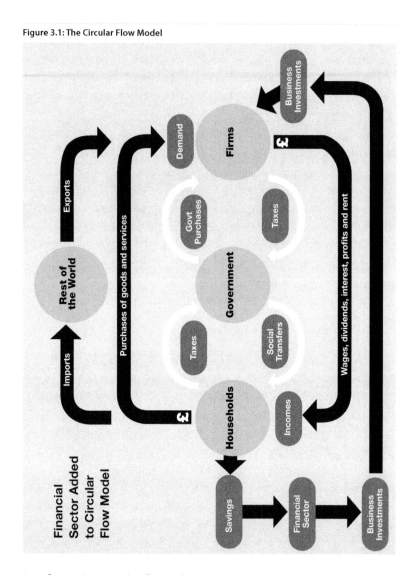

It is from the circular flow of income that we start understanding how a nation calculates its GDP.

Gross Domestic Product

Gross Domestic Product (GDP) becomes clearer after we first visited the circular flow of income, since the two are intertwined. We all hear this term thrown around in the media and in social circles, and many use the terms Gross National Product (GNP) or GDP without perhaps an understanding of what they mean. The difference is that GDP measures the value of goods and services produced, and sold within a country's borders, by citizens and non-citizens alike. GNP measures the value of goods and services produced by only a country's citizens but both domestically and abroad. So, for practical purposes lets stick with GDP.

Simply put, it is the size of a nation's economy, its total spending of goods and services in a year. All expressed in U.S. dollars, the U.S. GDP in 2019 was 21.5 trillion, Canada was 1.7 trillion, the European Union was 18.3 trillion, China (their numbers are always skewed and suspect) was 14.1 trillion, Germany was 3.9 trillion, and Japan was 5 trillion. So, one might ask, how do we calculate the GDP?

Below is the classical formula taught in business schools—and don't worry, you will not be inundated with complex math formulas, but it starts with the following equation:

$$GDP = C + I + G + (Ex - Im)$$

When we break down the above formula's components, everything starts making sense, especially after having a reasonable feel of the circular flow of income:

- C = total spending by consumers
- I = total investment (spending on goods and services) by businesses
- G = total spending by government (federal, state, and local)
- (Ex - Im) = net exports (exports - imports)

We often hear that the economy is growing, but this might affect certain sectors or investment asset classes as opposed to spreading more equitably with other sectors. For example, there might be a large demand for people working in IT or people who design artificial intelligence, while the housing or retail sector might be contracting. This is why, when government numbers are pointing toward growth, some company owners question it if their industry is sluggish, while other sectors have more robust economic growth. Or it is quite possible that some industries have substantial pressure on the earnings because they might not only be experiencing sluggishness, but are in perfect competition, which is a knockout combination.

How Government Fudges GDP Numbers in an Inflationary Environment

When the growth of the GDP is announced, it is a talking point for fostering votes, as it is widely applauded by the capital markets and the plebeians as a sign of prosperity, even though it might not affect one's personal lot in life, since it is a sign of growth in the overall economy and not by industry. In 2021 the U.S. GDP increased by 5.7 percent, but at the same time January 2021 to January 2022, CPI inflation was closer to 7 percent.[2] Hence, an argument could be considered that the GDP did not grow, but inflation numbers grew with associated higher costs for goods and services, negating the GDP growth argument, since 7 to 5.7 percent would be a shrinkage of -1.3 percent. However, the real inflation numbers on things we buy, according to Shadow Government Statistics, is closer to 15 percent, and then if we go by this, we can calculate that a 5.7 percent GDP growth minus 15 percent puts the real GDP at -9.3 percent growth. It could be argued that the GDP numbers make deflator adjustments for price changes, but this is based on the CPI index, which is not a measurement of practical effective inflation when one shops at the supermarket or experiences the spike in energy and household costs.

2   "U.S. Inflation Rate," Y Charts, accessed March 27, 2022, https://ycharts.com/indicators/us_inflation_rate

This means the real value of the currency is dropping, resulting in higher prices of the same goods and services in relevance to the currency, hence, coupled by lower consumption rates causing overstated and distorted GDP numbers. This not only masks the real GDP, but with a higher GDP, the debt to GDP numbers do not look as tragic, and you will find talking heads from government to media espousing a host of these erroneous assertions. Regardless of what the GDP number is to debt, it does not change the actual amount of the debt owed by government.

Back To Our Regularly Scheduled Program

There is a genesis that has nourished intellectual thought to "fiscal stimulus," meaning the government theory that they can inoculate against the peaks and troughs of the business cycle through government expenditure. The stimulus is diametrically opposed to economic proponents of the laissez-faire approach, which is the theory or system of government that upholds the autonomous character of the economic order, trusting that government should intervene as little as possible in the direction of economic affairs of the state. This is in line with the Austrian School of Economics and Milton Friedman's Chicago School of Economics.

There are some other things to note on a macroeconomic level. The concept of fiscal stimulus really belongs to a man named John Maynard Keynes, even though presidents Hoover and Roosevelt were intervening at the earliest stages of the Great Depression, before Keynes, who we visit in Chapter 4, published *The General Theory of Employment, Interest and Money*. Diametrically, Keynes was in conflict with proponents of free market mechanisms posit by Adam Smith, the architect of modern economics, who is discussed in Chapter 8. Still, Keynes had a great respect for the natural mechanisms of the free market.

The argument is really about what economic philosophy can bring the levers of the economy back into equilibrium, while ensuring that there is the most efficient allocation of capital and resources that fosters an increase in consumer and societal welfare. It is this juncture and two schools of thought where the battle has lied since the Great Depression, a confrontation that can be compared to a Mexican standoff, or perhaps a perpetual sumo wrestling match between the two boulevards of thought. So, this might be a good time to introduce these economic thinkers.

During an economic contraction, can the government and the Central Bank help or further distort the market mechanisms through monetary and fiscal stimulus? It can easily be argued that it has a very mixed record of leaving a hangover of public debt—over $30 trillion as of early 2022—leading to money printing and the subsequent economic tragedy of inflation. Conversely, to proponents to the Austrian School of free markets, they subscribe to a laissez-faire school of thought, meaning to let the natural mechanisms of the free marketplace put pricing, production, demand, and supply formation back into equilibrium by rinsing out the distortions. Liquidationists rely on the timeless genius of Adam Smith, the father of modern economics, who proposed the invisible hand that naturally cures marketplace demand and supply back into equilibrium. Politicians with rarely any business experience have trouble understanding this and show up with accolades and fiscal tools not really knowing what to do or how to cure the troughs of the marketplace. However, to be fair, they are under pressure by the electorate to be seen as doing something to relieve the pain but are most proficient at taking a cold and turning it into a pneumonia, as they self-congratulate themselves for a never-ending litany of failures, and ask for higher budgets to architect their next colossal disaster, as the citizens of Rome cheer on!

To understand the tenets and the politico of fiscal stimulus and demand-side economics, it brings us to probably the most renowned economist of the 20th century. So, without further ado, in Chapter 4, I introduce to you none other than the man who gave intellectual propensity for government participation of remedy for the sometimes-rough seas of the free markets: John Maynard Keynes.

The difficulty lies not
so much in developing new ideas
as in escaping from old ones.[1]

In the long run we're all dead.[2]

The markets are moved by animal
spirits, and not by reason.[3]

—John Maynard Keynes

CHAPTER

Keynesianism

John Maynard Keynes

John Maynard Keynes (1883-1946) was perhaps the most prominent 20th century economist, schooled at Eaton College, originally trained in mathematics and the classics, then at King's College, Cambridge, where he was inspired by his economics professor, Alfred Marshall, to shift his higher education to politics and economics. His career included being a civil servant with the India office in Whitehall, eventually returning to Cambridge, where he taught economics until 1915. He worked in the British Treasury, became an economic advisor to Prime Minister David George Lloyd, and was the key British representative during Bretton Woods in 1944, where he proposed a global currency to be named the Bancor. However, the Americans, being the real victors, would not forgive Britain its war debts and worked to weaken the pound sterling reserve status, and diminish the clout of the Imperial preference system of low tariffs among British Commonwealth countries. Simply put, the Americans wanted to enjoy the spoils of the war and replace the pound and ensure the U.S. dollar as the reserve currency of the world, which still stands today. In many ways both in the first and second wars, Britain by being not forgiven for wartime loans, which were at higher interest rates than other countries, paid the most reparations of sorts including the loss of empire. Keynes' last major mark was when, in 1945, he negotiated a multibillion-dollar loan granted by the Americans to Britain.

Up until his 1936 publication of *The General Theory of Employment, Interest and Money* the position of government, in respect to the economies of the West, was laissez-faire, since there was little political appetite in interfering in the natural economy, outside of setting property rights and rules of commerce. Certainly, Keynes was not a

---

1   John Maynard Keynes, *The General Theory of Employment, Interest and Money* (London: Palgrave Macmillan, 1936).
2   John Maynard Keynes, *A Tract on Monetary Form* (London: Macmillan and Co., 1923).
3   John Maynard Keynes, *The General Theory of Employment, Interest and Money* (London: Palgrave Macmillan, 1936).

liquidationist like Andrew Mellon, the Treasury Secretary for Hoover. Keynesianism put an end to the laissez-faire economics as we know it—he was not a socialist, so to speak, and did not subscribe to the Platonism, the philosophy of Utopia as described in Plato's *Republic*. On the contrary, he had great admiration and fascination for the remarkable resilience of capitalism, even though he was a proponent in creating artificial demand, and labour price formation. This brings us to the inner workings of Keynesian economics.

Keynes was a demand-side economist and did not believe that the natural forces of the marketplace would quickly return into equilibrium, meaning demand and full employment when market pullbacks occurred (recessions). Instead, he promoted the school of thinking that once an economic downturn sets in, regardless of the reason, the fear and gloom that it generates among businesses and investors will tend to become self-fulfilling and can lead to a sustained period of depressed economic activity and unemployment.

In *The General Theory of Employment, Interest and Money*, Keynes posits the belief that the market's natural mean reversion toward full employment is a misconception. Hence, government interventionism is therefore necessary to overcome economic slumps. In practical terms, this meant governments running deficits to create public works projects to increase wages, decrease unemployment and subsequent demand, without considering that demand causes higher wages, and inflation. It should also be noted that he was a product of his times, meaning the Great Depression hit the UK severely, so his search for outside of market remedies was a natural outcome of his thinking. Keynes was, in many respects, the man who gave intellectual inertia for government to tinker with the mechanisms of the free markets, and the father of fiscal stimulus.

During periods of economic woe, Keynes advocated a counter-cyclical fiscal policy in which the government should undertake deficit spending to make up for the decline in investment and boost consumer spending, in order to stabilize aggregate demand. Key takeaways are as follows:

- Keynesian economics focuses on using active government policy to manage aggregate demand to address or prevent economic recessions.

- Keynes developed his theories in response to the Great Depression, and was highly critical of previous economic theories, which he referred to as "classical economics."

- Activist fiscal and monetary policy are the primary tools recommended by Keynesian economists to manage the economy and fight unemployment.

- Aggregate demand is more likely than aggregate supply to be the primary cause of a short-run economic event like a recession.

- Wages and prices can be sticky, and so, in an economic downturn, unemployment can result.

What Keynes did not consider was the specter of inflation, specifically stagflation in the 1960s and '70s, which had the effect of dispelling Keynesianism among economists by the 1980s. (Stagflation is the combination of high unemployment and inflation.) In particular, Milton Friedman from the Chicago School of Economics, argued with clear empiricism that government interference in the free markets agitates economic downturns, creates price distortions, and that government meddling is a "net negative" on the economy.

In his preface to the German edition of *General Theory*, Keynes writes:

> *Nevertheless the theory of output as a whole, which is what the following book purports to provide, is much more easily adapted to the conditions of a totalitarian state, than is the theory of production and distribution of a given output produced under conditions of free competition and a large measure of laissez-faire.*[4]

4 Bertram Schefold, "The General Theory of a Totalitarian State? A Note on Keynes' Preface to the German Edition of 1936," *Cambridge Journal of Economics* 4, no. 2 (June, 1980): 175-176.

Keynes' legacy was that he was the perfect protagonist for government to have carte blanche in spending themselves out of a recession, which unfortunately transitioned to the chicanery of permanent oppressive taxation with the outcome of a largess government self-congratulating themselves for each successive folly, while living off the avails of the industrious. Fiscal stimulus as we know it, regardless of its validity, is the hallmark of John Maynard Keynes. But in defense of Keynes, he never foresaw or would approve the toxicity of unsustainable government debt, loss of the individual psyche, and an untenable welfare state together with which is a drag on the economy, especially in the new millennium with accumulated deficits.

Now, with this new appreciation of Keynesian economic philosophy, some admittedly valid and some with shortcomings, we are able to understand the Keynesian multiplier.

The Keynesian Multiplier

The multiplier effect was in essence a fiscal tool used since the Great Depression as a way of inoculating the pubic from economic downturns, by creating aggregate demand or perhaps deepening, widening and prolonging the downturn in the business cycle, depending on what your school of thought is about the government's role in the economy.

To best explain the Keynesian multiplier, imagine that the government came up with a shovel ready project, like infrastructure, and they built the Hip Hop Centre for the enrichment of culture and profanity for $10,000,000, and it employed 10,000 workers, paid $1,000 each to build it (forget about the cost of cement and raw materials for this example). Then, let us look at the activity of Walmart Wally or Snoop Dog Smog or Blogger Shaky Shakira, as they now have $1,000 each to spend. Let us assume that the marginal propensity to consume (meaning spend) is 75 percent of their income, (after all, why live in America if you can't flaunt it?) and the marginal propensity to save is 25 percent. This simply means that in this case, 75 percent of all money received will be spent.

Let's say Snoop Dog Smog, who received his $1,000 for his labor, and we established that the common savings rate was 25 percent, and the spending rate was 75 percent, went out and bought a $750 custom suit, (like Elvis's golden suit), and then his tailor Franky Flash buys an air conditioner with 75 percent of the $750 he received from Snoop Dog Smog, which amounts to $562.50.

In turn, the air conditioner seller donates 75 percent of the $562.50 to a political party, which amounts to $421.88, and the politicians put together a group therapy session with a psychiatrist to deal with their "compulsive lying disorder" for $316.41. After listening to these politicians for two hours, the psychiatrist became unhinged and decides that she needs some therapy from listening to politicians and pays her professional colleague, Dr. Brain, to recalibrate her brain for $237.30.

Without boring you with the balance of calculations, it took multiples of 17 transactions of diminishing returns to get to zero, but before it got there, the original $1,000 multiplied after 17 transactions turned into $4,000 (don't worry, I did the calculations).

Then in theory, consider that if all consumers acted the same way with all other factors remaining equal (ceteris paribus), and we have $4,000 x 1,000 employees = $40 million created from $10 million of government spending on our hypothetical Hip Hop Centre project. You now understand the multiplier effect, but at the same time, Milton Friedman of the Chicago School of Economics and Murry Rothbard from the Austrian School would argue that if you didn't tax people at such oppressive rates in the first place, the economy would grow more exponentially, consumption would be higher and quickly revert to mean reversion. Later in this book, we will be visiting the anti-Keynesian economic thinkers, as the puzzle comes together.

Just to give you a deeper understanding of this, there are two elements to the multiplier, namely, the marginal propensity to consume and the marginal propensity to save. And without getting too mathematical, the marginal propensity to consume formula is as follows, based on 75 percent consumption:

$$\text{Multiplier} = \frac{1}{1-\text{MPC}}$$

$$\text{At 75\% Consumption} \quad \frac{1}{1 - 0.75}$$

Multiplier is therfore   4

Consequently, what the above calculation insinuates is that for every dollar spent in fiscal stimulus, the effect will be to increase spending by four times. There are a few caveats here to consider, because economics, just like life, is not always black and white, and is often grey. In our example, not all consumers will spend 75 per-cent—some will consume more if the liquor and cannabis store is open, and some less. Then we ask the question, if the consumer is given $2,000 of helicopter money as a fiscal stimulus, and it is spent on imports via Amazon, how does that create value added employ-ment and wealth in your domestic country, while your factories are idle, and collecting dust on the backs of dated equipment?

One might deliberate, if the Fed decided to lower interest rates to zero, which they nearly did during the 2020 pandemic meltdown, what if consumers saved their fiat printed helicopter money? What if the consumer confidence index tanked? What if the low interest rate button was so overused that it desensitized the market and the real economy? Then, is it not quite possible that the government, equipped with a fancy fiscal rifle, would be shooting blanks in a Dodge City gunfight with inflation?

We now move to the most insidious hidden tax that easy mon-ey creates: Inflation.

And when money circulates there in greater abundance than among its neighbours, a national Bank does more harm than good. An abundance of fictitious and imaginary money causes the same disadvantages as an increase of real money in circulation, by raising the price of land and labour, or by making works and manufactures more expensive at the risk of subsequent loss. The crafts which require the most time in training or most ingenuity and industry must necessarily be the best paid.[1]

−Richard Cantillon

CHAPTER

Inflation and Its Many Faces

Richard Cantillon

No conversation about inflation can begin without consideration of Richard Cantillon (1680s-1734), an Irish French economist best known for *Essai Sur La Nature Du Commerce En Général*, (*Essay on the Nature of Trade in General*). At an early age, he became a successful merchant and banker, and in the early 18th century, he funded and speculated in John Law's Mississippi Company, where he built a fortune. It is not certain when he wrote *Essai*, but most believe it was around the year 1730, where it was circulated only in manuscript format, but was formally published in 1755, after his death.

Cantillon's *Essai* is considered the first treatise on economics, while his works on the political economy heavily influenced Adam Smith. What makes Cantillon's works not only important in his time, but more than ever relevant today, is his writings on monetary theory, especially where he brought to the forefront the velocity of money in an economy, meaning how quick it moves through the canals of an economy. Simply put, you can expand the money supply, but it has consequences of not being spent or overspent in respect to savings and consumption.

Essai is where he developed the relation of money supply (fiat money printing) to inflation, first stating that new money first had a localised effect in creating higher prices, and then those that received the money first benefited most, while the latter benefited less.

This is the exact trap we see in the modern U.S. economy, where liquidity is not leading to desired consumption because people took helicopter money and out of frustration mostly spent it on Amazon, vis-à-vis China, with the effect of clogging up container traffic from China (container costs are up five-fold assuming you can find one) leading to inflation. Even if you can find a container to ship from the UK, it is hard to find drivers that rather stay home on government money. It is the money printing causing inflation and shortages, the Covid narrative is the deflection that allows this

---

1   Richard Cantillon, *Essay on the Nature of Commerce in General*, trans. Henry Higgs (New York: Routledge, 2001).

travesty to continue. The concept of relative inflation, or a disproportionate rise in prices among different goods in an economy, is commonly known as the Cantillon Effect. This is the classical and timeless teaching of the Cantillon Effect.

It is more relevant today than ever, with the increase in prices trickling down the supply chain, we see inflation stemming from the demand on all sorts of products such as shortages on semiconductor chips that are required to build appliances, automobiles, phones, computers, and a host of electronics, all of which are increasing in price. Money printing by Central Banks creates inflation, which causes distorted asset price bubbles in homes and equities, as well as a further wealth divide.

When "too much money chases too few goods", you get inflation, and this is the Cantillon Effect—it is for this reason that Richard Cantillon is essential to understanding inflation. But there is more to the *Essai*—it is here where we first see the use of the word entrepreneur. Cantillon split a society into two categories: one being fixed income earners, and the second entrepreneurs, who earn non-fixed incomes. He stated that entrepreneurs paid a known cost of production, with a tolerance for unknown income while correctly predicting or creating consumer preference and arbitrage. Cantillon did not further develop the role of the entrepreneur—this was done later by Ludwig von Mises, the Austrian economist, in his 1922 book *Socialism*, where he proposed that an economy cannot have equilibrium and growth without the entrepreneur, something that Marx did not even fathom. In 1934, John Maynard Keynes discusses the entrepreneur in *The General Theory of Employment, Interest and Money*, as it relates to wage formation. Later, Murray Rothbard further develops the entrepreneur in his 1963 book *America's Great Depression*, where he states that entrepreneurs are in the business of forecasting changes in the market, both for conditions of demand and of supply.

So, with the intellectual economic works of Richard Cantillon, we can begin to better understand the architecture of inflation, and the dynamic flows of money and human risk in the way of the entrepreneur. It is this gift that defines Cantillon's legacy.

Inflation's Devastating Consequences

Inflation is the concept of higher prices for products and services in the face of stagnant wages. It affects people on pensions, the shrinking middle-class, the working poor, those on government subsidies as a way of life, and students, while it degrades the concept of fiat money being a store of value. In a nutshell, it results in the consumer paying more for less. People who are schooled and disciplined in the growth of wealth are less affected, since they take refuge into hard assets, as well as using hedging strategies.

Inflation has a long history, going back to sustained inflation due to gold discoveries by Spain during the 15th century. In the 20th century, we saw inflation after World War II and its aftermath, as was the case in Hungary in 1946. Perhaps its most astounding example was German hyperinflation in 1923, during the Weimer Republic, where it would take barrels of fiat money (German Marks) to buy a loaf of bread, and often by the time a person reached the front of the line, they would need even more money to make the purchase.

The cause of the Weimar Republic's inflation was that its key industries were confiscated by France and Belgium, its gold reserves were depleted, and it had unsustainable war reparations from World War I. John Maynard Keynes, who accompanied Prime Minister David Lloyd George during the Versailles Peace Conference of 1919, was deeply troubled by the political and economic price imposed on Germany by the victors, and as a result published his 1919 book *The Economic Consequences of Peace*.

Germany's economy was devastated after World War I, primarily due to hyperinflation because of money printing to attempt to satisfy war reparations, which needed to be paid in foreign currencies or gold. This led Germany to print money to purchase gold, in order to convert the gold into a foreign currency that would satisfy the victors' reparation demands, which resulted in the collapse of the Deutsche Mark, and subsequent hyperinflation and the wiping out of the middle-class.

History has a habit of rewarding the most successful hero with its unintended consequence of producing tyranny within the soul of the savour. This was certainly the case with the Romantics of the 18th century who abdicated safety for excitement, which they received their fill of from the French Revolution that produced Napoleon. In Germany, the most successful hero to save the country from economic woe was Hitler, who did just that, but at the price of tyranny.

It is doubtful that the National Socialist German Workers' Party, formed in 1920, and then led by Hitler from 1921 to 1945, would have gained political momentum without the unbearable price of reparations imposed upon Germany. It is true that the French and Belgians were especially vindictive toward Germany after World War I. But the genesis of World War II inadvertently laid in the inter-ally debt of the peace, where loans were not forgiven by the Americans, and it was historically customary for allies in war to forgive debt. As Michael Hudson states in his book *Super Imperialism*, in the economic monetary strategy of American Empire the only challenge that lay in America's way of empire was Britain and the pound sterling, which was firmly embedded in its imperial preference economic trading order within the Commonwealth countries.

America was owed $12 billion in intergovernmental allied debt, of which $4.7 billion was owed by Britain. Conversely, Britain was owed $11 billion by the allies, much of this by Russia, which became uncollectable after the Bolshevik revolution of 1917. In essence, when America put pressure on Britain to pay its inter-ally debt, Britain exerted pressure on its European allies, who in turn choked Germany. By far, Europe suffered the most human loss of life in World War I and in exchange for keeping America out of the war until 1917 resulting in saving American lives, in turn Europe thought this could be traded for the forgiveness of inter-ally debt, but the Americans would have none of it. President Wilson, through isolationism, had left the American Army unprepared for a war on the scale of Europe. But with resources such as labour, money, and manufacturing capacity for arms production, the position of the United States was, why fight the war themselves when neither the loss of American life or money spent would be recoverable?[2] It was a political strategy

2   Michael Hudson, *Super Imperialism* (London: Pluto Press, 2003).

immersed in classical American isolationism, in essence it shifted the burden both in lives and economic costs to Europe.

In January of 1923, Conservative British Prime Minister Bonar Law sent Montagu Norman and Stanley Baldwin to Washington to negotiate these loan agreements with President Warren Harding's Secretary of the Treasury, Andrew Mellon.

The intent and the outcome further weakened Britain's Empire that was already exhausted on all fronts after World War I, as the Americans imposed British loans at a 3.3 percent interest rate, while only 1.8 percent on Belgium, and 1.6 percent on France.

For these reasons Britain did not share the fruits of victory and miserably lost the peace, while seeing the steep erosion of the Empire that gifted the world with the English language, Magna Carta, systems of commerce, the industrial revolution and America's founding fathers.

Going forward, we shall see how America had its own battles with inflation, although nowhere as severe as what was experienced by the Weimar Republic.

The U.S. economy, and much of the rest of the world, has had some epic sumo wrestling matches with inflation, which was stubborn from 1916 to 1920, at an average of about 15 percent, and came back again during the latter part of World War II in America. Fast forwarding for a moment, inflation reappeared again in the 1960s in the single-digit realm, playing havoc during the Nixon and Carter years. At one point, Nixon took the playbook from John Maynard Keynes and implemented a socialist doctrine in the early 1970s by evoking wage and price controls, meaning the government felt it could, by decree, forcefully control wages and prices. In effect, the result was that they were willing participants in creating distorted price formation, only to be brow-beaten back by natural market mechanisms. Even though Nixon was an ardent proponent of the free markets and detested communism, which he intellectually states in his book *1999*; however, he unwittingly was practicing a form of socialism or communism, as his strange choice by manipulating the means of production, and more specifically price formation. This type of thinking is against the natural price formation delivered by the free markets, and its effects were devastating.

Eventually, U.S. Fed Chair Paul Volcker slayed inflation in the late 1970s and early 1980s with a bold initiative of double-digit interest rates that contracted growth through monetary policy. The option of tapering asset purchases since 2008 is off the table. Why? Because an increase of interest rates at any significant level would collapse the equity markets, broad asset classes, and most governments, almost overnight. This is touched upon in detail in Chapter 15 as we discuss the correlation of deficit spending and sovereign government debt default.

The Phillips Curve

To explain the relationship between inflation and unemployment, which was said to be the missing link of Keynesianism at the time, was the advent of the Phillips curve. Named after the New Zealand economist A. W. Phillips in 1960, the Phillips curve identified a systematic relationship between inflation and unemployment. Simply put, there was a trade-off between inflation and unemployment. If you wanted low inflation, it was at the expense of higher unemployment, and if you wanted low unemployment it would result in higher inflation.

This was easy for most policy makers in Washington to grasp, to add to their repertoire of interfering in the free markets with unintended consequences, as we shall see later.

Figure 5.1: Phillips Curve

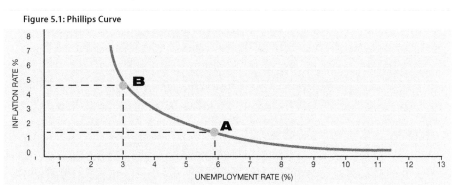

In theory, policy makers had to pick a balance between two evils, since there is no such thing as zero unemployment, the trade-off in the above chart shows at point B, 5 percent inflation for 3 percent unemployment, and inversely in point A, we see 6 percent unemployment with a trade-off of 1percent inflation. But sometimes modeling and reality do not make the best of bedfellows!

Stagflation and the Phillips Curve

The Phillips curve was held within the intellectual thinking of economics in the 1960s as a prevalent analysis of the relationship between inflation and unemployment. However, cracks at its very seams started to appear by the early 1970s, when we witnessed the decoupling of the inverse relationship between high unemployment and low inflation. A strange thing happened, we saw the phenomena of high unemployment and high inflation that contradicted the tenets of the Phillips curve, hence the introduction of the term "stagflation". This meant that policy advisors could no longer rely on the trade-off between inflation and unemployment.

Stagflation became undeniable by 1975 when CPI inflation hit 9.1 percent and unemployment reached 8.5 percent, while the GDP contracted both in 1974 and 1975. Keynesian economics could not explain these factors.

Milton Friedman, who won a Nobel Prize in 1976 for his contributions on consumption, monetary history, and theory, as well as addressing the nuances of stabilization policy, did not subscribe to the Keynesian model of "demand pull " inflation but posited that it was monetary in nature—in other words inflation driven by the money supply and interest rates. Friedman argued that the Federal Reserve should pursue a constrictive monetary policy, since without money supply, inflation's fire would suffocate from lack of monetary oxygen, and it would follow that Friedman must have been influenced by Richard Cantillon's 18th century works. It is reasonable to support Friedman's thinking when considering the 2021 inflation genie that the Fed has unleashed, and of course they will not be held to account by the financial legacy media.

The role of the Fed is to be independent from the U. S. government Treasury, which it was, but no longer is. Consider former Fed Chair Janet Yellen, who now heads the U.S. Treasury, who received millions of dollars in speaking fees from Wall Street firms and is indebted to Wall Street as a result. This is a clear conflict of interest, especially as Fed Chairman Jerome Powel continues to keep the printing presses running. There was a time when the Fed was less politicized and operated outside the influence of the US government, and as a result, government had to spend within its means.

Paul Volcker, Chairman of the Fed from 1979 to 1987, put Friedman's monetary theory into practice in 1979, by driving interest rates into double-digits, which brought inflation under control by the mid-1980s at the expense of contracting the economy into a recession.

We started seeing severe inflation again in 2021, not only in CPI index at near 4 percent, and hitting near 8 percent in early 2022, but in asset price inflation in stocks, raw materials, and real estate assets in the 20 percent range. However, with a $30 trillion debt, an increase in interest rates would lead to a debt default by the Treasury. Besides, there is no political capital to increase interest rates in a meaningful way. If Fed Chairman Powell increases interest rates and tapers the money printing in any meaningful way— the political and economic implications would tank the economy beyond recognition as the whole Ponzi scheme would crumble like a house of cards. As of May 2022, Powell has started to increase interest rates, but this is just political window dressing, for the problem that the U.S. Federal Reserve and government created through Wild Wild West fiscal and monetary policy since 2008. It is at best delusional to think that a slight rise in interest rates or even 100 basis points would have any meaningful effect on inflation, while at the same time it is tanking the stock market. The debt is considered in Chapter 15 in some detail, where it becomes clearer that any meaningful increase in interest rates would collapse the economy and asset prices.

To be fair, Paul Volcker did not have to deal with near $30 trillion debt, which has turned into the quagmire of our times, and is the looming noose around the neck of tomorrow! It simply takes monetary flexibility off the table.

Volcker believed Milton Friedman's statement that "Inflation is always and everywhere a monetary phenomenon."[3] In other words, he believed prices could not increase without an increase in the money supply. To get the economically devastating effects of inflation under control in the 1970s, the Federal Reserve should have followed a constrictive monetary policy. This finally happened in 1979 when Volcker put the monetarist theory into practice. A monetarist is an economist who holds the strong belief that money supply is the primary factor affecting demand in an economy.[4] Volcker drove interest rates to double-digit levels, reduced inflation, and sent the economy into a recession. This is impossible to do today because of the debt, which is again treated in Chapter 15.

Today we are seeing the U.S. Fed drastically increase the money supply with the purchase of U.S. Treasury bills, being the willing accomplice to the Treasury's intoxicated spending with no realistic chance of paying all this debt back.

Phillips curve hardline apologists argue that it has shifted to the right, but by the 1980s Keynesianism's flaws were painfully evident. However, it is still used by the government to convince itself that by interfering in the market they are doing more good than harm, leading to some command economy characteristics that includes a heavily subsidized electric vehicle industry.

John Maynard Keynes was in some ways a tragic hero. Milton Friedman once said that if Keynes lived another 10 years—some say the stress of Bretton Woods shortened his life—he would be horrified at how extreme government intervention in the economy had become. Freidman went on to say that "Keynes had the

3   Milton Friedman, *The Counter-Revolution in Monetary Theory: First Wincott Memorial Lecture, Delivered at the Senate House, University of London, 16 September, 1970* (Minneapolis: University of Minnesota, 1970), 24.
4   Adam Hayes, "What is a Monetarist?" Investopedia, updated March 23, 2021, https://www.investopedia.com/terms/m/monetarist.asp

standing force of character and personality to reel in his disciples."[5] And because Keynes was not afforded another 10 years of life, economies would have averted the macroeconomic disequilibrium in wages, asset prices, especially inflation, and the resulting largesse and addictive government, on the verge of financial collapse! If Keynes was alive today, in a defense of Keynesianism, he might just repeat what he purportedly once said to a reporter.

"People will do the rational thing,
but only after exploring all
other alternatives." —*John Maynard Keynes*[6]

Types of Inflation

There are two schools of thought in respect to inflation: the Keynesian and Monetarist's arguments, some of which have been touched upon.

Keynesianism believes that inflation is the result of "demand pull," where high demand for goods and services exceeds the capacity output of an economy at current prices. This includes the possibility of higher wage increases and further union concessions (when unions were relatively powerful before America's manufacturing decline). But in the case of the public sector today, they are almost impossible to get concessions in a recession—of course, this is at the expense of the public purse. The big problem with this approach is that it conveniently ignores monetary policy, where higher interest rates beat back inflation, or lower interest rates increase inflation, at least in the historical sense. Further, this approach does not consider increasing the money supply. Keynes

5   "Milton Friedman Discusses John Maynard Keynes," Common Sense Capitalism, November 17, 2010, YouTube video, https://www.youtube.com/watch?v=_9DH07MBG_w
6   John Maynard Keynes, "Liberalism and Labour," *The Nation and Athenæum*, February 20, 1926.

believed that wages do not drive inflation, but demand pull does, and that salaries react to inflation, and not cause it, especially in a scarce resource environment.

The monetary theory of the cause of inflation posits that inflation is derived from "cost push." For example, wages go up with unions and then this is pushed to the consumer, or business to business (B2B) sectors. It believes that a small group of companies within certain closely-held industries can dictate prices, and a good example of this is the price increases achieved in the computer chip business, which is dominated by Intel, Taiwan Semiconductor, and AMD. Another example is how resin companies (resin is needed to make plastic bottles and smart phones), at the first sound of oil price increases (oil is needed to make resin), will impose price increases to blow molders (bottle makers), which will be passed on to the final producer. Thus, with higher plastic bottle costs, the shampoo/body wash and vitamin manufacturer will be forced to pass on the increase to retailers. Companies like Proctor & Gamble can pass this increase on to retailers, since P&G has strong brand equity and channel strength. Remember, even if oil drops from $80 a barrel down to $20, the resin company will barely reflect this in their price, because it is no different than taking back a dog's bone.

As an afterthought, in my opinion, both schools of thought have respective validity and shortcomings, even though I personally lean closer to Friedman in his cost push assessment of inflation. However, I must add that lower interest rates and an increase in the money supply will stimulate demand, until it reaches the saturation point as the cause of inflation becomes monetary in nature. What both economists might have missed is efficiency gains in the way of the industrial and office automation as well as advancement of manufacturing robotics, software engineering and the general increase in white collar productivity, which all in theory stabilizes inflation. Then if we do direct labour costing as a component of finished goods and services, labour per units of finished goods or services may be shrinking because of widespread gains in automation and AI. A good example is cable companies that make automated calls for payment, while the "chat" customer support system employs a combination of a robot or a live person handling five customer support calls at the same time. Hence, your labour cost component is spread over higher output of efficiency.

With all this being said, what should also be considered is the pressure of eight billion people on one planet driving up the demand for resources such as energy, food, and raw materials for finished goods affecting final price output, to the point where the West is no longer able to export its inflation to low-cost producers in Asia. I am not sure that cost push or demand pull really accounts for the effects of a growing planet with high demand for energy and key element resources for production, which is producing a hungry furnace that is fanning the flames of inflation.

Low Monetary Policy and No inflation. Could This Be Magic?

Yes, it looks like the Riddler has Batman in a head-spin again, because up until 2020 and since the mid-1990s, we were experiencing the combination of low (CPI) inflation, relatively low unemployment, and GDP growth, with the exception of 2008 to 2009, when the U.S. government inadvertently helped precipitate a market meltdown, partially by allowing the government-owned Fannie Mae and Freddie Mac to backstop bad real estate loans. Fannie May and Freddie Mac are government entities that purchase low down payment mortgages off lenders freeing up capital for banks to make fresh loans, with an initiative to help people get into homes often with lower down payments. For an encore, the easy money policy that the world is addicted to has burst the asset bubble again in March of 2020, and has since re-inflated asset prices through accommodative monetary policy, which is conveniently pinned in its entirety on the pandemic. This covered up the alarming issues of September 2019, where the Fed had to drop interest rates for international banking liquidity in order to keep the repo market flowing, while a recession was in clear play. To be fair, the exogenous shock of the global pandemic greatly contributed to the latest economic tragedy, but one cannot conveniently ignore the elephant in the room—namely, asset class bubble distortions caused by artificially low interest rates since 2008, which are fostering poverty and intergenerational economic exclusion, with an outcome being the phenomena of the wealth divide.

Taking a deeper dive with these assertions of cause and effect, the health of world economies has never really recovered from 2008-2009. This is evidenced by the Central Banks not being able to take the patient off life support in the way of low interest rates, and go back to mean reversion interest rates, which is historically in the 6 percent range. The Fed tried to shrink its balance sheets by slowing selling their bonds instead. In May of 2016, the Fed started increasing rates from 0.037 percent, to as high as 2.4 percent in the summer of 2019, but then started dropping interest rates closer to 1 percent by year-end. Why? Because their models showed a pending recession or a slowing GDP—this in addition to buying repos in Europe. This is, of course, forgotten in light of the COVID-19 pandemic.

The audience might ask the magician, "how have we been having low inflation and low monetary policy together?" The genesis of the answer really lies in China joining the WTO in 2001, of which President Clinton was the primary architect, and then-Senator Biden was a strong supporter of. The thinking was that China would develop Western values as part of a peace dividend theory. The key to our higher living standard in the West was simply that China's low-cost goods increased our living standards and increased the basket size when cashing out at Walmart. When you can get more for less, it increases a nation's living standards, so what we did was export our inflation and carbon footprints, as we now hypocritically wag our fingers at China's ecology, and we imported their unemployment. This was the trade-off, as the Radio City Rockettes kept dancing, why ruin the festivities!

Twenty years later, there was a price to pay: much of the manufacturing in the West, and more specifically America's heartland, has been decimated as jobs were lost, wages never recovered, and opioid use skyrocketed. Hillary Clinton put a dagger into their hearts and ruined her presidential aspirations by calling these people deplorable—the same deplorables that did some of the most dangerous work in factories, died in battle for erroneous wars under the obfuscated mantra of patriotism, and built infrastructure that helped lift America.

Yes, we laid down for China as they pick-pocketed our intellectual property and hollowed out our manufacturing industry with no Sheriff in town to administrate justice. After all, who cared about such a tragic trade-off when inflation was tamed and Walmart shoppers filled their carts. With low prices, the consumer was getting more for less, mega-corporations imported and rid themselves of higher and more regulated costs, while the savage beast of inflation had disappeared into the magician's mystic hands. However, as the British Empire found out, "when a nation loses its manufacturing, it loses its inventiveness,"[7] one reason that our engineers have little experience in the plants is because of this, and the detachment from the factory floor does not allow

7   Lawrence James, The Rise and Fall of the British Empire (New York: St. Martin's, 1994).

them to learn from the hands-on technicians to help them better teethe and go up the learning curve. On a micro scale, these are the building blocks of a nation's manufacturing competitive intensity.

It was the loss of manufacturing that greatly contributed to the fall of the British Empire, and it is fair to note that Germany has kept its manufacturing and produces more than likely the finest engineers in the world. But there is more at play here, and where we looked at labor as the cause of inflation, at least in the monetary view, we can now replace labor with automation. In 1961, General Motors used the first industrial robot in their New Jersey plant, which was invented by George Devol Jr. in 1954. Sadly, this is another industry that America lost to the Japanese and the Germans. Today, Rockwell Automation, FANUC Robotics, and a host of others worldwide, manufacture these robots for as low as $35,000, or $4 per hour over four years to run based on a payback analysis—and these robots don't form unions, don't call in sick, aren't woke, don't spend idle time on the social media, and can outproduce modern day Luddites. Thus, assuming raw material prices don't inflate as we are now seeing in 2020-22 in the way of commodities, industrial robots, and those who know how to set them up, and keep them humming might be the greatest inflation slayer of all time! So, perhaps the new battleground in a nation's competitive advantage is not only the quality and quantity of their labor and stock capital, but the quality and quantity of their industrial robots, CNC machines, and, of course, AI.

It is also interesting to note that Germany, which has kept its manufacturing base, is proficient in the industrial robotics space, so much so that German robotic manufacturer Kuka was purchased in 2016 by Midea Group of China.

So, when we consider industrial automation, an idea that was founded in America back in the 1950s, and its loss of American leadership in this space reads like a Greek tragedy except this time in an empty theatre.

Other Explanations of Inflation

Realizing that we have travelled a long road with a reasonable narrative that efficiency has tamed inflation, by historical standards, and it is this great leap forward that has exponentially increased production possibility frontiers that David Ricardo, the British economist, first discussed in the 19th century. More importantly, the cumulative outcome of increased economic efficiency has increased living standards, while coinciding with the consumer's innate predisposition to increase their welfare in life, meaning wanting "more for less." Adam Smith, the father of free markets in the 18th century, discusses this in some detail, as prescribed in his book *The Wealth of Nations*.

It might be convenient to walk away from the section on inflation and move on to unemployment, but this might leave us with just a shallow understanding of inflation and its many interpretations. Why? Because there are some more things to consider here, and that is, how inflation is measured, and is it an empirically valid economic litmus test? Dealing with certain alternative truths was not discussed in my MBA economics textbook, and anyway, the exams were so academically rigorous that we all lived in fear to make sure we made it, and many did not.

The classical measurement of inflation is the Consumer Price Index (CPI), and then one might ask, how is the CPI put together, and what are its components and weights? The CPI includes a host of items, such as foods, consumer goods, electronics, energy, car rentals, shelter, fruits, housing, mortgage costs, electricity, childcare, ISP providers, cable, phones, and the list goes on. If you are statistically curious, it is based on a Laspeyres Index, which I became proficient at during my quantitative studies, and you can find out more about inflation by doing a search under "Canadian CPI Basket of Goods and Services 2020."

In finding some type of logic, how can we now reconcile low interest rates with low inflation? Consider the relationship of the Phillips curve that showed us low inflation meant a tradable of high unemployment, and vice versa, and at one point in the 1960s and '70s, we had stagflation, which means high unemployment with high inflation. I hope the Riddler has not made you dizzy, but we were in the age of low unemployment and low inflation, in a low monetary policy environment—well, that's before the economic meltdown of 2008, when unemployment spiked to 9.9 percent in 2009, stayed stubbornly high until 2018, when it was driven down to a more manageable range of under 4 percent, where the Fed believed it could affect unemployment through the money supply. Then came the more catastrophic 2020 exogenous shock due to the pandemic, which helped spike unemployment to 14.8 percent in April of 2020, where perhaps the real number was closer to 20 percent effective unemployment.

The burning question becomes where did the inflation go? Has someone taken the time to file a missing person's report? Has someone called in the FBI to find this missing entity? Has the Riddler taken over Gotham City, and is it possible Batman is eating potato chips, while watching reruns of professional wrestling, playing online video games, and having a text fight with the sumptuous Cat woman? Is Commissioner Gordon just another idle bureaucrat?

Well, as mentioned earlier, the simple answer is that we exported our inflation to China to ensure we get cheap goods, while importing their unemployment. We even exported our carbon footprint to China. Don't touch that dial and don't get dizzy with all this hip economic speak, revelations are coming! Read on! We lived good—we lived for today, and personal savings became a blasphemous relic of an antiquated period. It seems the bone strengthening economic experiences of the greatest generation that endured the Great Depression were not propagated to future generations, since the lessons of living within our means as households and government spending has been discarded. Has the cultural weakening of our collective souls not drawn from the lessons of the past, while only allowing the seductive winds of the present?

The citizens of Athens wanted more for less, and they wanted it now, so the Fed, which first turned on the money supply in 2008, went full throttle in March of 2020 when the stock market cratered. This most impressed the applauding participants who rode the credit and asset price inflation bubble (especially Wall Street aristocracy and holders of real estate), back into fabled prosperity. People felt wealthy, as their intrinsic sense of perceived worth was as good as their last BMW payment. Facts don't matter, but endorphin-induced material possessions do, as our cupboards runneth over with trinkets from Dollar Tree, and earbuds to tune into affordable iPhones, because of overseas low-cost manufacturing. This would not be possible without China, while we tuned out the future of our civilization, as we ignore the pending peril just to have one more dance with the addictiveness of the present. But this party is over now, as the bouncers are starting to remove the last of the most inebriated from Bourbon Street.

But if we are to believe in "cost push" inflation as prescribed by Monetarists, this might be supported by the experience of inflation in your firm that you work at or run. For example, what happens when you get a price increase, and you cannot pass it on in the trade, and your competitor got the same increase, and said they will absorb it to keep market share? What if you are buying in UK pounds and the Canadian dollar depreciates against the GBP? You have perhaps experienced channel inflation, and when you try to pass it on in the channel, your competitor is willing to work on razor thin margins, or maybe you have a sharp CFO, and you hedged your currency exposure.

Have you ever tried to get a price increase from Walmart or Amazon? It is like getting in the ring with Spartacus or unwittingly signing up for a sumo wrestling match at Ryōgoku Sumo Hall in Japan, and your opponent has 300-pound advantage. Or better still, once you present inflation to your customers, they might want to slay you in the Roman Coliseum as the Senators look on in amusement. What if at the news of the price increase, your customers exhibit neanderthal chest beating and growling sounds? The financial tragedy on many firms is that afterward the outcome erodes your profit margins and your brands, while many services often go into perfect competition, to the point that the lower margins diminish the equity of your brands if it is not price inelastic, meaning the demand is not strong enough to warrant a price increase.

What if raw material costs go up and this is not reflected in the official inflation numbers? These numbers are reflected though in the Producer Price Index (PPI) that measures domestic manufacturing, which was 9 percent in March 2022 TY/LY.[8] What if inflation is being imported through a cratering U.S. dollar, compliments of Fed money printing resulting in Chinese factories asking for higher prices? How about the Producer Price Index (PPI) showing a 30 percent increase in April 2022 from the same period last year? And what if this is compounded by higher container costs from China, which was $3,800 up until 2019, and rose above $20,000 in 2021,[9] and climbing to the point that ships can't leave the harbor due to congestion? Sadly, none of this is hypothetical but it is the stark reality we face today, as people became overly consumed by a politicized virus (until the next crises comes along), as they sat home, collected helicopter money, watched Netflix, ordered online, ate and drank too much, and exhibited docility to overreaching government. The result is that ordering from home, they grew the balance sheets of Amazon, which has acted like a pimp of sorts for Chinese-made goods. And, as of early March 2022 ordering corrugated boxes to ship finished goods in, experienced a seven-week lead time!

We have been in the age of hyper-consumerism 2.0 since 2000, which has delivered the taming of inflation, the advent of hyper-affordability complements of China, meaning we dumped the heavy burden of inflation on their backs, which they gladly accepted, but still, there are tradables for the future of tomorrow. In many respects, Consumerism 2.0 resembles the renaissance of 1950s America after World War II, the golden age of consumerism, in the era of large, ostentatious cars. However, the difference being that America was the workshop of the world after World War II,

8   "U.S. Producer Price Index," YCharts, accessed March 27, 2022, https://ycharts.com/indicators/us_producer_price_index
9   Luna Sun, "China's Shipping Insiders Brace for Another Full Year of Rising Freight Rates Having a 'Profound Impact on Trade,'" China Macro Economy, December 19, 2021, https://www.scmp.com/economy/china-economy/article/3160158/chinas-shipping-insiders-brace-another-full-year-rising

with 50 percent of global GDP, with a record of innovation in the last century that is historically incomparable, from the first flight, electrification of cities, Henry Ford's assembly line, solid state circuitry, Atanasoff–Berry computer, software, the satellite, internet, the personal computer, advanced engineering, tooling, the Moon landing, CNC, Robotics, AI, advances in physics and mathematics—the list is endless. When all is considered, the correlation between American inventiveness tied to manufacturing is intellectually and statistically undeniable.

One might notice that since the year 2000, many things became more affordable, such as iPhones, laptops, desktops, clothing, and industrial tooling that are used to manufacture machines—even low-quality pipes made in China that are used in new condominium buildings that leak after four years, because of poor and weak metallurgical composition (if buying a condo, ask for a QC metallurgical certificate on the pipes). The list continues with PCs, running shoes, electronics, earphones, as well as advanced technologies, even though China is behind in advanced semiconductor chips. China is even taking away some of Silicon Valley's social media lunch money with TikTok, to not only further addict but also affect one's health.

Take the case of a Wall Street Journal article, which states:

> According to a spate of recent medical journal articles, doctors say the girls had been watching videos of TikTok influencers who said they had Tourette syndrome, a nervous-system disorder that causes people to make repetitive, involuntary movements or sound.[10]

The taming of inflation was and is due to China reducing the cost of manufacturing to much of the world, and what the consumer received was more for less, which is an innate urge of humans, but there are setbacks. Consider the hollowing out of American manu-

---

10   Julie Jargon, "Teen Girls Are Developing Tics. Doctors Say TikTok Could Be a Factor," *Wall Street Journal*, October 19, 2021.

facturing, loss of jobs, a diminishment of inventiveness, espionage of intellectual property by China, along with low interest rates that propelled the marginal propensity to consume. With no savings and no end in sight, they could only see the lustful Romanticism of the night. Our innate desire to live beyond our means in the present is the savage within us that is conveniently swept under the rug. There are consequences and social ills in all this apathy, as we are transforming into a safe society that has trepidations to meet the future, because it has lost its confidence, while it is the safety of a civilization that leads the blind into the caustic hands of tyranny.

But, when all is said and done, the story of inflation came back after a hiatus from the 1980s, as we are seeing it in other forms that are not reflected by the CPI. Do we not feel it on our skin with grocery bills when we purchase vegetables and fruits? Should we be looking elsewhere into inflation as for an explanation that considers asset price relevancy?

The underlying issues of the hidden underground city of rising prices that is not often considered, forces us to perhaps look at things with a different lens.

The Renaissance of Inflation

For those who lived through the 1970s and '80s, the current theatre production of inflation is not a new Broadway show. The only difference is the type of inflation we are starting to see now is caused by a combination of fiat money printing and a Treasury that spends like drunken sailors at a port of call. Subsequently, we are now living in a time where a population is so addicted to the perceived safety of government handouts where self-reliance is a blasphemous word next on the cancel culture's chopping block, and companies being bailed out as a reward for unsound business practices. This is a toxic brew for an economic meltdown.

The result is a renaissance of inflation, and it is not transitory while it is already showing signs of stagflation. And when we look under the hood, we are seeing raw material prices going up.

To take a deeper dive as to the cause and effect of inflation, a May 2021 article in Barron's provides some insights.[11] Scott Taylor, CEO of Pallet Central Enterprises, says that wood pallets that were costing $7.50 each are now being diverted to the West coast, leading to pricing of over $20.00 each. In order to keep warehouse staff, Taylor has given three wage increases in four months. Home framing and plywood for home builders has gone up four-fold and is playing havoc with home builders and affecting new home prices.

The question then becomes price elasticity of new home prices, but what is driving the shortage? In a Forbes article, Bill Conerly says that it certainly is not raw materials, because we have lots of that.

> It is because existing mills are having difficulty recruiting labor in not only the wake of the virus, but primarily it is back-breaking work, the young are advised to go to college instead; the government keeps issuing helicopter money, which in many cases pays more than these jobs; mills are in remote areas, where the youth are leaving, not migrating to; glue shortages; and truck drivers are in high demand to move the goods. It is this combination of factors that have driven random lengths wood framing prices from $350 per thousand feet to $1,500, which are not captured in the CPI inflation index, where sawmills are simply not able to keep up with new homebuilders' demand. The chart below starts giving a more accurate picture of framing costs.[12]

11   Lisa Beilfuss, "Inflation Is Here and Hotter than It Looks. Why It's Time to Worry," Barron's, updated May 17, 2021.
12   Bill Conerly, "Why Lumber and Plywood Prices Are So High—And When They Will Come Down," Forbes, May 21, 2021, https://www.forbes.com/sites/billconerly/2021/05/22/why-lumber-and-plywood-prices-are-so-high-and-when-they-will-come-down/?sh=757d32a84b71

Figure 5.2: Framing and Lumber Prices

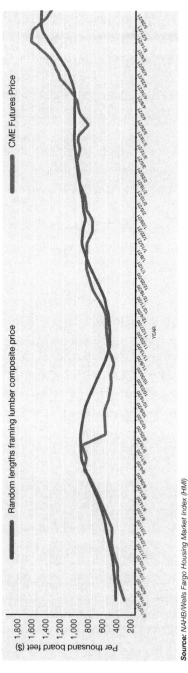

Source: NAHB/Wells Fargo Housing Market Index (HMI)

When all is said and done, this looks like a combination of cost push inflation, where commodity prices are increasing, and demand pull, with a concomitant increase in wages.

For many firms, labour is their highest cost center, and it is typical that companies are reluctant to increase wage costs because they are nearly irreversible, according to many Wall Street economists. Hilton Hotels CEO Christopher Nassetta stated that in 2021, labour shortages were constraining their recovery, which has been especially acute in the hospitality space.[13] The story of wage inflation comes particularly to light where Domino's Pizza drivers in some cases are being offered $1,000 signing bonuses, in addition to a $25 per hour wage, while Federal Express is offering a $500 signing bonus. Small businesses are particularly hit hard, where Procopio Companies, a U.S. commercial real estate builder, is having trouble filling positions with skilled trades despite offering a $20,000 signing bonus. Plumbers are commanding $170,000 annual salaries and construction estimators are being paid $150,000 per year, while small retailers are having major challenges hiring, in addition to the lockdowns.

All these wages will create a tidal wave of inflation that is not transitory, as the Fed would want us to believe, because the acute increase cannot be retarded back, while the cumulative effect of this inflation is a tax on the consumer.

When we look closer, it becomes clear that we have "cost push" wage inflation. When the government attempted to manipulate wage formation through minimum wage fiscal policy in 2021, it lacked political capital to pass congress. Incidentally, this is the same type of wage price formation that failed miserably during the Great Depression, which resulted in further exacerbating and contracted the economy. Never to give up on wage increase ideas, as we shall see, it was accomplished inadvertently through helicopter money.

13 "Hilton CEO Christopher Nassetta at Skift Global Forum 2021," Skift, October 20, 2021, https://skift.com/2021/10/20/hilton-ceo-christopher-nassetta-at-skift-global-forum-2021/

U.S. and Canadian governments' next self-congratulatory cosmic vision would only add to their unblemished record of failures, namely, to drop fiat helicopter money, with the net result being wage inflation, which sits squarely on government's shoulders. It was this helicopter money that had wider ramifications of unleashing the inflation genie by creating logistical bottlenecks and hyperinflation with international containers. Why? Because many at home getting their daily dose of media fear, alleviated their anxiety by ordering on Amazon, to buy even more Chinese goods. After all, why work, when one can make more money by sitting at home, watching Godzilla vs. Kong on Amazon Prime, helping their immunity against the COVID-19 virus with a buffet of junk food, while finding a higher consciousness with alcoholic spirits, and cannabis. Then to cap things off, many were coerced into taking an experimental MRNA jab in exchange for the freedom, to participate in a society, with the caveat being that there is no legal recourse under EUA against the pharmaceutical companies. In defense of Hoover and FDR, at least they had work programs that built infrastructure, as opposed to encouraging idle lethargy during the Great Depression.

Unquestionably, the inflation, along with economic distortions we are seeing, now sits squarely on the combined shoulders of government and the Central Bank's fiat money printing. However, the official narrative will more likely point to firms as the villains, for the plebeians to feast on, as their all-you-can-eat official buffet.

Home Price inflation

The story even takes more twists and turns as the plot thickens. When we look at the anatomy of easy money, the mainstream media business script readers look at the CPI inflation index published by the St. Louis Fed, which is at over 8 percent, well above the Fed inflation goal of 2 percent, as the barometer of inflation the Fed and the MSM attempted to sell a narrative of transitory inflation, meaning temporary, as the economy adjusts back into equilibrium. Then this brings us back again to the Richard Cantillon effect, who in the

18th century predicted the relationship between the money supply and inflation. Simply put, his prophecy of too much money chasing too few goods, as the result of expanding the money supply, is more relevant than ever, in helping to explain inflation.

But the story of different types of inflation starts rearing its ugly head that is driving a host of things well beyond just wage disparity. Namely asset price inflation and its comparative relativity of the false sense of wealth effect it creates, when compared to fiat money.

Let's start with the price of homes, where Case-Shiller index, which measures national home prices in the United States, has gone up from 213 basis points in March of 2020, to 243 basis points in March of 2021, for a total of a 14 percent increase. Then from March 2021 to March 2022 we see another 20 percent increase.

Figure 5.3: S&P/Case-Shiller U.S. National Home Price Index

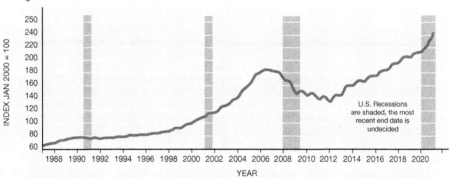

Source: *S&P Dow Jones*   fred.stlouisfed.org

But the story gets more interesting when we consider the most heated markets in the U.S. that paint an even more inflated picture. Cities and surrounding areas in Boston, Phoenix, Tampa and the likes are reporting home price increases in the 20 percent range. According to the Wall Street Journal, even some of the zip codes in the poorest neighbourhoods with median home prices at $100,000 are experiencing acute increase of 42 percent since 2018 to April 2021.[14] In Youngstown, Detroit and other economical-

14   Ben Eisen, "Housing-Market Surge Is Making the Cheapest Homes the Hottest," Wall Street Journal, May 12, 2021.

ly strapped neighbourhoods, local entrepreneurs are purchasing these homes on the cheap, fixing them up to flip them, or better still, live in them to help revive the neighbourhood.

In Canada the story is much the same. Vancouver and Toronto home prices have appreciated approximately 20 percent from March 2020 to March 2021.[15] Subsequently, the same holds true comparing 2021 to 2022 year to date, but single detached homes have cooled. Even outlier areas such as Hamilton, Oshawa, Hamilton, Brantford and the likes are seeing much higher prices—surprisingly, quieter markets in the Maritimes are seeing noticeable appreciation in home prices as well.

Many homeowners feel the wealth effect, and as a result, their marginal propensity to consume is psychologically favourably impacted. However, the adverse effect is that it shuts many out of the housing market, and there is much virtuous speak of the wealth inequality gap, which is really caused by the Central Banks and government working together, to further aggravate distorted asset price barriers to entry. Specifically, it is done first with the dual blessings of the Treasury and U.S. Federal Reserve through interest rates (monetary policy) that distort asset prices, making homes unaffordable for the working poor, but perhaps even more tragically for Gen Z and Millennials, through the phenomena of intergenerational poverty. As of 2021, the U.S. Central Bank is purchasing $40 billion per month of mortgage-backed securities to further inflate the housing bubble with the effect of doing an encore of the 2008 capital market meltdown. In other words, today they are encouraging reckless lending that is exasperating inflated home prices, while buying potentially toxic securities in the way of these mortgage-backed securities.

It is this wealth inequality gap which government will never be able to resolve, but only create and aggravate, which becomes even more crystal clear later in this book when we look at the history of the Great Depression and economic pullbacks.

---

15 "Canadian Housing Market News," WOWA, accessed March 27, 2022, https://wowa.ca/reports/canada-housing-market

What Is a Home Really Worth?

When taking into account the value of your home, consider that the future savings of your low-cost mortgage is built into the higher present value of the price of your home today. Here's a numerical explanation: to keep the numbers simple, let's say you bought a home in the Toronto area worth $1.5 million in a 2 percent mortgage interest rate environment, and you took a mortgage of $1,000,000 amortized over 25 years. In this scenario you would pay $271,000 in interest over such a period. If interest rates were in mean reversion (normal historical levels that puts asset prices in equilibrium) rate environment of 6 percent, you would pay our $932,000 in interest over the same 25 years. The difference in the savings is $661,000, and if you deduct the differential on the interest savings, it means your $1.5 million home is really worth $839,000. This is a pristine example of distortions of economic valuation and the toxic cause and affect of intergenerational poverty as a result of money printing.

You can do this yourself with an online mortgage calculator, and the concept of future value savings without getting into more complex discounted cash flow models.

As a side note, once you understand the time value of money, as Warren Buffet says, you will become wealthy, cautious, and become patient about putting aside your insatiable human wants and instant gratification and respect the time value of money in investment vehicles.[16]

Looking at some other paradigms of inflation, on a relative basis, let's say that home prices have increased 20 percent in one year, and last year you had $1,000,000 of cash sitting in the bank hoping to buy a house in one year—when that year passed, the same house you contemplated to buy which was $1,000,000 is now $1.2 million.

16   Warren Buffett, "Chairman's Letter," Berkshire Hathaway, Inc., February 27, 1987, https://www.berkshirehathaway.com/letters/1986.html

In essence, what happened is that your $1,000,000 is now worth $800,000, with respect to last year's relativity of purchasing power of real estate as an asset class, or differently put, it is a devaluation of sorts on your fiat money. In other words, you lost $200,000 on the currency you held in cash, and this is called "currency inflation." It is one of the reasons that currency does not hold value in relative to other assets. Put differently, currency is a depreciating asset, especially in light of effective purchasing power. You can apply this exercise to your grocery bills, for example, from 2020 to 2021, to 2022 by comparing your documented receipts for food shopping, and then compare this against the Feds CPI inflation index, which sits around 7.9 percent. As the evidence of effective inflation mounts, the CPI index which is the convenient barometer the Central Banks and government uses, lacks plausibility. This brings about asset price relevancy as we now consider a plethora of comparables.

Asset Price Comparative Relevancy

Let's say you own your house, and you are titillated that in one year that $1,000,000 house has gone to $1.2 million, but that is only in respect to fiat money, especially when we compare it to other asset classes. Consider the following line of thinking: as of the end of May 2020, crude oil traded at $36 a barrel, meaning that it would take 27,777 barrels of crude oil to buy your house one year ago. As of April 2022, crude oil is trading at $100, which means it would take only 12,000 barrels of crude oil to buy your house. Yes, your house went up $200,000, however, oil went up 277 percent, meaning the $1 million of oil is now worth $2.8 million. The end result is that a hard asset like crude oil outperformed the appreciation of your home by approximately $1.6 million. Once we look at things with this type of a lens it might cause one to scratch their head, as to which train ticket to buy. To replicate this, all one would have to do is purchase either a perpetual futures contract, or for the less adventurous, buy a non-leveraged oil ETF such as USO or put down 20 percent and buy $1 million of Bloomberg crude UCO (two times the price movement of the spot price) symbol ETF, and pay about a 2 percent margin loan rate. Before friction costs, depending on the scenario, your return would be $1.8 million. In all these options, one has a much more liquid asset that you can convert into fiat, while at the same time, if you did this, you could buy that $1.2 million house for cash and have at least $600,000 extra left over to take the family out to see the premier of *Godzilla vs. Kong*. There are a host of "what if" scenarios you can try, both through leverage and otherwise, depending on the financial instrument you utilize.

The argument made here is that your home is increasing in value against fiat money only, but decreasing in value against a hard asset like oil, over a two-year period. It should be noted that real estate has liquidity issues, especially in a pullback, that many are in denial of or have not experienced.

As we are now flirting with the idea of looking at inflation through a different lens, let's consider another asset class, namely the Nasdaq. The Nasdaq exchange was founded in 1971, and the name is an acronym for the National Association of Securities Dealers Automated Quotations. Originally it was brought out as a stock quotation system, and traded over the counter stocks (OTC), which are stocks that are not officially listed that dealers trade and can lack the liquidity of IBM or P&G.

It eventually merged with the London Stock Exchange, and by the late '90s the advertising slogan was "the stock market for the next hundred years" as it became the first market in the U.S. to trade online. It then evolved into the exchange today that is best known for its technology related stocks.

On January 2, 2020, the Nasdaq was trading at 9,150. In the subsequent COVID-19 pandemic meltdown of March 2020 it tanked to 7,700. This, of course, caused the crowd to miss the final act of the play as they were running for the doors in the burning theatre. What they didn't consider in their moment of panic is that the Fed was turning on its money presses to reinflate the stock market. In January of 2020 the Fed had approximately $4.2 trillion of assets on their balance sheet, and by June 1st it increased to $7.165 trillion, meaning in 4 months they printed near $3 trillion out of thin air to reinflate the markets. Certainly, considering that it was an election year the executive branch was in one ear of Chairman Powell and the Wall Street banks in the other.

Figure 5.4 shows the Fed's ballooning balance sheet.

Figure 5.4: Federal Reserve Board - Recent balance sheet trends

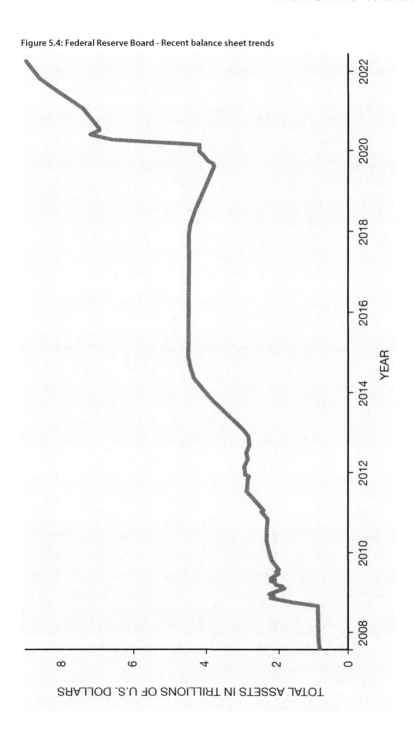

All one had to do is realize that the Fed was going to use the pandemic as the excuse to print money, and make it appear that the ineffective government lockdowns was helping people and businesses it crushed through sheer incompetence. (Sweden fared better without lockdowns in comparison to much of Europe and the U.S.; see worldometers.info that supports this). The real agenda was to reinflate the markets, save Wall Street, bail out public companies to reward incompetence through crony capitalism, and, of course, feed the plebeians with some scraps in exchange for votes, docility and optics. However, in the next meltdown that will probably start in the bond market, the Fed's one trick pony of printing money will run out of steam.

The prudent watched the Fed monetary policy, stuck around as the Nasdaq closed at 14,000 at the end of April 2021, an increase of 57 percent year over year. This means that if you invested $1 million, the value of your investment in one year would be $1.57 million. In this scenario, you could have bought the $1.2 million house and had $370,000 left over. Some will say that you can leverage a mortgage on your home, which is true, but you can also buy on Nasdaq through QQQ with 20 to 25 percent down without jumping through all the hoops the bank will put you through on a mortgage, which sometimes feels like you are being cross-examined before a grand jury.

Switching assets, what if in April of 2020, you invested in gold, a traditional hedge against inflation. Analysing this scenario, where the price in April 2020 was $1,736, and the price in April 2021 moved to $1,900 for a gain of 9 percent. You would have ended up with an increase of net worth of $90,000 compared to a real estate purchase with a net profit of $200,000, excluding friction costs, such as selling fees. It seems that gold is underperforming against effective inflation, such as home and oil prices, perhaps because not only is it manipulated on the gold futures market, or quite simply, a technological disruption in the way of Bitcoin that is challenging its 5,000-year record.

What if in May of 2020 you started accumulating Bitcoin, which has a scarcity limit of just 21 million units? You didn't tell your friends, because they are stuck with money managers who have under-performed the S&P for 10 years, just like Warren Buffet. And after all, they are convinced that Bitcoin is a Ponzi scheme, without realizing that the U.S. dollar and fiat monies in general with absolutely no backing or finite characteristics, historically have all ended up at zero with no exceptions, going back to the time of the Romans, who diluted silver leading to a currency debasement. Consider that by the time Egnatius Gallienus, who was Emperor from 253 to 268 AD, the Roman denarius coin, which was once nearly 100 percent pure silver, had been debased to 5 percent silver coating, and when scratched, revealed a poor copper interior—it eventually went to 0.05 percent silver per coin. It was this type of debasement that led to hyperinflation, where soldiers demanded higher pay, (after all, why fight for ideology) complemented by higher taxation with the result being that outside of its local areas, Roman coins had no value. In the end, the citizens of Rome resorted to a barter system, as the currency collapsed, as did the empire.

The U.S. dollar is just doing a "rinse and repeat" of the Roman coin that eventually went to zero value.

Bitcoin is now quoted internationally in markets, while support-ed by a wide array of Wall Street funds. Let's look at the following analysis:

You bought $1,000,000 worth of Bitcoin in May of 2020 for $9,641, and it is quoted at $40,000 in May of 2021—you would real-ize a gain of 4.14 times, meaning your Bitcoin in U.S. dollars would be worth $4,148,000, leaving you with $3,148,000 left over after you purchased the $1 million house. Now equipped with this extra money, you can take a break go all out, and take the family to Dairy Queens this weekend, and watch reruns of High Plains Drifter, or better still, transition to an official Bitcoiner and appear with Michael Saylor of MicroStrategy and become a YouTube celebrity.

By looking at things through a comparative asset lens, we can empirically validate that fiat money is losing its value against real estate but is gaining against gold. However, real estate is depre-ciating versus oil, Bitcoin, the S&P, and Nasdaq. Hence, real estate is losing money against most asset classes with the exception of gold. Understanding that owning land is intuitive to our emotional architecture since Greece in antiquity first gave peasants the same rights in 594 BC under Solon to land ownership, thus sharing some of the privileges of the aristocracy, understandably this attained right has not been lost on us 2,600 years later. However, if you insist on investing in real estate this can be more easily done on the stock market, and unlike selling a second home which can take time especially in a spooked market, you can instead buy into a host of Real Estate Investment Trusts (REITs), such as Mid America Apartment Communities, where you can sell your shares in seconds, while enjoying real estate's leverage privileges, of course with more liquidity. At the same time, if real estate is dropping you can short REITs.

Figure 5.5 shows the performance of various asset classes since 2019.

Figure 5.5: Asset Class Price Comparisons 2019 to Nov. 2021

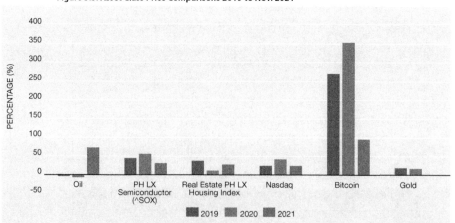

This brings up the question: Is Bitcoin the fastest horse in the race? As billionaire hedge fund manager Paul Tudor Jones asked, "Why are Wall Street banks jumping on the bandwagon?" Bitcoin is discussed in more detail in Chapter 16.

What we have done here is taken a tour of classical inflation and practical inflation through considering the changes of various asset classes. And now, if we cross-reference other asset classes as opposed to fiat money, we are enriched with not only a clear lens of comparative asset class valuations, but with a 360-degree perspective. The point being that asset price inflation, when compared to fiat alone, might be giving us a false sense of wealth, while real inflation is not always captured in the official CPI numbers.

It seems that we have been on this path before, specifically the exogenous shock caused by lenient monetary policy in the 2008-2009 housing and capital markets meltdown, which resulted in the mechanical gears of the capital markets seizing from lack of liquidity, and desperately needed lubrication from the Fed. As a prescription, the Fed reduced interest rates in 2009, with the effect of reinflating the housing market by 2017 beyond its original highs, and the Dow by 270 percent in the same period, without looking at the systematic risks and the unintended consequences of asset price distortions that the Wild West interest rates cause. After all, a decade of near-zero rates has helped pump up the S&P 500 Index to about 22 times the projected earnings, close to its highest level since the 2000 dot-com stock bubble.

Inflation is a tax on citizens, since the plebeians have to pay more for the same goods, and when prices on everything go up, the government marginally collects more taxes on the same products due to higher prices, even though the tax rate has not gone up, especially in an economy that is precipitously inflating. It is a play named Bubblicious, which has been running on Broadway since at least 2000—the applauding minions on Reddit, Twittersphere, and the lords of Wall Street ensure a guaranteed sellout to this theatrical suicide.

It is this specter of asset inflation through money printing that contributes to a wider wealth gap, while reducing purchasing power, as illustrated in Figure 5.6.

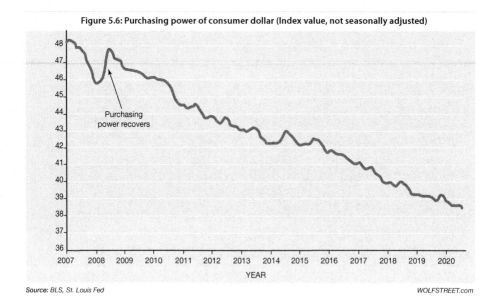

Figure 5.6: Purchasing power of consumer dollar (Index value, not seasonally adjusted)

Source: BLS, St. Louis Fed

WOLFSTREET.com

When purchasing power is diminished, it is further evidence that fiat money is not a stable store of value over time. At the same time, it suffocates the fruits of labor and inventiveness. If the working poor and Gen Z and Millennials want to pull themselves out of spiraling and relative intergenerational poverty, they will have to attain a combination of asset classes, ranging from equities, real estate, precious metals, agriculture, and Bitcoin. Without knowledge on how to manage money, and slowly create and accumulate wealth, the ill-fated ideas of wealth redistribution will even lead to wider societal poverty and division.

Containers, Helicopters, Covid Anxiety, and Inflation

It seems that the Covid-19 phenomena, to be followed by another crisis, is being used as a veil for the government and the Fed to print currency, as citizens are being showered with money that is created from thin air, generating distractions for people. But in reality, the agenda is for the Fed and Wall Street to buy assets with easy money that will exasperate the wealth divide. As an example, the Wall Street Journal reported that Blackrock Capital, Invitation Homes, and American Homes 4 Rent are buying complete subdivisions for rentals from home builders such as Horton, which implicitly build these subdivisions to sell them in one bulk sale to Wall Street![17] These are bidding wars that exclude the average middle-class buyer, drive up prices, suffocate the dream, and deconstruct the cultural fabric of the working person and the nation as a whole, while the builder spends less on romanticized marketing collateral material!

As we are witnessing, money printing has a host of inflationary consequences, and one that might not be as obvious, the COVID-19 crisis is the perfect diversion for government donning a fireman's hat as they play the hero, for what they exasperated tenfold. The result is that they are feeding the inflation fire and causing a bigger mess. How? With all the helicopter money printing, people are being pacified, while not being cognitive of the developing inflationary horror show now playing at a theatre near you. And we are in act one still. With these helicopter funds falling magically from the sky, they were and are attaining anxiety relief by having an orgy of purchases on Amazon and the likes, which has resulted in demand on all kinds of goods, from electronics to strainers. With massive orders being given to Far East manufacturers, it is leading to bottlenecks in Chinese and Vietnamese shipping ports. According to the Wall Street Journal, the situation is further aggravated because large ships carrying empty containers back to China are held back outside ports for a week as the crew awaits testing for COVID-19.[18] The Chinese port of Ningbo-Zhoushan was closed in August 2021 for two weeks after a COVID-19 outbreak, creating a bottleneck at

---

17   Ryan Dezember, "If You Sell a House These Days, the Buyer Might Be a Pension Fund," Wall Street Journal, April 4, 2021, https://www.wsj.com/articles/if-you-sell-a-house-these-days-the-buyer-might-be-a-pension-fund-11617544801
18   Costas Paris and Stella Yifan Xie, "COVID-19 Closure at China's Ningbo Port is Latest Snarl in Global Supply Chains," Wall Street Journal, August 20, 2021, https://www.wsj.com/articles/covid-19-closure-at-chinas-ningbo-port-is-latest-snarl-in-global-supply-chains-11629451800

origin, while on the other side of the Pacific, in Los Angeles, ships were backed up for weeks at times to get unloaded.

We can blame it on COVID-19, but it is only a small part of the story—this demand is due to money printing causing steroid driven demand on labour and issues with equipment shortages, as both are static, while demand has increased, thus the delays and associated costs.

Another barometer of quantifying inflation is the Producer Price Index (PPI), which measures the average change over time in the selling prices received by domestic producers for their output. From March 2021 to 2022 the PPI has spiked by 11 percent, as it is considered a reliable leading indicator of where the CPI is headed.

In March of 2022, I experienced this first-hand with my imported container. Sailing from China to Vancouver takes about 16 days, and now it takes 55 days. Once the vessel with my container arrived in Vancouver, it was kept on the ship for three weeks off the coast of Vancouver waiting to be unloaded due to bottlenecks. When the container was finally unloaded, it sat at the railyard for three more weeks, costing further premium to have the container moved on the rail for shipping across Canada. To add further pain, in addition to an $18,000 freight bill, the steamship company presented my company with a supplemented $8,000 charge for port congestion and getting space on the ship—in this environment fair play and rule of law need not apply!

All this results in lost sales, which is termed opportunity costs as these lost sales are gone forever, and dents the bottom line of companies, that on a macro scale will affect the price of shares, because of supply chain bottlenecks. Or in the case of private companies that have lines of credit, these losses show up on a bleeding income statement, which will have your banker breathing down your neck, and even threatening to call the loan.

Some companies such as Walmart, Home Depot, Costco, and Target have chartered their own smaller ships that can hold 1,000 containers, as opposed to larger steamships that can hold 20,000 containers. These smaller chartered ships come at higher costs per container to ship, but at least the seasonal merchandise arrives on a timelier basis, while these smaller ships can detour the most congestive ports in America for offloading. There are also now energy shortages in Europe, China, and America, raising prices for natural gas, oil and related energies, causing further shortages on goods, leading to even more inflationary pressures on semiconductors, cars, gadgets, appliances, food, and a host of consumable and durable goods. (Note that this was even before the war in Ukraine, which will further aggravate energy costs.)

The inflation is not just on containers, because even if you can find a container, there is a shortage of truckers to move the containers from the factories to the ports for loading. In fact, this is the case in the UK, where it is very challenging to find truckers to move goods to the Port of Liverpool, because many have left the workforce or are being compensated by government, causing wage inflation. Hence, firms have to bid for truckers in real time, further escalating wage inflation and shortages on the shelves.

As another personal example, in my business, I have experienced 40-foot container costs from Port of Ningbo-Zhoushan in Zhejiang Province to Vancouver go from $3,500 in November 2019 to $25,000 in mid-2022. The financial acuity of this across 50,000 units of widgets being imported equates to a cost of over $0.50 per unit on a product costing $0.50, which in practice exceeds one's profit margins after factoring in the selling price. Even if you can pass on the cost to the retailer, which in the case of Walmart resembles getting in the ring with André the Giant at Madison Square Garden—even then, the consumer might not accept the price increase, especially if it is a non-essential item that is price elastic, as the family is struggling to put food on the table.

Figure 5.7 illustrates the container crises.

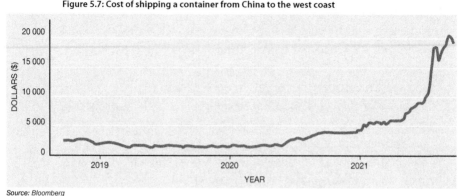

Figure 5.7: Cost of shipping a container from China to the west coast

Source: Bloomberg

The Victims of Inflation

The poor are the most acutely affected by inflation since many of them are already shopping at discount stores, so they have enough money to pay their bills. And their basket can include food items as well as a host of gadgets and widgets for their home. Recently, under this heavyweight of cost push inflation, Dollar Tree had to increase their price strategy from $1 to $1.25 on nearly all items, and they are now even opening a $1.50 section. Shareholders were exuberant at this news in late September 2021, and it resulted in their underperforming stock moving up nearly 20 percent in the span of two days. However, effective inflation in this scenario is devastating for the poor that rely on Dollar Tree and other price format retailers to simply exist in their day-to-day lives, while the middle-class go to their selected retailers including dollar stores to help drive down the total costs of their shopping basket.

In summary, by looking at some of the causes of inflation we can easily surmise that those most affected are the poor, who are on fixed incomes, and most sadly those who have retired with little or no savings, which accounts for the bottom 50 percent of America. In an attempt to illuminate that tragedy, it is these same poor who might be single mothers who are barely able to feed their children; many elderly who fear shopping at night because of violence in their neighbourhoods. This is the economic and cultural genocide that government in concert with the Fed have caused, and these are some of the tragic outcomes of easy money.

Unquestionably, government in coordination with the Fed has caused this container inflation to add to their long uninterrupted litany of failures, as well as other inflation through money printing, and the tragic result is that a lot of decent folks are living with the unintended consequences.

A September 2021 article in *Barron's* discusses how container costs have gone up tenfold.[19] The title should have read, "Government is further punishing the poor and the middle-class through money printing, leading to inflation, despair, and instability."

The MSM and the White House have an alternative truth, specifically that the economy is pumping on all its gears, and this is the cause. This is rubbish—the clogging in Los Angeles, Vancouver and other ports is caused by artificial demand that the Fed money printing and government fiscal policy caused by helicopter money. This has resulted in a shortage of chassis to transport the containers inland, while drivers are overworked with long hours, while ship unloaders are in shortage, hence, driving up wages by way of cost push, with prices spiking on the retail shelves. Of course, the victims are the poor and the diminishing middle-class.

Simply put, with a weakened manufacturing core domestically, helicopter money is going to employ Far East manufacturers. If it gave fiscal stimulus for creating demand for U.S. manufacturers, that would be another story, since this would organically grow the GDP and its subsequent benefits. However, we are no longer living in the 1950s where American manufacturing ruled the world, as most have offshored since. But today, we need to ask, who are we strengthening with this helicopter money—China, Amazon, or the United States?

---

19   "Will Shortages Ruin the Holidays?" Barron's, September 26, 2021, https://www.barrons.com/visual-stories/will-shortages-ruin-the-holidays-what-to-know-01633138094

This is the result of the Feds increasing their balance sheets by over $4.5 trillion since 2019, which is showing up with acute inflation that far exceeds the 8 percent CPI narrative. In essence, inflation is closer to 14 percent according to shadow stats.[20] As of 2022 the prophesy has been actualized, and it is a burning inferno with no easy way out, because with a $30 trillion-plus deficit, higher interest rates would literally collapse the U.S. Treasury, which is discussed in Chapter 13.

In the end, monetary inflation punishes the poor and decimates the middle-class. To believe that government and the Fed will solve this is akin to calling the axe murderer to the scene of his crime to act in the role of the medic, to help resuscitate the patient.

What we have here is a classic case of money printing that Milton Friedman articulated in the 1970s. Naturally, this brings us full circle back to the Cantillon effect of the 18th century, namely "too much money chasing too few goods."

Meanwhile, Back in Gotham City

Back in Gotham city, Batman might want to listen to the Riddler, because maybe he isn't actually a felon. He is perhaps in his moment of intellectual desperation saying to the caped crusader that inflation in the economy is not transitory but is here to stay, as he articulates asset classes that have been discussed earlier in this chapter. The Riddler, who is forever stigmatized as the villain, speaks desperately yet eloquently to the deaf ears of Batman, as he proposes that the unprecedented and addictive easy money that now defines the fabric of Gotham City will turn the metropolis of hope and order into the ruins of Pompeii.

---

20   James Mackintosh, "Inflation Is Already Here—For the Stuff You Actually Want to Buy," Wall Street Journal, September 26, 2020, https://www.wsj.com/articles/inflation-is-already-herefor-the-stuff-you-actually-want-to-buy-11601112630

The Riddler, in his strangely revealing affinity and regard for the citizens of Gotham City is passionately trying to stimulate the shackled citizens who are addicted to the docility of their fallen spirits, and to energize them into the visionaries that once built an incomparable Western civilization. When unmasked, the Riddler is perhaps a true champion of the proletarian, as each riddle he creates reveals the rot and corruption of the fiat money system built on a toxic mountain of villainy and cronyism. He then asks questions that are masked as riddles: How did all great civilizations fall? Does all fiat money go back to its intrinsic value of zero? It is these riddles he asks, without a clear possible answer, because all seems so irreversibly obfuscated, as Batman seems overwhelmed.

But somewhere in his incomparable perception, the Riddler is asking Batman how he attained all these material assets like the Batmobile, Bat Helicopter, and how is Robin the Boy Wonder being compensated? Batman, the caped crusader, who is really Bruce Wayne, a man brought up in pampered privilege, is himself already tormented by his dual personality disorder. Batman struggles with his true agenda, which is to enrich the coffers of Wayne Enterprises and perhaps license his Batman brand. The same Bruce Wayne who, from his privilege of inheritance, has created wealth through a fiat money printing system that has inflated his assets, and even the Riddler, with a 190 IQ being a pauper, can only dream of such wealth accumulation. Batman is tormented yet addicted by his privilege as he increases his ostentatious wealth through the Bruce Wayne Foundation, that depends on money printing.

The Riddler then starts connecting the dots as to Batman's real nature and agenda and who he might really be. Again, he asks Batman about his source of funding and his association with Bruce Wayne and Wayne Enterprises, as he also accuses Batman of being a member of the high priests of Gotham City's aristocracy. He then asks Batman, "Why does your friend Bruce Wayne sit on the board of governors of the Central Bank? And is it true that you dined last week with Jerome Powell, and Janet Yellen to strengthen your cabal associations at the Central Bank? What are your ties to Wall Street banks, and views on money printing that is causing a wealth divide? Is it not true that you have friends in Silicon Valley at Google, Twitter, Facebook and LinkedIn that will censor truth at your very whim, so the gaslighting of Gotham City's citizens continue?" The Riddler, who had read *The Age of Surveillance Capitalism*, knew the relationship between government and Silicon Valley. He asks if his Bat Computer was merged with Google and Facebook, gathered private information on the citizens of Gotham City without their knowledge? Yes, the Riddler was connecting the dots of this toxic brew of crony capitalism, and it seems that the caped crusader was not really a champion of truth, justice, and fair play. The Riddler even threatened to spill the beans to Catwoman, whom with Batman was having a secret affair.

After hearing these words, Batman breaks out into a cold sweat, trembling at the horror of truth, and after composing himself, he uses the prepared words of the aristocracy's Orwellian playbook of propaganda, accusing the Riddler of being a spreader of misinformation! He then messages his Cabalatocracy associates in Silicon Valley, the self-proclaimed ordained adjudicators of truth, resulting in the Riddler being de-platformed on YouTube, Instagram, Facebook, Twitter, and even had Amazon ban his book of Riddles from 1966.

Without any further deliberation, Batman insidiously tosses the Riddler and truth into an incarcerated grayness buried into the tragedy of opaqueness. But in his parting words, the Riddler, behind bars, emphatically proclaims to Batman that 2,400 years ago the Greek philosopher Thrasymachus said, *"Justice is nothing else than the interest of the stronger."*

So now, it is perhaps a good time to move on and introduce inflation's first abused and marginalized cousin, namely unemployment.

CHAPTER

6

Unemployment

In the 1792 book *The Social Contract,* Rousseau, who greatly influenced the architecture of the U.S. constitution and the romantic era, inadvertently stated the importance of employment and the necessity of man's need to be industrious for the state's survival by declaring the following:

> *In all the governments of the world, the public person consumes, but produces nothing. Whence, then, comes the substance it consumes? From the labour of its members. It is the superfluity of individuals that supplies the necessaries of the public. Hence it follows that the civil state can subsist only so long as men's labour produces more than they need.*[1]

Work represents dignity, pride, and a sense of purpose, while building the framework of a stable individual psyche and communities. All work is dignified—it helps define the national fabric, the lack of it is a national demoralizer, and to have this taken away is economically and psychologically devastating.

Unemployment often coincides with a recession, which means a contraction in the GDP for two consecutive quarters but can survive without one. Unemployment is the villain that costs politicians elections, since it is the labor force's primary barometer of the economy—that is, unless fiat helicopter money continues to be printed and keep the labor force staying home in a state of docility, and demoralization. The size, and more importantly, the quality of the labor force, in its diversity of useful education, skills and inventiveness defines the competitive architecture of a nation.

Economists have created a classification of different types of unemployment, but before we look at these, first let's take a look at the tragic state of personal finances. We start by considering the alarming state of things, when, according to the site GOBankingRates, 69 percent of Americans have less than $1,000

---

1   Jean-Jacques Rousseau, *The Social Contract, or Principles of Political Right,* trans. H. J. Tozer (Hertfordshire: Wordsorth Editions Limited, 1923), 79.

worth of savings, and 45 percent have no savings at all[2]—put another way, most are living paycheck to paycheck, and if they lost their job or government assistance benefits, their whole house of cards would collapse. Sadly, this cannot sit well on one's sense of self, emotional well-being and household security. According to the U.S. Census Bureau, 65.5 percent of Americans own homes, and millennials are starting to make some headway at 38.50 percent,[3] while the total debt, including mortgages, credit cards, home equity lines, student loans is $14.6 trillion, according to the New York Fed consumer credit panel.[4] Why is it then that the greatest generation that came out of the Great Depression had more savings in the 1930s than today? Perhaps, as unpopular as this sounds, the Greatest Generation had strong bones weaned on hardship, and even though they were less formally schooled, they had better life instincts and lived within their means. After all, intelligence can be measured in many ways, it seems.

Any shifts in employment levels will leave many consumers at peril with a high level of household debt in difficult circumstances. Any adverse shift in the employment market we are seeing since 2020 will have devastating ramifications, both economically and socially. The astute reader can now see the effects of low monetary policy and the collateral socioeconomic damage it is causing both in savings and consumption, based on unsustainable credit. Households' spiraling credit debt will eventually meet the reaper in the moment of reckoning.

2   Cameron Huddleston, "Survey: 69 Percent of Americans Have Less Than $1,000 in Savings," GoBankingRates, December 16, 2019, https://www.gobankingrates.com/banking/savings-account/americans-have-less-than-1000-in-savings/
3   "Quarterly Residential Vacancies and Homeownership, Fourth Quarter 2021," U.S. Census Bureau, February 2, 2022, https://www.census.gov/housing/hvs/files/currenthvspress.pdf
4   Jeff Cox, "Household Debt Rises to $14.6 Trillion Due to Record-Breaking Rise in Mortgage Loans," CNBC, February 17, 2021, https://www.cnbc.com/2021/02/17/household-debt-rises-to-14point6-trillion-due-to-record-breaking-rise-in-mortgage-loans.html

Re-electing a prime minister or president usually depends on the business cycle, and if the unemployment rate is above 4 percent, the theatre goers will not approve of their leaders, as they will usually vote primarily for their own economic self-interests—sadly, many believe government creates the jobs market. However, government's primary role is to create a business environment where hiring by firms is conducive to business and its ability to create jobs.

The story of unemployment directly affects our social fabric, and it is no accident that we have an opioid crisis of the middle aged and youth, walking the streets aimlessly in a state of idle confusion and justifiable delusion and anger at their lot in life, while three generations living off the avails of the welfare state in exchange for docility, resulting in the breakdown of the family structure, passing off for societal progress is an intellectual fraud in exchange for votes. These genuine and tragic social problems are attributed to unemployment, causing lost hope, idleness, and following false digital icons of virtue. To be under the impression that government creates jobs means that you drank the Kool-Aid from a toxic and manipulated narrative. It is this sad place that we see ourselves at, where we lack the moral and intellectual resolve to heal back into equilibrium.

We now move to the four types of unemployment:

1. Frictional
2. Seasonal
3. Structural
4. Demand deficient

Let's elaborate on these four different types, bearing in mind that an unemployment rate of under 4 percent is considered full employment by policymakers, including the Fed.

1. Frictional Unemployment

Frictional unemployment is the process of workers changing jobs, meaning it is transitory, or when one simply quits their job from boredom, better opportunities, or getting out of a toxic work environment. In the normal course of things, many do not qualify for unemployment benefits, and accordingly do not show up on the jobless numbers. It is fair to say that some could financially be in a better position to be able to leave a job without another one already lined up, or possibly they are the subordinate earner in the family, or perhaps a millennial is ready to reoccupy mom's basement and take up a career trading derivatives, which might not be a bad idea, assuming that they are lucky enough to be the 1 percent that makes money as a day trader. To many, corporate life is so mundane that folks of all ages decide to make changes by opening an online business, and no one can blame them when we are no longer operating in job market our grandfathers did.

However, on the other side of the coin, many people who can simply leave a job and find another one at their leisure are more than likely highly-skilled and sought-after in the labor market. The question then becomes, what portion of the labor force does this constitute, as it does not show up on the national statistics?

Well, it seems that many people now on augmented unemployment, as mentioned in the inflation section, are staying home as opposed to working, and if they are skilled, it takes some big perks to snag them out, as is the case of construction, plumbing, electricians, coders, estimators and the likes. Even Domino's Pizza drivers are picking up higher wages as a result of government competing with the private sector by creating incentives to stay home, with the result of acutely driving up wage inflation. I realize that some will say these artificially higher wages are great, and that government helped. Then I ask, are you prepared to pay $35 for a medium pizza, or will you just decide to cook at home? Is this not a classic case of "cost push" inflation? This is a typical example of the effects of money printing causing distortions in the labour market where the victim is inflation.

2. Structural Unemployment

Structural unemployment is a term employed by economists to describe situations where the jobs are available but are not aligned with the skill-set of a certain sector of the workforce. For example, the job market might be looking for more IT professionals or digital advertising reps to call on packaged goods companies, which may not be aligned with a laid-off 51-year-old auto assembly line worker, or a steel worker's skill-set. It is actually a sad state of affairs when this happens, and government ideas about retraining an older worker into becoming an MIT mathematician at 51 years old belongs in the scene where Dorothy meets the Wizard of Oz. Another example of structural unemployment is that there is very little need for parking lot attendants, when most parking lots are now automated, and those that can maintain the automation might be in higher demand. Subsequently, the market might be calling for an industrial robot set-up and maintenance technicians (I actually know a few) who are highly trained and skilled, where there might be a shortage of this skill-set. Contrast this to the vast supply of graduates of degrees in soft unemployable subjects who spent four years being knowingly duped by the university, and well compensated professors for the pleasure of having their hard drives reformatted into idealogues.

Structural unemployment is the pain many of the so called deplorables have endured—a name coined by Hillary Clinton. Unfortunately, many formerly employed in casual labor such as factories and the auto industry are in a precarious position. Many civil service jobs with little skill required fall into this category—however, they are protected by militant public service unions that push for their protection regardless of the economy in exchange for votes. Any politician that touches the architecture of this entitled civil service racket sitting the shoulders of the industrious (public purse), will be met with accusations ranging from dictatorial to being a job killer, as the guillotine awaits their re-election prospects. We could turn around and drop this on the shoulders of China and be done with it, but this only explains part of it. Since the 1960s, starting with

Japan, industry by industry has been decimated in America, from television sets (does anyone remember RCA, Admiral, or Zenith TVs) radio, solid state, electronics, phones, and computer assembly. Now the same is happening to Japan, as China is doing the same to Japanese manufacturers who have gone up the food chain and are forced to employ more industrial robots.

As a side note, my wife's cousin explained how he went into a Mitsubishi factory in Japan that worked in the dark 24/7 to save lighting bills, since industrial robots do not need light to perform their work.

Since 1947, there has been a transition of a steady decline in American manufacturing that once represented 33 percent of U.S. payrolls,[5] that also played a big role in creating the middle-class. Much of this loss in manufacturing is due to the rest of the world catching up after World War II, and rebuilding their economies in the 1950s and '60s. Figure 6.1 visually tells the story.

Figure 6.1: Manufacturing's share of employment

Source: Bureau of Labor Statistics

5   LiLi Chen and Paul Morris, "Is U.S. Manufacturing Really Declining?" St. Louis Fed, April 11, 2017, https://www.stlouisfed.org/on-the-economy/2017/april/us-manufacturing-really-declining

There is a combination of causes for America's manufacturing decline: suffocating regulations, the learning curve gap being narrowed, the automation of factories, higher wages (which even China is experiencing now), and certain sector of manufacturing jobs that can be done cheaper overseas. But there is more to the story—due to international hyper-competition, traditional recruiting grounds for unions, specifically manufacturing overseas with less stringent labour regulations, and corporations are under pressure to produce financial results to increase share prices, a self-serving consumer, as well as youth, who rather go to college as opposed to participating in a perceived declining sector.

There are hard questions that one might ask:

- What type of a future in an automated world does an unskilled worker have?
- Did they not see the future or not bother to invest in their skill-set?
- Was this the fault of the free markets?
- What happened to unions protecting jobs?
- Did the consumer not act as a market participant in their own self-interest?
- What role can the government play, if any, and will they make it better or worse?
- Is this a replay of British Industrial Revolution with a new cast of Luddites?

These are the large conundrums of our times, in terms of finding an avenue out of relative poverty that economists, businesses, entrepreneurs, and those that want to be dynamically and gainfully employed need to come to King Arthur's round table to discuss, or perhaps the dynamics of what is left of the free markets and human covetousness for self-maximization, to help put it all back in equilibrium. The victim in all this turmoil is the middle-class, and we are seeing their slow and painful funeral procession, as it seems they have been given their last rites.

When looking at official employment numbers, once their unemployment benefits run out, they are no longer considered part of the unemployed, and fall off the government unemployment numbers, and may move to part-time work or welfare assistance instead, or tragically living on the streets.

3. Seasonal Unemployment

Seasonal unemployment is the most intuitive type of unemployment—it might include construction, fishing, and tourism, and is usually quite cyclical, while at the same time, during peak working months, one might experience substantial overtime. Because of its easy-to-understand nature, I will not further elaborate on it.

4. Demand Deficient Unemployment

Demand deficient unemployment is probably the toughest type of unemployment for policymakers to deal with since it is not structural in nature. Simply put, there is a weak demand for employment. It can come from weak consumption, which is what really drives demand and we saw this in the 2009 great recession meltdown, where unemployment peaked out at 10 percent and stayed stubbornly high for years and did not come down to 4 percent until about 2017. In the 2020 current pandemic meltdown, the unemployment rate officially hit a high 14 percent as of the first quarter, but again, as of March 2022 is running at 5.5 percent—however, according to other sources the number is closer to 24 percent.[6]

During the pandemic meltdown, it could be argued that the cause of unemployment was the virus, and we can be done with this, and once the economy opens, all will be well. However, the

6   "Alternate Unemployment Charts," Shadow Government Statistics, accessed March 28, 2022, http://www.shadowstats.com/alternate_data/unemployment-charts

situation is much more complicated than this, since the economy was slowing down in the fourth quarter of 2019 as mentioned prior, was evidenced by the Central Bank's repo purchases and the typical Fed response was to further expand the money supply by lowering interest rates, which is highly debatable in creating the type of demand that will drive generic consumption and create jobs, when the Fed rate was already near 2 percent. Typically, by increasing the money supply, the Fed would want the lower interest rates to move into the marginal propensity to consume and stimulate the job market. But if unemployment is structural, it would have little effect, and if it is demand deficient and the manufacturing sector is being hollowed, the stimulus will seep into China via Amazon. Subsequently, this could cause even more distortions in the broad economy. Even if one is still manufacturing in America, higher wages through inflation and challenging regulations are being offset through robotics and AI to gain efficiencies. Hence, if the Fed mandate is accommodative monetary policy to tackle unemployment, monetary policy alone is too broad a stroke that cannot create skillsets. Consequently, this is a very real limitation of monetary policy that challenges the Fed's ability to provide stable employment.

As the economy started to reopen in Canada in 2022, with many organizations barely hanging on, such as the highly volatile restaurant industry, many will shut down before the lights go back on, since countless were operating on one week of cash flows and shaky balance sheets, even before the meltdown. Intuitively, workers in this sector are suffering from demand deficient employment prospects for a host of reasons. For example, many servers rely on tips, and if restaurants were forced to switch to "take out only", it is not tip conducive, while for a period of time, they were also burdened by ensuring that only the vaccinated were served, was a job description they did not sign up for. In Canada, small businesses were locked down, especially retailers, however, Walmart, Costco, grocery chains and liquor stores were allowed to stay open. This was not only unfair, but it is also in contravention of The Competition Act in Canada, secondly, the irony was that the same amount of people was crowded into less stores.

The same can be said of the business travel industry, where online platforms such as WhatsApp, Zoom, and Team Viewer have replaced much travel, affecting the future for flight attendants—the list is endless, and firms are quite comfortable with this type of communications methods and its associated travel cost savings, while it is a no-brainer for the millennials and Gen Z. Hence, even though the virus is now endemic, the demand for airline travel might be reduced permanently in the foreseeable future, since technology substitutes and shifts in consumer and business tastes may replace much of the need to travel. Will the timeless need for the face-to-face meeting be replaced by technology, and at what cost and what loss? At what level and how many industries will this affect? How will our socialization change? What if the vogue of working at home, with its advantages and disadvantages have management thinking that if you can do your work at home, they will pay you less? What if you were not missed enough during your absence, and the company comes to the conclusion that you were taking up space with little productivity gains? Or what if your job can be outsourced overseas, as your boss discovers Fiverr and Upwork for candidates overseas that will work for 20¢ on the dollar? No one knows what lurks in the dark unknowns of fate, but many possibilities exist.

The government remedy in 2020 was a broad prescription of Keynesianism, which in this case means that many governments were giving out loans (remember government is borrowing this money as they are broke themselves), to businesses on the condition that they use these loans to hire back their staff. This is naïve, since a business that has had a three-month revenue shock, first needs to reestablish top-line revenue and be past the breakeven point, which is the natural point where they can start rehiring. While at the same time, even with the helicopter money, the Fed is sending cheques in the mail, one would think it would be used for basic needs, as opposed to luxuries like travel, and eating out. Consider if an unemployed person's first priority is to put food on the table, and not buy the latest iPhone for Johnny Rocket. Hence, how will this affect Apple and Android phone sales? Surprisingly, phone sales, computer peripherals, and depression alleviating purchases on Amazon went up, as well as social media use since it is a refuge of sorts from the isolation of the lockdowns, and as of 2022, we are seeing the psychological effects this has had on individuals. Quite simply, people are traumatized waiting for the next crisis.

What is important is that the emperor is perceived to be doing something, as he gives carte blanche to the Central Bank to print fiat money, which eventually fosters inflation, further validating the works of the 18th century economist Richard Cantillon, who said that larger money supply chasing fewer goods will lead to inflation. But in the art of politico, why present facts in the face of emotion? It is imperative that the senators of Rome be perceived as preparing medicine for the economy, even if it causes the patient to become more ill, as long as they can continue their self-congratulatory traditions in the wake of infinite failure, is the modus operandi as the musical notes of Keynesianism in E minor play in the distance. The question then becomes, do we get stagflation or inflation, and how will this affect the job numbers? Because, when all is said and done, there is a strong relationship between inflation and unemployment.

The marginal propensity to consume is acutely affected by the consumer confidence index, and we can see that in the pandemic meltdown the middle-class has little, if any, savings to consume. Government measures to jump start the economy will lead to even higher debt levels, in both households and government, with major exhaust trails called unmanageable government debt, (over $33 trillion by the end of 2022 in the United States, and over $2 trillion in Canada).

What is incredibly intolerable is that the talking heads of the mainstream media, as part of the Cabalatocracy—a syndicate of media, Silicon Valley, Wall Street, Hollywood, universities, the government, and corporations creating a false narrative—is covering up fiat money printing that is leading to a tidal wave of inflation, in combination with oppressive taxation, and the very real possibilities of sovereign debt default in major economies, which will lead to contractions on market demand and subsequent consumption.

(The Cabalatocracy and its distinguished members are introduced in Chapter 13.) Even Europe, which has had some titillating bouts with unemployment with its nanny state, is no longer a sustainable economic model, of "whatever it takes" money printing apparatus of the ECB.

Realizing that demand deficient unemployment has taken us off on a tangent, it was merely to illustrate the effects of a sick economy, external forces that facilitate this type of unemployment. We now start to dissect the validity of official unemployment numbers narrative, which brings us to the doorstep of effective unemployment.

Effective Unemployment Numbers

When the unemployment numbers are put together, there are some wide gaps in the labor force that are conveniently ignored. For example, if your unemployment benefits run out after nine months, you are taken off the unemployment rolls (U3 unemployment). There is more to consider if we are to have deeper insights as proposed is the following:

- What if you are a part-time worker who does not qualify for unemployment?
- What if you are a contract worker?
- What if you are a consultant?
- What if you were a part-time server who makes $1,000 per week with tips?
- What if your business failed and you do not qualify for unemployment?
- What if you have been looking for work for 15 months, and dropped off the official unemployment number?
- What if you work in the underground economy?
- What if you are a teacher sitting at home during the pandemic meltdown, and you are still getting paid, under the guise of remote learning?

■ What if you are in the civil service and given a paid leave, as in the case of the current pandemic?

Again, the real effective unemployment rate and the official unemployment rate would give us different outcomes, often void of empirical reality, and one that is obscured in political gain that might be best relegated to the fictional section of the library beside *Alice in Wonderland*.

A couple of things to remember here: the official unemployment rate is defined as U-3 rate in the U.S. by the U.S. Bureau of Labor Statistics, and just before the current pandemic, was under 4 percent as of February 2020 spiked to 14.8 percent in April of the same year, and as of April 2021 had come down to 6 percent. The real rate though often referred as the U-6, a broader definition of unemployment than the official unemployment rate gives us a different picture, where in April 2020 the U-6 unemployment was at 23 percent, compared to the Great Depression of the 1930s, where it peaked to 25.6 percent. By April 2021, the unemployment measured by the broader U-6 was 10.4 percent, and closer to 7.6 percent as of March 2022, but for the same month Shadow Government Statistics calculates effective unemployment at 24 percent.

Figure 6.2 shows the U-6 unemployment rate from the St. Louis Fed.

Figure 6.2: Unemployment rate

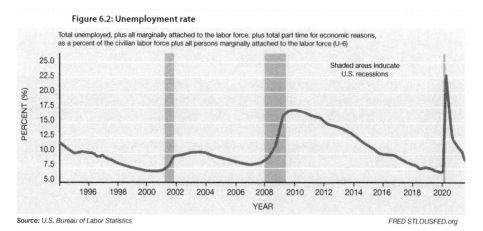

Total unemployed, plus all marginally attached to the labor force. plus total part time for economic reasons, as a percent of the civilian labor force plus all persons marginally attached to the labor force (U-6)

Source: U.S. Bureau of Labor Statistics   *FRED STLOUSFED.org*

However, if the U-6 unemployment rate is not enough, we can turn to additional statistics, as shown in Figure 6.3 that uses additional measures including discouraged workers.

Figure 6.3: Unemployment rate – Official (U-3 & U-6) vs ShadowStats alternative

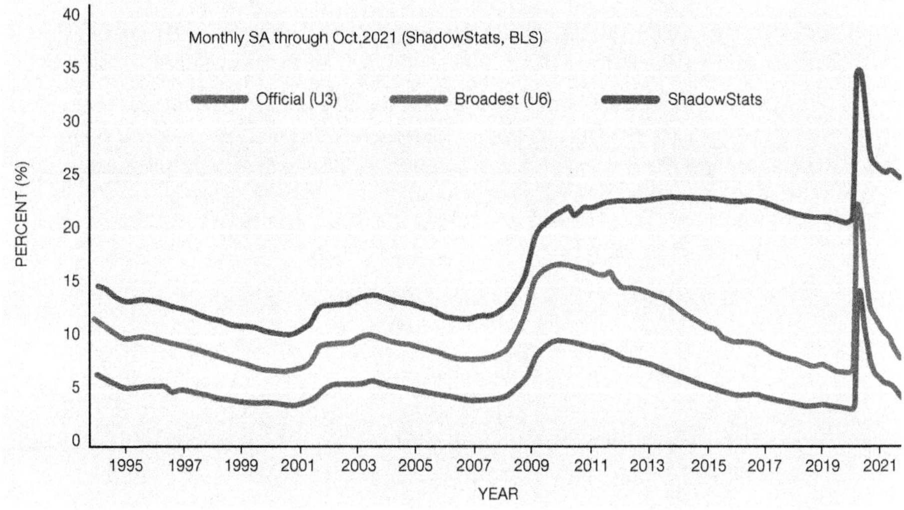

Source: ShadowStats

So, when we add in all the factors, it is closer to 25 percent, even in March of 2022, and probably higher, and when we include public sector workers who are getting paid for staying home, or teachers passing off remote learning as education. Many teachers I know have readily admitted that they cannot see student reactions through Zoom meetings which they said diminishes the learning environment. At the same time, how are all the COVID-19 stay-at-home strategies affecting industrious output of labor, while realizing that people can be replaced by virtual assistants in developing countries like the Philippines at a fraction of the price.

Some Final Words on Unemployment

Unemployment and underemployment are tragic—what we see in the numbers does not reflect the deep societal tragedy of not having gainful employment and a sense of purpose. Many have been displaced, not by only the recent economic pullbacks, but by the hollowing out of traditional industries in America's heartland. It is this loss for hope that has greatly contributed towards an opioid crisis with no end insight, as perfectly decent people fall from the graces of what they once had as they walk aimlessly around, passing the days of their lives in a trance of unexplainable pain. It is in the inner cities where we see a loss of hope, rampant drug or alcohol addiction, crime, intergenerational welfare addiction in exchange for votes, and the cratering of family structures, caused by government stemming back to the great society of 1965. Much of this can be healed with employment that will help resurrect the spirits, economic well being, and used as a foundation to give purpose in life. Unemployment is simply a scar on a nation, while it depletes oxygen from the soul.

Universities and colleges are producing idealogues, living in the denial of 130 million tombstones that Marxism and socialism delivered in the 20th century. Not realizing in the exuberance of youth that the end game is being saddled with student debt, a worthless degree at the benefit of lining the pockets of the faculty and ending up being victims of a syndicate built on a kleptocracy of universities and government working in orchestrated cooperation that facilitates this result. Specifically, student loan racketeering where government is backstopping student loans, to facilitate faculties, and universities teaching soft courses to indoctrinate the young and restless as idealogues with worthless degrees that have no line-of-sight employable relevancy.

The end result is, little career prospects, no skills, or a real full cultured education—their best hopes lay between being a barista, a professional protester, or a poorly-compensated brick thrower at a demonstration. Students are understandably frustrated, but instead of pointing at the society only, in their cult of victimization, they should perhaps visit their unaccountable professors, with little tolerance for the marketplace of ideas. It follows then to ask them why they wasted four years in college having their impressionable hard drives reformatted into the cult of victimization, Marxism, the abdication of self-reliance, and accountability, and various other fallacies taught at universities. Better still, just like a defective washing machine that you want to get your money back on, why not hire a law firm and launch a class action lawsuit against the faculty and the professors personally for a refund including opportunity costs? Why not make academics accountable for their failed ethos for which they have many? Why not hold universities accountable for the intellectual fraud they are committing with what can be considered racketeering? In the end, the real victim of all this is truth!

I accept that these are my personal views expressed here, but to be clear, I advocate the beauty of literature, music, the classics, Rousseau, philosophy, history, and the likes should be taught, learned and appreciated, because they are glorious, enriching and an important part of our human culture. We are no doubt living in a magnificent age of technology that is a double-edged sword that can give us progress, freedom and slavery, while creating unemployment in a disruptive era that is rapidly shifting the ground. To meet this new age, a society also needs skilled people, may it be in coding, software, IT, AI, modern and classical trades—I have one in tooling and machining, which is how I know the factory floor—international business channels, maybe interplanetary, marketing, and so much more.

Perhaps these gaps in skills can be best taught in intensive, hands-on courses with the duration of six to twelve months that are offered in private tech schools, and or community colleges, which seem to be more in tune with industry needs, while being taught by people in these technical fields. Further, there are multitudes of excellent courses to supplement education online, as well as companies like Google (who no longer are asking for degrees), Apple, GE, and the likes offering these hands-on courses in their corporate universities. These types of education are now being recognized as the types of skills that employers are seeking, to ensure they can hire someone who can hit the ground running.

At the same time, people with these skills are snapped up quickly and paid handsomely for their services. And if loans are required from the public purse, it should be in a field where the student can benefit from a robust and rewarding career prospect, as well as contribute to the community they live in while contributing to the competitiveness of the nation's strategic architecture.

We are perhaps seeing a new paradigm shift and we might be renting out our skills through sites like Upwork, LinkedIn, and Fiverr. Then again, we might emancipate ourselves from safety, and boredom, to danger, and possibilities, and it is here where entrepreneurs live as they pursue the future of tomorrow. It is here where I have lived!

In antiquity, during the Hellenistic period of the city states, there was freedom and disorder. Then during the ruling of Alexander the Great and Phillip II ushered in the Macedonian period of subjugation and disorder, and finally after the death of Cleopatra the Roman Empire instituted subjugation and order.

In the lost Romanticism of the Roman Emperor Marcus Aurelius, in his works of meditations, he proposed "freedom of the governed," and later John Locke proposed a social contract with the governed, while Adam Smith lay the economic foundations where we still immerse our daily lives.

CHAPTER

Bretton Woods and the 1944 Mid-Century Reset

A New Order Born out of Antiquity

We have been loitering for quite a while in the unemployment and inflation sections, so it is perhaps a good time to take more of a historical macro perspective to figure out how we arrived at the current world order, or lack thereof, depending on one's views. This naturally brings us to the summer of 1944, in a near mythical place called Bretton Woods, New Hampshire.

After the two World Wars of the 20th century, an American Empire emerged, immersed in the philosophy of liberal doctrine with the boldness of considering the collaboration of "freedom and order." To create this vision, America, along with its participative disciples, lay the architecture of the new colosseum of Rome, but this time without bricks and mortar.

The new colosseum was built on ideas and economic systems, the solidity of gold, the elimination of mercantilism, loans for the fallen, but still was not able to deliver peace as a result of war. In many respects, this new empire was a continuation of the British Empire but, unlike Europe, was built on philosophies, not history.

This was the great reset of the 20th century that still shapes our world today. It is in this story of Bretton Woods that we find the genesis of the present, and for this reason we must consider it.

One might have heard the term Bretton Woods tossed around by some in the media, or referenced it in newspapers, business shows and online platforms. Simply put, the international order and economic systems Bretton Woods Conference created that summer of 1944 is astounding, and in essence, the foundational architecture of the world economic order some 75 years later. Put differently, it was the mid-20th century reset that helped define America's liberal doctrine. Today, the world we live in, its international institutions of commerce and economic systems are still actually affected by this. Being versed in this will help one to truly understand the world we live in today, and how it affects one's life, as an individual and in business.

Our story starts in July of 1944 Bretton Woods, New Hampshire, with an all-star cast from over 40 nations, but the lead actors were from the United States and the United Kingdom, and Canadian Prime Minister, Louis St. Laurent, who was also present during the negotiations.

Let's go back into a time capsule and note some of the attendees—consider economist John Maynard Keynes representing the UK, who incidentally was riding off the accolades he received especially from government in the economic tenets proposed in The General Theory of Employment, Interest and Money that argued that fiscal policy should be used in facilitating artificial aggregate demand in economic contractions, believing governments could cure or soften economic downturns that he felt the free markets couldn't in the way of a quick return to full unemployment. It is at the Bretton Woods Conference that Keynes gave the intellectual fuel for governments to attempt to interfere and remedy the business cycle that we live with today through bloated government, and acute deficit spending as a way of fiscal governance, which Keynes was not intellectually aligned with, since he felt that Treasury debts should be paid back after the fiscal stimulus.

The United States was represented by Dean Acheson, the Secretary of State under Truman, who helped create the Marshall Plan and the Truman Doctrine, that was really inspired by Churchill, who was ridiculed after he delivered his famous Iron Curtain speech at Westminster College in Fulton Missouri, on March 5, 1946, and was passed off as a xenophobe of the emerging Cold War with the Soviets. (Churchill wrote his own speeches and had the finest grasp of the English language). It is also important to mention the presence of Harry Dexter White, a senior member of the U.S. Treasury, who was dominant at Bretton Woods. White played a key role in creating the International Monetary Fund (IMF) and World Bank and was believed to be compromised as a Soviet asset, which was later confirmed to be true by released FBI documents. During Bretton Woods, White and Keynes had some arduous sumo wrestling matches over the world reserve currency, where Keynes argued that an international currency should be created, which he named Bancor. In the end, the U.S. dollar became the world reserve currency and superseded the British pound. It was this conference that American monetary imperialism took hold, after all, they had near 80 percent of the world's gold reserves. As the British and Romans found out, once a nation state loses the international reserve currency status, the decline of their empire follows, as we are seeing with the beginning stages in United States today.

Simply stated, it was a summit of its time, but then, what was the new world economic order that resulted from this conference and its resultant international institutions? The Bretton Woods meeting agreements resulted in not only the U.S. dollar being the de-facto reserve currency of the world, but four distinct pieces of commercial diplomatic architecture that still affect the economic order of today. They include the following:

- The international currency Pegged Exchange System backed by gold
- The International Monetary Fund (IMF)
- International Bank for Reconstruction and Development, better known as the World Bank
- General Agreement to Trades and Tariff (GATT, that later evolved into the WTO)

The Rise of the U.S. Dollar—The Adjustable Peg System—The Gold Standard

Prior to the adoption of the Peg Exchange System, there were wild currency fluctuations in currencies, especially during the Great Depression, and a stabilizing system for currencies was needed to act as a stable store of value, medium of exchange, and a unit of account. In 1944, Bretton Woods created an economic order based on a peg exchange system to alleviate these currency fluctuations that played havoc with international trade. What this means in practical terms, is that if your firm in Sweden owed $500,000 in USD, and the Swedish krona dropped 20 percent in a month when the goods were paid for, your liability would increase by $100,000.

Clearly, this type of fluctuation was a destabilizing force in commerce, while fostering flash crash transactional inflation/instability in pricing, so a new system was developed at Bretton Woods to foster stability based on an adjustable peg mechanism. The Bretton Woods system of currency valuation is what brought forth the U.S. dollar as the reserve currency of the world. The reason for this is the United States was by far the most dominant economy in the world, which commanded 50 percent of GDP, while it held the bulk of the world's gold stock. And when one owned gold, one could dictate the currency of the world going back to the Romans. Simply printing fiat money based on trust will eventually devalue a currency, as the U.S. Fed is currently doing.

Here is how it worked—don't worry, I won't bring out any advanced regression analysis models, and correlate R^2 variables to the ANOVA table. From the 1940s to 1960s, gold was valued at \$35 USD per ounce, the GBP equivalent of £12.5 per ounce. Hence, the exchange between the two currencies were £1.00 = \$2.80 $\therefore$ 35/12.5.

Under the pegged exchange system of currency management, the currencies were allowed to fluctuate up or down 1 percent. However, in practice, the issue was that if imports increased in USD denominations, and you were in the UK, eventually in a classical sense, the pound would drop, due to a lower demand of the pound, and higher demand of the U.S. This could mean that the GBP would drop below the 1 percent established threshold under the Bretton Woods monetary system, and to support the pound, the Bank of England would have to buy up pounds, and at the time the Fed or BOE simply could not print pounds without gold or USD reserves. It is here that the IMF came into play in defining its initial purpose, and what very few people realize, was that the IMF's principal function was to be the guardian of the "adjustable pegged exchange system," which, in essence, is the Bretton Woods monetary system. Hence, the IMF would provide liquidity in USD to the UK, so it could purchase GBP driving the Pound back up within the ± 1 percent strata. Conversely, if the pound became too strong because of exports, the Bank of England could sell pounds until it brought it back within the ± 1 percent strata.

The whole idea behind this was to curtail currency manipulation to attain advantage in trade, while it should be noted that trade is what drove currency demand in the world of the 1940s, since more sophisticated financial instruments like futures, swaps and the likes were not yet part of the economic instruments available. Put simply, the pegged exchange system was to curtail wild swings in currency and stabilize pricing in world trade, which included having ramifications of harnessing the beast of inflation!

The time of Bretton Woods can perhaps be remembered in romantic nostalgia in a relatively simpler post-war time, where world trade in goods has gone through dynamic growth since 1950 from $61.8 billion, to 2020 where it is worth $17.5 trillion.[1] (To give perspective, Bezos, Gates, and Musk are worth at least six times the value of world trade in 1950). To add to the present equation of things, world trade services equate to about $4 trillion or 22 percent of trade in goods, since we are living in a world of outsourced call and technology centers, as well as entrepreneurs offering their services on platforms such as Fiverr and Upwork. Of course, services include much more, such as accounting, IT, creatives, and legal service where baseline sophistication is outsourced, as well as transport services internationally. Naturally, these numbers do not include the black market for stolen goods, illicit drug activity (not including pharmaceuticals), services such as gambling, hiring an enforcer to collect on vice debts, or evening services of passion.

Figure 7.1 is a visual graph of 70 years of trends on trade of physical goods.

1 "Trends in Global Export Value of Trade in Goods from 1950 to 2020," Statista, May 2021, https://www.statista.com/statistics/264682/worldwide-export-volume-in-the-trade-since-1950/

Figure 7.1: Global Export Value of Trade in Goods 1950 to 2020

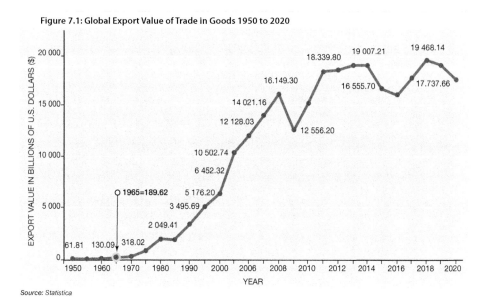

Source: Statistica

We live in a different era today, far removed of the time of great thinkers like Keynes, Churchill, de Gaulle, and Friedman. Gone are the days of Truman, Khrushchev, Kennedy, and Nixon. The economic dynamics today have veered away from the currency determinism of Bretton Woods, where the valuation of currencies is no longer a derivative of physical trade. More specifically, we live in a complex financial setting today, where the physical trade of goods no longer plays the historical role of currency determination with hot money, futures (often referred to as the derivative paper markets), exotic derivatives, swaps, Libor, repos, demand for equities and the likes amounting to well over $2 quadrillion, by best estimates. For example, of the total value of world physical gold estimated at $10 trillion, the paper markets that trade gold through derivatives are estimated to be just under $1 quadrillion—in other words, 100 times the size of the underlying gold asset, admittedly no one knows the exact amount. But what we do know for sure, is that J.P. Morgan and other Wall Street banks have been caught suppressing gold prices through shorting futures contracts, and paid fines of nearly $1 billion for manipulating gold prices. The moral of the story: just pay the fines, don't do the time, and contribute to the government's coffers.

In the name of hope, we take solace that virtue will be better re-warded in the next world as opposed to this one. The outcome is that the futures market is determining the underlying asset, hence suppressing price discovery where the inverse should be true.

In this era, the paper markets in all asset classes overshadow markets for goods and services. Hence, exports and imports are no longer the lead players of what drives currency valuation.

One can see that there was hard currency support under the Bretton Woods system, albeit with little to no flexibility in terms of money expansion, even though the IMF was created to relax the rigidity of the Bretton Woods pegged exchange system. Then, in 1967, the devaluation of the British pound was the beginning of the end of Bretton Woods exchange system, and eventually, in 1971, President Nixon took the U.S. dollar off the gold standard and transitioned the dollar into fiat money, what was to be a temporary measure—which has now been going on for over 50 years. Many call the closing of the gold window to de-couple gold from cur-rency, as Bretton Woods 2.0.

The closing of the gold standard was done for several reasons, but the main one was the foreigners were exchanging U.S. dollars for gold, depleting the U.S. gold reserve since the Europeans were un-der the impression that the U.S. had already started printing money without gold backing in their vaults, which was a plausible assertion.

The Jamaica Accords in 1976 allowed gold to float freely in the markets against fiat money to create currency price stability pro-visions of GATT, and for optics, the accords included solutions for currency manipulation that was blended into the GATT, that in the-ory, has survived into the WTO. The interesting takeaway was that gold, when de-linked from currencies, shot up like a rocket from $35 per ounce in 1971 to near $800 per ounce by 1979—in essence, gold was hedged against the inflationary effects of fiat money, and inflation indeed was the story of the 1970s, again caused by the government.

As of 1971, the printing presses had permission to create fiat money, with occasional intermissions, such as the Paul Volker years to take a break and lubricate the gears. The hard money gold standard, where money could not be printed without gold backing, created currency stability—it ensured governments lived within their means, and living within their means usually does not allow tyranny to rein while having less money to bribe voters. Smaller budgets lead to smaller government, and in history going back to antiquity, oppression is often at the hands of large government. With a hard backing of currency, there would be no opportunity to creating $6 trillion of so-called stimulus packages from 2020 to 2021 that is approximately the size of almost two years of U.S. Treasury revenue.

Now, with the decoupling of gold from the dollar, we can see how governments worldwide have accumulated debts of over $100 trillion, and this does not include legacy costs, while Central Banks have purchased toxic assets such as Greek bonds, and as a result, one of the major Central Banks could easily collapse. As a remedy, Central Banks or Treasuries purchasing a combination of gold and Bitcoin for hard asset backing may not be farfetched. However, if bribing voters with fiat money borrowed in their name keeps politicians in power, more power to the emperor, always looking for a cause for people to receive benevolence, in exchange they will receive tyranny. Because, once the subjects are hooked on government, the true victims become "intellectual clarity" and "self-reliance", which at the present are blasphemous thoughts.

Getting back to Bretton Woods, it brought us more than the monetary system, it brought us the protectorate of the pegged exchange system, namely the IMF that magically turned into the international lender of last resort.

The International Monetary Fund / International Lender of Last Resort

The International Monetary Fund's original articles were negotiated in Bretton Woods in 1944, and it is arguably the second most remembered institution that is current speak—the first being the WTO. The IMF has a love-hate relationship with benefactor nations.

Yes, the IMF does good, and it often does harm, as we shall soon see. As noted earlier, the original principal function of the IMF was to act as the guardian of the adjustable peg system of providing liquidity to protect against wild currency swings, and not to bail out chronic debtors with leaders who could not manage themselves, much less the affairs of a nation.

Just to give a backdrop on the original articles of agreement on the IMF, it was to establish an international code of financial behavior for members both in the pegged exchange system and liquidity requirements. The current position IMF finds itself in as the international lender of last resort which it never had a mandate for in the 1944 Bretton Woods articles, and it has been hurled by history in a role it was never meant to fulfill.

Okay, so before any mud is slung or glory bestowed upon the IMF, both of which are admittedly deserved, it might be a good idea to take a peek into how the gears and circuit boards of the IMF work.

Each country pays a subscription quota, which originally was a combination of gold and home currency, and later evolved into just currency once it was taken off the gold standard. Eventually, they created Special Drawing Rights (SDR) based on a basket of currencies. Another key mechanism is the quota each country contributes, which is a reserve tranche, so in theory, means that they can borrow back the money they contributed.

In 1974, the IMF went from supplying short-term liquidity to an Extended Fund Facility (EFF), in which member countries received longer term financial assistance.

The table below shows a list of key IMF developments.

IMF developments

1952	Standby Arrangements
1962	General Agreement to Borrow
1963	Compensatory Finance Scheme
1969	Buffer Stock Facility

1969   First Amendment
1970   Introduction of SDRs
1972   Committee of Twenty
1974   Extended Fund Facility
1974, 1975 Oil Facility
1976   Jamaica Accords
1976   Trust Fund
1978   Second Amendment
1979   Supplementary Financing Facility
1981   Enlarged Access
1986   Structural Adjustment Facility
1987   Enhanced Structural Adjustment Facility
1988   Compensatory and Contingency Finance Facility

There is a wide array of loan types that the IMF gives out, including but not limited to, standby arrangements, flexible credit lines, precautionary liquidity line, rapid credit facility, standby credit facility instruments, and debt relief, to help shore up a nation's balance sheets in the poorest of countries. Unfortunately, many cases of lending are to chronic debtors who would not qualify for a $1,000 Visa card—case in point Argentina, much of Africa, Greece, and the list goes on. You will notice that government officials still get paid while the country is collapsing, mostly due to their inept management and chronic corruption, to the point where this way of life trickles down through the population, resulting in its subjects' inclusion into a culture of participative kleptocracy.

The IMF is mostly financed by the United States, and in too many instances, it results in the taxpayer financing the IMF to give the powerful and corrupt foreign government officials money to subjugate their poor. In other words, our poor and middle-class pay tax dollars to the IMF for the rich third-world dictators to subjugate their poor. Case in point, during the Ethiopia famine of the 1970s, much of the aid dropped from the air by the British and Americans was horded by local government officials and exchanged for land ownership of the victimized farmers. The IMF even lent to genocidal thugs like Robert Mugabe in Zimbabwe in

2009, which in the estimation of his critics, ended up in the hands of this brutal dictator to inadvertently help bolster his party, and quite possibly, his Swiss bank account, which is a must have luxury of the kleptocracy.

This does not mean the IMF has not done good—it did, especially in its early years. During its history, it bailed out nearly half the countries in the world, including the UK during its financial crisis of 1976. It can be argued that the IMF imposed disciplined financial approaches to government expenditure, or at least tried to, admittedly with mixed results. However, as mentioned earlier, from the outset, the key mandate of the IMF in 1944 was to provide liquidity for the world pegged gold backed exchange currency system, not to put on a fireman's hat and reward bad behavior in every financial crisis.

To be fair, the IMF has bailed out some chronic dead beats such as Argentina that defaulted on sovereign debt nine times in its history, and three times in this century. As of May 2020, Argentina could not pay the interest on $500 million that has come due, while it is trying to restructure $65 billion in bonds, and yes, this is the same country that introduced the 100 year bond, which at best, belongs in the new soap opera *The Naïve and the Restless*, but hey, if they can make money trading the bond well below face value, as Goldman Sachs does, all the more power to them.

The IMF has a tough job, which is probably overwhelming for many career bureaucrats, most of whom have never run a business. They visit developing countries and act like the messiah of ordinance, while staying at five-star hotels at the expense of the taxpayer. But in all fairness, the 1997-1998 Asian crises bailout has been a success, since the economic reforms imposed by the IMF have ushered in an era of prosperity in the new millennium. Further, there are a host of situations where the IMF has helped avert a complete collapse of nations, both in the developing world and in Europe, that is mostly self-inflicted by a combination of corruption and large governments, which seem to be inseparable bedfellows since the Greek city states.

When an economy is on the verge of collapse, it leads to much social unrest, so every government that wants to stay in power should have funds for an ample supply of riot helmets, well paid enforcers in uniform, a good diet of propaganda, along with a contingent of working water cannon trucks. In fact, this is what happened in Greece when the bankrupt government wanted to implement austerity. This did not sit well with the serfs, as they demanded their junkie fix of highly addictive social entitlement that created the mess in the first place, and as a result, ECB and IMF backed loans, Greece is looking at $500 billion debt level, with a debt to GDP ratio of 242 percent. Hence, at the next European cup, finance ministers from various countries can start the football match ceremonies of seeing who can kick the can down the field furthest.

The moral hazard of knowing they are going to get bailed out, the so-called leaders have created some poor financial governance, and abdication of fiduciary accountability, which is not necessarily the fault of the International Monetary Fund, or other lenders of last resort.

Conditionality

The IMF, like other monetary institutions, has a set of rules, especially since it is indirectly funded by taxpayers. Attached to loans are a set of covenants and conditions established to promote good fiscal governance, something that might be missing in the present world, particularly when we consider that the Russian debt to GDP ratio is just under 20 percent. In contrast, most Western economies are at well above unsustainable levels of over 100 percent debt to GDP ratio, as they have been spending like sailors at a New Orleans house of ill repute!

Examples of conditionality might include reducing the money supply by 6 percent, or reducing its government expenditure by $10 billion, or reducing a country's debt to GDP ratio from 180 percent to 120 percent. Thus, imposing this on chronic debtors such as Greece, with an electorate riveted on highly addictive entitlements and policies, is challenging. Hence, weaning them off this puts the

IMF in the awkward position of being socioeconomic entitlement addiction counselors, or putting it diplomatically, custodians of economies. And there are many instances like this when the financial measures imposed by the IMF have merit for incompetent governments and an electorate who are in denial, or simply do not care about fiscal limitations if the public purse puts them in a position where the IMF is accused of politically interfering in a sovereign country's domestic affairs. The IMF loans are in U.S. dollars, it further subordinates borrowers as catalysts for American monetarism geopolitical leveraging, since loans are paid back in U.S. dollars; let's say the Peso in Mexico declines, the total value of the loans in Pesos goes higher. This of course has countries like Mexico coming back for new financing to pay back the old financing. Hence, borrowers are financially enslaved to the IMF vis-à-vis the U.S. dollar, and fall into a debt spiral, much like borrowers of China's Belt and Road Initiative, and in changing global geoeconomics and political dynamics, at least borrowing nations get a chance to choose their masters. The caveat is that the IMF becomes a tool for political leveraging, and with the U.S. being its largest contributor, it can double the leverage, first through the IMF, and then its reserve currency status, to further strengthen its monetary imperialism. In other words, many argue that the United States pushes political agendas using the IMF as a vehicle. The argument against this is, spend within your means, or watch your entitlements and large government collapse under the weight of privileges you voted for.

It can easily be argued that this is exactly what a bank does when it lends a company money based on the health of its accounts receivable, cash flows and balance sheets. Subsequently, the bank might want to stipulate through loan covenants the amount of minimum working capital a firm has to maintain or ensure that shareholder loans remain at a level of minimum of one million dollars, or their directors not use private jets, while the stakeholders starve.

To be fair, it is almost always the same countries that have their hand out to the IMF, including Ukraine, which is run by corrupt leaders, democratically or not elected, complimented with underworld thugs. Consider oligarch mobsters like Kolomoisky and Zlochevsky, who own or formed Burisma, the Ukrainian energy company, the same one that Hunter Biden, with no experience in gas, engineering and oil sat on their board of directors, after his then U.S. Vice President father, Joe Biden, made at least five trips to that country. Now, waving the wand of anti-corruption, the IMF came to the aid of Ukraine in December 2019, with a $5.2 billion rescue package! (For reference, please see *Secret Empires* by Peter Schweizer, pages 58 to 63).

Many argue against both the monetary and fiscal policy that the IMF imposes, as well as its one-size-fits-all approach, and that some countries don't have profligate government issues, but have poor tax collecting mechanisms—good idea not to get governments in the habit of collecting too much tax, and we all know what comes next. While at the same time, the IMF imposing fiscal measures such as reduction in military spending can result in a general leading a coup d'état. This is a tradition employed since the death of Marcus Aurelius in 180 AD when the army realized its power made and unmade Roman emperors in exchange for cash. Hence, it may not be prudent to take military equipment and entitlements away from your military, since the emperor's trained pit bull might turn on its master and appoint a new one!

Under James Callaghan's labor government, even the UK received IMF assistance in 1976, to the tune of $3.9 billion, which was the IMF's largest bailout to date. The summary of the financial crisis was that there was downward pressure on the pound, which would result in runaway inflation. Subsequently, the IMF imposed certain preconditions on the loans, including, a cut of public expenditure by $2 billion, the IMF wanted $5 billion for repayment, while at the same time, the Bank of England had to reduce credit expansion over three years. Naturally, this was met with public discontent, remember withdrawing fiscally unsustainable government programs costs elections, but does create employment for riot police who are hopefully well compensated to receive and administer abuse, while enforcing the austerity. Subsequently, the current account deficit was reduced, while inflation was tamed from 26 percent in 1974 to

7 percent in 1978, and finally, the loan was paid back in 1979 by the Exchequer. It should be noted that there was a substantial flight of capital with an 83 percent top tax rate for the wealthiest, while some say this crisis led to Thatcher coming to power.

The United States has a federal accumulated deficit approaching $33 trillion in 2022 and the rest of the developed world, including Japan at GDP to debt ratio of 273 percent, and European Union approaching 100 percent, with Italy being a star spender at near 167 percent, and Canada, which is running on a toxic brew of government handouts, and a well-rehearsed diet of propaganda in exchange for votes, is approaching a debt of $2 trillion (Provincial is another trillion), that puts the country at over 150 percent of GDP. And, of course, how can we forget China, where its total corporate, household and government debt rose to 303 percent of GDP in 2019, according to the institute of World finance Bloomberg. This is expanded upon in Chapter 14.

All this will go much higher as governments are using the platform of the current pandemic to spend, instill societal fear, and will present the failed outcome with a combination of a tax bill, inflation, and depreciating fiat money. Eventually, when presented with the bill, the inhabitants of the decaying empire will be startled as they must take a break from the refuge of Netflix and intaking of life's stimulants, to come to terms with the pending tragedy!

This begs the question, if major financiers of the IMF such as the U.S., China, EU, UK, and Japan cannot keep their houses in order, what gives them the moral right to impose fiscal and monetary measures on borrowers? So, the moral of the story is do as I say, not as I do, and focus on my wagging finger, because I can print money, and you cannot, that is of course, unless gold or bitcoin takes over the old neighborhood.

Alternative Lenders

If a nation's credit rating is good, it will get international lenders or bond dealers falling head over heels to lend it money. However, this is not the case as in much of the developing world—sadly, at the expense of a nation's people, a perpetual all-star lineup of governmental kleptocracy, or lack of societal discipline, eventually seeps into a nation's culture over generations. Therefore, over time, its population unwittingly becomes part of the kleptocracy.

The IMF is often stringent with its lending covenants that just might lead to responsible financial management, and accountability. Hence, with a view of belching out nationalism and saying to the lender, "Just give me the money and don't tell me how to run my devastated economy." The problem is that many third world leaders and others from the developed world for the most part on a hot, sunny afternoon could not balance the books on a lemonade stand.

But thank goodness there are other lenders of last resort and this bring us to China who are quite willing to lend, but at what price?

The Chinese Debt Trap

Yes, once this Chinese debt trap hold is applied, not even Houdini can escape. Deception, passion, and desperation has been the story of much of human history as the passionate becomes intoxicated in a marriage of desperation, captivated in the deceptive arms of the savior and emersed into a dream of benevolence. All the while selling tomorrow for the ecstasy of today. It goes then that if a country leader wants to bypass international bond holders and the IMF, they can always fall into the seductive hands of China's Silk Road Initiative.

In a sense, China is becoming a third-tier lender for financially mismanaged nations where the funds have to be paid back in U.S. dollars, just like the debt crises of the 1980s that shook financial markets primarily in Latin America—meaning that when their local currency gets pulverized against the U.S. dollar by 50 percent, their outstanding debts doubled in U.S. dollars. This is the problem with fiat money, especially in emerging economies.

So, an explanation of the game is in order. For example, China will offer Ethiopia loans in U.S. dollars at much higher rates than the World Bank to finance road projects and the contracts, and as a precondition, these projects will be tendered to Chinese construction firms that are in turn owned or influenced by the CCP, not exactly a bastion of fair play democracy and transparency. Subsequently, of course, certain local firms get part of the action, who have most certainly bribed the host government that intuitively skims off the proceeds, and as with the Chinese firms, these are all at inflated prices, compliments of corruption that in many cases increase loans on the back of projects that are overpriced against the cost of the infrastructure initiative, especially when factoring in the cost of graft by the lender and borrower. And for being guests, China gets access to Ethiopia's coveted rare earth elements that are required for high-tech manufacturing.

How much China has lent other cesspools of corruption such as Sri Lanka, is kept under wraps by the China Development Bank with ironclad nondisclosure agreements? And for good measure, countries like Nigeria and other West African nations are having their media outlets bought out or highly influenced by CGTN TV and radio, and a host of other Chinese propaganda sites, which are a direct branch of China's Communist Party propaganda apparatus. But hey, the loans keep coming and the graft is good while breakfast with some propaganda goes down nicely, so why stop?

Take the case of Sri Lanka, where nonpayment of a loan has resulted in giving out Hambantota Port on a 99-year lease, on a debt-for-equity swap deal. So now a key revenue driver for a country being its port, has been taken over by China. Though to be fair to China, they usually show a much softer hand in these matters of coming to terms with deadbeat borrowers and find workout solutions that is easier to digest. Remember, no one notices Dracula if they are dressed like Robin Hood! And after all, buying the port through loan default seems like a more prudent strategy than the American strategy of confiscation of oil by battle.[2]

Turning our attention to Egypt, they now pay at least 38 percent of their budget toward interest on their loans, and past 50

2　Nathaniel Taplin, "One Belt, One Road, and a Lot of Debt," Wall Street Journal, May 2, 2019, https://www.wsj.com/articles/one-belt-one-road-and-a-lot-of-debt-11556789446

percent in cashflows when we include loans and installments.[3] Even as the Egyptian pound did a spectacular Acapulco cliff diving leap for 50 percent in 2016, Egypt continued to take loans from China in U.S. denomination, which should have been hedged by using derivative instruments. During this crisis, there were no cutbacks in privileged civil service jobs, (this sounds familiar, where the public sector is protected in the West during the 2020-21 meltdown at the expense of the private sector). After all, party leaders need to consolidate power, and having a civil service that is well compensated and accepts bribes to augment their pay while the emperor looks the other way, helps achieve it. The Egyptian government serenades a lovely evening melody to the local population called "Protectionism by the Moonlight" (mercantilism), in the name of saving local jobs, as they put it. Why? Because they are pushing a narrative to manufacture products domestically, for which the country does not have comparative advantage, but still this narrative is great for domestic consumption. The problem though is that many of these items on the import ban list will drive them into further poverty because of higher domestic production costs versus imports, but the optics look great even if they cannot produce them efficiently and at a low cost, which in turn becomes an inflationary tax on the Egyptian consumer, one that they can ill-afford. In addition, remember, import duties collected go into government coffers, which translates to mostly wasted capital.

Oh, but wait! A blind eye is turned to protectionism by the Egyptian authorities if the goods are made in China—they can sail right on through as part of a diplomatic trade-off for the soft loans they received from China. But if the products come in from the West, its entry gets rejected, as this writer experienced firsthand, and this might need some explanation, if I can weep on the reader's shoulders for a moment.

---

3   Yehia Hamed, "Egypt's Economy Isn't Booming. It's Collapsing," Foreign Policy, June 17, 2019, https://foreignpolicy.com/2019/06/07/egypts-economy-isnt-booming-its-collapsing-imf-abdel-fattah-sisi-poverty/

In 2017, my Canadian-made haircare brands were properly and meticulously registered at the Ministry of Health in Cairo by a highly competent local importer at a cost of over $20,000, which was happily received by the ministry. Registration is required with the Ministry of Health in Cairo so the product can enter the country—otherwise the container will be held at port with $300 per day demurrage charges.

We must have filled out a mountain of paperwork over months that eventually became years, and just when we were a few days away from my importer getting their license to import my brands, a new regulation would come up at the last minute, or it would sit in government bureaucracy. It was a game—the government would require more fees to finalize the registration, and then stall. Simply put, the goal post was being moved by the week.

The bottom line is that no matter how fully we complied with the Ministry of Health at the highest levels, they would not approve our application to import goods into Egypt. We even had a well-known local lawyer help us. The result was that my goods were excluded, but Chinese goods sailed on a corrupt carpet of economic nepotism. My Egyptian customer, a very decent competent team of local doctors, tried everything to get registration, but rules change by the minute in that country, as the wheels of corruption rob the nation, and specifically the youth from a prosperous future. This is how the world turns all too often.

Since we are on the subject of mercantilism, it might be a good time to turn our attention to the third component of Bretton Woods, namely the creation of The General Agreement of Trades and Tariffs (GATT), which is the predecessor of the WTO.

However, before considering Bretton Woods GATT, we need to visit the work of British economist David Ricardo, that inadvertently created the case for free trade that still stands today.

The Case for Free Trade

Our story begins with the British economist, David Ricardo (1772-1823) in his famous 1817 book *On the Principles of Political Economy and Taxation,* where he argues the case for free trade through what he termed as "comparative advantage" and introduced the production possibility frontiers. I will spare the graphs, but to break it down to simple terms, consider the following simple example.

If the UK could produce 1,000 cars a year, but 500,000 bottles of hairspray, and Japan could produce 400,000 cars a year, but only 10,000 cans of hairspray, would it not make sense that the UK should buy cars from Japan and Japan should buy hairspray from the UK? The outcome being that Japan has a comparative advantage in cars and the UK in hairspray. Therefore, if these two countries traded, the Japanese consumer would have stiffer hair (not a stiffer upper lip) at a lower cost, and the UK consumer would have cars at a lower cost with reliability, hence the shopper in both countries would get "more for less," affording them an escalation in personal material outcomes. Thus, on a global and multilateral scale, the fostering of free trade would ensure that the global consumer's welfare will escalate and help diminish poverty. In addition, countries that have cooperating trade practices of fair play, would be less inclined to consider war, but I will elect to stay with a more familiar scope of writing, and not consider its geopolitical ramifications.

Adam Smith argued that by giving everyone freedom to produce and exchange goods as they pleased (free trade) and opening the markets up to domestic and foreign competition, people's natural self-interest would promote greater prosperity than with stringent government regulations. In practical terms, duties and import tariffs are a tax upon the domestic citizen while they fill the coffers of government.

The Clustering Effect and the Competitive Advantage of Nations

There are, of course, a host of reasons a country might have advantages in certain sectors of trade and services. For example, in the UK they have a tradition of aerosol manufacturing. They have the chemists, machine mechanics, productivity engineers, and investment in the most efficient manufacturing lines.

As a side note, the UK also has expertise in complex suspension systems for autos that they sell all over the world, as well as surveillance systems and software. Incidentally, much of this was sold to China to keep an eye on its citizenry, as a key component of their social credit system, (Silicon Valley, through Google also offered services for the CCP to subjugate their own citizens).

Subsequently, the UK has both capital asset investment in equipment and personnel that has moved them up the learning curve, and the same holds true for Japan in cars, industrial robotics, medical technology, and heavy equipment.

Eventually, certain nations specialize in a host of industries where, over time, they have sustained competitive advantage over other regions and countries. Simply put, you can't make everything yourself, otherwise the Soviet economy would not have collapsed, and as would have China without adopting free market tenets at some level. Closed economies are referred to as autarky, which is a tenet of classical communism or mercantilism gone amok.

So, when certain industries are found in certain regions, this is referred to as the "industry clustering effect," where industries cluster in certain parts of the world or within countries. For example, consider the traditional Detroit corridor for the auto industry, where engineers, workers, part suppliers, industrial robot set up technicians, and a host of peripheral players need to come together to produce the final products or services. Other examples are Silicon Valley with high-tech, Bangalore, India for software,

Taiwan for Semiconductor chips, and Bitcoin mining formerly in China, which was centered around mountainous Sichuan and Yunnan provinces, where turbines churn snowmelt and seasonal downpours into electricity, or when rivers eased, miners packed their computers and headed north to coal-rich Xinjiang and Inner Mongolia. Because of this exit by Chinese Bitcoin miners, the industry is being received with open arms in places like Texas, and, of course, El Salvador (where Bitcoin is legal tender), which has geothermal clean energy, as it attracts the equipment and the specialized peripheral knowhow that will lift both these regions. Or take the case of Wall Street being the financial capital of the world, where the combination of Wall Street banks, venture capitalist, traders, derivatives, and the likes are peripherally supported by robot traders, market analysts, quants, and so on.

In the case of Silicon Valley and Bangalore, a host of support in software is needed, such as venture capitalists, entrepreneurs and related technology from computer engineers, coders, mathematicians, and people with marketing skills in the IT sector. In all these cases of clustering of the peripheral support follows, giving indispensable support to the final product or service. As a result, the supporting cast clusters around centers like this, which creates competitive advantage through specialized clustering. The whole concept of clustering was brought to light in the enlightening work of Michael Porter of Harvard Business School, who wrote his masterpiece book titled *The Competitive Advantage of Nations*. I highly recommended it, as it explores theories of competitive advantage of nations and firms.

It is this specialization that offers industry economic efficiency, since without it, the quality of output and higher prices would lead to diminishing returns for the consumer dollar, inflationary ramifications, pressure on consumption, and a diminishment in consumer welfare.

With a view of bolstering the case for free trade, it is understood that the bilateral example of Ricardo is somewhat of a simple explanation, even though I could have illustrated this in a multilateral model. Subsequently, there have been more advanced arguments to support the case for global trade. At the risk of sounding academic, I have included the following other trade theories with quick summaries.

Hechscher-Ohlin Theory

This rests on a factor endowment model where one country is abundant in labor, and the other relative to capital, and subsequently, it would make sense to trade. A good example is Japan and China in electronics, computers, and Canada in wheat, building nuclear plants, and natural resources. In summary, countries have a production bias in certain areas of manufacturing and services, and in a free trade environment, consumer welfare maximization will be the benefactor.

Technology Theories of Trade

Just as the name implies, it is differences in technology, stolen or not in the case of China, that affects trade patterns in manufactured goods among nations that are usually the result of differences in country technologies. In fact, Michael Posner argued this in his 1961 paper "International Trade and Technical Change,"[4] where he proposes that innovation is arbitrary, which is arguable, since the West has had the lion's share of innovation in the last 500 years, and it was certainly not arbitrary to build the world that we all live in today.

However, there are some valid points that exist today when Posner considered technology differences are temporary, and this temporary state allows enough arbitrage to foster meaningful trade. Hence, there exists country lags in technology, and the closing of this lag he termed "the imitation gap." Nevertheless, this theory

4 Michael Posner, "International Trade and Technical Change," *Oxford Economic Papers* 13, iss. 3 (October 1961): 323-341.

does not integrate labor or capital advantages in a nation. Case in point, America sells China advanced microchips, but even though America can manufacture computers, it chooses laptops made in China. To elaborate, there are two derivatives of the imitation gap, they are the reaction lag and the learning lag, and when both are mastered, the outcome is the elimination of the imitation gap.

Some Final Thoughts on Theories of Free Trade

It would be fair to conclude that a combination of technology, labor costs, skill level, quality of a nation's capital stock, such as workforce, skill-set, industrial robots, CNC machines, AI and automated efficiencies, and marketing of its brands, to make the world salivate. Since I mentioned marketing, is it not marketing and intrinsic gratification that makes one buy the latest smart phone or BMW? While at the same time, countries in the West have substantial regulations on manufacturing firms, where many companies rather outsource manufacturing abroad, or to subcontractors domestically. In fact, this is what Apple and Proctor & Gamble do. The question then becomes what is worth more, your brands, factories, or technologies? So, without invoking an extensive debate, and just before we go to GATT and the WTO, I present a case against mercantilism.

Why Mercantilism Fosters Mediocrity

At first, protecting one's markets is a great battle cry for domestic political consumption—that is, until the domestic consumer pays more for less, driving down their consumption power, and one's subsequent quality of material life, which is closely related to one's emotional wellbeing.

There is no example of protected markets that create efficient enough firms to be able to leapfrog on a global scale, meaning, a highly competitive domestic marketplace with little or no government created frictional distortions such as high duties, which drive up prices at the expense of consumer welfare. Competitors both foreign and domestic drives local participants to either become efficient or die, governments are of course the exception to this. So then, if a nation's theatre of companies is not efficient with its industry at home, how does it become efficient abroad? And who ultimately pays the price? Consider the following examples.

India

India has a long history of trade protectionism, dating back to 1947. Mahatma Gandhi believed in ruralism, as opposed to urbanization. He blamed European goods, thinking that is what drove out Indian jobs. As a shortcoming, Gandhi was not a proponent of free markets, and did not understand market systems—while he was a lawyer, he had little or no business experience. This seems to be the norm today of the global elite political class. His successors, who were dominated by family members, were chronic mercantilists and toed the same line, and eventually had to change their tune in the 1990s when India's level of economic distortions, largely driven by protectionism, caused an economic crisis, which forced India to turn to the IMF for a bailout. These loans came with conditions, including removing trade barriers, red tape and opening to foreign investments. In other words, India was asked to embrace natural market conditions.

These are a few examples of economic distortions that inadvertently encourage domestic manufacturers to be mediocre at the expense of the consumer, subsequently leading to more poverty, because the consumer is getting less for more. Whereas, the primary aim of trade is to foster comparative efficiency and output advantage where the consumer is getting more for less, this is the key driver of open markets that foster a diminishment of poverty. While at the same time, domestically competitive and efficient firms use accustomed competition as a springboard to enter foreign markets.

Tariff rates in India averaged over 150 percent in the 1950s, dropped to 56 percent in 1990, while in 2020 they averaged close to 6.7 percent. Consider the new car industry in India where duties and government fees, depending how it's calculated, can reach up to 182percent, (not including graft at customs). This inadvertently encourages Tata Motors to build cars that are not world-class—of course at the expense of impoverishing the Indian consumer, and holding them back in poverty, while reducing the purchasing power of the emerging middle-class. Much of Tata Motors' parts are imported at suffocating duty rates, so then how does this help the consumer? Also, all these duties and tariffs fill the coffers of a bloated government, supported by its favorite bedfellows: bureaucracy and inefficiencies. Subsequently, the outcome is a monopoly for Tata, which lobbies rigorously to India's government, at the expense of the nation's economic wellbeing for its citizens. This is not a slight against Tata, because they do have the opening price point in the auto industry, but merely to illustrate that it is protected against competition at a societal cost! In a momentary defense of India's government under Narendra Modi, as an exception in this day and age, has regard for its citizenry, which it should be commended for.

So then, how does the collection of duties help benefit the consumer? On the contrary, it encourages government to grow at the expense of the public purse with virtue signaling programs that almost always end up in failure and achieving the opposite of their goals. The result being oppressive mercantilism that diminishes consumer welfare, gives carte blanche to domestic manufacturers—the end game is that these protected manufacturers often rely on crony capitalism to get exclusive license within industries creating a monopoly of economic societal strategy. This is not only in India of course, Nigeria is known for this in bar soap manufacturing, where one or two competitors attain license (helps to have friends in government to get these licenses) to make soap while imports are not permitted, entrepreneurs skirt the duty by importing cars with bar soaps filled in the door panels and ensure that the customs officer is compensated for looking the other way. In fact, this is how my customer in Nigeria sold my Health & Beauty Care Brands there. These are some of the economic outcomes of trade protectionism that foster competitive mediocrity in their domestic market and lend itself to a spiral of economic stagnation.

Back to India, protectionism does not end with Tata Motors. India has strong trade protectionism for its retailers, many of them being mom and pop shops that constitute a strong political lobbying force. Subsequently, efficient retailers such as Walmart and Carrefour are literally excluded from India's $1.2 trillion retail market. In the case of Walmart, they can only act as wholesale "cash and carry"; according to the Wall Street Journal, India has laws in place forbidding large chains like Walmart to directly sell to consumers. The net result is that lack of competition harms the consumer and the broad economic welfare of the society, where few benefit at the expense of many.

Other Examples of Mercantilism

Revisiting Egypt, the country has another long history of mercantilism as well, with a current average duty rate of 22 percent and, as mentioned earlier, they allow Chinese goods to sail in, even though other country producers offer better for less, after all China did lend them money through spiraling debt traps to build the Cairo subway, and why not be nice to them in exchange? So as gratitude for the loans a bit of quid pro quo is in order by excluding other non-Chinese goods from being imported. As an example, what the Egyptian government will do is protect the shampoo and soap making industry by offering the license to one or two manufacturers under the guise of protecting domestic jobs at some expense, with a combination of licensing fees and graft to the ruling party of Al-Sisi, or whatever other power-hungry despot takes over.

Moving back to Ethiopia, where I have firsthand knowledge because of family ties, the government will grant a few people, sometimes one, a license within an industry, may it be flour mill, leather production, or chemical production. These companies will make monopoly profits at the expense of the greater economy, consumer and stakeholders. Simultaneously, the government will sing a tune of patriotism, by blocking imports, collect exorbitant licensing fees complimented by bribes. The result will be a distorted economy at the expense of the consumer and with a few firms making profits, until a new political party gets in power claiming it is going to clean up corruption, which means replacing the prior tyrant with a new brand of corruption, namely taking new bribes to move their exclusive arrangement to their cronies or take bribes from current license owners. So then, it seems that the swamp lives on with all types of new and interesting creatures inhabiting its murky waters.

Take the case of rare earth elements (REE) found in Ethiopia, such tantalum used for the electronics industry for capacitors and high-power resistors. This element is also used to make alloys to increase strength, ductility, and corrosion resistance. The metal is used in dental and surgical instruments and implants, as it causes no immune response. Chinese and German companies are in Ethiopia for this reason. Do you not think that Chinese and German manufacturers have market entry advantage in Ethiopia as a result? Is there not a trade-off? Do you not think that government members are not receiving graft? Do you think that if other exporting nations are excluded, does this not reduce consumer choice and societal welfare?

China

How could any study on protectionism be complete without considering China, which was allowed into the WTO by President Clinton—as bright as he is otherwise, he was naïve in his thinking that they would come into the fold of the Peace Dividend Theory. Steeping back in history, two great leaders I have studied, Churchill and Eisenhower, would not have allowed China into the WTO without more rigorous tenets of performance. I say this because both Eisenhower and Churchill governed and saw the savagery of war, and had not only deep visionary abilities, but understood the human psyche. A deal should have been negotiated where WTO privileges would incrementally be afforded based on incremental verifiable undertakings by the CCP. But regardless of personal views, the narrative was that as the West, and especially the United States was moving toward a utopian service industry as opposed to manufacturing which we could outsource to China, and other low-cost producers. Then magically for two decades America has been exporting her inflation and importing China's unemployment, which it eventually nullified up until recently. The thinking was that China would come into the fold of liberal democracies and savor at the thought of reading Jefferson and Locke.

The utopian vision has not worked out that well. Wolf Richter writes the following in a 2021 article:

> *Back when offshoring production by Corporate America to cheap countries was hailed as good for the overall economy, rather than just good for Corporate America, any fears about potentially exploding trade deficits were papered over with visions of the new American Dream: America was great at producing and selling high-value services—the financialization of everything, movies, software, business services, IT services, etc. Exports of these high-value services would make up for the imports of cheap goods. And trade would balance out.*
>
> *Today, we got another dose of just how spectacularly this strategy has failed. The overall trade deficit in goods and services hit a new all-time worst in August of $73 billion (seasonally adjusted), according to the Commerce Department today.*
>
> *The trade balance in services deteriorated to a surplus of only $16.1 billion, the lowest since 2011, while imports of goods reached the worst ever $239 billion, and exports of goods edged up to a record of $150 billion, thanks to $33 billion in exports of crude oil, petroleum products, natural gas,*

natural gas liquids, products from the petrochemical industry, and coal.[5]

Figure 7.2 tells the story.

Figure 7.2: Total goods & services trade deficit

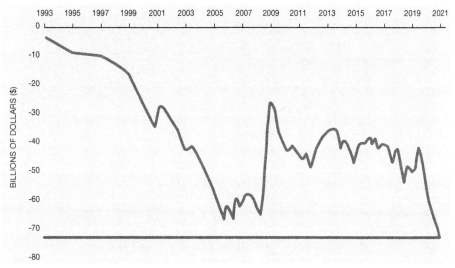

Source: U.S. Department of Commerce   WOLFSTREET.com

When the United States tabulates the trade surplus globally in services against the trade deficit in goods, it exported $64 billion in services, and imported $47.9 billion of services for a net gain $16.1 billion in service. However, the utopian promise of a flourishing economy has not quite panned out yet, when we consider the integration of the trade deficit on goods which is just over $90 billion in August 2021, and when we frame this against the net surplus on exports on service, we see a deterioration of a nations competitive scope.

5   Wolf Richter, "Just Keeps Getting Worse: Services Trade Surplus, the American Dream-Not-Come-True, Worst in 10 Years. Imports Worst Ever. Trade Deficit Worst Ever," Wolf Street, October 5, 2021, https://wolfstreet.com/2021/10/05/services-trade-surplus-the-american-dream-not-come-true-worst-in-10-years-imports-of-goods-worst-ever-total-trade-deficit-worst-ever/

Figure 7.3 gives us even more trending data.

Figure 7.3: U.S. Trade: Goods Deficit, Services Surplus

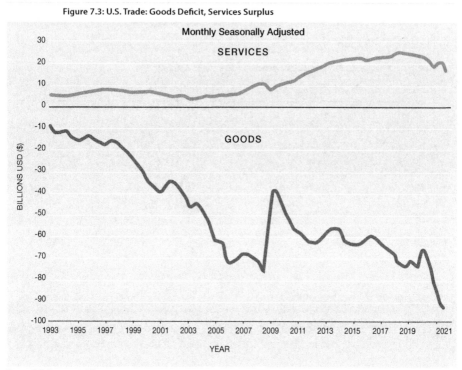

Source: U.S. Department of Commerce

WOLFSTREET.com

China has many examples of protecting its domestic industry, with a current average tariff of 12 percent on imports. But the bigger issue is non-transparent barriers to entry, such as lack of transparent regulation that exclude foreign players, that is until a foreign corporation decides to manufacture in China and shares its intellectual property as it gets undressed, which is part of the welcome to China hospitality package. Again, *caveat emptor*. Interestingly, the issue of non-transparent barriers to entry was not addressed until the Tokyo rounds of GATT in 1973, and then baked into the WTO articles.

China moves with five- and ten-year industrial plans adopted from Soviet times that only worked for a short period, as did Japan's industrial policy. Originally approved by China's State Council in

2015, take for example, the Made in China 2025 policy that specifically targets 10 high-tech industries. This comes with government subsidization and loans, and this alone goes against the tenets of the WTO and its predecessor GATT. The question is, can China really have a comparative advantage in every industry government central planning pursues? What if the market preferences shift, and how quick then can you swing resources? David Ricardo's and modern theories of technological trade exchange say otherwise.

For example, can China make the best computer chips in the world and surpass Intel and Taiwan Semiconductor Manufacturing Company? And if not, would its finished value-added product in laptops or AI suffer at the expense of the Chinese consumer and competitive industrial output? Can it develop the finest of 5G technologies without trade, and if so, for how long? Can government be proficient at picking winning and losing industries, and is there any commercial history to support this? Yes, it worked in Japan for a while but now they have gone through the Lost Decades. Can it rely on domestic consumption to fuel growth, and use the protectionism of infant industry arguments to close the imitation gap?

Consider the case of Google and YouTube, which are barred from China, or the Chinese consumers exclusion from these platforms, while business can only have limited access to them, and as a result locals have to use Baidu, which is a Chinese search engine and advanced technology company, all in one. What if the search results are not as deep and proficient as Google, and what is the economic effect of censorship on businesses and consumers? (Are we are not seeing algorithm manipulation in the West now with Google searches.) Did China really benefit from abruptly barring Google, which was launched in 2006 and banned in 2010 after the digital Great Wall of China blocked many of its searches? YouTube, which is effectively banned in China and is it putting China's industry, consumer and intellectual knowledge at a competitive disadvantage, because the ruling party considers it also a threat to its rule? After all, what is wrong with a little bit of American propaganda? And if so, how do we put an accounting number on this using qualitative and quantitative measurement? But now, home grown giants in China such as Alibaba (especially the flamboyant Jack Ma) and Tencent are having their paws slapped, since the Chinese Communist Party (CCP) will lay the law down for anything that threatens their propaganda and tyranny. The lesson here is, go about your business in China, but do not say anything outside the official government narrative makes one wonder if we are not starting to see the same in the West.

This brings up the question, are there drawbacks to censorship affecting the capital stock of a nation, especially when we consider that China's growing number of knowledge workers need access to global news and research, and Baidu is notoriously bad at turning up relevant results from outside China that the CCP does not ratify in its moral script? In effect, this is protectionism that Ricardo could not fathom, and it does create both economic and competitive distortions that harm the domestic economy in the way of higher costs and inefficiencies.

China's protectionist history could easily be a book on its own, but a couple of areas also worth noting are their banking and insurance industry that are rigorously protected with substantial drawbacks. For example, foreign banks are limited in China, while Chinese banks are forced to lend state owned zombie government-run companies that have sinking balance sheets. The idea is to keep lending to these companies so they do not have to write down the bad debt, because after the write downs, the banks would need to be recapitalized due to declaring the losses on their books or come clean and admit that they are insolvent.

Some of this is due to different accounting rules, and unlike the West, the Chinese banks do not write-off, or at least put in loss provisions for shaky loans over 90 days, while government officials do not want to deal with the blame of finally putting a zombie company out of its misery. This practice is antithetical to rigorous banking practices, and one must then ask that if it had initially opened its banking industry to foreign competition with an international standard of GAAP, stress tests, accounting and audit rules, would domestic banks be healthier and require fewer bailouts? Should government-run zombie companies be allowed to perpetually show up as a toxic asset on a bank's balance sheet?

Turning our attention to the insurance industry, China eventually opened its market to foreign insurance companies and its financial sector to foreign companies. For years, the Chinese insurance sector was simply not world-class and lacked the products and discipline of governance that European and American companies have. Many Chinese insurance companies are involved in high-risk investments, offering well above market rates for insurance premiums. Today, there are over 50 foreign insurance companies operating in China, and in 2019, new measures were implemented in liberalizing the market.

The result of liberalization by offering overseas insurance products for the Chinese consumer and firms allows consumers and competitors the benefits of rigorous competition, and access to better methods, systems, and operation of foreign institutions. By facilitating now 51 percent ownership, it has reduced barriers to market and fostered fair play after, shall we say, some pressure by the WTO, and other facets of commercial diplomacy. A good example of a foreign company operating being wholly owned by themselves and not with joint Chinese ownership is Tesla. Elon Musk is quite revered by the Chinese as he is at home, and it might be argued that he is the most revolutionary industrialist since Henry Ford.

The U.S. Auto Industry: An Awakening Moment

The golden age of the American auto industry—with large, creative cars with the latest creature comforts and technologies of their day—is now in the nostalgic past. The Harley Earl-inspired designs exuded the confidence of the nation with its large ostentatious tailfins, as if to say the 20th century was America's century. However, by the 1970s, the state of the U.S. auto industry had become quite insular in its success by dismissing small cars, coupled by reliability, build quality, and fuel inefficiency issues of domestic manufacturers. At one point, assembly line workers would leave pop cans in between the panels on Cadillac doors, which were only discovered when consumers complained—a real black eye for the Cadillac brand. What many cannot fathom today was that as late as the 1970s and early 1980s, even in the luxury segment, Cadillac and Lincoln carried higher brand cachet than Mercedes and BMW. In 1956, Lincoln produced a hand built Continental Mark 11 that sold for over $10,000, a higher ticket price than a Rolls Royce—Sinatra, Elvis, Nat King Cole, the Shah of Iran, and all the beautiful people of the era owned one. It is truly a stunning exhibit of industrial design and penmanship.

In the 1950s, American car executives and engineers would visit Europe and Japan and would sneer and laugh off the possibilities of small cars in America, even though the Volkswagen Bug and MG were big hits during the decade in the U.S. market, (MG was the car that first introduced to America handling through rack-and-pinion steering system). They went to teach in-process quality control to the Japanese and laughed off their small cars as serious competition—after all it was America's golden age, and that was projected by its cars that seemed to have captured the era. That is until the perfect storm of the OPEC oil crisis in the early 1970s resulting in gas lineups, as a fleet of reliable Datsun cars showed up to capture the shift in consumer preferences. When Lee Iacocca (a master salesman) the father of the Ford Mustang, proposed the future of smaller cars to Henry Ford Jr, it cost him his job.

Going back to quality issues, in one case, I picked up a new GM product in the 1980s that had an unstable idle, and when I mentioned it to the dealer on pick-up day, they told me to drive it for two weeks and create a list of issues the car may have, then bring it back for warranty adjustments and repairs. This was quite common, whereas the in-process quality control at the factory came up short and the responsibility was put on the dealer and consumer. Today, this would be completely unacceptable!

So, what drove American car companies to make world-class cars again, and in the case of GM be a market leader in China with the Buick brand? Was it the onslaught of foreign players in the 1960s and 1970s? The answer is specifically the Japanese and the German makers that forced a renaissance in excellence for American-made cars, which resulted in a significant increase in build quality that is on par with world-class today. This hyper-competitive home market has allowed U.S. car makers, especially General Motors, to leapfrog into the world's largest auto market, namely China, where they sold over 1.47 million cars in 2020, and are the number three auto maker in China with 7.5 percent market share, trailing Honda at number two with 1.63 million, and Volkswagen, which holds the number one position at 13.3 percent, with 2.6 million autos sold.[6] In fact, GM sells more Cadillacs in China than in their home market, while Buick is considered a premium brand in China.

It is highly doubtful this would have happened if the United States protected their auto industry. Did the U.S. consumer benefit by obtaining better cars for less? It is empirically irrefutable that if a company could not create competitive excellence at home, it could not abroad either.

Concluding Thoughts

Foreign competition drives excellence in a domestic market and forces domestic competitors to up their game or perish, while acting as a springboard to global markets. Subsequently, if you protect these industries with archaic reasoning, such as the infant industry argument, by helping it along until maturity, puts the consumer at economic peril while there is no evidence that government protecting infant industries works.

Nations need low tariff rates to import critical tooling, machinery, robotics and a host of other capital inputs, and if duty rates remained closer to 50 percent as they did after World War II, it would stymie the efforts of setting up local manufacturing facilities for both domestic and multinational corporations. All the while the

6   Bart Demandt, "China Car Sales Analysis 2020," CarSalesBase, accessed March 28, 2022, https://carsalesbase.com/china-car-sales-analysis-2020/

duties would go into the coffers of government as opposed to the natural forces of the free market where it would be expended in a more equilibrium manner.

If the consumer is getting more for less, their marginal utility increases and this helps them pull out of poverty in the way of higher standard of living, in respect to their consumption power. And this can only happen in a free trade and free market economy where consumer choice and fair play is not undermined.

We live in a different world today then the time of David Ricardo, Adam Smith, John Maynard Keynes, in respect to both theories of trade and the original economic paradigm of 1946 when the articles of GATT were created. We've gone from the manufacturing world to a service world. The theories of free trade in the world are on the cusp of yet another industrial revolution that have come under pressure since services are traded freely with the exception of VAT taxes which are imposed on certain services.

The world we live in today has engineers overseas exchanging ideas 24/7 on projects, and as more corners of the world become highly educated in technologies it puts pressure on the imitation gap. In today's service economies so much is outsourced such as call centres, engineering, law, IT, marketing, creatives, and the list goes on, as intercompany services outsourced across the globe as well as the through platforms such as Fiverr and Upwork, we are seeing unimpeded free trade in services.

The size of all service exports in the world is $6.5 trillion versus all trade in goods closer to $20 trillion. It is remarkable that services are offered in the spirit of complete free trade where the company or individuals offering these services are not impeded by duty, tariffs, and trade wars. But this is not the whole story, we now live in a world where financial instruments are traded with little or no impediments. Consider the total size of derivative contracts flowing through global financial capital centres in London, Hong Kong, Shanghai, New York, Zurich, and Munich worth approximately worth $1.2 quadrillion. And finally, a mention must be made of the $100 trillion plus size of the equity market.

The theory of how another industrial revolution will materialize in 30 to 60 years is conjectured at best, which might include the ability to program the mind and might defy the parameters of our current thinking in respect to imagining the future. Don't be alarmed by this, because at the outset of the second industrial revolution in the mid-19th century, no one could have imagined the coming combination of urbanization, flight, electricity, cars, skyscrapers, motion picture and the likes 30 to 50 years into the future. The question is not the technology, but the impairment to individual liberty!

How do these trade theories hold up in a new complex financial world market of services, against the tradition of goods against the backdrop of hyper-disruption? The only possible answer might come from the hidden hand called our imagination that enamors the psyche as to infer upon the future of tomorrow!

Now equipped with the case for free trade, it is only natural that we revisit Bretton Woods and the creation of GATT, which is the centerpiece of commercial diplomacy that followed World War II and underpins much of that global economic order that affects us to this day.

Commercial Diplomacy GATT and The WTO

Just after the World War II the adverse effects of mercantilism had devastating consequences on world economies, and political culture leading to substantial distortions and inefficiencies, where average global tariff rates were in the 40 percent range. According to many economists, it was mercantilism that created not only inflation after the First World War but was the primary cause of the global Great Depression. The Great Depression is discussed later in this book in some detail.

In some respects, mercantilism leading up to the Great Depression is similar to the ruthless mercantilism practiced today by China, where it has hollowed out Western manufacturing with a willing cast that includes firms, consumers, inventiveness, and knowhow, while not buying into the American post-war ideals of neo liberalism. To be fair though, America has fervently protected its agricultural industries since the first world war, where they imposed their agriculture on the Europeans while closing their markets.

It was the American liberal order and the British sense of fair play in commerce that gave intellectual fuel to challenge the decaying effects of protectionist measures. A proposal was prepared by the Americans—victory has its privileges—between 1946 and 1948 referred to as "The International Trade Organization." Ironically, the ITO charter was not ratified by Congress. However, the momentum to dismantle trade protectionism gained strategic inertia, and in 1947, an interim agreement was ratified by 23 countries, and it was this document that led to the articles of the General Agreement on Tariffs and Trade, commonly referred to as GATT.

GATT was the predecessor to the WTO, which was formed in 1995.

The primary goal of GATT was to dismantle barriers to trade, both transparent and non-transparent barriers to entry, with a view of fostering trade liberalization. It was a centerpiece of neo-American liberal world order and a testament to commercial diplomacy. There were many rounds of talks in GATT that eventually led to 128 contracting parties by 1994, which resulted in the treatment of 90 percent of world trade. But first let's take a quick look at some basic principles of the GATT articles.

Most Favored Nation Treatment (MFN)

This means that if you give a bilateral tariff reduction to one partner, it must be extended to all contracting parties. So now you know what the U.S. president is talking about when he rattles his saber and threatens to withdraw MFN.

Article 2 includes concessions made are binding and cannot be reversed, something like new taxes.

Protectionism must be transparent, specifically addressing non-transparent tariff barriers to entry such as overbearing regulations not imposed on domestic participants, only on foreign entrants. GATT plays the role to ensure that arcane regulatory registration is not used as a protectionist measure, which is used in many developing and developed economies. In the real world these barriers can be brought down by the importer offering favor in exchange for the registration ministry to ratify importing documents, practiced in the more corrupt countries. This type of graft is simply the cost of doing business, and if you stand up to it, will have your container sitting at customs for months.

Then there is the concept of the "free rider", which is addressed by stating that if your goods are given favorable rates, reciprocity should be extended. It is in a sense the principal underpinnings of fair play!

Between 1945 and 1964 there were five multilateral rounds of GATT and to save you from unwarranted prolixity, it might be best to focus on the three major rounds of GATT, with their challenges and accomplishments.

The Kennedy Round: 1964-1967

As the name insinuates, the Kennedy Round of GATT was named to honor the memory of President Kennedy. However, it was more than that, since Kennedy pushed for a new United States trade agenda, which resulted in the Trade Expansion Act of 1962, and concurred with the American liberal agenda of free markets and democracy, to foster economic and political stability. After all, the century had already seen two World Wars, a Bolshevik revolution, and China's fall into the totalitarian hands of Chairman Mao Zedong.

The Kennedy Round was held in Geneva—well, if the taxpayer is paying for it, why not have posh accommodations like royalty. Even socialists love to be pampered in hypocrisy of bourgeois Champagne surroundings in perks that the fruition of the free market provides, as the revolution percolates in the backdrop!

Many consider the Kennedy Round the golden age of GATT, as it involved more participating parties, while achieving reductions on a host of HS tariffs across the board (Harmonized System of product identifiers). Originally, the goal was to reduce rates by 50 percent, but it still reached an impressive 36 to 39 percent reduction. This was a significant victory, especially when we saw the effects of mercantilism in the first half of the 20th century, including war and substantial commercial hostilities, capstoned by economic calamities including two depressions and bouts of hyperinflation. It should be noted that the Kennedy Round, on a weighted average basis, tariffs were reduced to 7.2 percent, which is a far cry from the 40 percent range at the closure of the World War II.

Still, there were shortfalls and challenges ahead—the reductions were mostly on industrial goods, and after World War I we did not see a drop on tariffs on agricultural products from the developing world to export. Thus, domestic farmers were protected at the cost of higher prices on the shelves for agricultural products. Admittedly, this was a political conundrum that affected the tenets of providing efficient consumer pricing, and subsequent interest of the welfare of the subjects of the state. After all the key tenet of GATT and the American liberal order was to pull much of the world out of poverty since the thinking was that trading partners were less likely to participate in hostilities. There were other shortfalls as well, first was the rising protectionism in textiles, and finally "non-transparent barriers to entry" that had not been addressed at the time which was being imposed by the industrialized countries.

The problem of non-transparent barriers to entry was not confronted in a meaningful way until the Tokyo Round.

The Tokyo Round: 1973-1979

The Tokyo Round of GATT had its ambitious eye set on confronting the new protectionism, some of which include regulatory hurdles that are not required for domestic manufacturers, or specialized labeling requirements that helps ensure the host country manufacturer is somewhat protected. At the same time, with non-transparent barriers, it becomes difficult to dump excess or subsidized goods into a foreign country, which plays havoc on local competitors, but adorned by the consumer. Specifically, you will see a lot of this excess product dumped in U.S. and Canadian Dollar Stores, with little or no testing, along with no barriers to entry, and that's just the tip of the iceberg. Try this in South America, the Middle East, and China, and you will have more documents to fill out than a Philadelphia lawyer during a 10-year litigation trial. However, it is interesting to note that Vietnam is China's dumping ground for surplus goods—a few well-placed bribes will result in import regulations being thrown under the bus for favors, which usually does the trick, with the outcome being that the containers roll in like the half time show at the Superbowl!

New protectionism was mostly wielded by the industrialized nations after World War II. Today, this has been much more treacherously deployed by China and a host of other bad actors with examples shown earlier.

To frame the backdrop, in the 1960s non-tariff barriers had appeared in industrialized nations, but it was under the guise of export restraint, and in 1974, what accelerated the process was the Arab oil embargo on industrialized nations, especially the United States, which went into a deep recession with a double-edged sword of high unemployment and high inflation, commonly known as stagflation, that went outside the Phillips curve model. The issue is more complicated and will treat it more deeply in the history of financial Booms and Busts in the next section, but the West was already losing key manufacturing industries, such as televisions, transistors, textile, autos to Japan, Taiwan, Hong Kong, Germany, and the list goes on.

The new protectionism of non-transparent barriers to entry posed a profound challenge to the authority of GATT, and was equating to national protectionism, and the influence of domestic politics, which politicians must answer for.

Just as a side note, it was GATT that allowed the Marshall Plan, which was the socioeconomic boost, to give fuel to perpetuate into the economic recovery of Europe and Japan after WWII. Few people know that Italy was the low-cost manufacturer of Europe, further, after the War, United States had 52 percent of the world GDP, promoted free trade as an intellectual and economic mechanism of the American liberal order. Of course, there was a trade-off, namely the U.S. dollar unseating the British pound and empire by becoming the de facto global currency.

To give a good example of protectionism that transpired concomitantly during the Tokyo Round of GATT was Section 301 of the U.S. Trade Act. Section 301 gives American firms and citizens the right to formally petition the U.S. government where they considered American commercial interests had been damaged by unfair actions of foreign governments. This does not mean that the U.S. is not guilty of unfair trade practices, because it is, but still is the most open major economy in the world, (farming commodities excluded) and the UK comes a close second.

Eventually, the 1988 Omnibus Trade and Competitiveness Act gave more teeth to Section 301, where it allowed the investigative findings of the U.S. agency to advise on the retaliatory recommendations. Subsequently, under certain circumstances, retaliatory actions were mandatory, making it politically difficult for a president not to retaliate in the face of unfair trade practices, perceived or otherwise.

President Trump used Section 301 as his legal premise to slap tariffs on China.

By the time the Tokyo Round concluded in 1979, there were some successes of another 34 percent reduction in customs duties, amounting to a reduction to 4.7 percent. Incidentally, governments hate to lose any revenue such as duties, since it gives them less money to win the next election, presuming there is one in some countries.

To address the new non-transparent barriers to trade, in the Tokyo Round there were some other breakthroughs, that included the following:

- Subsidies and countervailing measures
- Technical barriers to trade
- Import licensing procedures (all developing economies love this one today)
- Government procurement opening up to international bidders
- Customs valuation price inflating
- GATT anti-dumping code.

Still, GATT's mechanism was no match for the rise of the new protectionism of non-transparent barriers to entry. Even with these breakthroughs, it was not enough to stem the tide, and by default, the Tokyo Round failed to effectively deal with the new protectionism. So, by 1986, it was time to make new reservations at five-star hotels, dine, debate, and put on their finest aristocratic attire and travel to the exotic locale of Uruguay.

The Uruguay Round: 1986-1994

The primary function of the Uruguay Round was to address the new protectionism, since the afterburn of mercantilism was having an adverse effect in lifting the economic fortunes of the less developed countries. Originally, it was designed to come to conclusion in 1990, however, it concluded in 1994. GATT's primary other aim was to attempt and reestablish itself as the agency of multilateral commercial diplomacy. The Uruguay Round had some very lofty goals that they hoped was to be resolved with 123 contracting parties, and the key ones can be summarized as follows:

- To reduce tariffs another 30 percent from its less than 5 percent mark at the end of the Tokyo Round
- Eliminate non-tariff measures, such as voluntary export restraints

- To create mechanisms to address the New Protectionism in terms of non-transparent barriers to entry

- Liberalization of natural resource-based products from the developing economies such as raw materials, non-ferrous metals

- Textile: reduction in tariffs; this was, and still is a highly protected sector, which at the time of the Uruguay Round, constituted 9 percent of world trade

- Trade in agriculture, against the lobbying efforts of local farmers and food as being a strategic asset of any country

- Bilateral safeguards (meaning countries could invoke bilateral agreements under Article 19, and this was primarily invoked by the Europeans and Americans first in textiles)

- Subsidies and countervailing measure, a Chinese favorite, and difficult to prove

- Stronger Intellectual Property rights (Turkey and China still contravene this to this day with blatant and documented examples of counterfeiting)

- Dispute Settlement mechanisms

- Trade in services: this was in place as the West was moving to a service-based economy with mixed results. Today with the internet, overseas outsourcing of customer service and tech-support, to mention a few, and sites like Upwork offering services on a global basis, it almost becomes impossible to enforce tariffs on services, if they exist at all, and quite possibly we are seeing utopian frictionless commerce that governments have not yet found a way to get their sticky paws on.

The Uruguay Round of GATT Establishes the WTO

In summary, the Uruguay Round did have some successes but was still not able to overcome the new protectionism of non-transparent barriers to entry. Furthermore, GATT did not have the mechanisms of legal enforcement and arbitration in place. Whatever developed during the end of the Uruguay Round helps explain much of our commercial diplomacy today. The United States and the European Union settled their differences primarily in agriculture categories in what was known as The Blair House Accord. Then, on April 1994, almost 123 contracting members of GATT signed an agreement in Marrakesh, Morocco—a favorite stomping grounds of James Bond—in what established the World Trade Organization.

The articles of GATT since 1947 still act as a legal umbrella, if you will, for the WTO. But the big difference between GATT and the WTO is the legal enforcement the WTO has, where GATT were a set of rules—the WTO is a permanent institution, its trade is not only goods, but intellectual activity and services, and its dispute mechanisms are much faster and more effective and automatic than GATT. Further, its legal basis is stronger than GATT, and the WTO commitments are full and permanent.

Now our journey of world free trade and commercial diplomacy lands us on the front steps of the WTO, and as we shall soon see, it faces an all-star lineup of bureaucrats and the likes.

The World Trade Organization and the Doha Round

The World Trade Organization holds more weight than its former GATT predecessor, and the original mandate of the Doha Round in 2001, was to reduce global trade impediment but had a special focus on the North liberalizing their markets to the South, meaning first world countries and developing economies.

Originally, the trade rounds were to be wrapped up by 2005, but with so many countries at the table and bureaucrats who get paid regardless of the outcome, things dragged on. After all, who could resist the never-ending supply of exotic locales, such as Doha, Geneva, Paris, Hong Kong, why not let the Champagne flow, complemented by all the culinary white-glove service, all of course, in the palatial surroundings of five-star hotels. Just be-cause they are espousing that they are there to help the down-trodden does not mean they must meet in proletarian surround-ings.

The Doha Round, with its lofty goals for more inclusion of the least developed countries, has arguably met with a litany of im-passes, and yes, failures. The first one that comes to mind is allow-ing China into the World Trade Organization during the Clinton presidency in 2001, with the thinking at the time that China's inclu-sion would pave the way for liberalization of its totalitarian regime, both socially and economically. Without imparting a bias leniency, Bill Clinton, who had successes as well as setbacks, was a Rhodes Scholar with no real business experience, like most politicians, and with a touch of naivety. He falls in a long line of seemingly brilliant academics/intellects who have a history of making poor decisions, including Henry Kissinger, Barack Obama, Alan Greenspan, Janet Yellen and Richard Nixon, who originally opened the door with Red China during the Cold War, while taking the U.S. off the gold standard. My critique is that Clinton should have allowed China to incrementally enter the WTO with preconditions based on per-formance clauses by way of key performance indicators (KPIs)—pre-conditions including economical, moral, and democratic, with a non-interference clause in Hong Kong, as well as intellectual property theft.

China should have had only incremental inclusion and as it liberalized its economic policies through actions and not words, the outcome would have led to a more stable and balanced world trade scenario. Anyone who thinks China subscribes to the British notion of "fair play" in commerce perhaps drank too much Kool-Aid served up daily now from China's CGTN, a mouthpiece of the Chinese Communist Party, and a host of other propaganda net-works of treachery, acting much like the Silicon Valley's Cabal and the MSM. *The Guardian* writes about examples of CCP propagan-da that includes Communist propaganda party inserts, opinion pieces into the *Wall Street Journal*, the *New York Times*, and the *Los Angeles Times*, where they pay these newspapers and many more, to gaslight the naïve.[7]

Realizing that this topic could fill a book on its own and we are steering off course a bit. However, with the information contained in this section's new-found knowledge of GATT, it is easy to see that the spirit of the Kennedy to Uruguay Rounds of GATT has been contravened with rampant, cavalier, non-transparent protectionism, meaning shutting out goods by using arcane and intentional regulatory hurdles.

Going back a bit, consider the Uruguay Round, China makes blatant abuse of IP laws, through knocking off and the theft of intellectual property, as well as technology, by insisting that foreign manufacturers have a Chinese partner and share this technology. This is in addition to alleged espionage activities including cyber-attacks in the West, both in academia and industry that is well documented by CSIS in Canada to garner industrial secrets. Further, consider Silicon Valley companies such as Twitter, which recently brought down 170,000 Chinese trolls and propaganda bad actors, are not allowed to operate in China, but WeChat, Baidu and TikTok, which are all Chinese companies, are allowed to operate in the West, while WhatsApp is not available in China. To be fair, the new propaganda wars are delivered through the social media, may it be delivered at the hands of the West or East, as corporations work closely with government in America, which amounts to a Corporatocracy, much like in China, to help deliver the official narrative that is not remotely plausible.

Another example is Skype, where it can be used on desktops but not on mobile phones in China, thus making it arcane in the mobile environment—this is intentionally done by the PRC, as well, YouTube, Google and Facebook are persona non grata in mainland China. This is not a problem, since the Silicon Valley cabal are participating in their own left-wing biased narratives that steers them

7 Louisa Lim and Julia Bergin, "Inside China's Audacious Global Propaganda Campaign," *The Guardian*, December 7, 2018, https://www.theguardian.com/news/2018/dec/07/china-plan-for-global-media-dominance-propaganda-xi-jinping

away from criticizing China as a tradable in exchange for market access, (NBA refrains from criticism of China as well in exchange for market access). Remember, in human history money always triumphs over virtue. Silicon Valley uses the First Amendment and Section 230 as useful catalysts—that is, until someone else's free speech does not align with their prevaricated narrative. The point being that the free flow of social media platforms constitutes the free trade of services, which should be a global platform without censorship by either Silicon Valley or the CCP in China. After all, a little propaganda with popcorn makes for excellent evening entertainment, just add salt and butter!

Back to the WTO, when accessing the Doha Round, the focal point was that agriculture subsidies and related sticking points is an area that the parties have not been able to come to an agreement on. This all came to a Mexican standoff in Geneva when protection of Chinese, Indian, African markets were challenged by the EU. Eventually, India and China's hard position was met with substantial criticism by the United States, particularly of India, who used the special safeguard mechanism to protect its poor farmers. There was also much discussion of pharmaceutical patent protection against the needs of the developing world for medicines at lower cost, as well as special and differential treatment. It is interesting to note that drug companies work on extraordinary high gross margins to recoup their R&D in one quarter, for example Pfizer 63 percent, Moderna 85 percent, Glaxo 66 percent, versus Tesla at 25 percent. For drug companies to justify such high prices can easily be debunked by dissecting their long sheet financials for R&D versus topline gross profit. To add to the bureaucracy, Congress withdrew the U.S. president's Congressional Fast Track Trade Promotion Authority under President Bush in 2007, and this meant that all deals with the WTO must be ratified by Congress.

The Doha Round effectively ended in 2006, when the European Union and the Americans refused to reduce farm subsidies, and again this goes back to World War I which is a contentious political subject, not only in the developed world, but the developing world as well. There have been incremental talks since, which can be construed as a continuation of the Doha Round but will let the scholars debate this point.

Some Final Thoughts on the WTO and Trade

It is indisputable that free trade and free markets have lifted billions globally out of poverty, by increasing consumer welfare, admittedly at some cost, many of which have been mentioned, however, like all things in the history of civilization there are trade-offs, but in the case of free trade, the benefits far outweigh the costs. After all, it was trade that allowed Europe and Japan to rebuild from the ashes of World War II, especially after being granted access to the U.S. market, this along with support of the Marshall Plan, with the trade-off being that they are enslaved to U.S. monetary imperialism and SWIFT system through the U.S. dollar still being the reserve currency. However, in addition to agricultural impediments to free trade, the Doha Round, by most measures, has been a failure for three systematic reasons, that include the following.

Non-Transparent Barriers to Entry

As discussed earlier, the non-transparent barriers to entry were first addressed in the Tokyo Round of GATT, later the Uruguay Round, and still has not been resolved, meaning countries can create regulatory hurdles, for which my personal experiences have been discussed that include China, Egypt, and Peru subsequently, there are enough bad actors to fill the library of Alexandria.

For example, if you wish to import body sprays into Canada or the United States, all you have to do is provide FDA approved ingredients in INCI format, which is the global standard, and your goods will easily be cleared by U.S. customs and the FDA. Conversely, if you try and export to China, you will be inundated with months of regulatory hurdles, redundant documentation including certificates of analysis, Beijing approval, providing copies of your formulations, and still your container could sit in the Shanghai Port for months, accumulating demurrage charges.

Another favorite technique for impeding trade is holding up courier samples at the border, whereas this is encouraged by the government as an unofficial policy, and China is not the only one, even worse actors include Egypt, Peru, Indonesia, and Pakistan, where customs agents will take the goodies home, or you might find your samples show up at a local flea market. Then again, you get some market penetration this way.

Sadly, the Doha Round did not come out with specific guidelines as to what quintessentially constitutes a blatant non-transparent barrier to entry, and this needed to be specifically defined. One method that might be employed is to impose countervailing regulatory hurdles on the country, but imposing this is very complex and in contravention of GATT and WTO provisions. As much as developed countries are depicted as the villain in the theatre in these WTO talks, it is fair to say that India and the likes, with their suffocating and blatant corruption put seizure on the wheels of commerce, and they need to look in the mirror hard, before throwing stones at the current commercial economic order.

The Renaissance of Bilateral Trade Agreements

We saw more bilateral trade agreements under the Trump administration, a good example of which were the current free trade negotiations between the UK and the United States, that are more than likely the two fairest free traders in the world, with Canada not being far behind. After all, the UK gifted the world with Adam Smith and David Ricardo, both of whom created the intellectual and economic tenets for free trade, while GATT was the brainchild of the American liberal doctrine.

As a side note, in 2016, when the UK was about to vote on Brexit, President Obama warned Prime Minister Cameron that if the UK left the EU, which incidentally is their sovereign right, it would result in the UK going to the back of the lineup for a bilateral free trade agreement with the United States. This comment made by a head of state was an affront to interfering in sovereign state matters. In essence, when all is said and done about the Euro and the continental Eurozone, it relies on the economic industriousness of Germany, hence the Euro is really the Deutsche Mark in another name.

Another bilateral free trade example that comes to mind is Peru and Canada, which has been effective since 2009. Still, it is a nightmare clearing samples through the Peruvian customs, where the products mysteriously disappear, either through corruption and/or non-transparent impediments to trade. The WTO has been hurled into a complex arrangement of regional trade agreements that create barriers to entry for outside players, or they are forced to manufacture locally to overcome these barriers. Below is a partial list of regional trade agreements:

- USMCA, formerly NAFTA, that includes Canada, Mexico, and the United States
- Central American-Dominican Republic Free Trade Agreement
- Asia-Pacific Economic Cooperation (APEC)
- African Continental Free Trade Agreement (AFCFTA), entered into force on 30 May 2019 for the 24 countries
- European Union (EU)
- Mercosur South American trade bloc
- Caribbean Community (CARICOM)

Intuitively, one might ask as to how things can be reconciled with the WTO acting as a central authority, this remains to be seen. Because in a world of national and regional interests, and balance of payments, the complexity of having a global free trade agreement becomes challenging, especially where there is a combination of bilateral and regional importance, complemented by a renaissance in mercantilism. If the current trend toward mercantilism ensues, which, as mentioned prior, helped cause the Great Depression, firms and consumers will be at the receiving end of macro and microeconomic distortions with devastating financial implications, as India and its consumers have well experienced. Again, this has been at the expense of citizenry in least developed countries stagnating in poverty by "paying more for less." Any poetic speak to the contrary is from politicians with either little or no understanding of commerce, or perhaps being under political pressure from constituents. So, depending on your leanings you can pick your narrative.

Multinational Corporations

Multinational corporations (MNC) will often jump the duty and trade barriers by opening production in markets or regions it wishes to do business in. For example, Volkswagen manufactures in Mexico as well as Chattanooga, Tennessee and uses the USMCA free trade agreement to bring vehicles into the United States and Canada duty free. At the same time, Tesla, which is warmly welcomed in China with majority stake, manufactures its cars locally to avert duties and other barriers to entry, as well General Motors manufactures in China for the local market, which is a bigger business for them than the U.S. market.

Of course, in many developing countries the MNCs have a low-cost labour advantage, and really this comes with a mixed bag. Why? Because many of these countries impose huge duties for importing raw materials like steel and parts, since governments are always in the business of growing their coffers, subsequently, becoming a net negative on the economy. India is a good example. Secondly, the local work force might have to move up the learning curve and modernize their skills and output. However, there are other considerations, when MNCs open plants, local employees are paid better by MNCs than domestic competitors, as is the case for Mexico, where Ford pays up to three times the local wages along with benefits, which increases the economic quality of peoples' lives in Mexico, this simply cannot be denied. Consequently, domestic firms lose some of their best staff to MNCs, often it leaves local companies that pay less wages to have some of their top staff poached, hollowing out the local companies' skill pool.

Finally, there are tangible contributions that MNCs bring to the table through increased spread of knowledge, such as technology, discipline, procedures, marketing, and tightness of organisational operations. Hence, the local quality of the labor stock goes up the learning curve with a higher collectivized skillset, while the local consumer is on the receiving end of better products and services, at more competitive prices.

On the balance, though, MNCs make positive contributions to the countries they operate in.

Intellectual Property and Knock-Offs

The Uruguay Round of GATT first started formidable talks on the issue of intellectual property. Traditionally, it is the West that has dominated inventiveness, from the first flight, calculus, Ford's assembly line, to the first digital computer, namely the Atanasoff-Berry computer (ABC), lighting cities, the phone, to solid state technology, television, radar, radio, software, smart phones, nuclear technology, first man on the moon, social media, and this list could fill a book on its own. Outside of cultural curiosity that questions authority, the primary reason for Western inventiveness is that Europe, (especially the Norwegian countries) and North America, have the most stringent intellectual property laws, including passing-off laws. Hence, if you are inventive in these geographical areas, you are protected and rewarded with the financial gains, and with financial protection and incentives, one can see why certain countries produce the lion's share, although this is starting to shift.

However, with the loss of manufacturing in the West, inventiveness is on the ropes.

In respect to IP protection, the international standard stems from two legal agreements, namely the Paris Convention for the Protection of Industrial Property patents, industrial designs, and the likes, and the second accepted legal international standard is the Berne Convention for the Protection of Literary and Artistic Works (copyright).

The agreement on trade-related aspects of intellectual property rights, (better known as TRIPS) which was created in the Uruguay Round of GATT, during the transition to the WTO, is an international legal agreement between all the member nations of the World Trade Organization. In essence, TRIPS backstops any gaps not covered in the Paris and Berne Conventions.

Trademark law, especially passing-off, is vigorously protected in the West, for example in Canada, this is covered under Section 7(b) and 7(c) of the Trademarks Act, and the same type of tort laws exist in the United States, Japan, the European Union, and the UK to offer more protection, there are industrial design laws. A good example is the case with P&Gs Herbal Essences' swerve hip bottle design, which is registered and protected. Some might remember the ads that used terms like "Hello Hydration"—do a quick search for a visual reference.

Specific areas protected by the various legal accords combined WTO TRIPS rules include:

- Copyright
- Trademarks
- Industrial designs
- Patents
- Layout designs of integrated circuits
- Trade Secrets
- Enforcement
- Technology transfer: Chinese companies demand this from foreign partners, and later transfer this into their products.

When someone tries to sell knock-offs or rip-off brands, one should expect a team of aggressive lawyers to send letters of toxic romance to the offending firm. Think of Coca-Cola's visual brand dress of red and white that is an indelible part of their quintessential look for over 100 years, and if this combination of colors that is part of the global visual lexicon is emulated and if it's called let's say Mecca Cola, Coca-Cola will send out a wolf pack of lawyers (notice no private label cola brands use red and white in their design). In the case of Coca-Cola, the brand look of combinational colors is indelible in the consumer's mind, while it is synonymous with red and white, in other words they own IP on these combinational colors in the soft drink business. Any attempt to emulate their brand dress would be considered "passing off" under tort laws. Another example is the orange color brand dress of the Tide detergent brand, which has been part of the consumer lexicon since the late 1940s, and any attempt to emulate this visual look in a retailer private label or independent Indie brand will guarantee an interlocutory court injunction, along with possible punitive damages.

On a personal note, I have been on the receiving end of Proctor & Gamble as well as Unilever's legal deliveries and speak from experience.

Consider the balance sheet on financials, what is worth more Coca-Cola's factory or its brand name? Or the value of a patented drug from Pfizer? Or what is Microsoft 10 operating system or Team cloud system worth as a brand? When one puts their mindset in this area of the Colosseum, one starts to see the future of Rome and its implications for economic valuation.

As we shall soon see, writing law either through international accords and further augmentation by WTO and the lack of global enforcement for the cultural respect that the West has for innovation, are two different things.

Take, for example, the fragrance of Chanel No. 5 and a knock-off firm that calls it Manal No. 5, or better still, they just might counterfeit it and call it Chanel No. 5, and even claim it is made in France. This shamelessly happens in Turkey, China, Vietnam, the Philippines, as well as a host of other bad actors all over the world. For example, you might make your watches in Vietnam, and the factory might run an extra 5,000 pieces and sell it on the black market, such as in independent ma and pa stores. Or even better, you can always find counterfeit goods on Alibiba.com as founder, Jack Ma, does some virtue signaling in Western talk show circuits—however, the CCP has reeled him in. Even Amazon has suffered from counterfeiting on its site with millions of individual sellers, it becomes tough to vet them all.

In Vietnam, certain retailers such as Pharmacity, Medicare, and Saigon Co-op will ask for customs documentation to ensure that the "country of origin" manufacturing and trademark ownership claims can be supported. In China, Watson Stores, Metro, and Walmart ask for full documentation on products they sell, to help avert counterfeit goods. Thus, these types of outlets have a high trust factor with local consumers and attempt to thrive on the equity of their brand name. But with counterfeits abound and a consumer who for the most part doesn't care, subsequently, retailing for global companies is a tough slog into unfamiliar neighborhoods in this new sandbox of emerging markets, where the local governments change the rules of play on the fly.

On my last trip to South Korea, I saw some blatant industrial design on cars that looked like a Rolls-Royce. In defense of South Korea, they are a stable democratic nation, as is Japan, that adhere to the rule of law. However, not to be outdone, China's Geely Motors has a blatant knock-off they call the Geely GE, which looks like a Rolls-Royce. China's cavalier attitude regarding trademark laws is without shame. Take, for example, BMW's partner in China, Brilliance Auto. As mentioned earlier, in China, a foreign company must have a Chinese partner, (Tesla is an exception) and naturally, a transfer of technology follows. After all, why innovate when they can steal? To pay respect to their partner, Brilliance Auto has now created a knock-off of the BMW X1 with their Brilliance V5. I am not sure that Western leaders with zero business experience did not see this when China was allowed in the WTO. When all is said and done, isn't leadership about vision and accountability?

After all, with weak or spotty industrial design laws that are poorly enforced in China—although this is changing—unless it benefits the Communist Party, why bother fighting it? That is, until a boisterous U.S. president like Trump comes along with actual business experience and starts his commercial war dance ritual. Eventually, the Germans, Japanese, and the British might take a tougher stance. In the absence of a world that lacks the leadership, and visionary skills of Churchill, this will have to do.

Moving to industry subsidization, which is against the tenets of the WTO articles, it brings up government ownership of China's banking system, and the enormity of its state-owned enterprise sector gives China the tools to illegally subsidize industries in ways that are difficult to detect. Bear in mind that state-owned banks in China made billions of dollars in loans to zombie shell companies to purchase aluminum from China-based aluminum giant, China Zhongwan, which was later dumped into the U.S. markets. These types of loans to credit unworthy companies would not be approved without high government endorsement by way of the CCP. This of course causes issues with the quality of loans on state-owned banks in China leading to financial distortions.

Take the case of Chinese aluminum giant, China Hongqiao Group, which is listed on the Hong Kong Stock Exchange, claiming to be the world's largest aluminum producer. Emerson Analytics released a report in 2018 alleging Hongqiao was vastly overstating its profits and committing widespread fraud. The tip of the iceberg on their financials is that their electricity bills—remember that you need lots of electricity to produce aluminium—was grossly understated. As a result, the stock was halted on the Honk Kong Stock Exchange, that is until they received fresh funding from state-owned CITIC bank, then mysteriously, after resuming trading, the stock was up 80 percent from its pre-halt close. Now we see where Robin Hood and Hertz Rental got its playbook on pumping up Chapter 11 zombie companies.

When we turn our attention to the capital markets, China has orchestrated hundreds of fraudulent listings on their exchanges that have swindled billions from both domestic and foreign investors. And why not when there is no sheriff in Dodge City!

Peter Navarro, an economist and former Director of Trade and Manufacturing Policy in the U.S., published a book titled *Death By China* in which he includes how China plays in the sandbox. Here are some key takeaways:

- China protects its home market from American imports with high tariffs, tricky non-tariff barriers, and constantly changing regulations.

- Subsidizing the exports of government-owned "national champions" to crush its free market competitors and dominate global markets.

- Preying on weak countries by padlocking up their natural resources with "debt traps." Examples include Ethiopia's rare earth tantalum, as mentioned earlier, but the list gets bigger in Africa and other regions, in an obvious effort to gain a global stranglehold on key resources like bauxite, copper, nickel, and other materials both essential and rare earths. These monopolies are not only being used to fuel China's industrial machine, but to punish those countries that would oppose its predatory policies.

- China subsidizes manufacturing with cheap loans and cheap energy, and by turning a blind eye to environmental issues, as well as health and safety standards, resulting in dominating industries, ranging from production of ships, to help control commercial marine traffic, refrigerators, to color TV sets, air conditioners, and computers.

- Theft of key technologies and intellectual property from the United States, Germany, South Korea, Japan and other countries; this includes cyber-espionage and forced technology transfer, down to massive open-source collection, and just plain old physical theft.

The combination of President Nixon's opening of relations with China in 1972—not that he shouldn't have—and President Clinton's naïve admission of China with nonconditionally into the WTO, or at least in increments based on behavioral output, has inadvertently created a rogue state that does not always trade on the principle of Ricardian comparative advantage. It could be argued that on these points alone, China has no business being in the WTO, but to be fair, China is the indispensable workshop of the world, and is an ascending power, that in many cases is doing the work we no longer have the grit to do in the West, while taking the heat for much of the world's ecology on the West's behalf!

This much is for sure, if the WTO wants to really establish itself with full credibility and a force for good in the new economic global order, it must not only establish, but enforce the tenets of fair play in commerce, as opposed to offering a diet of globally reaching propaganda.

Low Monetary Policy and the Mysterious Disappearance of Inflation in the West

Much of the loss of the manufacturing sector was doing a slow but pronounced swan dive starting in the 1960s, first in transistor radios, then in televisions, video cameras, electronics, industrial robotics, advanced tooling, watches and of course, automobiles to Japan, to name a few. At the time, the in-thing was to study Japanese management, and industrial productivity. Many of these inventions that the West created crumbled, complements of Japan's proficiency in production.

Eventually, Japan became a premium manufacturer and the developed world, meaning first the West, including Japan, started the new millennium by exporting its inflation and manufacturing mostly to the Far East, meaning China, while importing relatively little unemployment. Without global trade, global consumers who would not have been able to get more for less, thus, increasing the consumers marginal utility. But admittedly, there are trade-offs.

If we are to believe the methodology of core inflation numbers, it was this phenomenon of inflation disappearing that allowed low monetary policy in effect to fix the woes of the economy, by inflating asset prices. In fact, the Central Banks believe that low monetary policy can curb unemployment by using it as a monetary tool to stimulate the economy. Realizing that those subscribed on a left-leaning mindset would come to conclusions that it was profit seeking firms acting in their own self-interest, and quickly get on the social media to sharpen their Leninist spears aimed into the heart of capitalism. However, it is in our own self-interest, out of an insatiable appetite to obtain more for less that makes consumers a participative accomplice by emulating firms that practice the same self-interest. Meaning, when the righteous Gen Y and Millennials go shopping, they willfully turn a blind eye to the origin of manufacture, so this way they have more money to spend on clubbing, cannabis, video games, protest signs, their made-in-China iPhones and their Robin Hood apps that help them get financially wrecked on get-rich-quick stocks and futures by buying zombie Chapter 11 companies. So then, who is the villain here? Or does the good guy use the services of a villain to abdicate their own accountability in the name of facilitating their own self-interest? Greed and self-interest are willing bedfellows, with many accomplices to create the rot from within, with no clear remedy in the annals of our recorded civilization! After all, creating Plutonian utopia, as is written in the first five books of the *Republic* almost 2,500 years ago, has been elusive within the savage that lies within man.

The intricacy of World Trade is complex, but certainly the WTO has a role to play, and its predecessor GATT has by far been a net positive on the development of the world economy since Bretton Woods, in respect to fostering free trade as a mechanism to facilitate growth and diminish economic distortions because of mercantilism. The world is not perfect, and certainly humans are not, but the diminishment of mercantilism while being an ideal goal, has produced favorable results, including lifting billions out of poverty and helping to foster prosperity for many.

Now that we are on the topic of inflation, money printing, trade wars and toxic mercantilism, it might act as a springboard to introduce a brief history of financial booms and busts that is sure to create some titillating theatre!

A Brief History of Manias, Booms, and Busts

*Rome was built stone by stone,
but it expanded and waged wars as its
senators looted the remains of its glory,
as the citizens quivered when the news of
Hannibal at the Gates arrived. For splendour
had seduced the mind into an unassailable
denial of the tragedy. Rome rotted from within,
and it left behind lessons in the relics of
its grandeur, buried so deep that modernity
denies its very existence. Good governance,
interest of its citizenry, and prosperity for many,
was elusive after Caesar Augustus, where peace
gave way to disorder, and by the third
century Rome's fate was sealed.*

CHAPTER

This Time It's Going to Be Different

Adam Smith: The Father of Modern Economics

No stories about free markets, asset price, market distortions, natural equilibrium, and the nature of market participants can begin without a discussion of the father of modern economics and capitalism, Adam Smith, the moral philosopher who can provide the finest adjudication of the effects of government's role in distorting and agitating the natural economy. Here are a few of his quotes:

> *It is not from the benevolence of the butcher, the brewer, or the baker that we expect our dinner, but from their regard to their own interest.[1]*

> *By pursuing his own interest, he frequently promotes that of the society more effectually than what he really intends to promote it.[2]*

> *The greatest value he intends only his own gain, and he is in this as in many other cases, led by an invisible hand to promote an end which was no part of his intention.[3]*

Adam Smith (1723-1790) was a Scottish economic moral philosopher, who is considered the father of modern economics, and no discussion of economics can be complete without him.

Smith produced a timeless economic masterpiece of a five-book set in 1776 called The Wealth of Nations, comprising of near 1,000 pages, which one needs time and focus to digest. Much is owed to Adam Smith, as he deeply understood the human psyche, how it acts in its own self interest, and creates the invisible hand of the collective economy.

It should be a required reading by every government official elected or appointed, then again it should be read by everyone with

---

1   Adam Smith, The Wealth of Nations, Books I-III (New York: Penguin, 1982).
2   Ibid.
3   Adam Smith, The Wealth of Nations, Books IV-V (New York: Penguin, 2000).

a genuine interest in commerce and human nature. Smith's works incorporates self-interest, human behaviour, production efficiencies, mercantilism, psychology, demand and supply, price formation and how it naturally creates the economic dynamics of the marketplace. His disdain for slavery as an unfeasible system of production as the Romans found out was dealt with in the Wealth of Nations, which was shortly abolished by the early 19th century in British territories, while some of the world continued well after the Second World War.

To best understand The Wealth of Nations, one needs to break down his contributions that help explain the world around us in respect to both economic and social implications.

On the Division of Labour

Adam Smith felt that through specialization of labour, production efficiencies would result. During the cusp of the Industrial Revolution, much of which occurred in Scotland, he had the opportunity to observe manufacturing processes firsthand. It is here that he discusses economically integrating machinery with labour. In respect to manufacturing, Smith analyses a pin, that better efficiencies could be attained when he observed the following in Chapter 1, Book I: "One man draws out the wire, another straightens it, a third cuts it, a fourth points it, fifth grinds it at the top for receiving the head."[4]

He goes on to say that eventually the pin is divided into about 18 distinct operations, where some could perform a few tasks. It is the division of labour and specialization that gave industrial birth to the creator of the modern assembly line, namely Henry Ford, who increased consumer welfare like none other in his time, and this is what led to the advent of industrial engineering. Today we are seeing the integration of machinery with labour, in a more advanced setting where labour might have specialized knowledge in tooling integrated with software literacy to harness the advanced capabilities of highly developed industrial robotics. Even industrial

4   Adam Smith, The Wealth of Nations, Books I-III (New York: Penguin, 1982).

robots are specialized in operations, including welding, tooling, assembly painting and so much more.

On Mercantilism and Free Trade

Smith deplored mercantilism for being counter productive and was a proponent of free trade, thus had much influence on David Ricardo's works that mathematically broke down the benefits of free trade through comparative advantage, and the production possibility frontiers. In *The Wealth of Nations* under "Of the Principle of The Commercial or Mercantile System," Smith states the following in respect to government not interfering in trade: "We trust with perfect security that the freedom of trade, without any attention of government, will supply us with the wine which we have the occasion for."[5]

Prior to *The Wealth of Nations,* a country's wealth was based on the value of their gold and silver deposits. Smith argued that countries should be valued based on their levels of production and commerce that would require free trade. It was this concept that laid the foundations of GDP as the true measurement of a nation's wealth.

On Demand, Wages, Supply, Price, Equilibrium

Adam Smith laid down the foundations for the symbiotic relationship between demand, wages, supply, and price, which creates equilibrium. He extensively talks about the natural and market price of commodities in Book I, where he proposes the following: "These ordinary or average rates may be called the natural rates of wages, profit, and rent at the time and place in which they commonly prevail."[6]

It is from here that the tenets of natural price equilibrium are drawn, where Smith extensively discussed the interrelationship between demand wages, stock supply on price and profitability.

5   Adam Smith, The Wealth of Nations, Books IV-V (New York: Penguin, 2000).
6   Adam Smith, The Wealth of Nations, Books I-III (New York: Penguin, 1982).

He stated that if prices are too high or too low, they will come into a natural equilibrium, while discussing its relationship as to how extraordinary or weak profits will come back to equilibrium through the natural market's invisible hand.

In essence, Adam Smith documented the beliefs of natural real time price fluctuation, which we see today by the second, when pricing equities, bonds, and commodities, while inadvertently he laid down the foundations of price elasticity and inelasticity, which is a hallmark of microeconomics. Today, these are all incorporated in stock markets where if left alone, the buyer of the equity will have a window into price discovery. We see this every day when we go shopping where if certain goods become too expensive, the demand will precipitously drop until there is a price adjustment. For example, today we see an increase in car prices in the United States, where they currently average around $40,000—eventually when prices rise too quickly, there is it diminishment of demand. However, with distortions in the market through helicopter money being distributed in 2021 and a shortage of semiconductor chips that are required for cars, we are seeing bidding wars on new cars and used cars selling for more than their original sticker prices. The concepts of demand and supply, as it affects price, holds true in stocks as well as real estate prices that if left to natural interest rates, meaning the fed does not distort these asset prices, will return to price equilibrium, as it will become more affordable. Natural price formation, may it be for products, energy, labour, or service is the child of the market's invisible hand.

Adam Smith was the founder of liberal economic thinking and promoted laissez-faire, and understood that even though government had a role in the way of rules of commerce—however, its external actions to create market equilibrium has unintended consequences, as the market will always find its way back.

The ghost of Adam Smith perhaps haunted Keynes, but lives within us all, in our misguided denial of the invisible hand! The British Historian Lawrence James stated that with the loss of her American Colonies, the Empire was thought to be at peril by many in the British establishment. Smith, in *The Wealth of Nations*, after all, had questioned the costs of Britain's extended colonies and economic systems. However, equipped with the moral philosophies of *The Wealth of Nations*, Britain had a new intellectual energy that affected much of the world and allowed the Empire to flourish until the early 20th century.

The seduction of the present often ends in a river of tears, but economic history holds many extraordinary examples of how manias and booms evolve into busts, but to ignore history puts our ability to see the present in clarity at peril.

When one understands credit bubbles, the business cycle will help avoid the pitfalls of a personal and business economic tragedy. After all, the human tragedy of inequality is the result of a civilization that seems to always come back to economics.

Booms and busts, especially in asset classes makes for some astounding collection of protagonists in this theatre of tragedy with a plethora of actors that include the business cycle, government, monetary environment, and the innate seduction of greed.

The Anatomy of a Bubble

All economic bubbles start with the stealth phase where the smart money might first get into an asset class, the second phase is awareness, and this is where institutional investors start coming into the market. At the first two stages, it is still risk-off, and one might see a small sell-off in the market, which is really a bear trap. Then stage three starts taking the bubble into the mania phase, where laggards like the media—financial MSM is almost always wrong—start talking up the bubble, and as the public becomes aware, leading to fear of missing out (FOMO) there is a strategic inertia of sorts, where enthusiasm turns to greed, before it transitions to delusion, as a new paradigm or a peak occurs. It should be noted that when dealing with overbought markets, no one knows the peaking point—yes, many technical analysts think they do, where they diplomatically call possibly higher tops or lower support points. Just go to YouTube and watch all the technical analysts through their head and shoulders, peaks and the likes, almost always get the market wrong where they feel they can pick entry and exit points. The problem with this type of modelling is that there are no provisions for exogenous shocks or emotional group-think. It is always better to understand the direction of the market such as institutional and fed support and retraction.

The truth of the matter is that in the middle of the bubble, may it be the Nasdaq, dot-com crash, or October 1929, no one knows exactly when the bubble will burst, but the band will eventually stop playing—however, hindsight value always gives clarity. The decline usually comes with a temporary slide—that might be mistaken as a buying opportunity, and this is sometimes called a "dead cat bounce" where it spikes up for a while before turning into downward fear again. The classical case of this was when the Nasdaq had more froth than a Guinness on St Patrick's Day, going from 5,048 in February 2000, sliding to 3,700 by May, then coming back to 4,200 in July, and then taking a slow swan dive to 1,400 by July 2009, and did not recover to 5,000 until October 2016. What happened in 2000 was greed fuelled by irrationality that quickly turned to fear, which then became capitulation with Nasdaq's absurd valuations of P/Es of 103. In other words, the present value of the stocks had 103 years of earnings built into it, where the norm is 23 years of earnings.

The sad truth is that Nasdaq stayed flat or negligibly moved for 15 years, many sold in a panic, while the smart money headed for the doors early.

It is worth mentioning that the smart money and some institutional investors headed for the exit doors early. Many retail investors lost money in stocks and other asset classes, since they tried to pick the tops and bottoms, which, as mentioned before, is a flawed strategy, because no one knows the bottom or top, but instead jumps on the directional momentum, and takes profits without going through the emotional trauma of internalising greed into fear. Yes, one could have held the stock through short-term roller-coasters, but few have the emotional framework to hold in a middle of a firestorm. Much like riding a bull, you need to know when to get off and say, "I am happy with the profit I took."

Figure 8.1 is a graphical illustration of the anatomy of a bubble.

Figure 8.1: The Anatomy of a Bubble

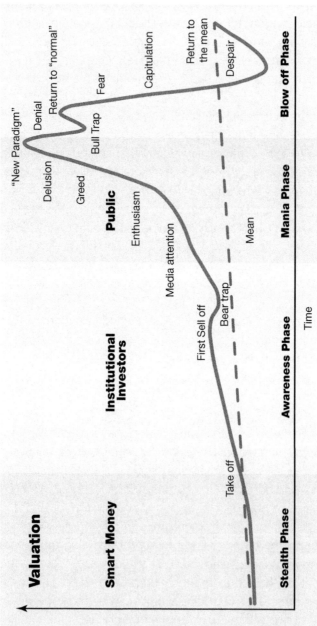

The 1921 Depression

Now, with a view of studying some relatively modern-day economic manias, pullbacks, and crashes, our story begins in 1921, when Warren Harding was the U.S. President. You might think that this is a typo, but the 1921 depression did occur, and it was short lived, and we shall soon see why. But first, we should discuss the causes.

As 1.6 million soldiers came home after World War I, it put substantial pressure on the labor market that had to make structural adjustments to accommodate this dynamic shift in the domestic economy. This resulted in wage stagnation, as well as low agricultural prices, because of European recovery of agricultural output, and governments, which were still teething on their learning curve, maintained a tightening of monetary policy that helped cause acute deflationary pressures on the economy, as they originally thought that they were still fighting inflation in 1919.

Milton Friedman and Anna Schwartz, in their 1963 book *A Monetary History of the United States*, were critical of mistakes in Federal Reserve policy as a key factor in the crisis. In response to post–World War I inflation, the Federal Reserve Bank of New York began raising interest rates sharply. In December 1919 the rate was raised from 4.75 percent to 5 percent. A month later it was raised to 6 percent, and in June 1920 it was raised to 7 percent. The Fed was thinking they were fighting inflation, but were actually fighting deflation, hence they exasperated the economic contraction, and especially the labour market.

In other words, the U.S. Federal Reserve did the exact opposite of what was required with respect to monetary policy by increasing interest rates at the most inopportune time. The Fed's incompetence is deeply rooted in economic history.

More specifically, factories that were geared for munitions and related wartime output had to retool and readjust into a consumer driven economy, and it is this adjustment period that was the cause of the 1921 depression. This adjustment period is a natural part of the free markets, as they had to react to the disequilibrium of a wartime economy, and remedy the distortions, to bring it back into market-driven equilibrium.

As a side note, some people believe that wars can bring countries out of a recession, but outside of the tragedy of the loss of life, wars result in governments collecting more taxes, debt, supplying ample propaganda at taxpayer expense, and wasting scarce resources on economic distortions that do not help in fostering a natural market equilibrium in a consumer driven demand and supply theatre.

It is also interesting to note that income tax did not exist in North America until World War I, when the U.S. imposed it in 1913, followed by sales tax in the 1930s. Not to be outdone, Canada imposed income tax as well in 1917 as a temporary measure to finance the war, while introducing corporate taxes on profits in 1916. From this an unsuspecting citizenry for over 100 years have given government carte blanche, which has led to our current oppressive taxation system on nearly all. I think when John Lennon wrote the song "Imagine," he should have included in the lyrics a verse about "Imagine a world with no income tax." But that was the world our great grandparents lived in. Low taxes or no taxes is all the fiscal stimulus needed to relatively grow an economy, but that train passed over 100 years ago.

During World War I, the unemployment rate was 1.9 percent, according to government economist Stanley Lebergott.[7] Eventually, just after the war, the unemployment rate went to 5.9 percent, and during the height of the depression, in 1921, to approximately 12 percent. At the same time, the Dow Jones, which had peaked at 119 points, dropped to 64 for almost a 50 percent decline. Relatively speaking, as of June 2020, official unemployment numbers were in

7   Stanley Lebergott, The Measurement and Behavior of Unemployment, National Bureau of Economic Research (1957), https://www.nber.org/books-and-chapters/measurement-and-behavior-unemployment/annual-estimates-unemployment-united-states-1900-1954

the 13 percent range, but the effective unemployment was over 20 percent. In the 1921 depression, to further amplify things, the 1918 Spanish flu pandemic (actually originated in the U.S.) infected approximately 500 million people worldwide, which was about a third of the global population at the time and led to 50 million global deaths, with 675,000 deaths being in the United States alone.

The depression lasted 18 months, from January 1920 to July 1921, and when a recession lasts this long, coupled by a deflationary GDP contraction of near 18 percent, it is agreed by most economists to be defined as a depression.

A Quick Analysis

The Bolshevik Revolution brought communists to power in Russia, and since communism had not yet revealed itself as a socioeconomic failure, it was allowed to exist as a credible economic organization of a nation up until the 1980s, when it collapsed under its own economic rot. In fact, communism was a growing ideology in the Great Depression right up until the 1950s, and is now experiencing a renaissance in academia, where there is a concerted effort to mask its many toxic and failed characteristics upon the human condition.

The big reason that communism gained traction was that the Soviet Union did not go through economic stagnation like the industrialized capitalist societies did during the Great Depression. The reasons for this were because it had created a planned economy that was insulated from monetary policy, exchange rate restrictions, trade restrictions, and static industrial technology, and its associated exogenous shocks. Further, during the Great Depression, the Soviet Union was rapidly industrialising and growing through its five-year central plans, while more industrialized economies were either stagnant or contracting during this period. The Soviet Union had created a temporary utopian autarchy of sorts, much like Plato's idea of utopia, meaning that with minimal exposure to outside economies, it was not affected by global economic shocks.

Communism was more of an ideological threat to capitalism during the 1930s than today, and a magnet for the formation of unions in the United States and Europe during that period, both in the public and private sector. Communism still had legs in the 1950s in its various forms like socialism in Latin America, Africa, and beyond. In the 1950s, during the Red Scare and McCarthyism, there were some communists and sympathizers in both academia and Hollywood. Even being accused of being a communist could have one blacklisted in the 1950s—as a comparison, it was much like woke cancel culture of today that seems to be getting some pushback. As a historical backdrop of the era, Premier Nakita Khrushchev of the Soviet Union during a cultural exchange in Moscow engaged into what is now referred to as the Kitchen Debate in 1959, with young Vice President Richard Nixon. Each espoused the virtues of their respective economic and political ideologies, while Khrushchev claimed that the Soviet Union would surpass America in production—Russian vodka can get one to make outlandish claims.

In the Kitchen Debate, Khrushchev claimed that Nixon's grandchildren would live under communism (he might be right yet) and Nixon claimed that Khrushchev's grandchildren would live in freedom. Against the backdrop of the Sputnik in 1957 that launched the space race, which America was behind the Soviets at the time, the economic comparisons seemed realistic, because the Soviet Union had still not shown its inner rot of economic structural distortions, the stagnations of a command economy, and the suffocation of the human psyche based on the ideologue of egalitarianism. All this and more brought the Soviet Union to its collapse in 1988.

The 1969 Moon Landing was perhaps the culmination as the pinnacle outcome of the Cold War era space race.

On a personal note, I bring you to a time of meeting Neil Armstrong, who spoke in Toronto in 2008 at a business function that I attended. He was a very humble and decent person. He was my childhood hero and I finally met him during his book signing. Later that day when I called my father to tell him I met Neil Armstrong, he was very excited because part of his legacy is that he made parts for the moon mission when he worked for General Electric in the late 1960s, while his best friend and mentor Levon Babluzian, an electrical engineer by training, had designed the reflectors that brought back the first pictures from the Moon Landing of July 22, 1969. The flag that was planted on the moon had Babluzian's name on it. So, all this was very personal for me.

I listened with unbridled intrigue as Armstrong explained how close the Soviets had come to landing a man on the moon first. After all, the Soviets had a plethora of brilliant scientists of their own, including Sergei Korolev who acted as the lead rocket engineer and Vladimir Pavlovich, pioneer of the rocket program in the USSR, as well as supporting educational institutes strong in mathematics and physics.

As Neil Armstrong spoke, I could feel I was in the presence of greatness and humbleness, all wrapped into a dreamy story that brought me back to July 22, 1969. I watched his hands tremble, since time and age had caught up to him—I wanted to reach out and touch him, my heart sinking, and wished that he could defy mortality because, like many of his generation, he gave to us so unselfishly.

He mentioned that little did we truly understand the gap that existed between President Kennedy's inspiring moon speech and the technology of the times in 1962. What makes it even more remarkable is that it was all done with computer memory chips that, at best, could not rival today's modern smart phone. Everything came together that day I heard him speak—it made life feel full, purposeful, and worthwhile.

The backdrop of the Cold War, as hallowing as it was, brought out the best in archrivals! Against the framework of the Soviet

Union being immune to the Great Depression, it allowed an intellectual sanctuary for communist agitators like William Z. Foster, labor organizer and politician, who eventually became a star member of America's Communist Party.

Returning to the 1921 depression in the United States, the government for the most part, still did not have a mandate to interfere in the business cycle, while the Fed was relatively docile at the time, and certainly was not the purchaser of toxic assets and purveyor of inflation, as is the case now.

Herbert Hoover, who served as Secretary of Commerce under President Warren Harding, believed in setting wage and price targets, as well as a host of other artificial economic price formations, according to economist Murry Rothbard. Later, when Hoover became president in 1929, and had carte blanche to implement his remedies, as the 1929 depression gave him a crisis to test his theories, as we consider later the effects of how his and Roosevelt's policies agitated, deepened, and prolonged the Great Depression. However, as Harding's Secretary of Commerce, Hoover could not persuade President Harding into departing from his laissez-faire approach, which coincided with Secretary of the Treasury, Andrew Mellon, who preferred more of a liquidationist approach, and was not a proponent of the government interfering in the business cycle. The government was not in the business at the time of bailing out unsound positions, and it quite frankly did not have the political capital as such.

The following speech by President William G. Harding at the 1920 Republican Convention gives a peak into his laissez-faire policies, with a view of letting an economy rinse out the rot, and revert to its natural structural equilibrium:

> *We can promise no one remedy which will cure an ill of such wide proportions, but we do pledge that earnest and consistent attack which the party platform covenants. We will attempt intelligent and courageous deflation, and strike at government borrowing which enlarges the evil, and we will attack high cost of government with every energy and facil-*

ity which attend Republican capacity. We promise that relief which will attend the halting of waste and extravagance, and the renewal of the practice of public economy, not alone because it will relieve tax burdens, but because it will be an example to stimulate thrift and economy in private life.

I have already alluded to the necessity for the fullness of production, and we need the fullness of service which attends the exchange of products. Let us speak the irrefutable truth— high wages and reduced cost of living are in utter contradiction unless we have the height of efficiency for wages received.

In all sincerity we promise the prevention of unreasonable profits, we challenge profiteering with all the moral force and the legal powers of government and people, but it is fair, aye, it is timely, to give reminder that law is not the sole corrective of our economic ills.

Let us call to all the people for thrift and economy, for denial and sacrifice, if need be, for a nation-wide drive against extravagance and luxury, to a recommittal to simplicity of living, to that prudent and normal plan of life which is the health of the Republic. There hasn't been a recovery from the waste and abnormalities of war since the story of mankind was first written, except through work and saving, through industry and denial, while needless spending and heedless extravagance have marked every decay in the history of nations. Give the assurance of that rugged simplicity of American life which marked the first century of amazing development, and this generation may underwrite a second century of surpassing accomplishment. [8]

If a president or prime minister gave such laissez-faire speech today it would be an affront to large government orthodoxy.

---

8   Warren G. Harding, "Address Accepting the Republican Presidential Nomination: June 12, 1920," The American Presidential Project, UCSB, accessed March 15, 2022, https://www.presidency.ucsb.edu/documents/address-accepting-the-republican-presidential-nomination-2

Successfully, they would be filleted alive, then tarred and feathered by digital virtue signaling mobs of the Twittersphere, as they would all tap away on their phones (modern form of ape-like chest thumping), frothing in vengeance. Since after all, large wasteful, ineffective, inefficient government, oppressive taxation, and depletion of self-reliance and self-flagellation is a birth given rite of passage that should never be emancipated from.

The Feds at the time were still stuck in inflation battle gear and should have increased the money supply in light of deflation. By President Harding taking such a hands-off approach and not mediating the business cycle, the result was that by the late summer of 1921despite the Fed's incorrect monetary remedy, unemployment was down to 6.7 percent, further fell to 2.4 percent by 1923, while by the same year the Dow Jones recovered to about 115 and went into a bull market run.

However, the empirical facts show that by letting the natural business cycle heal itself (it was not the business cycle that caused this depression in the first place), distortions and structural inefficiencies had been rinsed out of the economy. What the U.S. government did under President Warren Harding was to reduce the total federal government debt by 30 percent, to 20 percent of GDP, and pay off its war bonds, while keeping interest rates at a normal rate to foster savings, price equilibrium on assets, and normalized consumption. Put differently, Warren Harding was mindful that the government not become a burden on the taxpayer and show prudency and accountability on the handling of the public purse.

Figure 8.2 is a look at the federal government debt from 1920 to 1930.

Figure 8.2: Gross Public Debt

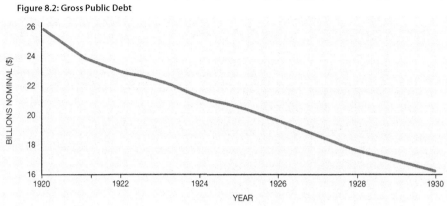

Source: U.S. Government spending.com

This was to be the last demonstrated case of the U.S. government not mediating and tampering with the business cycle, and the last time that America saw a true free market without distortive market interference. Simply put, this was the last natural recovery from a depression or recession.

In 1922, the government had demonstrated that by keeping out of the affairs of the economy, it was a net positive on the economy. Keynesians cannot remotely explain this, except to say it was an anomaly, but soon we shall see the genesis of government mingling in the private economy. So now it seems like a good time to look for the seeds that perhaps diminished the fruitful prospects for a true free market, as we investigate the policies of Hoover, and FDR, and without further ado, we enter the Great Depression.

The Great Depression

Everything faded into mist.
The past was erased the erasure was forgotten, the lie became truth. —George Orwell, *1984*

The official economic historians' view and commonly held belief is that FDR's New Deal brought America out of the Great Depression and the Depression did not have international origins. To challenge this is often met by dismay and/or an intellectual renaissance of Orwellian cult chants that suffocate empiricism and reason, both of which are blasphemous in the current orthodoxy. One has to dig deep to find historically buried obscurity, the clarity of economic truth and reconcile it with the modernism of lazily constructed convenient emotionalism. In this section, we unsettle, or at least reconsider this widely held orthodoxy of FDR's economic strategies during the Great Depression.

The Lead Up and Causation

The Roaring Twenties was indeed a time of unprecedented growth, with America releasing its industrial might from skyscrapers to industrial output, subways, planes, and a host of technologies that fostered confidence and expectations.

Without entering an academic dissertation, the Great Depression was caused by various factors, and it is a bit complicated. For example, on an international basis, European production recovered after the war, which drove oversupply, concomitantly, U.S. interest rates were lowered to assist in strengthening the British pound, for Britain to pay back intergovernmental WWI debts to the U.S. in dollars. Thus, decreasing the war debt burden in theory via currency translation gains for Britain. However, because of a stronger GBP, UK products were priced out of the market cumulating in the opposite effect, and exasperating Britain's balance of payment in U.S. dollar, meaning there was not enough profits through trade to pay down its war debts. Eventually the British pound was delinked from gold in 1931.

Five months prior to the October 1929 stock market crash, there was a decline in industrial production, when the production index went from 127 in June to 122 in September, October was 106 and by November, production index declined to 99. We can see these in the automotive numbers of 1929, when 660,000 units were produced in March of the same year, which in August, precipitously declined to 319,000, and in October only 92,500 autos were produced.

In the classic book *Manias, Panics, and Crashes* (a must read for students of financial history); Charles Kindleberger blames the decline in production on the instability of the supply of credit markets due to funds being channeled into a sharply ascending stock market.

Globally, prices for wheat, coffee, sugar, silk, cotton, and rubber quickly dropped, with the outcome of pressuring farmers on an international scale.

The Germans deflated their economy to help raise cash to pay for their war repatriations, which exceeded the total value of her industries, which were economically and psychologically unbearable, with the confiscation of coal and industrial centers by France and Belgium. In history, victors dictate the peace, as Belgium and France owed money to America, which greatly affected the untenable reparations on Germany. This led to depletion of Germany's gold reserves due to war reparations, needing to be paid in gold or foreign currencies. Thus, they attempted to buy gold with the German mark, which led to massive devaluation of the currency during the Weimar Republic—money printing always ends up bad. Naturally, this led to hyperinflation, since people spent their money immediately, because of increased price expectations, (we are seeing signs of this globally today) by the hour in some cases. Consider that a loaf of bread in Berlin that cost around 160 marks at the end of 1922, and by the end of 1923, the same loaf cost 200,000,000,000 marks. This meant that people would stand in line with barrels of cash for a loaf of bread, and by the time they reached the front of the queue, it might cost double. Then in 1931, President Hoover called for a delay in war reparations at the expense of French outrage, with some success.

Eventually, German economic instability led to the birth of the National Socialist German Workers' Party, bringing Adolf Hitler into power, that through industrial militarization, government controlling the means of production led to full employment. As the renowned philosophical intellect Bertrand Russell stated, "The most successful Hero, becomes the most proficient Tyrant."[9] Hitler was

---

9   Bertrand Russell, *A History of Western Philosophy* (New York: Simon & Schuster, 1945).

part of a long tragic lineage of Socialism and Communism in the 20th century that brought about unprecedented human tyranny, and when we include Mao Zedong and Joseph Stalin, the ideology led to over 130 million tombstones. Yet today we see the naïve temperament of our youth embrace these ideologies, as opposed to seeing it for what it truly is, which is old wine in a new bottle being served up in a new century for ideologues who want to grab power without accomplishment or merit!

Back to America

In March of 1929, just before leaving office, President Calvin Coolidge called American prosperity "absolutely sound", and said that stocks were "cheap at current prices,"[10] which excludes him from the visionary Hall of Fame. Then the bottom fell out of the stock market, starting in September 1929 and the decline accelerated in October.

What happened in America was the combination of easy credit—the 10-year Treasury yields were under 4 percent, which incidentally was the work of the Feds and government policy, combined with a massive technological shift, very similar to the one under way since 1995, with the acceptance and practical adoption of the internet, the birth of online shopping that accumulated into the dot-com crash of the year 2000. Similarly, during the 1920s, we were seeing the widespread adoption of automobiles, the electrification of cities, radio broadcasting, refrigeration, urbanization, the production line, the beginning of commercial flights, mass transit, and a host of materializing technologies helping to drive the Dow Jones that moved from 94 in 1924 to 381 in 1929. Against this backdrop was a low inflation environment, with wild speculation on the Dow, since margins were as low as 10 percent, meaning one could put 10 percent down on a stock and control it, but the problem was that if the stock moved down 10 percent, one lost all

10   Cornelius C. Bond, T. Rowe Price: The Man, the Company, the Investment Philosophy (Hoboken: Wiley, 2019), 46.

their money, or if it went up 10 percent, one doubled their money.

Against this setting, there was the paradox of inflation that was actually very low—in 1926, at 1.14 percent, and in 1928, the economy was experiencing deflation at -1.72 percent, and by 1932 was at -9.8 percent. Treasury yields declined steadily to 2 percent by 1944. During the Roaring Twenties, even the shoeshine boys were giving advice on stocks, so, it might be a good time to borrow a term coined by Fed Chairman Alan Greenspan that might be relevant here, when he described the Nasdaq pricing valuations as "irrational exuberance"[11] before it dove 70 percent over a few years, starting in 2000.

Milton Friedman argued many years later that it was the Feds that allowed the Great Depression to go into full inertia, because they did not increase the money supply in 1929, which in his view would have helped prevent bank failures.

Many years later, on November 8, 2002, at an event honoring Milton Friedman, Fed Chairman Ben Bernanke came to the following admission:

> *Let me end my talk by abusing slightly my status as an official representative of the Federal Reserve. I would like to say to Milton and Anna: Regarding the Great Depression, you're right. We did it. We're very sorry. But thanks to you, we won't do it again.[12]*

The Great Depression was international in scope, as Europe was not allowed preferential tariffs into the U.S. market in the 1920s due to American trade protectionism taking away Europe's ability to export to facilitate revenues in order to meet their war debt obligations to the United States from World War I. European wheat cost

11   Alan Greenspan, in a speech given to the American Enterprise Institute, December 5, 1996.

12   Ben Bernanke, "Remarks by Governor Ben S. Bernanke at the Conference to Honor Milton Friedman, University of Chicago, On Milton Friedman's 90th Birthday," November 8, 2002, https://www.federalreserve.gov/boarddocs/speeches/2002/20021108/

less than American wheat that lead to the Fordney Tariff imposing a 38 percent tariff, which was at the expense of the American consumer and European farmer. Again, just to revisit, the British pound, at the insistence of the Americans through higher interest rates, was artificially set high to pay off its debts in lower cost U.S. denominations. This resulted in British products being priced out of the market, while the high sterling put pressure on domestic wages leading to a series of general strikes in 1926.

Before the Great Depression had made its way to America, it had already started in overseas markets by 1928,[13] hence affecting American exports, as trade wars started to take their toll. Major stock markets abroad had already peaked—Berlin in 1927, London and Brussels in the spring of 1928, Tokyo in the mid-summer of 1928, Switzerland in the fall of 1928, and Paris and Amsterdam in early 1929.

In summary, the Great Depression was caused by depressed world agriculture prices, speculation, lack of Fed easement of monetary policy, the beginning of the end of the British pound as the global currency, unsustainable war reparations, wild currency fluctuations due to going off the gold standard, the perversion of fiat money, hyperinflation, and distorted asset prices leading to mercantilism (trade wars), and subsequent trade distortions, at the expense of consumer welfare, price distortions, macro factors leading industries to misaligned industrial output.

The Depression Begins

The stock market crash of 1929 was the catalyst that propelled the Great Depression, and most people's starting point of reference. But what caused its prolongation, depth, widening, and agitation was government. The Great Depression is the epic turning point

---

13   Michael Hudson, *Super Imperialism: The Economic Strategy of American Empire*, Third Edition (Islet, 2021).

in history of what shifted us from small government that did not interfere with the natural equilibrium and mean reversions of free market mechanisms, to the addictive tenets of large government that today obfuscates the ethos of self-reliance and individual freedom, which is the hallmark of American liberal democracies. It is this paradigm shift that is lost upon students of economic history.

President Hoover took the helms of the presidency in March 1929. Even as the Treasury Secretary under President Harding, Hoover always had a strong belief in government playing a central role in the economy, including creating commissions on unemployment, and felt that government could promote efficiency in the economy, while minimizing waste and even be involved in production, since he was a mining engineer by training. Perhaps if he was an industrial engineer Hoover might have been more versed in efficiencies, as Henry Ford was with the advent of the assembly line. But to associate government with efficiency and conservation is a fictional book not yet written. Later, Hoover even started delving in the imposition of price setting for produced goods, and while holding a straight face, he proposed that wages took precedence over profits, as opposed to the inverse relationship being the economic driver.

By the time Hoover took the baton and passed it to his partner Roosevelt they took a deep recession and turned it into a depression. I do believe this statement needs to be supported and elaborated upon, so I take this opportunity to better explain the Great Depression, its participants and what makes for tragic theatre.

A Brief Look at the Times

To give a backdrop of the times, the Bolshevik Revolution had created a political crosswind in Europe of communism and socialism, where collectivism was gaining ground. Even as early as 1920, U.S. Steel had a Mexican standoff with a strike, led by communist labor leader and a noted agitator William Z. Foster. Eventually the American public figured out the strike was Bolshevik inspired and took the side of U.S. Steel. Alternatively, there were liquidators who believed that liquidating weak firms and letting the natural winds of the free market rinse out distortions of market failure regardless of the cause, was the remedy, and they had the empiricism of the 1920-21 short-lived depression to support their position. As mentioned prior, William Z. Foster was chairman of the Communist Party USA from 1945 to 1957. Political leanings aside, this much is for sure: between 1929 and 1934 the GDP contracted by about 40 percent. The unemployment rate went from 3.2 percent in 1929, steadily climbed to 16 percent in 1931, then ascended to 25 percent in 1933 and stayed in double digits until 1941—it normalized under 4 percent in 1943, hardly the hallmark of the government's New Deal success. When we delve further, the lower unemployment numbers in World War II were because the soldiers were sent to fight, and if they didn't go into the military, the unemployment rate would have stayed well above a stubborn 10 percent. Subsequently, during World War II, women were called in to work in factories, while men were taken off the unemployment numbers because of military service. To think that the New Deal solved unemployment is at best hallucinatory and suffers from logic being built on a platform of emotion and romanticism, as we shall soon see when we dissect empiricism from folklore.

The Hoover New Deal

Hoover bought into the 1928 book by William Trufant Foster and Waddill Catchings, The Road To Plenty, which was in many respects an economic line of thought that was Keynesian thinking before The General Theory of Employment, Interest and Money. It was from here that hatched the Hoover-Foster-Catchings Plan. It was hailed by the press as prosperity insurance, while free marketers heralded it as a fictitious socialist attempt to ignore the laws of supply and demand. Hoover had bought into the idea that depressions are caused by underconsumption and low wages, which is something like proposing that stars are created by the night sky.

As stated earlier, Keynes' 1936 *The General Theory of Employment, Interest and Money* was not yet published during the onset of the depression, but yet Hoover was already unknowingly adopting some of the tenets of Keynesianism and its socialist first cousin, namely creating artificial demand. As far back as 1921, when he was Harding's Treasury Secretary, he adopted the prevalent theory that high wages created prosperity and were the driving force of consumption, and at the time, American workers were the highest paid in the world. However, the fallibility of this was that he ignored the facts that industrial profitability, productivity, demand on skills and capital investment is what grows wages, as well as the simple fact that this mindset subscribes to creating the cart before the horse.

A Peak into Hoover's Mind

In World War I, the railroads were seized by the federal government, and much like the civil service today, public sector wages were not in alignment with the natural equilibrium of private sector wages; this unbalance was at the expense of the public purse. Hence, the government ran the seized railroads and they concomitantly increased wages above market price, which is a classic case of price distortions. Eventually, in 1920, the railroads were returned to private owners but were left with a distorted wage structure that was diametrically opposed to the market prices. In 1921, during the violent railroad strikes, a court injunction against union violence was issued, (unions usually have hissy fits like this when you take some of their lunch money away). At the time, Herbert Hoover was a union sympathizer who fought against wage reductions during the 1921 depression and was appalled with the news of a court injunction. Eventually, he teamed up with Secretary of State Hughes, to persuade President Harding to remove the court injunction.

Once Hoover became president in 1929, he dragged the government into an unsound position of rescuing firms in the name of saving jobs. This was a U.S. government first, and his propensity toward fostering a moral hazard (we saw an encore starting in 2020), which resulted in the government getting involved in setting wage rates, public works, in what amounts to as the New Deal. Hoover wasted no time in tinkering with the business cycle.

As Hoover later recalled:

> *The primary question at once arose as to whether the President and the Federal government should undertake to investigate and remedy the evils... No President before had ever believed that there was a governmental responsibility in such cases. No matter what the urging on previous occasions, Presidents steadfastly had maintained that the federal government was apart from such eruptions... therefore, we had to pioneer a new field.*[14]

Hoover liked to have industrialists confer with him as to strategies for the 1929 economic shock, and on November 21, 1929, he brought legendary industrialist pioneers into the White House, some of which we know in folklore. The all-star guest list included Henry Ford, Alfred. P. Sloan of General Motors (incidentally, it was Sloan's thinking that introduced marketing segmentation), Julius Rosenwald of Sears Roebuck, Pierre DuPont, and Walter Teagle of Standard Oil, just to name a few. The industrialists wanted to create cooperation between industry and government. Hoover's position was that with unemployment near three million, wages must be kept high to foster consumption. Here is a peak into what he said to the industrialist round table on November 21, 1929:

> *[President Hoover] explained that immediate "liquidation" of labor had been the industrial policy of previous depressions; that his every instinct was opposed to both the term and the policy, for labor was not a commodity: it represented human*

---

14   Herbert Hoover, Memoirs of Herbert Hoover, Volume 3 (New York: Macmillan, 1937), 29.

*homes.... Moreover, from an economic viewpoint, such action
would deepen the depression by suddenly reducing purchasing power.[15]*

In a message to Congress on December 3, 1929, he fully displays his
cosmic vision and naïveté:

*I have, therefore, instituted systematic, voluntary measures of
cooperation with the business institutions and with State…
that wages and therefore consuming power shall not be reduced, and that a special effort shall be made to expand construction…. A very large degree of industrial unemployment
and suffering which would otherwise have occurred has been
prevented.[16]*

By any standard, Hoover was an interventionist who really did not
have a schooled grasp of market mechanisms, as it relates to economics, and did not see the validity of recovery in a laissez-faire
approach and obscured the natural cure with a cosmic sense of
economic self-righteousness. Hoover wanted to bring the business cycle under government control, and even nudged Henry
Ford to increase wages in the middle of a deep recession.

How Hoover Deepened, Aggravated, and Prolonged the Depression

Realizing that this claim needs support, we need a starting point,
and the roots of Hoover's thinking comes from his economic philosophy. Hoover felt he could disrupt price formation of labor un-

15   Murray Newton Rothbard, America's Great Depression (New York: Van
Nostrand, 1963), 211.
16   Herbert Hoover, "Annual Message to Congress on the State of the Union:
December 3, 1929," The American Presidency Project, UCSB, https://www.
presidency.ucsb.edu/documents/annual-message-congress-the-state-the-
union-0

der the belief that the consequences of the depression must fall on profits, not wages. This goes back to the cart before the horse which makes his thinking flawed, since it falls under the belief that high wages cause prosperity. In other words, he wanted to punish job creators, namely firms and entrepreneurs, which is surprising, since he did have a business background in mining and finance. Once he got into the game of price formation, it came back to bite him politically because the unions he empowered in the early 1920s were the same ones that he asked to hold off on asking for higher wages during 1929, which again, interfered in the natural supply and demand of labor.

There is more to the story with Hoover's Great Depression, as his presidency established the Federal Food Board (FFB), which was government created but run for the benefit of the food cartel. With falling wheat prices, the FFB advised farmers to sell wheat only slowly on the market, and in September of 1929, it lent more money to farmers to withhold wheat, yet the prices kept falling. In other words, Hoover did not let the market naturally clear the excesses of wheat. Shortly after the stock market crash in October, the FFB lent an additional $150 million to co-ops at full price of wheat to further encourage wheat off the market. For a time, wheat prices held up, and with the FFB backstop, farmers found it financially convenient and subsequently increased wheat production by offering more acreage to wheat growing, knowing it was going to be bought up by government guarantees. This led to a loss in world market share, with which the surplus of wheat spooked the markets, leading to a further decline in wheat prices. Then the Grain Stabilization Corporation was formed, and the farming cartel dumped surplus wheat to the GSC at full price, resulting in a cartel driven scam at a cost to the public purse, driving down prices even further. Also, as American wheat piled up, Russian and Argentinian productions drove down world prices.

Farmers were being told to increase production on the one hand, and then decrease wheat acreage on the other hand. Under no circumstance would this happen under natural demand and supply. By the middle of 1931, the FFB bought 200 million bushels of wheat from the farmers and eventually dumped it abroad for closer to 10 cents on the dollar, along with giving away 85 million bushels to the Red Cross, for a loss exceeding $300 million in 1931 dollars, which approached 10 percent of the U.S. federal budget in 1931.

The FFB was on a roll and really, why should one failure preclude them from creating another even bigger failure? Because, after all, a timeless government tradition is to create a new failure, so the spectators at the Colosseum are too consumed watching the gladiators and forget about the last failure. Hoover continued his misguided strategic inertia, masking failure and waste and repackaging it as success. After all, only the anointed have vision, as us mere paupers must be led for our own good.

The next disaster turns our attention to wool, as the FFB created the National Wool Marketing Corporation (NWMC). In order to firm up wool prices, the NWMC financed loans to wool farmers stimulating production, and with excess wool stock on the markets, prices became depressed, with the end result being that the NWMC had to sell all this wool at fire sale prices with a total loss of $20 million in 1931 dollars.

When it comes to farming, the story gets better when the FFB asked farmers to reduce livestock to increase meat prices, which backfired because the farmers were unable sell at higher prices for the reason that the consumer could not afford the higher prices. Attempts were made to stabilize butter and grape prices, but this failed as well. The FFB rabid failures seemed to have no end or exceptions, (remember they were not spending their own money), when they created a host of coops in dairy farming and tobacco to stabilize prices, which also ended in failure between 1930 and 1932, and the coops were eventually closed.

As Murray Rothbard puts it in his 1963 book *America's Great Depression*:

> And so, the grandiose stabilization effort of the FFB failed ignominiously. Its loans encouraged greater production, adding to its farm surpluses, which overhung the market, driving

prices down both on direct and on psychological grounds. The FFB thus aggravated the very farm depression that it was supposed to solve.[17]

But when one has a cosmic vision of organizing economies, colossal failures using the same ineffective price formation strategy gets in the way of the failed narrative, so it is imperative that government deflect reason and intellectual accountability. To alleviate surplus, all of which he created, Hoover recommended that crops be destroyed and young farm animals be slaughtered. Simply put, all these price and supply distortions mentioned would not have happened in a natural business cycle, since any demand and supply disequilibrium is naturally adjusted, and surplus clears the market. Later, President Franklin Roosevelt eventually socialized agriculture with even more horrific results.

Peter Schiff, a noted hard money advocate, stated in his 2014 book The Real Crash, that the last real good advice a U.S. President received from a Treasury Secretary was from Andrew Mellon, who came from a family of industrialists, and according to Hoover's memoirs, Mellon advised him the following:

> *Liquidate labor, liquidate stocks, liquidate the farmers, liquidate real estate.... It will purge the rottenness out of the system. High costs of living and high living will come down.... enterprising people will pick up the wrecks from less competent people.[18]*

In fact, this liquidation strategy would have alleviated much long-term distress for firms and citizens, by adopting the same laissez-faire policy of President Harding, where Mellon also served as his Secretary of the Treasury. Peter Schiff just might be right in his assertions.

---

17   Murray Newton Rothbard, America's Great Depression (New York: Van Nostrand, 1963).
18   Herbert Hoover, The Memoirs of Herbert Hoover (New York: Macmillan, 1951).

By 1932, Hoover was having doubts as to the effects of his public works projects that were costing $1,200 per family in aid and excluded the unskilled and the needy in more remote areas. To make things worse, the American Federation of Labor (AFL) was using a typical union trick by restricting labor supply, to drive up wages, which ended up driving up unemployment, or non-members into lower paying jobs. Subsequently, this led to more distortion in the labor market, and specifically wage formation and natural demand for consumption. At one point the American Federation of Labor, encouraged the young to stay in school and married women with husbands working in good jobs, to stay at home, so they could create a junta monopoly on wage rates. This suited Hoover fine, as he was not able to break out of his seductive trance from Foster and Catchings' Road To Plenty because he was a union sympathizer, and by keeping women home and the young in school, it drove down official unemployment rates, but this was at the cost of natural marketplace consumption, as few benefited at the expense of many.

Hoover even maintained wages on public buildings, did not reduce public wages, but instead reduced hours, which, in effect, is the same thing, and again this drove down demand by distorting the marginal propensity to consume (MPC) and savings, which is needed to drive consumption, and economic growth. Subsequently, Hoover, or Roosevelt, for that matter, were clueless about the money velocity problem, meaning, the lack of confidence was retarding spending trickling through the economy. Subsequently, the economy contracted further, and the battered consumer of the Great Depression had to bear the brunt due to an abdication of sound governmental policy by interfering with the tenets of the invisible hand.

The story of Hoover and Roosevelt only becomes more tragic as they bludgeoned any remnants of laissez-faire in government, introduced socialism, and turned their turrets on the free markets.

The next trick to resolve the Depression, as if this was the cause or remedy, was when the government-built ships in Naval yards and arsenals, instead of outsourcing it to the private sector, which would have saved money at the benefit of the public purse, not to mention efficiency. Meanwhile, the states helped create cartels and socialization of the crude oil industry, leading to price manipulation. Then, with a deficit of $2 billion, and no real option to money print, since the U.S. dollar was backed by gold at the time, Hoover turned to the Revenue Act of 1932 and created oppressive taxation, including reviving wartime excise taxes, sales tax on toiletries, gasoline, electricity, malt, jewelry, furs, and many more categories. The resulting increases in taxes was affecting consumption and contracting the GDP further.

Hoover further aggravated the depression, and specifically the marginal propensity to consume, and any chance of a natural economic recovery was thwarted by suffocating both the consumer and firms that create employment, with his taxation to help subsidize ineffectual governmental spending gone amok. These actions when ripped to the core, can best be described as socialism, so, no, it is not a new phenomenon in the United States today, but at least the reader can now start to understand its genesis. Put frankly, Hoover and Roosevelt created the kernel of socialism in the United States, which is antithetical to the U.S. principles of freedom. For anyone to blame capitalism with its admitted flaws for more frequent and deeper breakdowns in the economy in the last 92 years is misguided, because the natural phenomena of free markets have been mostly disabled as such after these two presidents. In other words, it is an intellectual stretch to think that we operate in anything resembling a free market today.

There is more to the story as the broad and acute taxation included transfer tax on bond transfers, which helped drive the Dow Jones lower from a peak of over 300 to under 50. These taxes included bank chequing accounts, communications, and, of course, the new Revenue Act of 1932 that affected the two primary income tax brackets, namely, 1½ percent to 5 percent that went to 4 percent to 8 percent, while corporate taxes were raised from 12.75 percent to 13.5 percent, and the wealthiest had their taxes raised from 25 percent to 65 percent, while the gift tax was reinstated. Hoover even tried to impose a retail manufacturers tax (VAT, or in the case of Canada HST), but manufacturers barked that one back into the dustbin of government overreach. One would think that with all the new taxes, government would have more money to squander, but in a shrinking economy, it ended up charging higher rates but collecting less. This is known as the Laffer Curve, that higher tax rates after a certain inelastic rate end up creating less revenue for government coffers. Arthur Laffer, a distinguished economics professor who taught at Pepperdine University, was in a meeting in 1974 during the Nixon/Ford administration when he sketched the Laffer Curve on a napkin for the pleasure of Dick Cheney and Donald Rumsfeld. The argument is really an integration of microeconomics' marginal contribution against the contraction of growth of the macroeconomy. Simply put, if the economy is shrinking, and government increases the tax rates, they end up collecting less tax dollars overall.

This gives the reader a peak in time to see how relatively low taxes of a small government economy was the norm, and how taxes can be described today as nothing short of oppressive. The increased taxes were in a reality a burden of inflation mechanism on both the consumer and firms, for the pleasure of government.

Of course, there were voices of reason and outrage to these taxes, consider the following from the St. Louis Chamber of Commerce:

> When governments seek to maintain the high levels of taxation they reached in good times in these days of seriously impaired income, the impending specter of higher taxes constitutes one of the chief deterrents of business recovery.[19]

But the train just keeps on rolling with a mountain of failures, and here are a few more situations, before we leave Hoover's economic record, and then dissect FDR's.

In 1930, the Smoot–Hawley Tariff Act was passed and signed by President Hoover, imposing crippling duties, and set the course for international mercantilism and trade wars that resulted with

19   Murray Newton Rothbard, America's Great Depression (New York: Van Nostrand, 1963).

average 40 percent duties by the end of World War II, which eventually, as discussed in Chapter 7, led to the formation of GATT in 1946 to dismantle such a distorted mess.

It must be noted again that duties were and are an inflationary tax imposed on already crippled consumers and firms that were increased under Hoover in the 1930s. The end result being a weakened consumer, a deterioration of consumption spending that further aggravated the Great Depression. This is evidenced when the Smoot–Hawley Tariff Act resulted in European markets retaliating with import quotas on American goods, as well as retaliatory tariffs that lead to a 50 percent decline in U.S. exports, while the importation of parts for industrial production affected the cost of goods for manufacturers, created cost push inflation, while at the same time, spooked the stock market further by helping to bring the Dow Jones down from 280 points in early 1930, to 70 points by 1933, resulting in a massive diminishment of the "economic wealth effect."

By 1932, the political drums of using tax money to increase public sector wages and public works programs continued to gain traction at the expense of the private sector, further debilitating the recovery. Public works projects, which were in vogue, found a supporting cast of agitators, consider the magazine "American City" called for low interest loans for such projects. Of course, this attained political traction from a wide cast of politicians in America, including Colonel John P. Hogan, who found support from the Construction League of America, and by the Associated General Contractors of America, as were both titillated at the thought of government subsidies to the construction industry. This further exasperated matters because of artificial wage rates as opposed to natural wage rates. To add more fuel to the fire, the public works programs were an inefficient use of public money, while it deprived private companies the capital it would require to recover from the depression.

With documentation from Rothbard's book America's Great Depression, when Hoover left office, the mess he left behind included production that had fallen over 50 percent, unemployment was at 25 percent, and a GNP that had fallen almost 50 percent.

These were not hallmarks of success, but a result of disastrous government meddling in the economy's business cycle. Rothbard says:

> Hoover's tragic failure to cure the depression and being passed off as a typical example of laissez-faire is drastically to misread the historical record. The Hoover rout must be set down as a failure of government planning and not of the free market.[20]

To continue this misguided policy as a remedy to the Great Depression, a new actor entered the stage that was to continue with the same prescription of economic barbarism, masked as sound policy.

FDR's New Deal—1933

Roosevelt's New Deal, which in essence was the continuation of Hoover's disastrous New Deal. As a backdrop, by the summer of 1932, three books of note were introduced in what formed the foundation of Roosevelt's mindset that promoted his intellectual reasoning and the flawed economic strategy of Roosevelt's New Deal: Stuart Chase's *The New Deal*, David Cushman Coyle's *The Irrepressible Conflict: Business vs. Finance, and George Soule's A Planned Society.*

These books called for heavy government spending and central government planning, which has become a timeless classic, much like a Beethoven Sonata. It is this thinking that gives inspiration to a new generation of socialist leaders who lust for power without accomplishment or merit, fueled by misguidance and envy. The real goal of these types is to act as a pseudo messiah of sorts for the proletarian, as a diversion for their real agenda, which is attaining power.

Roosevelt showed audacity and reckless abandon that could have stemmed from the fact that, like most politicians, they have

---

20   Murray Newton Rothbard, America's Great Depression (New York: Van Nostrand, 1963).

never run an enterprise. When we consider that the Federal Reserve did not provide enough liquidity, either with Hoover or certainly with Roosevelt, both of whom had the political capital to influence the Fed into increasing the money supply. Milton Friedman stated, and admitted earlier by Bernanke, that the Fed helped cause the Great Depression. Further, this would have helped create the liquidity that the banks so desperately needed, to stave off bank runs and loss of confidence by depositors.

It is blasphemous to criticize Roosevelt and the New Deal because it is baked into American emotional mysticism that obscures its tenuous foundation without considering an empirical dissection of its failed economic policies. Roosevelt's follies conveniently are ignored for the convenience of today's even more flawed economic programs.

FDR Aggravates and Prolongs the Great Depression

We start by asserting that FDR aggravated the depression by forming the National Recovery Administration (NRA) in 1933, which had a mandate for government and industry to cooperate in setting up fair practices and set prices. In essence, Roosevelt decided to meddle in price formation for consumers and firms resulting in creating unnatural profits for industry. It set minimum wages and maximum working hours. The outcome was that by withdrawing fierce market-based competition, and by guaranteeing profits for manufacturers, it resulted in price spikes on goods when the consumer could least afford it, and further exasperating the depression. Under the NRA, inefficient firms with unsound positions were kept afloat, profits were guaranteed, the cost of doing business went up, according to conservative economists, and unemployment stayed stubborn in the 22 percent range between 1933 to 1935 and did not recover until the U.S. entered the war in 1941. This is a classic case of the moral dilemma and government dictating price formation in the marketplace, in terms of employment numbers, it would be hard to argue that the New Deal was nothing but an unmitigated disaster, and not the hallmark of success, while it was an example of why government should not be in the business of employment creation and should leave it to the natural formation of the marketplace. The natural tenets of the marketplace would have brought employment back to equilibrium in two years versus 11 years to recover, and it was not because of the New Deal that employment recovered, it was due to America's entry into the war.

8.1 shows unemployment between 1929 and 1945.

Table 8.1: Unemployment between 1929 to 1945

Year	Unemployment Rate (as of Dec.)	Year	Unemployment Rate (as of Dec.)
1929	3.20%	1938	19.00%
1930	8.70%	1939	17.20%
1931	15.90%	1940	14.60%
1932	23.60%	**US WAR YEARS**	
1933	24.90%	**1941**	**9.90%**
1934	21.70%	**1942**	**4.70%**
1935	20.10%	**1943**	**1.90%**
1936	16.90%	**1944**	**1.20%**
1937	14.30%	**1945**	**1.90%**

The enforcement of price controls was not practical, and of course black markets grew because the consumer always votes with their pocketbook, and entrepreneurs see arbitrage opportunities. In 1935, the Supreme Court ruled that the NRA law was unconstitutional, and the cessation of the organization followed in the same year, behind it left a political landscape for decades of powerful unions that created monopoly on labor and wage inflation.

Henry Ford, the man who perhaps did more for consumer welfare, industrial efficiency, and the attainability of the automobile for the common man, did not join the NRA.

Additionally, Roosevelt aggravated the depression by using relief programs such as Federal Emergency Relief Administration as a vehicle for shifting money from frugal states to poorly run states, thus, giving them incentives for inefficiencies. Aid was also shifted into swing states and Republican states, to lull them into voting for him. This was again at the expense of the public purse and not the national interest.

The New Deal failed because there was a further increase in income tax during a depression, and the increase in tax rates brought in less revenue in 1936 compared to 1930, when tax rates were lower. Thus, if it was the government's role to increase revenue, they failed again—or perhaps Arthur Laffer should have been born earlier to educate the administration on marginal contributive revenue, as it correlates to tax rates. And these taxes were job destroyers, unless one thinks that governments create jobs and prosperity, by taking it off the taxpayer and redistributing into other areas, which always results in macroeconomic distortions.

The New Deal also failed because Roosevelt believed in central government control and bought into the tenets of centralized government. The natural price formations derived from supply and demand were not allowed to rinse itself back to its natural equilibrium. By not allowing a natural recovery, Roosevelt prolonged, deepened, and exasperated the Great Depression, while he squandered the public purse, and all those that it served as the financial victim of these ill-advised Keynesian artificial demand experiments. Communism had not yet shown itself to be a failure, and under any circumstances, Roosevelt did not believe in the natural mechanisms of the free markets, or Adam Smith's invisible hand, as Winston Churchill did. FDR aggravated the Great Depression by not allowing price discounting, which would have cleared market excesses, and bringing supply and demand back into natural oscillation. Inadvertently, he built on these litany of failures that deepened, agitated and prolonged the Great Depression when he signed the Anti-Chain Store Act (1936) and the Retail Price Maintenance Act (1937), it was again, at the expense of a cash strapped consumer who needed bargains, not central command price formation. Perhaps instead of signing the Retail Price Maintenance Act, it might have been more prudent to introduce an "Anti Large Government Act!"

The National Industrial Recovery Act forced consumers to pay above market prices for goods and services, while it required

firms to create cost structures above sustainable wage formation, causing further distortions in market mechanisms, leading
to more diminishment of unsound positions for both consumer
and corporations. The NRA pressured firms to mobilize and join
under federations, which were under federal control to prescribed
trade practices where production and consumption was to take
a central role, meaning, price and wage formation was distorted
against the tenets of the natural market. For those businesses that
subscribed to this quasi-Orwellian practice, would result in hanging outside their business a Blue Eagle logo to show they were
toeing the line in respect to doing away with hyper-competition.
The Blue Eagle logo was virtue signalling before it became pop-
ular, and stores that did not display it outside their window were
often recipients of consumer boycotts.

Franklin Delano Roosevelt had a personal admiration of Benito
Mussolini and his communist practices, which translated clearly in
his attempts to create a command economy in the United States,
under the auspicious of alleviating the hardships of the Great
Depression with a heavy and incompetent hand.

The New Deal failures were further augmented by the Agricultural
Adjustment Act, helping farmers by increasing the value of their
crops and livestock, while assisting agriculturalists to reap higher
prices when they sold their products. This included paying farmers
to reduce the growing of cotton by leaving the land allocated for
cotton empty, which acutely hurt the black community of share-
croppers. All this resulted in higher food prices on the shelves when
people could least afford it, which unintentionally hurt the poor,
the very people it was intended to help. This was similar to Soviet
economic planning where they would increase prices on wheat,
which would then result in a glut of wheat and shortages on other
crops leading to acute distortions and hardships.

All these failed programs that squandered the public purse had
the effect of increased prices without studying the elastic nature
of consumer spending and consumption at the time. In a nutshell,
it deepened, prolonged, created further hardship, and aggravated
the Great Depression. Not to stop there, FDR also confiscated gold

in 1933, under Executive Order 6102, where gold was forced back into the banks in exchange for $20.67 per ounce in currency, and for noncompliance, one could face a potential jail time of up to 10 years.

"Left to their own devices, government elected or unelected can turn into thugs, as for the most part vie for power without accomplishment, as FDR's confiscation of gold is a classic example!"

At the time, the U.S. dollar was backed by 40 percent gold, and the Fed needed gold to quickly increase the money supply, and this money supply was used to stave off failing banks, which were based on the unsound fractional banking system, which in effect holds true today. Roosevelt, right after signing Executive Order 6102, requiring gold coin, gold bullion and gold certificates to be delivered to the government, an action that revealed his hand. What FDR did to increase the money supply was change the fixed gold exchange price from $20.67 in 1933 to $35 per ounce by 1934, in essence bilking all holders of gold a net loss of $14.33 per ounce. This was not only involuntary confiscation, but fraud by the strictest of definitions, and used as a tool to drive the nation into an accumulated deficit of over 114 percent of GDP by 1945, which has never been paid back, but inflated over time. When dissected, FDR's strategy is programs for votes, just as we are seeing today, but at what cost?

According to Austrian School economist Murray Rothbard, the course taken by Roosevelt was the destruction of the property rights of bank depositors, the confiscation of gold, the taking away of the people's monetary rights, and the placing of the federal government in control of a vast, managed engine of inflation. This meant that if one had physical gold in the bank, one could not retrieve it, and could only be offered currency in exchange. A study of the stability of currency versus gold in the last 2,000 years shows that it is government issued currency which ends in tears, and by confiscating gold, FDR punished the frugal and those who wanted a store of wealth away from government, which is an innate right.

The better course of action would have been to let the shaky banks fail and not reward them for unsound positions and practices, put their frozen assets in the hands of depositors, which would eventually end the precarious practices of the fractional banking system that we still have today. Hence, to save shaky banks and other unsound positions provides us a culture that tolerates the moral hazard that we have evolved into. Meaning, we reward poorly run firms and households with bailouts.

By 1945, at the end of World War II, the United States had a total deficit of 114 percent of GDP, and to be fair to Roosevelt, it ballooned from 44 percent in 1942, just after the onset of the war to 259 billion, 114 percent in 1945, and to give it relative meaning, the GDP in 1945 was near 227 billion. However, from 1934 to 1941, the U.S. Treasury was running deficits on an accumulated bases hovering around the 40 percent range.

Still, by 1940 the New Deal failed to quell unemployment, which was at 14.6 percent, but effectively nearer to a rate of 20 percent.

Much of the deficit spending was hurled on the back of taxpayers, the prudent, and job-creating firms to pay for programs that failed, all of which have been specifically demonstrated in this area.

And finally, the return of the stock market wealth effect took over 25 years. In other words, the wealth lost during the 1929 peak of the stock market when the Dow was at 381 did not return to this level until November of 1954. If one calculates an average return of 7 percent on $1,000 over 25 years, there is an opportunity cost of $5,725.42 that the initial $1,000 investment would have turned into. Extrapolating this into a larger economy, the billions of dollars lost in the crash were an opportunity cost of the wealth effect that if left alone under a pro-free-market, Roosevelt would have created a quicker and more natural recovery, probably under three years. Simply put, Hoover and Roosevelt unjustifiably had a distaste for the capital markets and did not understand, or at least ignored, how a stronger, vibrant more natural free market would have propelled the recovery through the wealth effect, by letting the market clear off inventory distortion, while supporting natural wage and price formation for stakeholders, as opposed to their Keynesian romanticism.

The Great Depression: Some Final Thoughts

When all is said and done, it does not take a Stanford University economist to reason that the plethora of taxes and disastrous programs introduced by both Hoover and later Roosevelt in a depression, did not only lengthen and aggravate matters, but put the economy in contractionary disequilibrium. Keeping the pay rate of the civil service and feeding the workers in the private sector to the dogs is the ultimate government abdication of economic responsibility, showing an arrogant distaste of John Locke's social contract, which formulates much of the fabric of the American constitution. In fact, this is exactly what was done again in 2021, in exchange for votes and central control. From price manipulation in agricultural products that created higher prices when people could least afford it, to numerous demand and supply distortions at the expense of both consumer welfare and the diminishment of the public purse, irresponsible spending that resulted in 118 percent debt to GDP by 1946, that was only partially caused by the war effort.

The United States government had debt in 1929 of a very manageable $17 billion, and a consumer in the middle strata of income would be paying an average tax rate of 11 percent in the $8,000 bracket, and from here ballooned in 1946, with an average tax rate of near 40 percent in an inflation adjusted bracket, complemented by an accumulated deficit of $296 billion. These are not the numbers that an intellectually stable and balanced sober mind would find tolerable, or someone wanting to keep the fruits of their own labor. At all levels, this was antithetical to freedom, but with ordained thugs like the IRS, which are the enforcement arm of this folly passing off as good governance will and always collect more efficiently than Al Capone ever did.

This New Deal failure was accentuated by centralized price, supply and demand formation, leading to distortions by way of the National Recovery Administration that injured the natural mean reversion of the free market mechanisms, with wasteful ineffective public works programs with the end result being that it aggravated the depression. FDR attempted to bring the business cycle under government control, with disastrous consequences, leaving the U.S. with a relatively docile culture today that tolerates oppressive taxation, largess government, and squandering of the public purse passing off as good governance.

Put simply, the New Deal took one dollar and turned it into fifty cents, while the free markets would have pulled the U.S. out of the depression in a mere two to three years, as was the case in 1921 by doing what it does best, taking one dollar and turning it into three. The 1921 depression with a prescription of laissez-faire approach, cut short the pain for all. This in contrast to a litany of failed government programs, massive debt, as well as 12 years of distorted price, production, and demand formation all that deepened, prolonged and agitated a deep recession and turned it into a depression with a tragic folly of economic thinking that has shackled us to this day.

The cause and deepening of the Great Depression were created by government and it is time honest historians stop obfuscating truth by blaming the free markets.

Murray Rothbard so elegantly put it in America's Great Depression:

> The guilt for the Great Depression must, at long last, be lifted from the shoulders of the free market economy and placed where it properly belongs at the doors of politicians, bureaucrats, and the mass of enlightened economists. And in any other depression, past or future, the story will be the same.[21]

According to Jim Powell in his 2003 book *FDR's Folly*:

> The New Deal prolonged the Great Depression rather than ending it: The Social Security Act and labor laws encouraged further unemployment, while high taxes encumbered healthy businesses, and so on.[22]

---

21   Murray Newton Rothbard, America's Great Depression (New York: Van Nostrand, 1963).
22   Jim Powell, FDR's Folly (New York: Three Rivers Press, 2003).

Economist and Nobel Prize Laureate Milton Friedman praised Powell's work, saying,

> *Truth to tell—as Powell demonstrates without a shadow of a doubt—the New Deal hampered recovery from the contraction, prolonged and added to unemployment, and set the stage for ever more intrusive and costly government.*[23]

When all is said and done, the United States and the West hasn't had a real free market since President Harding, and it was the New Deal that robbed the U.S. from self-reliance and the individual spirit that built the West. Instead, the seeds of socialism were planted, as well as crony capitalism within the American free market system that it has still not recovered from. What we are left with is a perpetual state of government programs that are not only unmitigated failures, centrally planned, but are a socioeconomic drag on the free market economy, taking along other tragic victims that includes the individual psyche, and the industrious, all suffering with the afterburn of oppressive taxation, and government largess that serves to suffocate.

While free markets are not perfect, it does give the best opportunity for the individual, while it has lifted billions out of economic hardship. Subsequently, to shoulder the economic woes on capitalism, which since 1930 has regressed to a mere unrecognizable shell of itself, is erroneous, fallacious, and obfuscates the deserved accountability of the real villain, namely government.

A complete book could be written on the failures of the New Deal, and it has been, so I highly recommend that if this topic interests you further, to read Rothbard's *The Great Depression* as well as Powel's *FDR's Folly.*

We now travel to other financial crises, which often the culprits play the same tune, as the government capeador directs the citizens of Rome to look the other way, preferably at the private

---

23   Ibid.

sector, while the maestro hides behind the curtains in obscurity to hide his true villainous intentions.

CHAPTER

A Short History of the 1970s

Most decades in economic history are tumultuous in nature, and many people today still remember this decade that featured a rollercoaster of spills and chills with characters of the economic theatre that included inflation, gold, fiat money, price formation, and an energy crisis, making the decade a centerpiece for exogenous shocks.

Nixon Takes the U.S. Dollar off Gold

President Richard Nixon took the U.S. dollar off the gold standard in 1971 (referred to by some as Bretton Woods 2.0) as what was to be a temporary measure, and with it marked the end of the Bretton Woods gold pegged exchange system, the result essentially amounted to a free-floating fiat money based on trust, as opposed to the hard backing, and fiscal discipline of gold. This did not occur overnight—from 1975 to 1980 the Central Bank auctioned off gold at a very aggressive rate to try and indicate to the markets that gold was not relevant in a new era of fiat money. Even as late as 1979, the U.S. Treasury sold 412 tonnes of gold to suppress the price and attempt to bury it into historical irrelevancy. However, at some pressure being applied by the United States, the IMF in 1974 demonetized gold in its Special Drawing Rights (SDR).

Considering that gold was pegged against the dollar at around $36 in 1970, decoupling it with the dollar unleashed its historical function as a store of value where it soared to $800 in early 1980. In essence, gold was hovering in the $200 dollar range for much of the 1970s, the U.S. Treasury squandered an opportunity cost by leaving money on the table by dumping gold in the world markets below its intrinsic value. Regardless of the official line from the U.S. Treasury and the Central Bank, the markets had a mind of their own, and saw gold as undervalued, and a hedge against exogenous shocks such as oil, inflation, and the uncertainty of a U.S. dollar reserve status being un-linked from gold. In fact, by 1975 gold was trading at $183 resulting in a 500 percent increase in four years. Figure 9.1 gives a bird's-eye view of the history of gold in the last 100 years and provides encapsulating insights on the arbitrage of gold in the 1970s. The grey vertical bars show recessions where gold historically has appreciated.

Figure 9.1: Historical Gold Prices

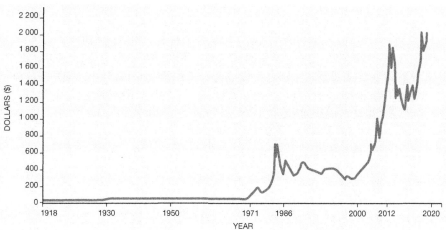

Source: Macrotrends

The year 1971 is important, as it is when the fiat money system was created in the modern area that has allowed governments to better print money to influence elections, military spending and wars to defend the dollar, and orchestrating coup d'état's while accumulating deficits that in contrast make Charles Ponzi a proponent of financial honesty and sobriety! 1971 was a turning point in U.S. economic history and signifies a new era. The U.S. dollar as fiat money turned 50 years old in 2021, and like all non-backed currencies, its intrinsic value is zero, and this is the primary reason cryptocurrencies like Bitcoin has risen to prominence. As an interesting side note, the average lifespan of a fiat money is 27 years, with the British pound at 300 years in various formats.

The official reasons for Nixon taking the U.S. dollar off gold was to devalue it, speculation by currency traders, and make foreign products cheaper to deal with trade imbalances, stubborn inflation, and unemployment hovering in the 6 percent range. The fans in Rome loved it as the Dow Jones was up 20 percent shortly after, Caesar was rewarded with a second term and the Colosseum glistened in glory, even if it was to be temporary.

The real reasons were two-fold: foreign entities were buying U.S. gold reserves in exchange for U.S. dollars, which was depleting the gold reserves of the United States, and it was felt that fiat money could provide much higher liquidity in times of economic crises for money expansion. Gold was putting restraints on government spending and forced government to live within its means, and gold is antithetical to larger government. But perhaps the big reason was that the Europeans were not allowed to physically inspect America's gold reserves and had valid concerns that the Americans were printing dollars prior to 1971 without a 40 percent gold backing.

As we shall see, once the faucets of fiat money were turned on, we start seeing the genesis of a rogue Central Bank that did not really manifest itself until after the year 2000 with an insatiable appetite for quantitative easing and toxic asset purchases, macro distortions, resulting in unsustainable public debts and institutions. The dual tragedy of deficit spending and fiat money helped usher in double-digit inflation in the 1970s.

OPEC Crisis

The OPEC crisis emulated from the 1973 Yom Kipper War. At the time, the Arab oil producing countries had 56 percent of world production, and the United States was a minimal producer. After much urging by Israel, which Secretary of State Henry Kissinger initially delayed, the United States supplied them much needed arms replenishment, which enraged the Arab countries due to U.S. support of Israel, whose fighting was led by Egypt and Syria. The Arab countries implemented an oil embargo on Western industrialized nations, including the United States, the UK, Japan, and the Netherlands. This led oil prices to move from $3.60 to $9.35 a barrel by 1974, and by 1975 oil went past $12, ending at $25 per barrel by the end of the decade. Keep in perspective that these were 1975 dollars.

What ensued were lines at gas pumps, inflation, stagflation, and increased costs of manufactured goods, since it takes oil to make many products, from plastics to aluminum, steel, bushings, tooling, lubrication, industrial coolants, mechanisation, hydraulics, electronics, and we have not even started to discuss oil consumption for transportation by cars, commercial vehicles, airplanes and the production and maintenance of EVs. By 1974, the U.S. pressured Israel to withdraw from the Sinai Peninsula and the embargo was over. It should be noted that Iran did not have an embargo to sell oil to Western countries, since the Shah of Iran was a close ally of the United States.

The oil crisis caught the American auto manufacturers—GM, Ford, and Chrysler, the traditional American economy's backbone—flatfooted with a fleet of large gas-guzzling vehicles when the consumer was looking for fuel-efficient cars. Lee Iacocca, the father of the Mustang and Pinto, upon his death in 2019 was referred to by Barron's as "The Last Emperor of Detroit."[1] In the 1960s, Iacocca warned Henry Ford II about a pending shift to small cars and as stated earlier, was eventually unceremoniously ushered out the door by Ford. In his time, Iacocca was an industrial visionary who understood the inroads that Volkswagen, Datsun, and other Japanese car manufacturers were making with a fleet of low cost, yet reliable cars. American auto manufacturers went to Japan in the 1950s to teach quality control. When they saw an abundance of small cars in Japan in the 1950s and '60s, many American auto executives chuckled at the idea of Americans driving such a small proletarian ride—when it came to American autos, big was beautiful, and not being ostentatious was, and probably still is, un-American. After all, it was America's century, and the 1950s was America's golden age.

Quite possibly the oil shocks, the last one being by Iran in 1979, coupled with American auto manufacturers building not only dated cars, but ones that were simply unreliable and poorly assembled, ushering in the decline of the U.S. auto industry and America's industrial might as we know it. By the late 1960s, the Japanese had taken over much of America's electronic industry, which America gifted

---

1   Richard Rescigno, "Lee Iacocca Was the Last Emperor of Detroit," Barron's, July 5, 2019, https://www.barrons.com/articles/lee-iaccoca-51562372956

the world, including television sets—very few remember Zenith or Admiral—radios, circuit boards and a host of related technologies. Hence, it can be argued that the oil shocks were the tipping point of the 1970s, steered in the beginning of the end of American industrial might at least in respect to manufacturing, but this trend was already apparent in the 1960s with the emergence of Japan, Inc.

Looking at some numbers by the St. Louis Fed, manufacturing accounted for 33 percent of U.S. employment in 1947, and 25 percent by 1969, and is under 10 percent as of the year 2021.[2] In terms of GDP in the United States, manufacturing as a percentage of GDP according to the St. Louis Fed has declined to under 10 percent as of 2021. This affects the inventiveness of a nation, where engineers are lacking the feedback of the production personnel, hence, leading them to design in a bubble. Of course, this is not the case in Germany, where they have kept much of their manufacturing. The middle-class is getting decimated, and in these numbers, if we dig deep enough, we find Hillary Clinton's deplorables. To be fair, manufacturing as a percentage of GDP is declining even in China, where it was 40 percent in 1980, down to 27 percent in 2019, while Germany and Japan's are stable at 20 percent between the years 2010 to 2020.

Going back to the 1970s, there were a host of factors that drove most of the world economy into a recession, including the U.S. dollar going off the gold standard, which would have tamed the inflation that ushered in a period of hyperinflation. To tame inflation required a slayer of beasts, the same inflation that government created needed a sheriff that was prepared to clean up Dodge City! Eventually, by 1980 a sheriff named Paul Volcker arrived to put an end to the government shenanigans, at least for a while!

To help give a feel for those who were not yet born, and for those who want to relive the 1970s, the timeline in Figure 9.2 gives us a more visceral feel of the era that helps us see repeated patterns of panic.

---

2   YiLi Chien and Paul Morris, "Is U.S. Manufacturing Really Declining?" Federal Reserve Bank of St. Louis, April 11, 2017, https://www.stlouisfed.org/on-the-economy/2017/april/us-manufacturing-really-declining

Figure 9.2: 1970's Timeline

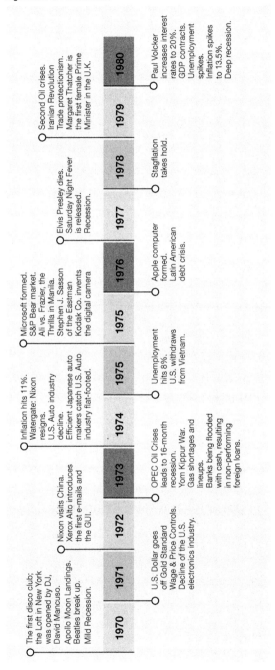

The first disco club; the Loft in New York was opened by DJ, David Mancuso. Apollo Moon Landings. Beatles break up. Mild Recession.

1970 | 1971 | 1972

U.S. Dollar goes off Gold Standard Wage & Price Controls. Decline of the U.S. electronics industry.

Nixon visits China. Xerox Alto introduces the first e-mails and the GUI.

1973 | 1974 | 1975

OPEC Oil Crises leads to 16-month recession. Yom Kippur War. Gas shortages and lineups. Banks being flooded with cash, resulting in non-performing foreign loans.

Inflation hits 11%. Watergate: Nixon resigns. U.S. Auto industry decline. Efficient Japanese auto makers catch U.S. Auto industry flat-footed.

Unemployment hits 8%. U.S. withdraws from Vietnam.

1975 | 1976 | 1977 | 1978

Microsoft formed. S&P Bear market. Ali vs. Frazier, the Thrilla in Manila. Stephen J. Sasson of the Eastman Kodak Co. invents the digital camera

Apple computer formed. Latin American debt crisis.

Elvis Presley dies. Saturday Night Fever is released. Recession.

Stagflation takes hold.

1979 | 1980

Second Oil crises. Iranian Revolution Trade protectionism. Margaret Thatcher is the first female Prime Minister in the U.K.

Paul Volcker increases interest rates to 20%. GDP contracts. Unemployment spikes. Inflation spikes to 13.5%. Deep recession.

273

Inflation and Stagflation of the 1970s

In Chapter 5 we were introduced to Richard Cantillon and money supply, and then the Phillips curve, which is in essence a defence of Keynes. By the 1970s the Phillips curve became unreliable since the combination of high unemployment and high inflation took hold, better known as stagflation, thus tarnishing the longevity of Keynesianism. In the 1970s we see perhaps some of the finest examples of both inflation and stagflation, which became the economic story of the decade. Again, much of it due to going off the gold standard, which is really a debasement of currency, much like what happened in with ancient Rome's silver coins 1,700 years ago under Emperor Egnatius Gallienus.

Inflation in the '70s showed its potency by way of a triple-hit for consumers as it diminished consumer purchasing power, because they were paying more for the same loaf of bread or litre of gasoline, which amounted to a tax or sorts. But it doesn't end there—inflation allows governments to collect more tax money in terms of overall amount without raising rates, assuming the GDP does not shrink.

Consider for example the following outcomes of inflation:

1. **Government gains during inflation.** Consider if the total consumer purchasing in the United States is $1 trillion and sales tax is 7 percent. The government collects $70 billion. However, if those same goods now cost $1.2 trillion, the government collects $84 billion.

2. **Income tax goes higher during inflation.** Let's say a salary of $50,000 a year at a 25 percent tax rate amounts to $12,500 in taxes, and if there is wage inflation (we saw this in the U.S. starting in 2021) the result is that wages increase to $65,000 because of cost of living, and the income tax at the same rate will be $16,250. In this scenario, what is not considered is that one is bumped into a higher tax bracket for twice the abuse.

In both cases above the increase in wages ends up in the coffers of government. Incidentally, in a reasonably enlightened society no one should be paying such exorbitant 25 percent tax rates to facilitate government. Even common street thugs cap neighbourhood protection fees at 10 percent, and they have a better history of delivering on promises.

Inflation clearly falls on the shoulders of President Nixon when he took the U.S. dollar off gold—it was pegged at $35 against the U.S. dollar, and by 1980 it had risen to $677 per ounce. What the world economy was saying simply that we are going to punish your new fiat money since it is no longer backed by gold. Put another way, if the U.S. dollar was backed by gold, the impact of higher oil prices would have been greatly subdued. How do we know this? Because by 1980 gold went up nearly 20 times it's 1971 valuation, while oil went from $3.77 per barrel in 1971, to $37.42 in 1980, a 10-fold increase. This brings us back to the relevance of asset prices that was discussed in some detail in Chapter 5. It goes then that if the Central Bank had kept its gold and exchanged it for oil during the crisis, it could have picked up oil for approximately half price. Probably the net effect would have been to drive gold to at least $1,000 per ounce by 1980, and would have simply exchanged gold for oil, therefore driving down oil prices via gold, while using hard money as a medium of exchange. Further, with the gold standard, the United States would not have imported so much inflation as it would have had a stronger currency, at least to tradable asset prices—when a currency weakens, the price of imports increases, which is inflationary. Further, many of the things imported, such as parts and oil are derivatives of finished goods, and on an accumulative basis, this drives up domestic prices.

On a practical basis, inflation plays havoc on companies' financial planning, often when cost increases in a firm's supply chain, the increase cannot be fully passed on. Case in point, try passing a price increase to Walmart, and let me know how you do after your brand gets delisted. Hence, cost increases, including wage increases that companies cannot pass on, diminishes profitability and depresses stock prices, or drives businesses bust, for those that do not have the clout, resources, or economies of scale, and this is what exactly happened in the 1970s. Then with depressed stock prices, we see a diminishment of the wealth effect, and simply put, if your asset prices go down, such as your stock portfolio, your marginal propensity to spend will erode, further contracting the economy. To fight inflation, interest rates go up, and historically, this drives down most people's primary asset, namely their home, which psychologically drives down further spending. When your home price goes up, there is an emotional inertia to spend more even though you might not be cash rich, but you feel asset wealthy in inflated fiat money, and this shows up in the marginal propensity to consume. This is a vicious Ferris wheel to be on, and it is tough to get off of.

Stagflation

Earlier, we looked at the Phillips curve, which gave only two scenarios, *high inflation low unemployment*, and *low inflation resulting in high unemployment*. But the myth of the Phillips curve was shattered when in the 1970s, we experienced the phenomena of high inflation and high unemployment. Defenders of the Phillips curve claimed it only shifted to the right, and thus asserting it was still a valid Keynesian inspired tool. In many respects, this line of thinking is the rationalization of the irrational.

The combination of a stagnant or contracting GDP, but specifically inflation and high unemployment together are referred to as stagflation, was not even considered in the Phillips curve, shattered and debunked Keynesian thinking, now buried into the economic history of the 1970s, along with disco and polyester. This complexity of stagflation changed economic thinking into uncharted waters, as policy makers pondered a new set of magic tools to surreptitiously avoid blame for the debacle created by fiat money. Nixon through perhaps visiting the ghost of FDR attempted to interfere in the business cycle with wage and price controls that created further distortions, as the invisible hand would have none of it.

In the case of economists, there was a visionary none other than Milton Friedman who warned of stagflation caused by the Fed's monetary policy. Friedman cautioned that inflation is monetary in nature and is everywhere, and this was in line with the 18th century economist Cantillon, who wrote extensively about monetary theory and warned of "too much money chasing too few goods" creating inflation. All being said, Friedman is the pioneer of modern monetary policy, where monetary policy role is to foster liquidity and stable prices, as well as protect the integrity of the dollar. We shall soon see how the Fed went way beyond this mandate.

It might give further insight to consider why stagflation occurred in the first place. In March of 1971, the Fed rate was 3.75 percent, and a Central Bank policy of relatively easy money was the seed that caused inflation against a backdrop of low growth GDP rate of 0.02 percent in 1970, and to further exasperate things, in 1974-1975, when the economy was contracting, the Fed probably going on lagging numbers increased the rate to almost 13 percent against the backdrop of 8 percent unemployment. We can just be lazy and put the two together as to the causation of inflation, be done with it, and get on to more important topics such as the rise and fall of disco—but there is more, because there is another element that needs to be introduced into the intellectual equation.

This brings us deeper into the tumultuous 1970s, where we have to visit Nixon again and his decoupling the U.S. dollar from the gold standard that allowed the U.S. deficit to grow from $371 billion in 1970, to nearly $1 trillion by 1980, while the lack of confidence in a non-asset backed fiat money eroded the U.S. dollar against hard asset commodities, such as wheat, oil, copper, steel, aluminum, plastics, gold, and silver. Concomitantly, inflation played havoc with company earnings and put the Dow Jones in a bear market. Studying the Dow, it opened the decade at about 750 points and had a wild ride up just over 1,000 in late 1972, then it skidded down to 600 points in 1974, closing out at about 830 in 1979, which meant that after inflation, people actually lost money on the Dow, especially when one considers this against risk-free investments in high yield bonds. Subsequently, the 1970s amounted to the longest bear market in history. Even in the Great Depression the Dow recovered more precipitously.

As disco music played in the backdrop in the 1970s, inflation and stagflation were the never-ending stories of the decade, and it was not until Paul Volcker, as Chair of the Federal Reserve, who had the intestinal fortitude to slay the beast of inflation by increasing interest rates to over 20 percent in 1980. Of course, this could not be done today, not only for political reasons, but because in 2022 if interest rates went to double digits the Ponzi scheme, passing off as the U.S. Treasury, would lead to massive U.S. government default and financial collapse within weeks, with the citizens of Rome being directed to divert their anger toward businesses, as opposed to the true culprit, namely the government and their self flagellating addiction to it.

To blame it on the free markets, or lack thereof since President Hoover, is an abdication of intellectual accountability. In an encore appearance, it was the Fed's abandonment of the gold backed hard money standard, along with their supporting cast in government, doing their best rendition of FDR by interfering with the business cycle, coupled by geopolitical events. It is this action that caused, prolonged and aggravated stagflation of the 1970s.

The 1970s were indeed a chaotic decade when Nixon took a page out of Hoover and FDR's books and tried to implement wage and price control in an attempt to control centrally planed price and demand formation, which the marketplace's invisible hand sponsored by Adam Smith slapped back with a dose of reality. But the backdrop had more than a few events that perhaps shaped our thinking today and enriched us with lessons from history: the OPEC shock that was caused by political policy in the Middle East, Watergate, the demise of the American auto industry, the loss of the American electronic manufacturing industry, gasoline line ups, Vietnam, the rise and fall of disco and the exit of Elvis from the American folklore, Three Mile Island nuclear disaster, an S&P bear market that eroded wealth and diminished the marginal propensity to consume, and some more moon landings. All this, of course, came with a constant background of uncontrollable inflation and stagflation. Then something happened that to this date economic historians cannot come to an agreement as to the cause, but the fragility of life gave a roller coaster ride to all who were present.

Once upon a time, roller coasters were made on wood structures with metal tracks that added a sense of nostalgia and a propagation of tradition. If one has ridden this old rickety emitting sound of a relic from a time gone by, with the smell of popcorn, barkers and candy floss filling the air with Coney Island or the CNE serving as a scenery, one might understand that it was a rite of passage of sorts. It is this visceral backdrop, a part of time that captures a bygone era that sits in our collective romanticism, and nostalgia that taught us the tough lessons of the roller coaster of life.

Eventually, our adrenaline vied for more and we needed a higher standard of exhilaration masking the madness that divorces ourselves from the denial of empiricism and reason in our quest for modernity. So, our next stop for spills and thrills was Magic Mountain, as we all stared in awe at the technological marvel that was to free our minds from the mundanity of human tragedy and deliver us into a democratization of a digital utopia. In our manifest destiny for enlightenment, we perhaps shackled ourselves into even more suffocating entanglements and vices in today's undeniable digital psychosis in the human journey of unbridled curiosity to discover the future of tomorrow.

It is this story that is told.

10

Roller Coaster Rides

The story of stock market crashes and subsequent pullbacks in the economy does not begin and end with the 1921 depression or the Great Depression of the 1930s—it has had even a more illustrious history, which brings us to the doorsteps of October 19, 1987, commonly referred to as Black Monday.

The 1987 Stock Market Crash: A Rendezvous with the Enigmatic

It is an enigmatic puzzle that is perhaps unsolvable to this day as to what caused the 1987 stock market crash. Was it the animal spirits of economics?

Our story begins in August of 1982, when the Dow Jones Industrial was at 776 points, and by August 1987, stood at approximately 2,700 points. This was an historical rally of the Dow index, and during 1987 alone, it had rallied over 40 percent.[1] Subsequently, the barometer of valuation, the price-to-earnings (P/E) ratio for the S&P was 21, which can be misleading at times but is still a good benchmark. P/E is the price of the stock divided by its earnings per share, and in most markets, when it starts approaching 20, it starts pointing to an overvalued market. Put differently, if the market or individual equity for stocks have a P/E ratio of 20, it has built in 20 years of earnings into the present value of the stock. P/E ratios are not always a correct barometer of valuation, but still serves us well for the scope of this conversation. However, in a non-public company, one would be lucky to get five times the earnings, unless one holds a high-tech stock in a private company, it could get snapped up by a private equity firm, even though it is losing money, be dressed for the ballet and sold to the stock market as a sterling example of buying the future now via an IPO, especially when the market is in a bubble. However, certain high growth

---

1   "Dow Jones—DJIA—100 Year Historical Chart," Microtrends, accessed March 29, 2022, https://www.macrotrends.net/1319/dow-jones-100-year-historical-chart

companies are rewarded a higher P/E in the mid 20s and better for a host of reasons, include being an industry leading company such as Amazon, at near 60 P/E.

So, when a stock price drops, in a classical sense, it is because earnings projected into the future drop. For example, the S&P went for 21 P/E in April of 1987, then to 12 in December of 1998, and this would indicate a very attractive market for the "long-term buy-and-hold" investor. So now we go back to Gotham City to find the villains that destroyed stock market value, its associated wealth effect and discuss how and why it happened.

On October 22, 1987, better known as Black Monday, leading up to it, the stock market put on a gain from January 1987 at 2,100 points and peaked in August at 2662, a gain of approximately 27 percent. Then on Black Monday, the stock market lost 508 points, or 22 percent of value in one day, which is still the largest drop in the Dow history by percentage points, and it sent shivers into international markets, from London to Hong Kong. The Dow eventually went as low as 1,938 points by late November, wiping out substantial wealth in the world economy. The larger concern was that this type of erosion would have ubiquitous ramifications, leading to a recession on Main Street, since, by definition, they were not decoupled, unlike the 2020 onward stock market bubble.

The causes cannot be pointed to one issue as a standalone as capital markets became quite complex after the 1940s. Some say the devaluation of the U.S. dollar played a big role as part of commercial diplomacy of the 1985 Plaza Accord, to offset U.S. trade deficits with G5 nations, while others say market makers—market makers open up the markets and help created volume and subsequent liquidity for the capital markets—were initially not backed by banks when they ran out of capital to kickstart the markets, and when stocks slipped, they were too reluctant to purchase in a dropping market with no bottom in site. Yet there is a body of thought in the belief that a relatively arcane computerized programed trading system was overwhelmed, while floor traders in the stock exchanges were backlogged for hours with orders they could not execute. Just to throw more variables into the equation, the weekend prior to Black Monday had a pent-up demand to sell, while the futures market with a closed stock market in the morning could not accurately price the value of equities and derivatives.

The tale of woes included the U.S. dollar being talked up—this is a technique Central Banks Chairs and Treasury Secretaries use to psychologically talk up the dollar, often resulting in a stronger dollar. You will hear phrases such as "we are supporting a strong U.S. dollar policy," coupled by higher interest rates to increase demand on the U.S. dollar during this jaw boning exercise. At the same time, Central Bank rates went from 5.80 percent in October of 1986 to 7.58 percent by October 1987, driving up the cost of capital.

Eventually, the Central Bank stepped in to calm the markets, when Fed Chairman Alan Greenspan stated the Fed would provide liquidity support that the market badly needed and started purchasing assets in the open market (this is just the relative beginning of the Fed's outward participation in the economy) and provided additionally liquidity to the market makers. By November, the Dow started recovering and the jittery mood slowly subsided with the easing of interest rates, by about 50 bases points (½ of 1 percent), to the 6 percent range. This resulted in the Dow recovering to 1,975 points by Christmas 1987, and by August of 1989, it had retraced to its pre-crash level of 2,700 points. This is actually an excellent comeback when we consider that Central Bank rates during the recovery period were as high as 9.8 percent. Comparatively, it took the Dow until August of 1954 to retrace its losses from the 1929 October peak, which is an incredible opportunity cost for the investor, while being an unprecedented erosion of the time value of money.

The 1987 crash recovered even though the Fed rate, which peaked at 9.89 percent in April of 1989, indicates the economy was able to withstand normalized interest rates, yet maintained realistic asset values and did not require near 0 percent interest rates used as life support. In reality, it might have been the bull taking a breather and letting Adam Smith's invisible hand readjust price distortions to get a handle on asset price realism.

Figure 10.1 shows the Dow in the 1980s with key events.

Figure 10.1: Dow in the 1980's

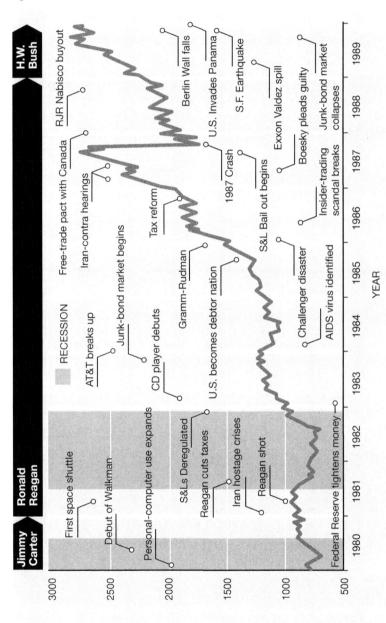

Source: Word Press

Consider what would happen today if we went to 6 percent or to 8 percent interest rates—every asset class would collapse, there would be defaults on U.S. Treasury bills, which would lead to an openly bankrupt government, as opposed to a non-declared bankrupt government. This would mean that in a perfect world government and its civil service accomplices would also be looking for gainful employment in the private sector—it is perhaps that time we could have a conversation about more civil, less oppressive tax rates, like perhaps 4 percent, similar to where it was in 1920. But with an insolvent government running a hungry furnace, it is but a dream.

Figure 10.2 shows interest rates from 1954 to 2020. The shaded areas show recessions.

Figure 10.2: Interest rates from 1954 to 2020

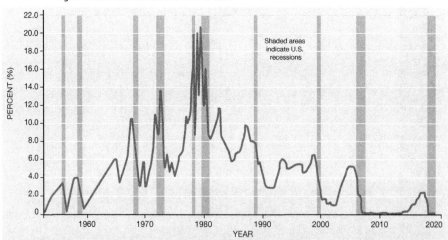

Source: Macrotrends.net

The scare of a recession, a relatively mild and temporary by-product of the free markets, did not materialize during the 1987 stock market meltdown, which would have given carte blanche for government to interfere in the economy and make things worse. Today, according to contemporary conditioning, when recessions occur, government and the Fed must immediately interfere in the market to mask the symptoms of a sick patient, as opposed to letting them naturally recover. If left to its own vices, a bottle of Pepto-Bismol or Tums would get people through a bumpy ride, as opposed to misguided government interference in the free markets, that always end up in an ulcer.

Of course, government will congratulate itself, like professional wrestling's perceived heels do, when they cheat and beat up the hero. And much like professional wrestling, the results are pre-determined, namely exasperation, disappointment, and failure that is passed off as success with a free hangover. The only guaranteed outcome is that the cure to the current crisis builds the foundations to create an even larger crisis on the horizon, as the encore performance down the road will be even more epic, as we travel on the expressway to the mother of all Ponzi schemes!

But, unlike tickets for professional wrestling and gladiator fights, fiscal stimulus does not provide the citizens of Rome their money's worth.

When we put all this together, stock market crashes scare off a lot of investors, with the result being that it probably changed the attitude toward the market for almost a generation of individual investors who only thought of price market ascension, not descension. The total wealth effect lost was $500 billion in 1987 dollars. But as we shall soon see, the skillful matador and magician distracts the ever more enamored citizens of the amusement park, leaving them in a state of collective torpidity and mystic illusion. In the next awakening they are presented with the titillating exuberance of more roller coasters, inflated balloons and tears!

Nasdaq 2001: The Dot-Com Bubble—A New Century, New Technologies, Same Exuberance

Earnings matter!
The future lay with Nasdaq—its promise in misty-eyed optimism for the future of tomorrow, and all its glory and tragedy neatly wrapped into the collective vision of the day. Much like the earlier

part of the 20th century, which had produced incredible technologies, including Henry Ford's modern assembly line, flight, wireless, telephone, radio, television, software, computers, the internet, solid state circuitry, storage, electrification, and of course steel framed buildings that created America's skyscrapers. Let us not forget that it was Thomas Edison who demonstrated wireless communications with wireless messaging in 1880, and in 1893 Nikola Tesla demonstrated the radio in St. Louis, and in 1898 he demonstrated a radio-controlled boat in a pool of water in Madison Square Garden. Eventually, wireless made its way to the British Navy in the early 1900s by way of the Italian inventor Guglielmo Marconi's equipment, in 1899. Much of this is mentioned in my first book *Newspaper Boys Always Deliver*, but this much is for sure, we sit on the shoulders of giants.

The Nasdaq was the catalyst that was designed to provide the future of tomorrow, though it borrowed some technology from the prior century, including the humble beginnings of the ARPANET in 1969, which stands as the engineering foundation of the Internet, as we know it today.

In mid-March of the year 2000, the Nasdaq market closed at 5,078 points, with an unprecedented P/E ratio of 189, against a backdrop of relatively accommodative Fed rates hovering in the 5 percent range, setting an all-time high. The big reason of such a high P/E ratio is that the dot-com companies were unprofitable and were using Wall Street money to burn cash at incredibly high rates, to the point where the cliff was right around the corner.

In fact, the market from January of 1995 to March 2000 had gone up over 600 percent, an unparalleled jump that made the 1929 runup look pale in comparison, which again was a time where breakthrough technologies of early 20th century were coming to commercial fruition. The decline started in March 2000 and became readily apparent by April of the same year, when the tech-heavy Nasdaq came down to 3,800 points, and the slow and painful train ride down to the bottom of the mountain all the way to 1,139 in September of 2002. When all was said and done, there was wealth erosion of $5 trillion (in 2000 dollars) over a 24-month period, and when assets fall, even if it is on paper, it puts large pressure on the "marginal propensity to consume, as well as the psychology of the economy."

When asset prices fall, it not only changes the psychological behaviour of the stock market, but it directly is co-related to consumer demand, as it affects the velocity of money in the economy, as consumer behaviour shifts. In other words, when assets prices drop, people hoard cash, and the psychology of the economy shifts. The whole paradigm of behavioural finance is affected as greed can turn to fear, and hope can turn to despair, much of this has to do the with the wealth effect! In terms of consumer behaviour, people often turn to their credit cards because even if one cannot afford the dream, they still want to look the part and chase luster as opposed to building wealth.

This, of course, can cause a contraction on the economy in the way of a recession. In behavioural finance, if one's assets go up in value, even though one might not be cash rich, the psychological willingness to spend accelerates and the opposite is true as well. It is this behaviour that creates the marginal propensity to save, and it is an intricate part of consumer spending, and market psychology when the capital markets are overcome by fearful money, as was the case with the Nasdaq crash. It is important to remember that greed can quickly turn to fear, much like a prized fighter who wins the first five rounds, then gets hit in the sixth round and is not able to psychologically recover, and the momentum changes as confidence shifts.

The Nasdaq went into a bear market, and took until May of 2015 to recover its losses from the March 2000 peak. In other words, it took 15 years to recover the initial investment from its height, which is a devastating opportunity cost, meaning if an investor could get 9 percent (average historical yearly return on equities), on alternative investment of $100,000 in 2000, their money would turn into $364,000 in 15 years. Thus, the investor forfeited $264,000 in opportunity cost into future returns on investment (ROI). This of course is the time value of money, which is outside the scope of this book. So, the "buy and hold" strategy in investments can be a rough road as was the case from October 1929 to 1953, as well as from 2001 to 2015 for the Nasdaq. It is important to note that people who do not understand or respect the time value of money do so at their own peril.

Figure 10.3 is a visual depiction of the trail to tears!

Figure 10.3: The Nasdaq 1992 to 2015

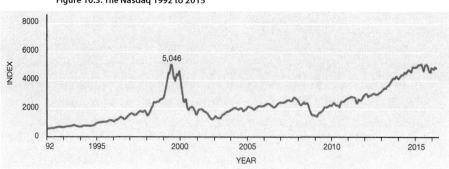

Source: *Yahoo Finance*

So, What Happened?

The simple way to articulate what happened is to say that it was like watching the movie *Scarface*, Tony Montana's moment of glory as he thought he could have it all, that is before the Colombians came to crush his coke-infused hallucinatory dream and reset the channels of distribution for the Miami cartel business, in a very persuasive way.

When the beat is so good, the strobe lights are on, the DJ keeps spinning the tunes, including the timeless hit single "This time it's going to be different," and the euphoria is this good, one only thinks about the glitter of the present with no consideration for the tears of tomorrow. Guests that are sober and present with reason, are not welcomed to the festivities.

While everyone rode the fast train and could only see Mount Everest, nobody wanted to listen to the sober man in the room, even though he held the keys to monetary policy, namely the Chairman of the Fed. December 5, 1996, is a momentous day in the history of Central Bank speak, when Chairman Alan Greenspan did his best rendition of Nostradamus and gave a famous speech in which he stated that "irrational exuberance" had begun to play a role in the increase of certain asset prices, namely the dot-com mania.[2] Four years later, the Nasdaq crashed and eventually lost 80 percent of its value as a stock exchange.

From a monetary policy standpoint, Greenspan started increasing interest rates in the latter part of 1999, to clear some of the badly intoxicated out of the room, or at least try and remove them in a more orderly fashion, but unfortunately, this is not how manias end. Finally, Greenspan understood that he was not the appropriate enforcer to bring asset prices back into equilibrium and called for the services of Adam Smith and the invisible hand, who, as a Scotsman, had an enviable and impeccable record of dealing with price distortions—often at the hands of a frothy malt—that comes with overextended markets. Yes, eventually Adam Smith the pub bouncer, not the moral philosopher, showed up and kicked out the delusional patrons back onto Reality Street by delivering the age-old prescription of price equilibrium and the ghost of the invisible hand!

Rationalizing the Irrational

Financial markets have a history of rationalizing the irrational in moments of euphoria, and this really emanates from groupthink. There was a host of tricks, euphoric expectations, and rhetoric that fueled the mania.

Venture Capitals (VCs) financed multitudes of businesses with often little regard to its sustainability or profitability, considering they were new and that they could repackage these ugly ducklings as IPO beauty queens. By October of 1999, Morgan Stanley stated

2   Alan Greenspan, "The Challenge of Central Banking in a Democratic Society," Remarks by Chairman Alan Greenspan at the Annual Dinner and Francis Boyer Lecture of The American Enterprise Institute for Public Policy Research, Washington, D.C., December 5, 1996, The Federal Reserve Board, https://www.federalreserve.gov/boarddocs/speeches/1996/19961205.htm

that the top 199 internet stocks were valued at $450 billion with revenues of only $21 billion, with loses of $6.2 billion. It did not matter that some of these dot-coms were bleeding $50 million a month—after all, the rhetoric and its associated playlist inferred that people were getting on the ground floor to exalt themselves into the future. And many retail investors did, as the smart money including institutional investors who took an early exit as they often do before the bubble bursts. Still, the key sales pitch was that this was like the beginning of the 20th century, when there were hundreds of car companies in North America and elsewhere that eventually rationalized to the big three, with Henry Ford being the most sustainable act. After all, hardly anyone remembers Nash Motors that went out of business in the 1950s, or Handley Motors that made cars between 1921 and 1923. History is civilization's house of wisdom, the shrewd study it to makes sense of the present and future.

A Look at Some of the Actors and Their Follies

With these types of valuation and irrational exuberance, it might be a good time to look at the anatomy of the bubble. Take Priceline.com, which was going to empower the consumer with a bid on everything from hotels, airline tickets, car rentals and even mortgages, and had an IPO that almost hit $10 billion on its first day. The only problem was that it was bleeding over $140 million in the first few quarters, and consumers ended up paying more during the bid process, as William Shatner, who delivered the future with the 1965 Star Trek, could not do the same as the Priceline.com pitchman.

Warning signs were abundant for the rational mind and by March 2020, *Barron's* published an article questioning the survivability of many of these start-ups that the VCs had dumped on retail investors at nosebleed valuations.[3] At the time, there were terms being tossed around such as cash burn rate, which means going

3   Jack Willoughby, "Burning Up," Barron's, March 20, 2000, https://www.barrons.com/articles/SB953335580704470544?tesla=y

through cash they had on hand, and their enormous month-ly losses, many had only a few months of cash to go before the bailiff came calling to put an end to these circus shows posing as businesses. In fact, Amazon was bleeding so badly, they had seven months of cash on hand, but had an ample supply of will-ing lenders allowing them to morph into the world's best-known online retailer, while many don't know that Amazon was at best marginally profitable until 2016.

Some did not do so well, such as Pets.com, which raised $82 million in February 2000, ended up losing $620 million in their first year, and went out of business nine month later as their cred-itors and investors were left barking, while their directors received $250,000-plus severance packages to hang around and mop up the spill then close the doors. Or consider Webvan.com, the on-line grocery retailer with a senior management team with zero experience in the grocery trade, which lived from 1999 until its demise in 2001. In the process, they burned through $1 billion (of course, management continues to get paid as Athens falls) in 18 months by building the future, which included their bankruptcy and a stock price that went from $30 to six cents and left a group of investors with empty grocery carts! In all these cases there was plenty of groupthink from within the companies themselves, and their investors where many ended up at Dollar Tree looking for an umbrella as the torrential rains poured.

Then there was the case of Boo.com (1998-2000), an online clothing retailer that went from a staff of 40 to 400 and concur-rently expanded from London's Carnaby Street to eight cities, with only one little problem, it only had total sales of $680,000 in its first three months. Subsequently, it burned through $30 million per month and six months later, the morticians arrived, but not until VCs lost a total of $180 million, leaving them and their advertising creditors without a wardrobe, and naked.

Since you asked, I will deliver you one more story of fairy dust turning into tales from the crypt.

During the early days of internet in the mid 1990s, well before Google, the thinking was that the person who controlled the web browser market controlled the empire and beyond. Younger readers might think Netscape is some sci-fi movie coming out to kill the pandemic, but it was the dominant web browser in the 1990s, even beyond. In the 1990s, Netscape commanded 90 percent of market share for browsers and fell to 1 percent by 2006. It was acquired by AOL in 1998 for $10 billion, which shows how many in the C-suite make bad decisions, even though their job is to envision the future. Today, Netscape sits on the books of Facebook at zero value. Eventually, Microsoft Explorer became the victor, and held that position for over 15 years when it was bundled with Windows 95, which means Microsoft gave away the web browser for free in exchange for online notoriety of the day.

But there is more to this Harlequin romance novel, as the numerical magicians came in and stated, "Are you going to believe what you see or what I am telling you?"

Accounting Tricks

The matador and the cuadrilla work together to distract the bull, as the audience in the stadium is treated to some more Kool-Aid, masked as reason as part of the admittance ticket. New techniques have been brought into financial speak, such as obfuscating revenue and accounting tricks to keep the audience on the edge of their seats.

At one point, dot-com travel companies such as Expedia and Priceline were declaring top-line sales on the full price of the hotel booking, as opposed to saying that they receive a commission fee on their services. For examples, if in a given month, they sold $10 million of airline and hotel reservations, they would receive a 7 percent commission for sales revenue of $700,000. Well, that is not how they wanted to present the bride, with a straight face they claimed with CPAs in tow, that the revenues were $10 million, not $700,000.

Their argument was that the material profitability remained unchanged no matter how they declared it. But the technique was employed to theatrically create top-line growth by highly upwardly distorted revenues that were not the travel agency's top-line revenue, but the property of the airlines and hotel's revenue. Wall Street then provided lots of hype for this line of thinking for the plebeians to lap up and stare into the cosmos.

The technique was employed to show majestically high revenues, making people believe that profits would soon follow, to give euphoria another last great hope. But wait, there is more that is borrowed from the creative and fictional section of the library, as they discovered a brand-new bag to pump show tickets.

Profits Don't Matter

When they checked under the hood, old timers from the old economy were perplexed that share prices would rise with no profits in sight. What a wrestling match for the WWE world championship with the main event being *no profits vs. high share prices*, accompanied by their directors, nefarious managers pulling salaries, exuding virtue, as the patient hemorrhages. But wait, remember that thing called customers, yes, the ones that drive profits? So, the next trick of the matador was to distract the room full of the enamoured that never let facts get in the way of emotions, with the concept of putting a value on customers, as opposed to brands and free-cash flows.

So, the illusionist's next ploy entails putting a value on customers. For example, Priceline.com might have a million customers who give them $100 per year gross profit each on average (many others were at a loss, incidentally), they then multiply it by 10 years for a customer value of $1,000 per customer. The next part of the trick is to multiply $1,000 x 1 million customers, for a market capitalization on the company of $1 billion, as Wall Street talks up their books based on this new valuation technique. This was another flavour of Kool-Aid that many drank as stock traders pushed their books to obscure the speculative euphoria, and to mask the empty vessel that was being passed off as investment. Yes, the retail investor getting their daily dose of the financial news mistook the last great hope as an investment and wasn't even provided the courtesy of a Kleenex to absorb the tears to come!

The concept of putting a value on customers is done by running a customer lifetime value (CLV), which I did once when I sold a medical business for a client. In *The Practical MBA For Marketing*, I take a deep dive in valuing customer profitability.

But wait, in the shameless ecstasy of accounting and the illusion of marketing expenses posing as investments that are part of propelling revenue, the magician had more sinister plots as the investors and the SEC were in a state of comatose with no doctor in sight. Better revealing this expense trick, it was a perversion of the strict definition of marketing expense. What many of the dot-coms were doing was claiming that couriering and preparing orders is branded packaging, and not stated as operating or shipping expense on their financial statements, instead, with a straight face, they claimed that it was a marketing expense. Because packaging the parcels and throwing in free delivery was a form of marketing, and subsequently they were attaining market share. The idea behind this was to show the audience that they were spending huge on marketing, and naturally hope and change would arrive with profits, if only they were given more cash to burn, and pay incompetent founders and management with deep six figure incomes for burning down the house. But this is how things are done in the age of robber barons, in what is becoming a strange strand of capitalism.

The Morning After

When all was said and done, many in the audience that were attending the play called "dot-com" before the slow but tragic ending, were suffering from a bankruptcy of logic as the actors were immersed in a sea of denial. In the end, what started as a serenaded gondola ride in Venice turned into the epic horror of Pompeii just before its tragic manifest destiny, as few were able to make it to the fire escape!

Eventually, Adam Smith showed up with his timeless invisible hand and delivered the painful lesson of mania and offered a brew of sobriety. Heavy-handedly, as is always the case of inflated asset prices, the invisible hand put Nasdaq into price equilibrium, in what was a majestic swan dive that took two years, as the last of the intoxicated men with lipstick on their collars and their scantily dressed women with smeared makeup and messy hair, were escorted out of that 1995-2000 Nasdaq party into the paddy wagon of realism.

The Nasdaq closed at 5,078 points in March 2000 and took a flamboyant dive to 1,139 in Sept 2002, followed by a street full of tears. When the dust settled, the mania caused wealth destruction of $5 trillion of market capital, and soon its unwanted cousin arrived in 2001, namely a recession, which made a grand entrance with the crowd running to their local 24/7 Walgreens to obtain hangover remedies.

This is not to say that there were no clear winners that had sustainability if they hung around for the ride. Fifteen years later when the market distilled back into economic realism for what was to be the sustainable, what emerged was Amazon, Facebook, Google, YouTube, Apple, LinkedIn, and a few others. When we consider hindsight value, it is where we see who the winners are, but this was not so easy back in 1995. The phenomena of seeing things clearer in the stock market with the passage of time is referred to as hindsight value, and in this case finding the winners in the aftermath of losses, then holding on for over 10 years while having a vision of the future is another matter. Why? Because most investors have spaghetti hands, meaning at the first sign of fear they run for the fire escape. In the case of Amazon, and Apple they stayed flat for 9 years, and Google for 10 years, and this would be frustrating for most investors to hang on to long term hope. Hindsight value is different than intellectual intuition.

I guess this time it wasn't really different, and it seems that occasionally old school ideas like profitability and P/E multiples did matter, even though that did not seem to be holding true in 2021 but is making a comeback in 2022! The Fed did not have the political capital of ushering in the moral hazard of bailing out bad actors and the fallen at the time; in President Harding's tradition of laissez-faire, they were fed to the sharks, and all those that swam with them, including investors.

Eventually, a new show appeared on the horizon with a new balloon that inflated so large until some kid came along to burst it, and this time, the finest musical masterpiece since Rachmaninoff's Piano Concerto No. 2 in C minor was played in front of mesmerized audiences, as the next scene aptly named from a theatrical master-piece *Too Big to Fail* was all the rage of Broadway, in what became the new vogue.

And this brings us to 2008, with Barack Obama doing an encore of FDR, as benevolence to this day seemed to mask the tragedy of truth.

It was a sultry, smoky jazz tune with a sound and look of Julie London, as she caressed the emotions of the never-ending party, and with guests dressed in the finest of attire no one knew the indelibly stunning lady had a heart full of lies. But the home she was in looked so full and yet was so empty.

CHAPTER

11

The Great Recession: A Crisis of Liquidity

The backdrop, according to Ben Bernanke:

> Barney Frank wanted to know where the Fed was going to get the $85 billion to lend to AIG. I didn't think this was the time to explain the mechanics of creating bank reserves. I said, "We have $800 billion," referring to the pre-crisis size of the Fed's balance sheet. Barney looked stunned. He didn't see why the Fed should have that kind of money at its disposal.[1]

Home Prices and Sub Prime

The 2008-2009 meltdown has its roots in the U.S. and international housing asset market that was at the core of this debacle, and to not include government and consumers as willful accomplices would not be consistent with the facts. After all, firms do not have a monopoly on greed. According to Zillow, between 2002 to 2006 the value of U.S. residential real estate had increased from $18.9 trillion to $29.2 trillion, or 190 percent of GDP.[2]

As a side note, according to Zillow, as of late 2021, the U.S. housing market was approaching $40 trillion, and with a GDP of $21.2 trillion, it equates to 189 percent of GDP, which puts the real estate market to pre-2008 meltdown territory. If or when the real estate market melts down again, this time the fed has very little room to decrease interest rates, and now with 30-year mortgages past 5 percent interest rates in the U.S. and near 4 percent in Canada, a good supply of Kleenex might be in order. My advice, stay tuned, and don't touch that dial, and if the real estate bubble bursts, watch government and the Fed in full harmonized orchestration blaming anyone else but themselves.

1   Ben S. Bernanke, *The Courage to Act: A Memoir of a Crisis and Its Aftermath* (New York: Norton, 2015).
2   Treh Manhertz, "The U.S. Housing Market Gained More Value in 2020 than in any Year Since 2005," Zillow, January 26,2021, https://www.zillow.com/research/zillow-total-housing-value-2020-28704/

Looking at Figure 11.1, as a broad national measure, we start seeing how prices went up from $189,000 in 1998 to $322,000 in 2007, a 70 percent increase, and then plunged to approximately $260,000 by early 2011.

Figure 11.1: Price For New Home Sold in the United States

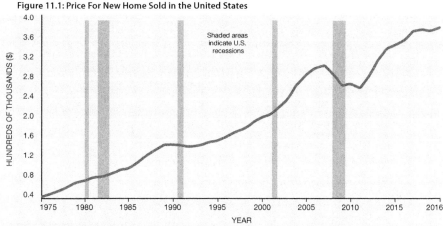

Source: *St. Louis Fed*

We could stop here and look at the broad index of housing prices and be done with it, but what is not stratified in our sample size, was the big cities where the most expensive caviar was being served with white glove service, of course. While at the same time, rural areas did not escalate at such a rate, thus, the broad housing index does not give a clear picture. To see the carnage in real estate asset prices, one needs to look at larger cities.

Average San Francisco house prices went from $251,000 in 1998 to $600,000 in 2005, and then plunged to $467,000 by 2011—in Los Angeles, the tear maker plays out the same way with the average prices in the $195,000 range in early 1997, and by 2006, had peaked at $687,000, a 268 percent increase. Not to be outdone, New York City went from $274,000 in 1994 to $774,000 in 2007. The story of the buildup of the bubble was the same in much of Western Europe, with Iceland experiencing real estate price increases into epic proportions, and of course, Dubai prices skyrocketed with both oil from surrounding GCC states, and international flow of funds to help the cause.

To provide the supporting ensemble for the full orchestral effect, after the Nasdaq crash and 9/11, the Central Bank started preparing the groundwork for the next meltdown with the Fed rate from 6.5 percent in October 2000, down to under 1 percent by October 2003, led by Maestro Greenspan, in E minor! And this was the type of fuel that every bubble needs to inflate. In the meantime, for political expediency, the U.S. government utilized Fanny Mae and Freddie Mac, who provided liquidity, pressuring or enticing lenders, as part of other government programs, to lend to unqualified home buyers, ending up with toxic balance sheets. Further, under National Affordable Housing Act of 1989, (governments give great names for failed policies, since it was monetary/fiscal policy that causes home asset price bubbles), lenders were further encouraged to underwrite loans to unqualified consumers that would not pass basic financial stress tests, at the time, housemaids were getting approved for $600,000 homes with no down payment.

More actors were in the backdrop in what really amounted to a subprime mortgage meltdown. Take Countrywide Financial, for example, the largest mortgage lender in the United States. Countrywide was led by a dynamic entrepreneur from the Bronx, Angelo Mozilo, who was the genius rainmaker in his time, and as the story goes, everyone likes a winner. Between 2002 to 2005, Countrywide sold 1.5 million securitized debt obligations, which means taking a pool of mortgages, grouping them in a batch and selling them to Wall Street banks, who then use adjectives such as Collateralized Mortgage Obligations or Collateralized debt Obligations (CDOs), and repackage the ugly bride into the princess of Instagram. These were then sold to retail and institutional investors, since the word collateralized insinuates financial soundness, it was not a hard sell. At the height of the housing crisis, Countrywide was found guilty of defrauding federal mortgage giants, Fannie Mae and Freddie Mac.

According to prosecutors in the office of Preet Bharara, the U.S. Attorney of the Southern District of New York from 2009 to 2017, Countrywide Financial ran a scheme called "Hustle" before the collapse, aimed at funnelling a rapidly deteriorating portfolio of home loans on to Fannie Mae and Freddie Mac. However, the government's Fannie Mae and Freddie Mac were themselves catalysts and helped precipitate the collapse, by backstopping high ratio mortgages at the expense of inflating home asset prices for the poor, who they were supposed to help. The outcome was distorted asset prices due to government meddling in the natural forces of supply and demand. This being said, the Hustle program by Countrywide cut back stricter underwriting review procedures for loans, leaving little controls, where even the borrower's income went unverified. The end result was that Fannie Mae and Freddie Mac lost $848 million on loans they bought from Countrywide Financial.

With this said, many lenders were offering sub-prime mortgages at higher rates to bolster up their revenues and balance sheets, meaning, they could charge higher rates of interest to buyers with weak credit scores and virtually no down payment.

Everyone got into the act of the subprime game, both domestically and internationally, as long as home asset prices were going up, what could possibly go wrong? There was a host of subprime lenders, including Ameriquest, New Century Financial, and American Home Mortgage, and even Bank of America got into the act.

After all, lenders could sell their mortgage portfolios to obtain additional liquidity and then by soaking, rinsing, and repeating create new portfolios and sell those to the capital markets as CDOs or CMOs. All this worked very well until 2007, when lenders started seeing defaults in their portfolios, specifically in subprime mortgages. The problem with the mortgage products was that they were being sold as large packages to Wall Street banks, some good loans were included, as well as many underperforming loans. Dissecting which loans were good and bad was like trying to find a needle in a haystack. What exasperated the meltdown situation was that mortgage lenders could not find liquidity in short-term loans, or the commercial paper market (commercial paper is short-term loans to finance short-term debt like 90 to 180 days that firms can tap into the capital markets for). Eventually, as the toxicity of the loans became apparent, many of these lenders were sold at fire sale prices, including Countrywide Financial, who ended up being on the receiving end of a "bank run," as depositors withdrew money out in droves, from their banking arm. Eventually, this led to Countrywide being purchased by Bank of America for $4 billion, which they later regretted. Why? Because even though the sale was approved by the Treasury department, the prosecutors went after Bank of America for the hit on Countrywide loans, meaning Countrywide's liabilities became part of the deal, as government official changed the rules of the playing field in mid-game. This, of course, turned into a king size headache for Bank of America, and left Jamie Dimon with lots of buyer's remorse. Not to absolve the actions of Countywide, but consumers who acted just as cavalier at the seduction of greed, as willing participants in the fraud of sorts, ended up underwater—mortgage exceeded the price of the property.

To be rewarded for their imprudent actions, these consumers were kept in their homes, because they were backstopped by the Obama administration, which weakened lender property rights, as did FDR during the Great Depression. By weakening lender property rights in essence results in the capital markets looking for easier avenues of lending, that can have the effect of drying up the mortgage market, hence driving prices down further, which has the opposite effect of the intended outcome! The outcome of this ill-advised government remedy was to further alleviate liquidity, since creditor rights, backed by property assets, were being rapidly deteriorated. In the case of General Motors, bond holders were forced into an illegal subordinate position, who ended up with a haircut of near zero cents on the dollar. Bond holders from a legal and fiduciary standpoint are the most secured creditors in a joint company legal structure, and again in the long run, actions like this can drive up the yield on commercially issued bonds due to higher risk.

The Origins of Too Big to Fail

There is a history behind this since it helps explain the present, and it is worth revisiting it again in greater detail, since it has relevancy to 2009, and beyond. It is this playbook that was developed from both

Presidents Herbert Hoover and FDR, who attacked property rights of creditors in the 1930s, with a federal drive to weaken bankruptcy laws, as many states adopted compulsory debt moratoria in early 1933, and sales at auction for debt judgments were halted. In the early 1930s, courts in many states were politicized to the point where they prevented insurance companies from exercising foreclosures. This happened simultaneously with the currency crisis, where gold was hoarded both domestically and internationally. As FDR was about to be sworn into office, there were dark rumours circulating in 1933, that his radical advisors wanted to take the U.S. dollar off gold, and this further aggravated the currency crisis. Unsound banks were bailed out, as opposed to creditors making good on their property rights of deposits, as States imposed bank holidays by fiat and allowed the banks to stay open without paying nearly all depositors.

Many National Banks that had worked hard to have relatively solid portfolios with adequate liquidity, did not wish to participate in this moral hazard, called a bank holiday. In fact, they were coerced by government in the 1930s. H. Parker Willis, a noted economics advisor and first secretary of the Federal Reserve Board states the following in his 1934 book *A Crisis in American Banking*:

> *In many cases, the national banks...had no wish to join in the holiday provisions of the localities in which they were situated. They had, in such cases, kept themselves in position to meet all claims to which they might be subject, and they desired naturally to demonstrate to depositors and customers their ability to meet and overcome the obstacles of the time, both as a service to such customers and as an evidence of their own trustworthiness.*
>
> *There followed what was deemed...the necessity or desirability of coercing...the sound banks of the community into acceptation of the standard thought essential for the less liquid and less well-managed institutions.[3]*

3   Murray Newton Rothbard, *America's Great Depression* (New York: Van Nostrand, 1963).

It was March 4, 1933, where every state in the Union declared a bank holiday, and it was President Roosevelt that illegally closed all banks during the one-week moratorium, which is typical thinking of people who have never run companies as part of their curriculum vitae. FDR took away depositor rights, as well as later seized gold at fire sale prices of near $25 per ounce, with the result of abandoning a truly hard and sound money system. According to Murray Rothbard:

> "Certainly, it is true that fear of Roosevelt's impending monetary radicalism, and Senator Glass's investigations forcing Charles E. Mitchell in 1934 to resign as President of the National City Bank, contributed to the banking panic."[4]

In essence, America could have reverted to a sound hard monetary backed banking system, as opposed to the fragility of fractional banking that we see some 87 years later, with its tragic history of bailouts.

This was the economic history of the ideological foundation of "too big to fail," which fundamentally rewards incompetent stewardship of firms, and especially shaky banks built on the fiduciary fragility of the fractional banking system. This is partially how we came to this tragic place.

The Capital Markets Freeze

The subprime mortgage market was the genesis of the 2008 financial meltdown, but there is more to the story, as the plot thickens, and the theatre darkens in anticipation of even more horror, when news arrived of the capital markets that came to a grinding halt in the way of having little liquidity.

Our story continues with AIG, the world's largest insurance company, when regulators looked under the hood and noticed

4   Ibid.

they were awash in toxic derivatives known as credit default swaps (CDS), meaning they were issuing options and other derivatives in the event of mortgage defaults. What this means is that people were hedging and wagering that mortgage securities would go into default, and when mortgage related instruments crashed, such as Collateralized Debt Obligation (CDO) and Collateralized Loan Obligations (CLO), the purchasers of these swap exotic derivatives would be paid off handsomely. The only problem was that AIG was issuing unlimited swaps that exceeded the size of the mortgage collateralized debt obligations market, and when these collateralized debts went bad, (yes sometimes collateral goes bad), they were not in a position to pay out, which spooked the markets further and halted the mechanisms of the capital markets' liquidity. In many respects AIG could not pay out the insurance payments of people who hedged, which can be thought of as an insurance policy in the event of mortgage instruments going bad. AIG eventually received a $68 billion bailout from the U.S. Treasury (today the Fed prints double this per month to bail out the U.S. government and other market participants), which, of course, borrowed the money from the Central Bank, since the government itself was, and is, certainly now in worse shape than those they bailed out. The mantra of the day was, certain companies were "too big to fail," which then reverts us back to the moral hazard argument, meaning do we encourage bad actors (poorly run firms) with unsound positions, by bailing them out?

On a global scale, it became a domino effect, as Iceland's economy collapsed under heavy leveraging, both in the private and public sector, while suffering a decline of 29 percent in real estate, while Ireland's real estate collapsed 40 percent further exposing lenders to high ratio mortgages. In England, we witnessed sights of bank depositors lining up at Northern Rock Bank, which was optically very disturbing for British fiduciary prestige.

Then the news poured in that U.S. investment banks were shaky, overnight lending for LIBOR and Repo dried up, further exasperating a liquidity crisis. Legendary investment banks, Merrill Lynch and Bear Stearns were sold at fire sale prices, the former to Bank of America and latter to J.P. Morgan Chase. Morgan Stanley and Goldman Sachs were also on the ropes and were given a lifeline by the Fed in exchange for being a commercial bank.

The big story was Lehman Brothers, whose hedge funds and investors bailed out on them, while the capital markets would not renew short term IOUs. Hence, Lehman Brothers was very slow in raising capital to counter the decline of their net worth, and for a host of reasons that were mostly due to lack of political manoeu-vring; when all was said and done, the U.S. Treasury did not bail them out, as someone had to be made an example of. Once the news spread on the demise of the Lehman Brothers, the capital markets froze, since very few wanted to lend—subsequently, li-quidity disappeared and a host of equity classes declined in value, most notably stocks, where the Dow came off its September 2007 high of 17,000 and slid to 8,600 by February 2009. When we add up the losses of both the equity and real estate markets, it wiped out $19.2 trillion of the wealth effect, which devastated consumers, investors and firms. For those who think real estate assets cannot take a haircut, they have not read up on the Great Depression to the Great Recession or are not closely watching the Manhattan real estate market, from 2016-2020. Simply put, nothing goes up in a straight line forever, as a quick look at the Dow and its real estate component will attest.

When it came to asset classes escaping the Great Recession from carnage, the old song by Martha and the Vandellas eloquent-ly says it all: "Nowhere to run, nowhere to hide!" All safe bets were off, from blue chips, banks, tech, to real estate, as the whole house of cards folded. At one point, there was no financing available on new cars at competitive leases, as I remember one General Motors salesman put all his stock money into GM shares only to see it become worthless. Many in the hardest hit regions in the United States had homes that were underwater. Later, the Obama administration found it politically expedient to try and stop fore-closures, which when stripped to the essence, rewards people for reckless, undisciplined, and imprudent financial behaviour. This again brings us to the moral hazard dilemma, meaning should government who then borrows from the Fed since they are insolvent themselves be bailing out reckless consumer behaviour, (realizing they were not all reckless) those living beyond their means, including making non-income verifiable mortgage applications? Respectfully, we will let scholars debate this, since we are not going to be compensated for doing modern renditions of Socrates.

Bailouts and Back to the Moral Hazzard

There were multitudes of companies that were bailed out by the U.S. Treasury, notable mentions include General Motors for $50 billion—GM eventually paid back the U.S. Treasury, via giving the Treasury shares in lieu, (that the Treasury has since sold, which in turn squandered the cash on trying to get re-elected as opposed to reducing the accumulated deficit and bring down taxes)—and Chrysler for $10 billion which has since been paid back. Not to be outdone, the government created a $200 billion bailout for Freddie Mac and Fannie Mae combined, while Citigroup received $45 billion, Wells Fargo $25 billion, Goldman Sachs $10 billion, Bank of America $45 billion, J.P. Morgan Chase $25 billion—the list also includes government-run entities outside of Freddie Mac and Fannie Mae, such as the Illinois Housing Development Authority (notice the word authority in their name) that skimmed the taxpayer for $750 million.

Now we get back to the moral hazard argument—why should the taxpayer be bailing out and rewarding unsound business practices? Going back to President Harding in the 1920 depression, the idea in a free market neo-liberal society is against the government interfering in the economy, manipulating the business cycle was not even intellectually fathomable, as is a bygone 5 percent tax rate, which was enjoyed in the era up to the 1920s. So, the concept of government interfering in the American economy is a great depression idea, and the policy of the Central Bank purchasing unsound positions really gained traction during the 2008 great recession. The economy has never recovered from the great recession, especially in terms of asset distorting monetary policy, otherwise we would see normalized interest rates, which would have stopped government and consumers from living outside of their means.

Some argue that bailing out firms is corporate welfare, which has merit, while others argue that national strategic interests such as Boeing, Westinghouse, Rockwell, Google, Bank of America, and the likes help to compose the competitive architecture, both domestically and internationally, and to let any of them perish would diminish the industrial might of the West.

On the other hand, it should be noted that almost all this money has been paid back from the borrowers, and the Obama administration did not use the proceeds to pay down the original government debt obligations, but leaned more on the taxpayer, by employing monies to either buy votes or further government bloat. Of course, this line of thinking is a government tradition, regardless of one's political stripes.

When we rightly vilify corporate welfare, it can also be argued that pretty much the whole public service sector should be included in the story. Too many government programs are bloated, inefficient, exasperate the problem, wasteful, are largely unnecessary, and these ideas especially the entitled civil service have been living off the avails of the public purse and the industrious, as this story can be traced back to Rome and modern Greece. The question is, have there ever been layoffs in the entitled public sector, especially in Canada and Europe on any economic downturn, since all the pain is borne by the private sector and its employees? When have public employees and people on three generations of propagated welfare, as a way of life, been cut off from their untouchable excesses during a recession or otherwise? Are we really all in this together?

When the Great Recession was over, at least technically, it wiped out $19 trillion in loss of asset prices and led up to 30 million people losing their jobs. However, the story does not end there, since the Great Recession gave the Fed carte blanche, via the U.S. Department of Treasury, to interfere in bringing the business cycle almost completely under government control by purchasing un-sound positions in the public household and corporate sectors, while addicting economies to low monetary policy that distorts and inflates asset prices, and encouraging reckless government spending, whereas the national debt went from $9 trillion when Bush left office, to $20 trillion when Obama left office. The ending result is that the taxpayer has nothing to show for it, except words, delusionary moral convictions, failed government programs and an unmanageable financial reckoning that will eventually come home to roost.

The government's interference in the economy, which includes the Central Bank, causes distortion in asset prices that is an unin-tended attack on the working poor, middle-class and the youth, who are being excluded out of asset classes. This is the essence of inequity, the rest is propaganda noise for plebeian consumption from the MSM, in the desperate search for the villain that opaques the true cause and effect. Put differently, it is government that creates institutional poverty, from Lynden Johnson's Great Society programs to chronically failed public education, because every government needs two basic things to stay in power, control over education, and a good diet of propaganda.

The outcome is a bankrupt social security system, to systematic multi-generational poverty, the formation of permanent ghettos as a way of life baked into U.S. culture, all of which degenerates the individual psyche, rewards the abdication of responsibility and accountability in an oasis of failure and wasted resources, in ex-change for votes. Any CEO of a business would be long gone if they ran their company in this manner. One train wreck is followed by another, even before the carnage can be cleared from the last by the repair crew. These are further discussed in chapter 13, under the causes of the inequities leading to the wealth gap.

As we shall see, the addiction to cheap money laid the foun-dations for the 2020 meltdown, and in essence, if the economy had ever recovered from the 2008 meltdown, it could have easi-ly been able to revert to mean interest rates (natural rates at 6.8 percent), as opposed to addictions at the 2 percent range. If the economy had really recovered, it would have been taken off re-suscitative low monetary policy, while ensuring that governments spend within their means with limits on national credit cards and putting asset prices back into equilibrium. It is these low interest rates that are specifically responsible for intergenerational poverty, complements of reckless government spending, and an addicted population of expecting without giving. In the end, this safe society will foster weakness, which is not a prescription for great a civilization to thrive.

When history reflects within the lens of critical thinking, the Great Recession will be considered the pivotal moment of when government and the Central Bank used this exogenous shock in a moment of pragmatism to gain authoritative confidence, at the expense of freedom. There are many excellent books about the Great Recession for further reading, but now it is time to go to the next chapter of our sick patient, namely the economy, which has never really recovered from the 2008 meltdown. The evidence is sluggish GDP growth of 2 to 3 percent a year, a reinflating of the housing and stock market bubble that got us into this mess in the first place, unmanageable government debt obligations, and household debt as of late 2021 near $15 trillion, according to the New York Fed.

But the magicians' hands of the main-stream financial media, a distinguished member of the Cabalatocracy, which is formally introduced in Chapter 13, passes a narrative in denial of truth and intellectual curiosity. Much like the decaying years of the Roman Empire, it masks and denies the systematic tragedy passing off as glory, as its citizens join in its looting, as mass psychosis sets in.

We now turn to a new song in 2020, but with a different beat.

The citizens of Pompeii could not believe their eyes as Mount Vesuvius, once again some 12 years later, erupted in anger. The plebeians had thought the aristocrats, senators, and men of commerce had stabbed the beast of the great recession, never to appear again. Hastily, the magicians of the empire were summoned from the Temple of Saturn, where lay within it the Aerarium of Rome's public treasury. But for how long could the banking temples continue to mask the nakedness of its empire and contain the rot that lay within its silver linings?

For what were its citizens to believe, the savagery of the truth, or the empty mirage that was created by its centralis ripam, showering them with gifts that mysteriously appeared from the thinness of the night? To hide the true face of the beast, once again, the aristocracy handpicked magicians used to create the mirage of paper wealth as her Central Banks lulled her citizens with gifts that put them back into sedation and docility. In the aftermath, the plebeians, the senators and aristocracy had joined together in the inclusion of pillaging the empire's treasuries, as the Barbarians at the gate amused at the self-flagellation.

The Empire's Achilles heel was bare to see for her enemies abroad and within.

12

The Phantom Returns with a Tragic Encore: The 2020 Meltdown

The Economy has Never Really Recovered since 2008

The underlying economy has never naturally recovered from the 2008 meltdown and has been on life support with unsustainable rounds of quantitative easing, perpetual low monetary policy and Keynesian denialism, masking the primary symptoms of an ill patient who has never really left the ICU. In reality, government finances are even more ill than the economy, where it is government prescription that is inadvertently keeping the patient alive on medication, which disguises the underlying decay of the economy, while denying government's own insolvency. In summary, what we have is a government that is unquestionably a net-negative on the economy, while being under insurmountable debt. In other words, government has lost its social contract for good governance, with respect to the welfare of its subjects, which unfortunately is the case since antiquity, with rare exceptions.

There is a whole backdrop to this story as it begins well before the March 2020 meltdown. The Fed has been trying to increase interest rates for a decade after the 2008 meltdown, where it was near zero from 2008 to 2016, since the economy was, and is, on monetary "easy money" life-support. Gradually, in late 2016, it started lifting interest rates, where in 2018 it reached 2.4 percent. At the time, *Barron's* and the *Wall Street Journal* posted a slew of articles that discussed the effects it would have on equity prices. At the same time, normal interest rates mean that government, firms and consumers will live within their means and make sound decisions. Normalized interest rates also promote confidence in the dollar, equity markets and the economy, and signals that world economies are coming off life-support after 13 years. However, the policy we are seeing is similar to Bank of Japan that has tried to print its way into prosperity, which has resulted in weak GDP growth and a federal deficit of $15 trillion as of 2022, and a debt to GDP ratio of 283 percent. The story doesn't end there with Japan, as the Nikkei index (Japan's largest stock market) has just recovered to its 1991 levels, taking 30 years on this long arduous road, coupled by tragic tale that the Bank of Japan is the largest shareholder at $470 billion of the Japanese stock market, while it owns 48 percent of Japanese government debt, and the Japanese government owns 55 percent of BOJ shares that trade under the symbol 8301.T. When we look at the complex financial intricacies of its inter-economic relationships, not only is it unsound money policy, but it is also a house of cards waiting for the big bad wolf to blow down Goldilocks' home!

In the case of the United States, the federal debt is approaching $31 trillion as of early 2022 and not counting legacy costs, it can still easily reach $40 trillion by 2024.

There is an abundance of evidence that the U.S. economy and much of the world was heading into a recession before the current pandemic, because in the last quarter of 2019, the Fed moved rates from 1.9 percent to 1.55 percent, based on sluggish GDP growth. As much as the citizens of Rome want to believe the narrative, the reality is that the pandemic was the pin that burst the reinflating of the 2008 bubble that manifested itself in February of 2020, and greatly exasperated a recession that was on the horizon. Consider that GDP growth was at 3.18 percent for 2018, and then tanked 2.3 percent in 2019 down in the U.S. The Fed, as well as Wall Street, knew that the U.S. economy was headed for a recession. But what really creates concern is the repo market, (this needs explanation for those unfamiliar with the repo market, which incidentally, is not the same as repossessing cars and other assets).

When we are dealing with billions of dollars sitting in cash on the bank's books, they might lend the cash to another financial institution in favour of securities (U.S. Treasuries or EU bonds), for typically an overnight rate of profit, based on trust. The following morning, the receiving party would give back the cash to the original holder, along with overnight interest. Banks often lend each other money overnight for some fee, and if it involves overseas, they go by the LIBOR (London Interbank offer rate), and or repo rate. The repo market acts as a lubricant for the capital market, to ensure cash flow (CF) and financial instruments work smoothly.

Here is what was happening in September of 2019: the U.S. banks were reluctant to lend overnight to the European banks, since they were concerned about getting paid back (Europe is another zone, due to unsustainable entitlements, is for all definitive purposes, insolvent). At one point, even until today, the health of the Deutsche Bank is being questioned as to its credit worthiness, and some call it a zombie bank, and if it collapses, the Eurozone would be in shambles and the financial 10.0 earthquake would be felt globally. Subsequently, what the U.S. Central Bank has done since September 2019, is purchase near $1 trillion of securities (often Treasury bills) and give the holders of the Treasury bills cash in lieu, namely, overseas banks. So, the Fed has now got into the business of propping up foreign banks by printing fiat money from thin air, which they do not have and lending it to unsound banks overseas, to facilitate lubricating the gears of the repo market that would have collapsed otherwise. If this should be done or not is another matter, but this is clearly outside the mandate of the Fed, and an astute reader will clearly comprehend that this would not have been considered in 1921, when President Harding did the right thing by not dragging the taxpayer into unsound positions, especially under a hard backed gold standard system. The uncomfortable position the Fed has backed itself into is being market makers for the repo market and facilitating unsound cash flows of the international banking system, with the outcome being a moral dilemma of sorts.[1] Admittedly, this is the cost of defending the U.S. global monetary system and hegemony.

But there is more to the story, as the evidence of the pending eruption of Mount Vesuvius started mounting. A strong predictor of recessions historically is the 10-year inverted yield curve—this is the barometer that both the St. Louis Fed and the markets keep a very close eye on. It is a reliable predictor that has preceded many recent recessions, sometimes by a few months to just over a year.

Traditionally, long-term bonds hold higher yields than short-term yields in financial markets. The yield curve is the difference between the yields on longer-term bonds in this case the 10-year Treasuries,

---

1   For further information on the repo purchase by the Fed, see https://fred. stlouisfed.org/series/RPONTSYD

and shorter-term three-month Treasuries. A yield curve inversion happens when long-term yields fall below short-term yields.

How this works is that if bondholders believe that the economy is robust, they will hold short-term bonds, knowing that interest rates are going up, resulting in higher yields. However, if bond buyers believe the economy is heading downward and interest rates are likely to drift lower, they prefer to hold the longer-term bonds, to lock in higher yields.

Figure 12.1 is a visual representation of how this happened to the inverted 10-year yield in May of 2019.

Figure 12.1: Yield Curve Inversion: 10 Year Treasuries vs. 3 Month Treasuries

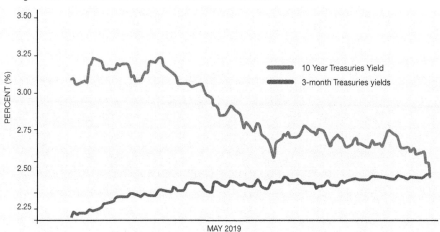

Source: Bloomberg

In May of 2019, the 10-year yield curve inverted, and the Fed wasted no time in reducing interest rates from 2.41 percent in May, to 1.55 percent in December of 2019, and this along with the issues in the repo market were well before the current pandemic, because their data indicated a pending recession, which is a natural outcome of the business cycle that rinses out its distortions. However, in the climate of the current politico, it would be blasphemous if the government didn't tinker with the business cycle.

A recession in the political environment of the last 50 years is intolerable and can mean the difference between losing and winning an election. Government's cures are fiscal stimulus, and the Fed's is monetary stimulus, which in the long run interferes with natural recovery. It is this addiction to easy money that for decades has cascaded into artificial remedies with the result being near permanent structural issues in the economy that are covering more dirt on the underlying decay. The outcomes are insurmountable government debt, higher taxation, centralized power, and inflation, suffocating a true recovery. The effect is that Wall Street and all asset crises depend on easy money to maintain the pricing distortions. Only the natural business cycle can rinse out distortions and inefficiencies out of the market, which seem to be driven by mostly government and its Central Bank monetary heroin dealers.

In summary, we can see now that an economic pullback was on the horizon, even without the help of the pandemic. This is evidenced by the inverted yield, reduction of interest rates since August 2019, and the toxicity of liquidity issues in the repo markets. Concomitantly, the GDP was contracting by 0.77 percent, based on early economic information Fed Chairman Jerome Powell had in 2019.

In an unstable world economic system based on fiat money, there seems to be no political capital for a recession, that if left to its own vices, would rinse the distortions out of the market—instead, what we have is a reinflation of a bubble in all asset classes being mistaken for sound economic policy. It can be best compared to an athlete who breaks their leg before the final game, and they jab a freezing needle to temporarily alleviate the trauma, but in the end, the leg must be allowed to heal naturally.

By the government interfering in the business cycle since Hoover, it has resulted in a 90-year Ponzi scheme with no way out of this house of cards. Admittedly, recessions are a part of the natural business cycle of an economy, and it seems that the weakened collective psyche of a nation cannot fathom some short-term pain for long-term gain. On the contrary, the subjects of the empire like short-term gain for long-term pain, because they are inoculated from understanding the reality of both and can no longer differentiate. It is this cultural conditioning of perceived safety, complements of government, along with Central Banks accomplice that has caused this uncertainty of the false wealth effect through money printing.

The victims are numerous, from the deplorables, because of the hollowing of America's industrial heartland, resulting in an opioid crisis to offset the abandonment of hope; permanent no-go zones in inner cities, where government programs have caused the decay of the American Black family's structure, which was intact and solid regardless of adversity prior to Linden B. Johnson's Great Society, which created multi-generational welfare addiction that destroys the human psyche with no light at the end of the tunnel. We are now seeing intergenerational poverty of a despondent youth, namely Gen Z and Millennials that are dealing with acutely inflated asset prices. All of which is caused by government and its intoxicating cohort, fiat money printing! Much of this is discussed later in the wealth divide.

In 1970 the accumulated U.S. deficit was $371 billion when Nixon was president, by the end of the Carter presidency in 1980, it was $908 billion, when Reagan left office, it went to $2.6 trillion, the first Bush brought it up to $4 trillion in 1992 when he existed the scene. Clinton kept a clean fiscal house where he actually had surpluses, and the deficit only grew at a relatively lower rate to $5.6 trillion by 1999. The second President Bush brought the national debt to $10 trillion by 2008, and when President Obama left office in 2016, the deficit doubled to $20 trillion. President Trump brought it up to $27 trillion, and the current administration is on track to finish their first term at $40 trillion.

During the Obama presidency, money was paid back to the Department of Treasury after the liquidity crises in the capital markets that included bailing out General Motors, Chrysler, and the likes, however the funds were not used to reducing the national deficit, which would be the hallmark of good governance. In fact, the last time government had a balanced budget was under the Clinton administration. In the great recession and onward, money was squandered and not employed in improved infrastructure, increased global skillsets for the tech labour market, national math scores, STEM education, nor the teaching of literature and history.[2]

The current pandemic is perhaps the greatest economic Hail Mary in the last 100 years that, in summary, is taking our eyes off the underlying economic decay that was there all along and is now revealing its Ponzi architecture. The pandemic was only the pin that burst the bubble, and it is the bubble that the Fed has reinflated through exorbitant fiat money printing, obscuring the reality that the current pandemic is being used as a catalyst to propel another disastrous government outcome in its response of the politicisation of science.

The stock market is the collective conscience of the marketplace, and it rarely gets fooled, although its emotional participants do. In early 2020, things happened fast—on January 1st, the markets started precipitously declining because they had already priced in a recession into the value of stocks, after digesting the 10-year inverted yield curve, reduced interest rates and the repo market that the Fed was already providing liquidity for. Even with distorted asset prices, the market found room for price discovery, to see if it could value the markets on reasonably priced assets, built on discounted cash flow financial modelling.

The story of the March 2020 shock of a pandemic includes asset prices, which were driven down by psychological implications. This resulted in substantially exasperating the situation, until a bottom was formed on March 1, 2020—market bottoms can only be accessed as hindsight value—where the Nasdaq dropped 19 percent, the Dow declined 29 percent, the S&P 25 percent, and Bitcoin did a swan dive for 45 percent.

By the second quarter, GDP had dropped 32.9 percent, the worst quarter to quarter dive ever recorded in U.S. history, far exceeding the Great Depression. Unemployment skyrocketed to U3 rates of 14.8 percent, probably much higher when we consider

2   Kimberly Amadeo, U.S. National Debt by Year," The Balance, February 3, 2022, https://www.thebalance.com/national-debt-by-year-compared-to-gdp-and-major-events-3306287; Kimberly Amadeo, U.S. Debt by President: By Dollar and Percentage," The Balance, February 7, 2022, https://www.thebalance.com/us-debt-by-president-by-dollar-and-percent-3306296

the self-employed, consultants, and people taken off the numbers when their UI benefits ran out; the number is closer to 20 percent. Politically, it is tough to get re-elected on these numbers, since the incumbent will be blamed by the media spinsters and assorted talking heads that will together reformat the hard drives of the plebeians with an emotionally plausible new narrative. After all, the financial and political press are rarely held to account, because they are nearly wrong about everything. Hence, in the absence of a mirror to consider the horror of themselves, they desperately seek a villain to point their fingers at. Thus, in a networked society, their brand of nonstop propaganda, which is essentially a "war on truth," will make them as irrelevant as CNN, which saw a 68 percent decline in viewership in 2022 compared to the previous year.[3] Jobless claims usually average about 220,000 per week, and the first week of March 2020, U.S. jobless claims skyrocketed to 5,985,000, and for the year 2020, the new jobless claims totaled 18.9 million, compared to 2019 that totals 2.65 million. These numbers far exceed, in absolute and relative terms, of joblessness during the Great Depression.

In 2021, total jobless claims are averaging 660,000 per month, for a total of 3,305,000 only until the month of May. By February 2022 the claims dropped to nearly 200,000, but this can be misleading, since all the heavy loss of jobs occurred in 2020-21 and many of those have fallen off the unemployment numbers, once unemployment benefits run out.

In desperation, the citizens of Rome vehemently asked for the return of the senators' magicians to inoculate them from the pain of the day, only to create ghastly horrors of future distortions that appeared sooner than their conscious thought. The senators, men of commerce, and the lenses of public obfuscation redressed the beast in angelic attire and sold this ghastly metastasized, re-attired monster to the addicted plebeians, as the soother of pain!

---

3   Mark Joyella, "CNN's Ratings Collapse: Prime Time Down Nearly 70% in Key Demo," Forbes, February 21, 2022, https://www.forbes.com/sites/markjoyella/2022/02/21/cnns-ratings-collapse-prime-time-down-nearly-70-in-key-demo/?sh=4765e7726dda

Eventually, in the distance in the modern moment of America, the helicopters appeared bearing gifts, that first enamoured, then soothed, and then subjected in exchanged with what seemed like wealth dispersed from the heavens.

Inflation Re-enters Our Lexicon

Inflation was a slain beast for almost 30 years, first by Volcker and then China in the way of lower priced goods, only to reappear as the fiat money spilled all throughout the economy. When too much money chases too few goods, we get the inflationary Cantillon effect. So, it just might be a good time to look under the hood to see what is really wrong with the engine that is making knocking sounds.

Government will rig inflation numbers for only so long to claim core inflation is not affected. Products such as household appliances, electronics, ear buds, clothing due to low-cost Asian manufacturing, so far has allowed inflation and monetary policy to remain low. But this is coming to an end for many reasons, consider some of the following aggregates: the first one being that container prices from the Far East to L.A. port was approximately $2,500 to ship are now $21,000—further, labour costs in China have increased significantly, the Canadian and U.S. dollars have weakened against China's RMB, while commodity prices for metals, oil, plastics have gone up past 400 percent, and are all inflating against paper non-backed currency. Some of this is captured in the JOC-ECRI Industrial Price Index, which is up 55 percent year over year while the Producer Price Index (finished goods) at 11.6 percent to year as of October 2021, but it still does not capture the essence of industrial inflation, which will crash land onto the heads of consumers! In 2022, oil is up 47 percent in March, while the PDBC ETF, which contains energy, precious and industrial metals, gasoline, agriculture, related futures contracts and the likes, is up 33 percent, while the RJA ETF, which contains agriculture derivatives, like wheat, soybeans, corn, cattle, soybeans and more, is up 21 percent as of March 2022. To blame this entirely on the Ukrainian crisis is misleading and does not align with facts, as these agricultural commodities were moving up in price prior to the conflict. And to spin a story that the war caused inflation and the consumption of this bald-faced lie makes one wonder as to one's state of mind. Cash is moving into energy and food, which will explode through the roof, as the stock market is under pressure in 2022.

Even corrugated cartons have gone up three-fold and have a three-month lead time since the mills are running behind, and this is causing bottlenecks in producing finished goods. Why? Because Amazon is now replacing Walmart as China's favourite 'go to' customer, leading to a heavy demand for packaging material for its online business, while at the same time, people are staying home and ordering in, which is increasing the demand on takeout boxes. Consequently, much of this helicopter money being disbursed to the consumer is being diverted to China in the way purchasing gadgets, as consumers are sitting home and being sent printed money in exchange for pacification and votes, while they gorge on Netflix and junk food.

Also, there is a shortage of semiconductors that require highly advanced plants with large investments and knowhow that rely on multitudes of components including resin, which is a chemically refined derivative of oil, wafers, Zener diode, and a variety of rare earth elements used in semiconductors and electronics. It is not surprising then that places like Ethiopia, Tanzania, and other parts of Africa are being seduced and ravished with infrastructural gifts by China, Germany, and others. China currently holds the world's largest reserves of rare earth at 44,000 metric tons.

The global chip shortage is due to high demand items such as laptops and printers, and this shortage threatening to do the same to other top-selling devices that include smartphones, as the extra cost of smart phones will be amortized into phone plans for having the privilege of keeping up with the Jones's with the latest iPhone. After all, even the proletarians want to appear bourgeois—all of which have seen demand skyrocket during the pandemic. Acer & Asus are expecting to increase laptop prices in

2021 by 10 percent, while HP has raised personal computer prices by 8 percent, and printer prices by more than 20 percent in one year, according to Bernstein Research,[4] while Dell is under pressure to increase prices, and we are only in Act 1 of inflation. All this is caused by money printing spiking natural demand out of economic equilibrium.

The story of consumer electronics does not end there—companies like Broadcom Inc., which specialise in communications circuits used in iPhones and Samsung Electronics, had to raise prices because of the supply chain. Considering the higher cost of up to 15 percent on silicon wafers used as the architectural foundation of chips, plus resins and associated metals used, result in putting enormous upward price pressure on semiconductors. As people spend more time playing computer games during the pandemic and beyond, a secondary market for Nvidia Corp. graphics cards has emerged, where arbitrage entrepreneurs can sell it for more than the original retail price. According to Supplyframe, Inc., the price of microcontrollers, (a small computer on a single metal-oxide-semiconductor integrated circuit chip) that are used for smart technology such as cars, fridges, as well as a variety of gizmos, is broadly up 12 percent on its 20 best selling microcontrollers.[5]

Household appliance prices have drastically increased, as I found out recently when my five-year-old European stove had to be replaced. Even though I had a warranty, it only covered the original cost, which was $3,000 in 2016, and in 2021 was $6,200. This means I had to pay the difference of $3,200 out of pocket. The moral of the story is if you buy a warranty with full replacement, ensure that you can get a contract for future value with an inflation component built into it.

---

4   Asa Fitch, "Chip Shortages Are Starting to Hit Consumers. Higher Prices Are Likely," Wall Street Journal, June 21, 2021, https://www.wsj.com/articles/chip-shortages-are-starting-to-hit-consumers-higher-prices-are-likely-11624276801
5   Ibid.

When the pandemic first hit in March of 2020, boatloads of cars were parked at the ports and dealerships, as well as domestic manufacturing storage facilities that were overflowing at the brim. Now, auto manufacturers have cut back on production because of the shortage of semiconductor chips that are required to build autos, where supply has dropped with many dealers having skeleton inventory demand. What the automakers have done to offset less sales, is to sell their most profitable higher-end cars to make up for the lost topline revenue, so the markets won't punish their stocks during earnings season. Subsequently, the opening price point for a car in the U.S. is closer to $30,000, and many are selling over MSRP, while two-year-old cars are selling for the same price as new cars in the most sought-after models. Then consider the increase of oil that has driven up car prices, including electric vehicles (EV)—approximately 80 barrels of oil are required to produce an automobile, while four times the amount of copper is required to produce an EV, versus one that runs on fossil fuels.

Just to add to the good news, China and Europe are bidding up the price of energy, especially in the natural gas sector resulting in not only higher prices but shortages. Now Europe that has been egged on by the U.S. into sanctions on Russia, is going to be on the receiving end of some substantial natural gas and oil price increases, which will more than likely lead to gas shortages. And if Europe is forced to pay with a stronger ruble, the inflation will be even more exasperated. Back in China, factories are rationalizing as to which products they can make—energy demand will go up even further when the ports reopen—while many factories are closed, because with no energy they can't produce goods. Of course, this will show up later in the economic numbers, and if we were to believe the U.S. Central Bank that inflation is transitory, comments like this belong in the fictional section of the library beside *Alice in Wonderland*. Later, in 2021, the Fed admitted it was not transitory, and in 2022, inflation is on fire at 8 percent based on the CPI, but effectively closer to 14 percent, according to Shadow Government Statistics.[6]

6   John Williams, "Alternate Inflation Charts," Shadow Government Statistics, accessed May 7, 2022, http://www.shadowstats.com/alternate_data/inflation-charts

All these are a combination of demand pull and cost push in supply chains—the aftereffects of monetary inflation caused by fiat money printing. In essence, commodities as of 2022, are inflating against an eroding U.S. dollar that is recklessly printed.

For people mounting an argument that the USD index has recovered to 98, I do concede this point. However, this is only in relevance to the more battered currencies the USD basket is being compared to such as the Euro, CAD, Yen, and the likes, while the USD is the reserve currency giving it some stamina, even though it is losing clout in light of the Ukrainian conflict, since we might be seeing the sales of commodities in RMB, Rubles, and the Rupee, as other countries are building a parallel monetary system away from the United States. This being said, the reason we are seeing inflation is that fiat money, broadly speaking, is getting battered against commodities, finished products, and wages. To support this, please revisit Chapter 5 on inflation where asset prices such as homes, Bitcoin and the likes show a surge against the USD.

Figure 12.2 is a chart of the U.S. dollar index since 2017, which tells only part of the story as it excludes asset price comparison to fiat money.

Figure 12.2: U.S. Dollar index since 2017

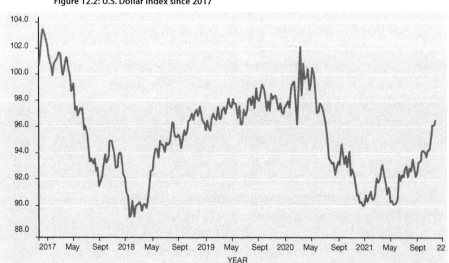

Source: *Trading View*

Helicopter money, a predecessor to Universal Basic Income (UBI), where $2,000 cheques are being dropped off by the government, to encourage more people to stay at home in the United States, and not to be outdone, Canada is no slouch when it comes to welfare and entitlement, was bearing gifts to its subjects by sending CERB cheques where make-believe monopoly money is managed, complements of the Bank of Canada. The end result is, increased product orders on Amazon, which is a catalyst along with Walmart, to help increase the U.S. trade deficit, not to mention that these gadgets could not be cost efficient if made in America. On another note, when people are staying home, they are losing their sense of emotional frame, and offsetting this collective type of psychosis of sorts by spending. As more businesses were starting to reopen in 2021, people got used to staying at home working, and otherwise, leading to an artificial labour shortage leading to cost push wage inflation—in the UK a shortage of truck drivers is leading to containers being delayed from factory doors to port, delaying exports.

The outcome is that with little money velocity, this type of fiscal stimulus is causing labour shortages, and it is no wonder the Fed chairman finally admitted that inflation had gone up to 5 percent in May of 2021—as of April 2022 it has gone up past 8 percent in a year, with no end in sight. The reality is that inflation is closer to 15 percent on things we buy in our everyday lives.

We are experiencing cost push inflation, or demand pull if you will, which does not account for demand being created by monetarism, but when using a Laspeyres index, we see the fix is in because these basic items do not appear in the core inflation numbers or have a very small weight. At this point, economists standing with billowed chests can no longer claim only 8 percent CPI inflation in the economy, since the consumer knows better, because they feel the difference in their pocket when they go grocery shopping, go to restaurants or purchase life's essentials. Hence, deniability of inflation or using erroneous claims of transitory inflation by erred government fiscal and Central Bank monetary policy makers of the obvious is shameful, it erodes credibility in our institutions, leading to wider societal instability.

All this fiat money printing again reinforces the timeless economic intellectuality of Richard Cantillon, where he explained causation of inflation, as *too much money chasing too few goods*, better known as the Cantillon effect in his 1755 book, *Essai sur la Nature du Commerce en Général*—something we are experiencing now.

Canada's Reckoning

Once a currency dives, even core inflation is affected, especially since the country is importing much of its inflation, and regardless of the manipulation by moving individual items out of the core inflation index when they become volatile, the government will have to come clean and admit we have substantial inflation in the economy. In the case of Canada, in order to defend the Canadian dollar, the Bank of Canada would be forced to increase interest rates, put simply, it cannot print money without devaluing the currency, because it does not have reserve currency status. This is exactly what happened with the BOC recently in 2022, when it increased interest rates by 50 basis points.

Now with gold and Bitcoin lurking, both of which are hard individual instruments, as opposed to sovereign state expressions of money as a medium of exchange and a store of value, then it becomes possible that money and state might separate due to an abdication of government fiduciary duty.

Sadly, the outcome of this governmental and Central Bank fiscal and monetary interference is that sadly everyday we are seeing folks that are hard working and very decent people, show up at our food banks where they need help.

A look at the Architecture of Canada's Suffocating Tax Environment

There has been a fair bit of talk about oppressive taxation in this book and it might be a good idea to give a Canadian perspective where people are basking in its Socialist utopia.

In Canada, federal taxes when blended with provincial for those in the $64,000 to $75,000 the tax rate is about 35%. Then one can add about 6% for Employment Insurance contributions and Canada Pension Plan. The abuse doesn't end there, and then one gets soaked for another 13% HST at retail (VAT), Property tax and hidden energy taxes when at the pumps and house energy, and it is fair to say that the takedown is nearer to 57% of income. By government taking the fruitions of one's labor is no different than confiscation of wealth in everyday life. Especially when we consider that, for the most part, these government services could be provided for 25 cents on the dollar from the private sector with an outcome of more efficiency and accountability.

Back to Housing Inflation

Housing prices are skyrocketing and have recently tapered off either for purchase or rent, as the U.S. Fed is purchasing $40 billion per month of mortgage-backed securities from Wall Street brokers. In Canada, the Canada Mortgage Housing Corporation (CMHC) is backstopping over 40 percent of mortgages for banks, while in 2020, the Bank of Canada quietly provided $40 billion of additional liquidity to Canadian banks to backstop any decay in housing prices that would put the banks' portfolios in jeopardy. However, the opposite happened where home prices shot through the roof.

We now have runaway inflation in the Canadian and U.S. housing markets, which is reflected in Toronto as of March 2022, the average price of a home is near $1.3 million, this means if ones own a home, it gives them somewhat a false sense of the wealth effect when compared to fiat money. The victims suffering from wealth inequity are the youth, where economic barriers to entry exist for Gen Z and the Millennials, with intergenerational poverty quite possibly being the outcome. Again, this is caused by money printing and low interest rates, and for government to actually speak about affordable housing is at best intellectual fraud that they themselves created. For our most trusted institutions to lie without impunity is afront to the tenets of democracy, personal liberty, equity and fair play.

Fiat money printing not only creates inflation but causes asset price distortions and always ends in tears. Also, our story does not end there, since higher interest rates on mortgages would drive down overvalued home prices, probably closer to at least 30 percent, rinsing out inflated home prices (this was calculated out in Chapter 5, on the future value of interest savings being built into the current value). This would, of course, lead to price discovery, but at the same time, play havoc on the banks' mortgage portfolios, who will then unload the loss on CMHC, and whoever bought mortgage-backed securities (MBS), landing on the shoulders of government, with the eventual victim being the taxpayer. When governments can no longer print fake monopoly money, the Ponzi scheme will reveal itself in a most tragic way that will make *Friday the 13th* look like a Disney production of *Bambi*! The scenario of the home market as it relates to expanding the money supply can be compared to the *Monopoly* board game, where traditionally $1,500 was given out as a starting point. Then if you decided to start the game with $4,000, you would see more reckless spending, and participants willing to offer money above the stated price of Illinois Avenue or the Boardwalk.

There are alternatives though, with a company called Home Partners, who were bought out in 2021 by Blackstone Group for $6 billion. Home Partners, which owns more than 17,000 houses, many that it bought during the 2008 meltdown, has a portfolio of homes that it rents out and offers its tenants the option to eventually buy them. True, it is a more complicated and expensive proposition, but at least it helps people become homeowners.

Whatever realtors tell you about supply and demand driving prices, the element conveniently excludes the easy money component that has created a venue for speculators, Wall Street banks buying housing developments, money launders and greedy bloated local governments that levy ridiculous fees on developers and builders, which in essence, is an inflation tax. In fact, every new lot being developed in the Toronto area, there is near $250,000 in land development costs, and this is before the foundation is poured. And you don't think government is the culprit?

When we assemble the components and connect the dots of housing inflation, it is due to easy money that is being orchestrated by government, causing much inequity. Sadly, the irony is that government has the audacity to say that we need affordable housing, when in fact, they have caused unaffordable housing. But big lies when repeated enough pass off as truth!

The housing inequity squarely sits on the mountain of government failures, because if interest rates returned to mean reversion, house asset prices would not be distorted, taking a powerful step towards more equitable wealth distribution. This is assuming that those who want homes have the required discipline, knowledge, emotion and accountability for their actions to attain and keep assets like homes. In acquiring assets, as in life, there are tradables.

But now it might be a good time to look under the hood of America, to analyze another engine that runs only on high-octane fuel.

Wall Street and The Fed Reinflate the Bubble

Near 0 percent interest rates make for a dramatic backdrop of absurd valuations within certain sectors of the stock market, as stories are weaved to make the worthless seem like wealth. There are problems that come to mind, one is that Wall Street analysts are not digging deep in the books and looking at comparative investment of a firm in R&D, upgrading of technologies and plants, or disassembling the strategic architecture of the firm. If the analysts did their homework, companies like Intel would be punished for inefficient deployment of capital resources by share buybacks, at the expense of antiquated factories, and loss of R&D to pump up current P&Ls.

But like a great magician or comedian, the repertoire that Wall Street's act keeps changing to keep the seals clapping, in appreciation for its latest theatrical performance with its producer, the Fed.

The dealers are talking up their trading books, and the story lines are being bought up like a hopeless romantic.

And its latest histrionic performance is somewhat of a repeat performance, but with some new salivating twists and turns that should be watched with Rolaids in hand. It seems that Wall Street's carnival is more interested in *Pump & Dump* schemes, where profitability at the expense of the future is not considered in the current climate.

But they are willing to value companies like Uber, dressing it up as a technology company, which is not exactly AI, while ignoring the fact that they have never made an operating profit, but with a market cap of $94 billion.

Or consider the case of WeWork, which is a company that provides small offices it rents in large quantities, and then subdivides into smaller areas for shared spaces for budding entrepreneurs. Their website also has an area that gives entrepreneurs advice on success, without thinking that perhaps they need it most themselves on how to run a profitable organization, as opposed to the checkered past of its founder Adam Neumann and his personal chefs, parasitically running off the avails of Japan's Softbank Investments, before he was given the boot with a $1.7 billion severance package, even though it was bleeding in the billions; that must have been negotiated by Trump's *Art of the Deal*!

Now WeWork is owned by a SPAC (Special Purpose Acquisition Company) that acts as a veil to hide the toxicity of what it owns, since the companies within its umbrella would never pass with the SEC—hence it allows the SPAC vehicle to raise more capital to keep this questionable act going. This strategy is similar to the 2008 collateralized debt obligations that had toxic assets buried in the deep dark basement where the SPACs burry the DNA within the SPAC. The bottom line is that they have repainted this old school donkey business model that lost $2 billion in the first quarter of 2021, and in excess of $10 billion accumulatively as a technology play, and even under the influence, it is a tough to buy the story. To add to the audacity of this WeWork, the zombie company went public in October of 2021, and has recorded losses in the same year of $4.4 billion—simply put, allowing a company with such decimated financials is patently an SEC fraud, as Wall Street banks J. P. Morgan Chase and Goldman Sachs were the main underwriters. As of March 2022, those who entered WeWork house of fools have lost near 50 percent since their October 2021 IPO. But Wall Street has an accomplished symphony that can play tunes that is skilled at seducing greed.

Wall Street is magical at spinning a story on companies like WeWork, but when you undress its strategic architecture, in essence, they are re-renting office space they do not even own, and in the case of Uber, another unprofitable company that lost $500 million in year ending 2021, that are acting as low technology surrogates for people wanting to drive and pick up some extra cash.

With Broadway shows closed during the pandemic, Wall Street has more than made up for the slack and ensured the patrons of theatre were not deprived, with its timeless masterpiece that is leaving New York and London's theatre district in envy with their timeless production *Pump & Dump*, along with its supporting cast led by the Fed, who supply the romanticised serenading *sound of printing presses* in the backdrop.

University of Florida professor Jay Ritter mentioned in a Bloomberg podcast that "80 percent of the companies that went public this year were unprofitable in the 12 months prior to the IPO."[7] It is not surprising that IPOs have never found a bubble they never liked, and with the theatrical Kool-Aid being served, it is standing room only, as magicians of Wall Street, including investment banks such as J.P. Morgan, Bank of America, Goldman Sachs, Deutsche Bank, and the rest of the supporting cast, help create the most epic event since the Beatles played Shea Stadium in 1964. And much like the concert, the overbearing screaming obscures the music in order for the matador to deflect the bull and manoeuvre his cape.

Take the case of DoorDash, the food delivery service that was launched in December 2020. With a first quarter loss of $110 million,

7   "80 Percent of Companies with IPOs in 2020 Are Not Profitable," The Tape, podcast, Bloomberg, hosted by Paul Sweeney and Vonnie Quinn, December 14, 2020, https://www.bloomberg.com/news/audio/2020-12-14/80-of-companies-with-ipos-in-2020-are-not-profitable-radio

and a loss of $466 million for the year, or $0.34 cents per share, and a market cap in June 2021 of $57 billion, and being down 50% in 2022, it is no wonder investors are well…. dashing for the door! Compare this to Domino's Pizza that showed profits or $487 million in 2020, with a market cap of $17 billion, and brand loyalty placing them at number 20 in the United States. It makes one wonder why someone became a CFA!

So again, is DoorDash a technology company or a delivery company, or the future? How do they come up with a market cap of $57 billion? Is it their brand name? No, because they don't even make the top 100 most valued brands on Interbrand list. Should unprofitable companies be allowed to go IPO? Well, that's not a problem according to Goldman Sachs and J.P. Morgan, who acted as lead book-running managers for the offering at $102 per share that flew 86 percent higher on the first day. Did Joe six-pack have an opportunity to get in at $102 per share like insiders did?

Is this giving capitalism a bad name? Are these the tenets of fair play that the British established in commerce? Should executives be working for pauper wages until the company becomes profitable? Without fiat money printing being washed into Wall Street by the investment banks, would these shenanigans being passed off as an IPO be tolerated?

Consider the case of Airbnb, which was founded in 2008 and has never been profitable, as a privately held company that went public in December 2020 with an IPO of $68 per share, loss of $4.4 billion, and as of April 2022, has been awarded a market cap of $110 billion. Compare this to Marriott Hotels that owns hard assets like real estate with a market cap of $45 billion, or Expedia Group that has a value of $25 billion, both of whom have a history of profitability, and in the case of Expedia, they can easily take a big chunk out of Airbnb's lunch money.

There are many examples of this and it seems that we are now in the stock market culture that is tolerating these types of absurd valuations with a straight face, in the hope of finding a greater fool to buy these much-overvalued companies. The more we look at these equity prices, the more it seems like we are having a renaissance from the year 2000 of the dot-com bubble—with similar euphoria and valuations, along with outstanding cash burn rates; perhaps it might be time for a whole new generation to wake up to a hangover, since foolishness gives us a more respect for history. Should a company establish profitability before going IPO? And, in fact, it seems like the cold hard reality has hit the IPO market as of January 2022 where, according to Wolf Street, some of the most hyped stocks are trading at up to 90 percent off their highs, and in the case of Moderna they have never brought out a successful vaccine with high-sustained efficacy. Here is a sample of IPO losses as of January 2022:[8]

- Moderna [MRNA]:   -62%
- Snowflake [SNOW]:   -29%
- Uber [UBER]:   -40%
- Cloudflare [NET]:   -57%
- Zoom Video [ZM]:   -73%
- CrowdStrike [CRWD]:   -42%
- Datadog [DDOG]:   -34%
- Coinbase [COIN]:   -48%
- Palantir [PLTR]:   -66%
- BioNTech [BNTX]:   -63%

The lower pricing in all these overhyped stocks is reflected in Cathy Woods ARK innovation fund that was the darling of 2020 with a spectacular gain of 267 percent, which has since done a swan dive as of May 2022 and lost 75 percent of its value. If one is interested in such things they should go on Yahoo Finance, pull up the ETF stock and look up holdings.

8   Wolf Richter, "Russell 2000 Drops Below Year Ago Level. Collapse of IPOs, SPACs, Housing 'Tech' Stocks, ARKK, etc. Progresses," Wolf Street, January 18, 2022, https://wolfstreet.com/2022/01/18/russell-2000-drops-below-year-ago-level-collapse-of-ipos-spacs-housing-tech-stocks-arkk-etc-progresses/

SPACs, the most hyped darlings in 2020-2021, have lost their luster. Hyped by celebrities, since we all know that they are authorities on financial valuations on assets, and if we listen to them, we no longer have to read the *Wall Street Journal* and the likes. Wolf Richter states the following:

> *These Special Purpose Acquisition Companies raised tons of money, often involving celebrities that hyped this crap in the social media so that the dumbest retail investors would swallow it hook, line, and sinker. After the SPAC started trading publicly, they bought start-ups at huge valuations. The merger caused the start-up to be the publicly traded company. Insiders made a killing in this process no matter what happened.*[9]

The idea of having your company acquired by SPACs is that you can avert SEC discloser that IPOs are subjected to, and then the SPAC will sell off these overhyped ugly ducklings to unsuspecting retail investors who think they are buying into the cosmos and the next great hope. SPACs are similar to the debacle of Mortgage-backed securities (MBS) from the Great Recession as you have to look hard to dissect the toxicity of the obscured holdings. Not to be outdone, hyped EV companies are now joining the implosion of ruin, many without revenues, they include:[10]

9   Wolf Richter, "The Collapse of the EV SPACs: Retail Investors Got Fleeced Swiftly and Spectacularly," Wolf Street, February 21, 2022, https://wolfstreet.com/2022/02/12/the-collapse-of-the-ev-spacs-retail-investors-got-fleeced-swiftly-and-spectacularly/
10   Wolf Richter, "Russell 2000 Drops Below Year Ago Level. Collapse of IPOs, SPACs, Housing 'Tech' Stocks, ARKK, etc. Progresses," Wolf Street, January 18, 2022, https://wolfstreet.com/2022/01/18/russell-2000-drops-below-year-ago-level-collapse-of-ipos-spacs-housing-tech-stocks-arkk-etc-progresses/

Table 12.1: Spac and IPO Implosions

EV SPACs & IPOs	Symbol	Price $	% from peak	Date of peak
Nikola	[NKLA]	7.79	-90.30%	09-Jun-20
Lordstown	[RIDE]	3.04	-90.40%	11-Feb-21
Romeo Power	[RMO]	2.06	-93.90%	24-Dec-20
Workhorse	[WKHS]	3.23	-92.50%	04-Feb-21
Quantum	[QS]	15.87	-88.00%	22-Dec-20
Faraday Future	[FFIE]	4.59	-77.90%	01-Feb-21
Canoo	[GOEV]	5.85	-73.90%	07-Dec-20
Rivian	[RIVN]	58.85	-67.20%	16-Nov-21
Lucid Motors	[LCID]	25.84	-60.20%	18-Feb-21

Source: Wolfstreet.com

A complete book could be written on this subject of so many companies in the storied market folklore that were pumped up and eventually dumped to the greater fool, with valuations that belong in the fictional section of the library besides *Alice in Wonderland* and *Harry Potter*! And eventually, the haunting ghost of Adam Smith will show up to put an end to these shenanigans, but not until many meagre spectators posing as gladiators are blood stained.

These are the outcomes of easy money as the bubble continues until alcohol inspired nights eventually come to an end and meet sobriety after investors run out of money. It is then that the bouncer unceremoniously throws the bankrupt patrons through the glass door as they land on the boulevard of broken dreams.

The rationalisation of the irrational is starting to look a like the year 2000 dot-com meltdown, only with different actors, but selling the same old wine in a new bottle.

Band-Aids Vs. Cures

To think that somehow the 2008 recession and its non-effective Keynesian remedies have been reckoned with is at best delusionary, because the same issues still plague us with no cure in sight and the list is long, including GDP growth at a sluggish 2 percent and distorted asset prices via addictive monetary policy that has reinflated the asset bubble. With 52 percent stock participation rate, it creates a wealth effect for the majority, especially if they were invested in technology stocks, but an inequity for the rest that is, and not the fault of the market. Therefore, it is imperative that people make sacrifices in terms of trade-off to current wants in order to participate in the equity market, regardless how small their monthly investment may be (assuming they don't buy right before the bubble bursts). As of early 2022, the tech flavour has waned, and it might be a good time to consider energies and food. With all this easy money in the backdrop, there is more to consider, specifically the unsustainable national debt approaching $33 trillion by the end of 2022, which exceeds America's GDP by near 40 percent. International Central Banks, most notably in North America and Europe, are desperately trying to sustain through money printing unsustainable bloated governments that have created unsustainable programs, on the backs of tomorrow for today.

The effect of this money printing and its first cousin, debt, will have devastating consequences. These are discussed further in Chapter 15.

At the time of this writing, the mainstream media and the Fed Chairman Powell have us believing that the current pandemic is the only cause of the initial stock crash of March 2020, that has since set all-time highs for the S&P, Dow, and Nasdaq. I propose that Covid-19 provided an ample deflection of the true agenda, and that is the Fed's money printing, the buying of hard assets at low interest rates by the Fed vis-à-vis through Wall Street banks, and then inflating the wealth effect to the upper stratum of society. Inflation accomplishes this, since high-net-worth individuals see hard asset prices go through the stratosphere, such as real estate, collectibles, equities and the likes. Sadly, we have not learned the lessons of 2008. So, it is here that I concur with Peter Schiff that the virus was the needle that burst the bubble, and that, for now, the Fed has successfully reinflated asset prices—that is until it seems like it is bursting again at the mere mention of increasing interest rates—for at least 65 percent of the population that might have either stocks and/or homes. The Fed's dual mandate is to promote stable pricing and employment, not to inflate the stock market to the point that equities have no price discovery, and it makes one wonder again, what is the point of being a CFA when price discovery is being abdicated based on quant measurements.

To consider this assertion in more detail, we need to look deeply at monetary policy, where between 2008 and 2015 the Fed rate has been near zero, and it was not until February of 2016 that interest rates started heading up, and by July of 2019 rates reached 2.47 percent. The relatively higher—stressing the word relative—interest rates then allowed the Fed to put back in their toolbox interest rate reduction. Since then, it went as low as 0.08 percent in 2020 and late 2021, where the Central Bank in March 2022 increased rates by 25 and then another 50 basis points, which is nothing more than window dressing in their denial of the inflationary Frankenstein's monster they and government created, and it looks like the 10-year yield is baking in some more rate hikes in 2022. Today there is very little separation between the Central Bank and the U.S. Treasury, since their actions are complicit.

Although the markets did not like their sweetener taken away, in 2019 the opposite line of thinking was that the economy was on the cusp of coming off life-support from 2008, while the markets could come to terms that the stock market could grow and stand on its own without extreme monetary accommodation. In other words, higher interest rates were sending a message of confidence in the economy.

Subsequently, the Fed was rebuilding its toolbox, while inadvertently signaling that the U.S. Treasury could no longer borrow at such low rates, while it had something to utilize in the case of its next recession and bubble, both of which were in concert with the Treasury. What is concerning about low monetary policy is that if the economy were truly healthy, it could easily sustain a 6 to 7 percent natural mean reversion interest rate environment. This would ensure that governments would not have the ability to run deficits, especially with the tapering of quantitative easing. The equilibrium outcome of normalized interest rates is less money made available for government, preventing them from bribing voters with money borrowed in their name, and putting a wrench in their follow-up act, which is even more oppressive taxation. Hence, the rug would be pulled away from government since it is easy money and oppressive taxation that is the essential lubricant for the wasteful wheels of government.

Normalized interest rate would recalibrate asset prices back into equilibrium, specifically in equities and home prices, as demonstrated in the Canadian area where I unmasked the true value of homes when we compared mortgages rates from 2 percent versus 6 percent, with the net savings of interest being baked into the current price of the home. Concomitantly, we would then see firms spend their capital resources more prudently, as opposed to manipulating shares through share buybacks, so the C-suite executives make their bonuses, which used to be and should be illegal again, while consumers would not be saddled with personal household debt of $15,058 trillion in 2021, according to the New York Fed. In essence, we are printing money to buy things we do not produce, and spending on imports that we simply can't afford to make in the West, and this is the GDP growth trap we are in. Hence, to grow GDP numbers we are in the state of relying on house price appreciation, especially in Canada, and this is not a sustainable strategy. The other issue is that if a country does not produce and mostly imports, how can it tame inflation through domestic producer efficiencies? Hence, it is at the mercy of foreign producers' efficiencies or lack thereof!

Higher interest rates would signal to the market that the economy could sustain 6 to 7 percent interest rates, which would foster long-term confidence in the markets, and more fairly priced equities, the responsible management of the U.S. dollar, while at the same time, Wall Street, Hong Kong, and Fleet Street would stop acting like easy money junkies, and more fairly price equities, and of course keep government in check, which is the most essential tenet in a free society, as oppression historically is government's most consistent outcome. It would follow then that younger people, Gen Z and the Millennials would be able to participate in home and equity ownership, due to prices that are valued fairly.

But the moment for this is emersed in nostalgic romanticism and its time has perhaps passed, since they might have to wait until the train stops at a station named sobriety. Because the Fed's response has been to reinflate the asset bubble that they and the Treasury caused and create a false wealth effect that makes 65 percent of the population with homes feel wealthy when compared to inflationary fiat money.

In another place called "A Town Without Pity" where the other 35 percent of villagers are kept, the sun never shines. It is here when they live in docility and in an emotional cloud when they receive their helicopter money, to soothe their primal needs. Each day they digest their prepared news, order an à-la-carte of daily Netflix, and gorge on an orgy of social media to sedate their sense away from the chance of finding hope. Occasionally when the villagers attempt to find truth, they are nulled back into sedation with another injection of self-flagellating entitlements, as they cannot fathom facing the horror of what lays on the horizon. As they come out of their homes, they shiver in visceral fear—their eyes are swollen with tears at the sight of the once revered middle-class that now lays mortally wounded in a pool of blood, with no superhero to save it!

Keep Printing and Buy It All

Through its asset purchasing program, much of it toxic, the Fed has ballooned its balance sheets from a manageable under $1 trillion in 2007, to $3.8 trillion in 2019, and to $7.6 trillion by of 2020. By the end of 2022, the Fed's balance sheets can easily reach $10 trillion. This is unheard of growth in a Central Bank balance sheet. The other question that is not being asked by the MSM is this: how could the Fed have bought such toxic assets, namely un-repayable U.S. Treasuries, propped up shares of publicly traded companies, commercial paper, and junk bonds? Then this begs the question: how sound are the assets on the Fed's balance sheets? The bigger question then becomes, as Jerome Powell jawbones about quantitative tightening in 2022, who in the private markets would buy these toxic assets?

They have gone on a buying spree, buying toxic assets, including propping up overseas banks through the repo market, purchasing municipal bonds (munis) that are junk status, buying U.S. Treasuries to finance the national debt, which in essence, is propping up the insolvent U.S. Treasury since 2008.

Then this begs another question! Are we at the cusp of modern monetary theory where we can print fiat money into infinity?

Modern Monetary Theory Explained

Modern Monetary Theory (MMT) is the concept of governments—especially if it's the reserve currency of the world—printing money and piles of debt, thus, when the old debt comes due, they just print more money to pay for the old debt, and at zero percent interest rates the Kool-Aid is so sensuous and seductive. And as long as technology reduces the cost of tomorrow with no core inflation in sight, we can keep interest rates low, we can act like Japan and print money, bribe voters and political parties infinitely until a non-transparent demagoguery is indoctrinated. This all works fine, that is of course, until inflation forces higher interest rates, which will be like putting a wrecking ball into this house of cards. Bill Mitchell, professor of economics at University of Newcastle, invented the idea of MMT in the 1990s, and as Thomas Sowell once commented, academics, especially economists, are not held to account for their failed ideas, which is almost always.[11] For those who believe in MMT, we can discuss monopoly money, the acquisition of boardwalk and the possibility that Elvis and Michael Jackson are still alive, and the end of economic price discovery. MMT is best left for academics to spoon-feed willing wide-eyed university students

11   Thomas Sowell, "Thomas Sowell Brings the World into Focus through an Economics Lens," Hoover Institution, YouTube video, December 19, 2014, https://www.youtube.com/watch?v=cdBn7MUM3Yo

looking for their next ideological fix. The bottom line is that all this money printing is causing hyperinflation not seen since the 1980s, with no end in sight.

In many respects, we are flirting with MMT in the Biden administration, where it seems few have watched the count on *Sesame Street* to get a basic grip on grade two level arithmetic.

All barbs aside, there are numerous problems with this house of cards called MMT, namely its fiscal policy is not necessarily monetary, it will also create currency inflation, and if the economy slows to a halt with a combinational bout of stagflation and inflation for good measure, or deflation, or a combination of all of the above, in the end, we might all be running around with worthless paper, which is becoming more realizable. The Fed would have nothing left in its toolkit except jawing the market, which was done during the Plaza Accord in 1985, to prop up the U.S. dollar. At the same time, if endless money printing policy required for MMT and UBI is such a great idea, why not abolish taxation? This way government could print money for their litany of failed programs, as it would create perpetual prosperity despite government, and is a splendid mechanism to ensure governments do not grow at the expense of the contractionary outcome of taxation. We can even have UBI as a supplement to welfare, to encourage people to stay home and produce even more mediocre results, as evidenced by the 2021 labour shortage.

UBI, in the way of free money to entice people, will be welcomed when free money is deposited into their digital wallets. It will first start out as the pretext for wealth redistribution, leading to a Central Bank digital currency tied to their passport, then vaccine card, their behaviour on social media, then social credit scores, even more oppressive taxation with digital trails, centrally planned purchasing criteria, and the freezing of their digital money if behavior is bad (case in point, people who donated to the truckers in Canada). In other words, society will live in a digital totalitarianism where personal compliancy will be the collective virtue for the plebeians and throw individual freedom under the bus.

To be fair to Hoover and FDR, they have to be given credit for exchanging money for public works that were built, like the

Hoover Dam and the likes, which were good for not only the efficiency of the country, but the lifting of the human psychological condition.

The Fed, by way of the Treasury and Congress, has been dropping helicopter money, a term first coined by Milton Friedman in 1969. Starting in 2021, there is a severe labour shortage in the United States that has caused substantial labour inflation, brought about by government. Why the shortage then? Because under the $2.2 trillion CARES Act, which included four-month federal boost to unemployment insurance (UI) benefits, adding $600 a week on top of whatever amount state programs already paid. Consider the following: in a typical state, where unemployment benefits often pay around $275 per week, that meant furloughed and unemployed workers could collect nearly $900 a week. In a state like California, which offers as much as $450 per week, and then combined with Fed programs, was potentially worth more than $1,000 of income for seven days of not working.

Details of the CARES Act, which stands for The Coronavirus Aid, Relief, and Economic Security, can be found at the U.S. Treasury department website. It is always interesting to note the communicatively soft language used in these highly propagandized acronyms. In essence, this is another example of government making a manageable situation into an unmitigated disaster, and in many respects, it resembles the oppressor acting as the therapist.

In addition to this, the Paycheck Protection Program (PPP) established by the CARES Act, is implemented by the Small Business Administration with support from the Treasury, which subsidized a portion of wages to keep people employed, even though firms were having their topline sales number decimated. There were naturally problems with PPP, namely that it suffered terrible implementation issues, such as unanswered applications and undisclosed caps. And in 2020, under Trump's $1.3 trillion package, it included sending $1,000 cheques to American households, which should have won him the election.

Clearly, the expanded benefits create unintended consequences like wage inflation, labour shortages, higher manufacturing costs, and increased home building costs that are being passed on, leading to several distortions in the labour market with serious macroeconomic consequences on inflation and productivity. All of which is showing up in prices in the real economy. It seems the ghost of Franklin Delano Roosevelt, along with his failed industrial recovery act lives within the halls of Washington, as the elated theatre goers give today's leaders a thunderous standing ovation for another encore called failure.

This brings a part of a long line of psychologically damaging programs that diminish one's sense of self. Then the question begs itself: how many people working want to help finance and help the government engineer a permanent underclass? Further, we have had a great test-drive with free government handouts since FDR and LBJ, especially with tragic outcomes and direct result of the Johnson's 1965 Great Society initiative. After all, in the great society, they just followed the model of Rome, of government needing a good diet of propaganda, and a monopoly on what is passed off as education to reformat the hard drives of another unsuspecting generation. Then what makes us think that UBI will not further exacerbate a toxic situation? What is the cost-benefit ratio of government attempting to manage the labour market and business cycle when it cannot even manage its own finances? Is our societal phobia of recessions (which are part of the business cycle) preventing the cleansing out of distortions, so new seeds that cannot sprout is creating a permanent underlying weak economy built on a house of cards? Is it industrious to create a society built on the lethargy of idleness? Is teaching a man how to fish blasphemous?

Regardless of what some of the young and impressionable think, there will be no safe space when the Ponzi scheme crumbles, because the government will not be in any position to assist them. While their intolerant professors who spent a career reformatting young impressionable minds through indoctrination, as opposed to critical and reasoned thinking, will be looking for gainful employment. Yes, these same professors, many of whom have not matured into adulthood themselves and live in an academia bubble, know full well that their thinly educated prodigies have weak career prospects. Accordingly, quite possibly, the youth's perceived victimhood and lack of career prospects was delivered at the hands of their professors.

When all is said in done, after four years of college, the primary accomplishment of education should be more than to recite Saul Alinsky's *Rules for Radicals*.

But all jabs aside, to condition people to stay at home as a way of life is an abuse on the human psyche's sense of who they are, while it destroys their self worth. And the social engineers who promote such avoidable human tragedy are a disgrace, as they wave their virtuous wands and sit in their castles far away from the fallout of ground zero. Safe societies crumble under the weight of their own weakness, and lack of confidence—great civilizations are built by people who are bold and know that risk builds accomplishments. We are meant to be industrious; it is a key manifest destiny of the human psyche.

The caveat emptor with monetary policy that calls for indefinite money printing is that it will cause a mass run on the U.S. dollar, putting an end to the concept of fiat money as we know it. Because fiat money can be printed without the creation of economic value, it remains unaccountable to fiscal truth in representing significance, as it would be limitless because of no hard backing, unlike gold or Bitcoin. Once upon a time, manufacturing and its first cousin inventiveness created the foundations of monetarism, and a nation's underlying wealth, which Adam Smith discussed.

Another way to create wealth though, is to inflate the stock market, which brings us to asset purchases and reinflating the stock market.

Asset Purchases and Reinflating the Stock Market

In February 2020, the Nasdaq dropped from an all-time peak to date of 9,732 points, to a low 6,879 in late March 2020, constituting a nearly 37 percent drop. Looking at the Dow, which still contains many industrial relics of American industry, including Exxon,

McDonald's and Coca-Cola, which incidentally was once the most valued brand in the world, we saw a precipitous drop from a peak of 29,432 on February 13, 2020, to a low of 18,600 on March 23rd, constituting a 37 percent drop in value.

As a side note, in May 2022 with the Fed taking its foot off the gas pedal, we are seeing a replay of a collapsing stock market that is spreading to the housing market as everyone is heading for the fire exits. Eventually, Wall Street will be calling for more Fed accommodative policy to save the markets.

Central Banks have made unheard of accommodative monetary policy that reinflated the Nasdaq north of 15,000 in 2021, where it has slipped to as low as 6,900 in March of 2022, and the Dow flirting with 35,000 as of June 2021. As of May 2022, the S&P is near Bear territory and the Nasdaq is off 37% from its high. Soon the markets will call the Fed for another monetary fix to reinflate the makers. The question becomes, is it true the Fed is now buying equities (stocks) directly to support the bubble with a trading desk, which is outside of their mandate?

Simply put, the recovery of the equity market did not happen because the underlying economy is recovering, with effective unemployment closer to 30 percent in 2020, which has since recovered in 2021, depending on who fell off the employment number, but in 2021 and 2022 there is a shortage of labour, especially in skilled areas. Still, in 2022 stock price fundamentals are not in line with discounted cashflows or enterprise value models—on the contrary, in 2020, the Fed created the formation of a slush fund for over $4 trillion, and why not, when all they had to do was turn on the printing presses and create pseudo wealth out of thin air. It was this announcement alone that helped reinflate the stock market and gave Wall Street a more warm and fuzzy feeling, while people on Main Street, especially those people who don't hold equities or homes, are having their wealth destroyed by effective inflation.

Subsequently, stocks rebounded because the Fed, through various asset classes, was on a buying spree, and the resulting increase in share prices is not based on any credible valuation methods, but on price manipulation of equities. Hence, someone taking their Certified Financial Analyst (CFA) classes must be scratching their heads when it becomes apparent that the fix is in, and discounted cashflow models have little bearing on equity prices. What we have here is the architecture of a bubble, and more than likely, it will not end well.

It might be a good time to consider in detail as to what the Fed is specifically doing. As mentioned earlier, the Fed is buying U.S. Treasury bills, municipal bonds, and other related government securities that otherwise could not be floated in an open market, since they are overbought or what might be unsound positions in the long run, as time will tell. With no Fed, these securities would have near junk status, and for the most part unsalable, since the market for them would lack liquidity. But then they started venturing into completely unchartered territories, such as providing loans directly or in combination with the Department of Treasury, or guaranteeing buying debt via junk bonds and commercial paper from companies who had created unsound positions. All these loans were substantially at a lower rate than market rates. They even mentioned that they have intentions to buy securities such as ETFs backed by credit card debt, student loans, auto loans and commercial real estate loans, guaranteeing the money market industry, which is worth over $1 trillion. And just to capstone it, the Fed was making direct loans to midsize and large businesses. This is the classical moral hazard, for, after all, the Fed has sedated the citizens of Rome with a mirage of entitlements, masking their true agenda of bailing out unsound positions reveals itself as cronyism. In the long run, the Feds could end up owning a huge chunk of the stock market, much like Japan, where price discovery could go the way of Michael Jackson's moonwalk!

Simply put, without the Fed participating in the equity markets, either through asset purchases or easy money, stocks would come down at least 30 percent almost overnight, as we are starting to see in 2022, and this is a conservative guess.

Bailouts and Share Buybacks

Since the beginning of 2012, the S&P 500 companies have bought back nearly $5 trillion of their own shares. Share buybacks lower the share count, and so earnings are divided by fewer shares to produce higher earnings per share (EPS) and thereby hopefully, a higher share price, without actually having to sell more or earn more.

Starting in 2020, the Fed has taken the unprecedented step of purchasing corporate bonds, shares, and some of the companies. Many of these firms listed decided to deploy capital for share buybacks, and now have their hands out to the Fed:

Procter & Gamble, the company that invented the consumer-packaged goods industry, which is now a slow-moving bloated relic, which is a reminder of when in 1979 Detroit, the big three automakers were lent $5.6 billion through corporate bond purchases.

The theatrical play even becomes more amusing when considering **Oracle**, which bought back $75 billion worth of stocks between 2016 to 2019 to pump its shares, including a bond issuance to buy back shares, resulting in depleted cash reserves on its balance sheets, and the Central Bank rewarded this reckless behaviour by purchasing $20 billion in bonds.

Carnival Cruise Lines was bailed out for $6.25 billion, while it might be sounder to let the cruise line perish or let it be taken over by a new company or entrepreneurs with clean non-debt-ridden balance sheets. When all is said and done, the ships will still be there, and the trained staff who are up the learning curve can be brought back when the dust settles.

Coca-Cola, a shamelessly woke virtue signaler, grabbed $6.5 billion after it bought back 150 million shares at over $200 per share in 2019. Its product includes nine teaspoons of sugar per can, which promotes diabetes, obesity, is highly addictive, and drives down math and academic scores especially in African American and Hispanic communities (hard to focus on a sugar fix), where pop consumption is the highest. In fact, Coca-Cola and Pepsi made concerted marketing effort after World War II to market to the African American community.[12]

How does one deal with **Boeing**, which the Fed helped directly with a $25 billion lifeline? Some will say they are being rewarded for bad behaviour and others will argue that it is a strategic industry that constitutes America's competitive architecture, assuming they can build planes that stay in the sky.

GM, of course, came back for an encore performance from 2008 and picked up $4 billion for its 2020 efforts.

Berkshire Hathaway even grabbed some Fed money with front row seats to the Central Bank purchasing frenzy, it even gets better, where in 2020, the Fed spent $5.7 million on debt in Berkshire Hathaway Energy, a subsidiary of Buffett's conglomerate.

"U.S. semiconductor manufacturing has declined to where it is now only 12 percent of the world's total," said Intel Corp's new CEO Pat Gelsinger in an interview with CBS on *60 Minutes*.[13] However, **Intel** has bought $84.5 billion of share buybacks since 2011 to juice their stocks, as opposed to investing in creating the best plants in the world. Subsequently, AMD chips are now more advanced than Intel's, while Taiwan Semiconductor has become the contract manufacturer of chips to the world. Simply put, instead of investing in plants, they invested in stock manipulation through share buybacks. Not to be outdone, the Intel's lobby group went into full

12   Marion Nestle, "When Soda Companies Target Minorities, is it Exploitation?" the Washington Post, October 10, 2015, https://www.washingtonpost.com/lifestyle/food/when-soda-companies-target-minorities-is-it-exploitation/2015/10/10/28df5870-6c63-11e5-aa5b-f78a98956699_story.html
13   Leslie Stahl, "Chip Shortage Highlights U.S. Dependence on Fragile Supply Chain," 60 Minutes, May 2, 2021, https://www.cbsnews.com/news/semiconductor-chip-shortage-60-minutes-2021-05-02/

swing and received a nice chunk, when the White House unveiled $50 billion in subsidies for semiconductor makers in the U.S., to address the shortages and U.S. exposure to foreign chip makers, as part of its $2 trillion infrastructure plan.

The success of Intel's lobbying became clear when subsidies for the semiconductor industry had bipartisan support in Congress, since corporate subsidies have nearly always bipartisan support. Subsequently, Intel had announced plans in March 2021 to invest $20 billion in chip-making plants in Arizona, and upon the news, the shares fell 1 percent. "Intel currently does not have the kno-whow to manufacture the most advanced chips that Apple and the others need," CEO Gelsinger stated.

Even ETFs got into the act, where $6.8 billion worth of corporate debt ETFs were also bought by the Fed, with the Central Bank pouring $1.8 billion into a single ETF alone.

The airlines are another example of abdication of capital deployment, where they spent billions on share buybacks to drive their shares up, which will ensure their C-suite executives would receive bonuses based on appreciation of shares, which is clearly stipulated in their employment contracts. Stakeholders who saw their airline shares go up before the 2020 crash, including Berkshire Hathaway, simply turned a blind eye to share buybacks, as the stock market was playing its tune. Eventually, Berkshire Hathaway sold their positions in the airlines only to see it go up again after the bailouts. In the last few years, American Airlines had buybacks of $40 billion in stock, and they received a Fed lifeline of $5.5 billion in 2020, with strict executive compensation and share buyback restrictions.

United Airlines bought back $11 billion in stock, and Delta Airlines bought $10 billion in stock. Should they be rewarded for such behaviour and be bailed out by the U.S. Treasury by way of the Central Bank?

Saving the best for last, U.S. airlines received $4.5 billion lifeline, and a separate $25 billion in March 2020 under the CARES Act, primarily in the form of grants to keep employees on payroll through the end of that month. The end game was that they were going to eventually go on jobless claims that was pushed back to manipulate job numbers and further aggravate distortions in the labour market. Even in late 2020, the airlines were getting money from the new "$900 billion package of coronavirus and non-coronavirus measures,"[14] which is 5,000 pages long that no one in Congress would have the time to read, but it kept some bureaucrats employed at the expense of the taxpayer. The package included $15 billion for airlines, which lasted for about four months before the well dried, presumably to get them to hire back furloughed workers, and with 40,000 laid-off employees.

So now that we are on the subject of PPP, firms were given money in 2020-2021, with loosely held stipulations that jobs would need to be preserved in order to qualify. Optically, this sounds like government holding a virtuous wand, as the townspeople applaud, but the reality is that in a crisis, firms need to retrench, remove lard, innovate, become nimble, and bring back their financials to respectability. Otherwise, government and the Fed are keeping zombies alive, again at the expense of broader societal diminishment.

All this creates distortions not only in the labour markets, but also manipulates the equity markets where it obscures price discovery of shares, while letting industry know that they are going to get rewarded for bad behaviour. Most people who fly often know that U.S. carriers are nowhere near the best airlines to fly with, when compared to world-class airlines like Singapore, Lufthansa, Swiss Air, British Airways, Emirates, Air France, and Korean Airlines.

This is a classic example of the moral hazard—if we just let these airlines go out of business a new breed of entrepreneurs would take over, younger, more creative, and bolder. The physical assets would still be there, such as airplanes, taxiing equipment and so forth, and they could start with a clean set of balance sheets, along with fresh corporate cultures, and more inventive

---

14   "Read: Text of the New $900 Billion Stimulus Bill," CNN Politics, updated December 21, 2020, https://www.cnn.com/2020/12/21/politics/new-covid-stimulus-bill-text/index.html

ideas. Subsequently, a new organization with a new vision could actually bring a lot of these airlines into a modern age, with a more versatile organisational structure, legendary customer service, the acceptance of cryptocurrencies—benchmark themselves against the most successful international carriers, while bringing their management information systems out of the prehistoric age.

By promoting a culture of commerce that tolerates the moral hazard of bailing out poorly run firms, we suffocate the future of tomorrow, and not fertilize the sprouts of innovation that promotes excellence in commerce and increases consumer welfare.

Banks and Share Buybacks

Never to be outdone in the game of share buybacks, we turn our attention to the usual suspects who practice misappropriation of capital, namely the big five banks that include J.P. Morgan, Bank of America, Wells Fargo, Citigroup, and Goldman Sachs. Cumulatively they have bought back a total $328 billion in shares, between 2017 to 2021. And according to the Wolf Street index, overall bank shares are down 23.5 percent since October 2021 to April 2022, as they burned through all this share buyback money, and it is this type of financial decision-making decay that is making one wonder about our economic institutions.

Figure 12.3 tells the story of share buybacks.

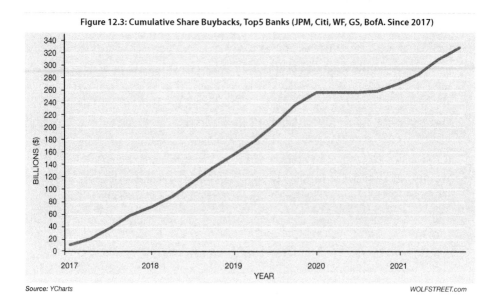

Figure 12.3: Cumulative Share Buybacks, Top5 Banks (JPM, Citi, WF, GS, BofA. Since 2017)

WOLFSTREET.com

In the first quarter of 2022 revenues for Goldman Sachs have precipitously dropped 27 percent, and income is down 42 percent in the same quarter, as shares are down about 25 percent. Investment banks rely on underwriting IPOs for juicy profits, as well as owning insider shares at lower prices than the retail investor can get them for, and now the IPO and SPAC dog and pony show market drying up without enough willing retail investors to get fleeced. Someone must have sobered up and figured out that companies that couldn't qualify for a line of credit at their local bank for $100,000 and losing $ billions per year might possibly not be worth billions in market cap value.[15]

Figure 12.4 tells the story of the IPO market.

15   Wolf Richter, "After Blowing $328 Billion on Share Buybacks since 2017, JPMorgan, BofA, Wells Fargo, Citi, Goldman Sachs Stocks Drop," Wolf Street, April 15, 2022, https://wolfstreet.com/2022/04/15/after-blowing-328-billion-on-share-buybacks-since-2017-stocks-of-jpmorgan-bofa-wells-fargo-citi-goldman-sachs-drop-to-2017-levels/

Figure 12.4: Number of IPOs per Quarter

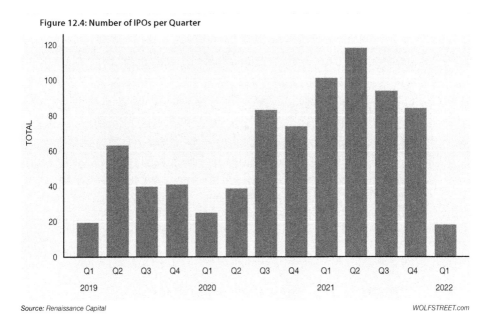

Source: *Renaissance Capital*

So, if we have another meltdown, assuming the government or Central Banks survive the next catastrophe, are the banks really too big to fail? This is the intellectual reckoning of that bring us back again to the moral dilemma.

Back to the Moral Dilemma

The share buybacks lead us back to the moral dilemma: should we continue to bail out firms and other bad actors, by rewarding them for poor management, lack of inventiveness, and misallocation of capital and resources? Should banks be allowed to fail, and the leaders held accountable, or do we fine them and give them a "get out of jail card" as is the case with J.P. Morgan for rigging the gold and silver market? Is it the government's job to pick the winners and losers at the expense of the public purse? Then again, should we continue bailing out the civil service and ineffective bureaucracy, and multi-generational social welfare programs that have destroyed the ethos of self-reliance and dignity? Must the private sector bear all the brunt of the layoffs, while the civil service is untouchable, and is this fair play? For how long are the taxpayer and the Fed going to bail out the government on a monthly basis for deficient cashflows?

The point is this, we all look for villains, which mainstream media misdirects, as to the true phantom. Because when clarity prevails, we might have the courage to look at the horror of what we see in the mirror, as we ourselves might be the most willing participants in this game of musical chairs because we deny the beast within. Then perhaps we should consider if all this behaviour is the hallmark of excellence of a successful civilization?

When large corporations are bailed out by the government, who itself is on life support from the Central Bank, it amounts to tarnishing capitalism as we know it, and paves the way for government on the road to tyranny, which is just around the corner to further interfere in the free markets, with even more disastrous results. Contrary to what some people believe about Trump, he delivered some left-wing Keynesian policies by implementing PPP, the predecessor to UBI. All this is taking a chapter from Hoover, FDR, and Nixon's wage and price controls, perhaps Obama's $10 trillion legacy of wasteful spending, could have been overshadowed by Trump if he had a second term, as we now have Biden, who thinks a balanced budget is a right-wing conspiracy theory.

Regardless of one's political views, the only question will be, who will preside when the Ponzi scheme of U.S. debt and fiat money printing house of cards comes tumbling down? Who will be sitting in front of the video game console to see the horror of the meltdown? Who will be holding the bag as the last participant playing musical chairs on the Titanic?

To be fair to the Fed, they have attempted to bail out, or at least smooth out cash reserves of smaller firms that are privately held. Subsequently, in 2020, a fund was set up by the U.S. Central Bank called Main Street Lending Program for $600 billion with a view of helping small and medium size businesses at LIBOR (London Interbank offer Rate) rates +3 percent ranges, for businesses in good standing for loans in the $250,000 to $30 million range, with all types of interest and principle deferments. Unlike directly lending $20 billion to Oracle, the Fed is not equipped to manage all these multiple loans to smaller businesses—instead it funnels these loans through the banks, where it guarantees 95 percent of the loan value to the banks in the case of default, and the banks hold 5 percent risk to ensure sound lending practices. At the same time, there are provisions for keeping employees on a "best effort" basis.

Here lies the problem, even with a 5 percent risk allocation, banks do not want to lend to many of these businesses, because many are on shaky ground with already pulverized balance sheets. For numerous businesses, the pandemic was just the tipping point, where in the case of restaurants, most have less than three weeks of cash-flow—sadly, too many of these businesses through the pandemic have owners that put up personal assets to save their child, such as home equity loans, and this lack of separation of emotion from logic can lead to a tragic personal outcome, in terms of pledged assets.

As a side note, these are things I personally learned when I worked as an assistant to a bailiff/repo man in the early 1990's—this was not the safest occupation to make a livelihood—where we put some businesses who were behind on rent for six months out of their misery by locking their doors. I asked Boyd Mitchell one night, (the bailiff I worked for), how he could change locks and destroy their dreams. He answered that he was not destroying dreams but giving them relief from a business that was personally draining the owner of resources and family. Boyd, a brilliant and eccentric man of few words said, "Finally the owner could come home to his wife and know the pain of seeing his business at the mortician was over, and there would be no need to get a third mortgage on the family home." And he was right, because in a sense, the bailiff gave the dreamers a chance to start with a clean slate from a dream gone bad.

Further, banks will always want personal guarantees in these types of loans, supported by hard assets like real estate, even if they are being backstopped by the Fed, and for a small business owner, it is an invisible noose. Eventually, many of these businesses will either thrive or perish, since it is the brutality of the marketplace, and unlike public companies, they cannot issue junk bonds and low-grade commercial paper, or sell insolvent IPOs to retail investors to keep the train going.

With the concept of paycheck protection, meaning to pay firms to keep people employed, implicitly brings up a philosophical question, namely do employees own jobs or does the market-place? I recently mentioned this at a party to someone with a civil service background, and he was under the school of thought that employees are not at the mercy of the marketplace, as firms, servic-es and products are—he subsequently thought that keeping em-ployees came before profits, and companies exist at the pleasure of employees. My initial position was that maybe he liked to dress up as Hoover and FDR for Halloween, but then I asked him if he was prepared to give up his life's work and accumulated personal assets to take the risks of losing it all, in order to keep employees, to support his assertions? I asked if he had any demonstrated his-tory of living at the edge of a diving board, like entrepreneurs do, and risk it all? He might have realized that armchair critics live in certainty, not uncertainty.

If we are to build Plato's utopia described in his *Republic*, how do we deal with a consumer who, at all material times, acts in their own self-interest of finding the maximum utility in their everyday quest in obtaining more for less, not less for more? Do we then ban them from shopping at Walmart and Amazon, and ask them to res-urrect Sears, K-Mart, and Macy's, all of which filed Chapter 11 before the current pandemic? Remember, this is the same consumer that will negotiate the price of a car where the sales rep ends up gross-ing $50 on a deal that he spent four hours on. It might be naïve to think the consumer is Bambi in the Woods and the consum-mate victim, where in fact the savagery of the market is reflected in themselves, since the consumer is the most integral driver of the marketplace. If one needs more convincing, go work in retail sales for five years, and let me know who has the bargaining power.

Perhaps the government can run retail and follow such suc-cessful models as Venezuela, Cuba, FDR's Blue Shield pricing, and the former Soviet Union as sterling examples. Better still, let's atone for our past sins and resurrect the horse and buggy industry and wipe clean Henry Ford's assembly line from history. After all, with the cancel culture, can we not ban progress and bring back the oil lamps for light?

And if so, it then naturally brings up the following questions for deliberation in respect to consumer behaviour and price formation:

- Do we ask people to pay more for their iPhones, in the name of reshoring jobs?

- Do we resurrect all the independent stores on Main Street from the graveyard that Walmart knocked out of the game since the 1990s?

- Is the consumer going to pay more out of guilt-ridden economic benevolence?

- Will this not put contractionary pressure on our economies, and create runaway inflation, stagflation, and structural distortions?

- Are governments good at price formation? Well, not according to the Austrian economist Murray Rothbard, who wrote probably the finest economic book on the Great Depression.

- Is there any credible evidence that price formation, which is centrally run, does not end in tears and disaster? How well did it work in the Soviet Union when people had to wait years for a fridge unless they had government ties?

- Does the market not provide price equilibrium and discovery, if left to its own vices?

- Did we not learn earlier in the Great Depression section that FDR's disastrous policy of fair price Blue Eagle logo program as part of the industrial act for companies that did not engage in cutthroat capitalism, ended up costing the consumer more, resulting to even deepen the Great Depression?

■ Do we reduce unemployment by asking women to stay at home, as Hoover did during the Great Depression?

In the end, we have to ask ourselves if this is our manifest destiny and should we hang our faces in shame because we innately want more for less as described by Adam Smith? It seems the ethos of Adam Smith still holds true when he articulated the following:

It is not from the benevolence of the butcher, the brewer, or the baker that we expect our dinner, but from their regard to their own self-interest. We address ourselves not to their humanity but to their self-love, and never talk to them of our own necessities, but of their advantages.
—*Adam Smith, The Wealth of Nations*

Are we not horrified when we abdicate the tenets of a great civilization by being too confused or cowardly to have allegiance to the truth? Will AI eventually learn on its own, ultimately make decisions for us to save us from the lessons of ignored accrued historicity? Do we let emotion as opposed to John Locke's empiricism find a marriage of reason? The caveat emptor is that we seem to be stuck in an intellectually idle place of the tragedy of building a foundation on an emotion of quicksand and passing it off as reason!

Yes, we want to find a culprit, but fear looking in the mirror and deny coming to terms with the savagery of our nature, which today, is intellectually blasphemous to do so. Much like the Wizard of Oz behind the mysterious curtain, it might be better to tweet 280 characters to help mask the horror of the calamity within the beast and sit in a sanctuary of digital cowardice.

The Fed and The Liquidity Trap

The Fed has puts itself into a liquidity trap that seems impossible to get out of, because, since the year 2008, it has become even more bold, and without the bat of an eye, has been purchasing both investment grade and junk bonds, to raise debt capital for companies, which is always cheaper than equity capital. In many cases, they are rewarding corporate leverage that was used to replenish cash that was squandered as part of the $5 trillion of share buybacks since 2012, which can end up creating further volatility, which shows up through suffocating price discovery. If the Fed even slightly closed the bond purchasing window, it would lead to a substantial collapse of the equity markets, along with a deep recession on this signal alone.

Up until the 2008 Great Recession, the Fed was rarely, if ever, in the business of bailing out corporations—when Long-Term Capital failed in 1998, even though the Fed felt this could threaten the financial system, it was careful about the optics of the bailout, since the economic and political culture had little appetite for direct interference in private markets. Subsequently, it treated the bailout softly and in a more clandestine way, to avoid any appearance of action.

But in 2020, the Fed is cavalier as it started purchasing stocks of companies, which would not have been tolerated five years before, not to mention even 12 years ago. Of course, this is not done directly, but through the Wall Street banks, with the outcome being successfully reinflating of the stock market and its equity holders to create a new wealth effect. This introduces a whole new dynamic that will lead to more frequent and severe recession, which is the very thing they are trying to avoid in the first place.

To add gasoline to the fire, the Silicon Valley cabal established censors, adjudicatures of truth—as long as it is their truth—had their hand out again in May 2021 when Congress approved $52 billion subsidy for highly profitable microchip companies to build strategic microprocessor plants. In the case of Intel, two of Chuck Schumer's former top aids were hired by Intel to lobby at a cost of $6.3 million, in addition to campaign donations of $6.7 million. This, of course, has the pretense of being in the national strategic interest. Not to be outdone, Jeff Bezos' Blue Origin space company was to receive $10 billion from the U.S. Treasury—the same

Amazon that dumped Parler off their AWS servers to censor and diminish competition for its Silicon Valley cronies.

When all is said and done, highly profitable Big Tech has been given a whopping $250 billion!

The stock market is addicted to not only easy money, but the Fed rescues and liberal inducements of liquidity, much like a heroin junkie who hides their needle marks. Any line in the desert sand that was previously drawn as to the Fed's mandate of stable prices and employment has been crossed, and they are not in a position to withdraw their accommodative policy, because if they did, the whole house of cards would collapse. Even back in June 2021, in the face of 5 percent inflation based on the St. Louis Fed's CPI numbers, when Fed Chairman Powell said that there would be slight tapering in 2023, the market took some time to digest the news, and then went into a hissy fit; much like a child having their toy taken away, even though they are grown adults. In early 2022 the Fed, with inflation approaching 10 percent, increased interest rates 25 basis points to at least be perceived as doing something about the inflationary monster they created and will more than likely increase it again over the year, maybe another 100 basis points. But this is too little to late and even if the Fed increase their rate to 2 percent, it would be behind the inflation curve that is approaching 10 percent. At the same time, this would drive the 10-year Treasury to past 4 percent. All this is all too little since to tame inflation, the Fed rate at minimum would have to be at the rate of near 10 percent, and if this happens, the whole house of cards would come tumbling down and they know it! For the financial media (especially Barron's and the Wall Street Journal) to not hold them to account along with government, is not only a war on truth, but further evidence that the fix is in.

This is the trap the Fed is in, and it cannot simply take its foot off the gas pedal, because capital market liquidity would come to a grinding halt that would make 2008 look pale in comparison. But if interest rates on U.S. Treasuries went to 5 percent, the $30 trillion debt load would put the government in a sovereign debt default position, which is the second part of the trap. We take a deep dive on this in Chapter 15.

This brings us to a place where we might need to analyze what the culture of capitalism really means and what it should mean. And are the bailouts propping zombie companies, much like the Chinese government at the expense of sprouting new firms that disrupt the present, while showing the future?

Capitalism Built America—Are Bailouts Ruining It?

People come to America to build, to be something they could not perhaps capture within their own culture and nation, to challenge the outer parameters of self-attainment, to explore possibilities that lay in the deep psyche of their aspirations. Like an unexplainable magnet, people are drawn to America with its capitalist culture that has lifted so many out of poverty, America's 20th century has perhaps been the most magical century in recorded human history.

America's capitalist culture helped provide the foundations of a country founded by people who had a healthy distrust for government and Monarchy, while understanding the fragility of democracy. The idea of America has provided a laboratory for innovation and a sanctuary for opportunity.

It was capitalist culture, not without its shortcomings, that brought the Industrial Revolution created in the UK around manufacturing processes, including textiles, iron, Stephenson's railroads, and steam engine technologies, which took its roots in Northern England and Scotland. It was capitalist culture that brought the second Industrial Revolution of advanced steel/alloy technologies, wireless, skyscrapers, electricity, electronics, flight, the internal combustion engine, television, the disciplines of industrial and electrical engineering, and advanced applications of chemicals for industrial use and so much more, most of which were American inventions.

The Third Industrial Revolution, sometimes known as the Digital Revolution, started in the 1950s with the advent of semiconductors, mainframe computing, personal computing, the internet, the cloud, advanced automation, global communications,

AI, electronic and computer engineering, the digital revolution, and the social media that defines the world we inhabit.

Was capitalism not the integral component that defined American ingenuity and knowhow? Would ingenuity have sprouted roots without capitalism, and protected intellectual property law? Was it not the free markets that cradled Henry Ford's ingenuity that allowed people to afford automobiles? Would An Wang, co-founder of Wang Laboratories, have created magnetic-core memory, the predecessor of the microchips in 1948? In 1886, would George Westinghouse, who lit up Great Barrington, Massachusetts for two weeks, have done so without a profit motive?

Nikola Tesla came to America and worked with Edison because free market commerce gave more opportunities for his creativity—in the same breath it was because of America's capitalist structure that fostered IBM mainframes in the late 1940s ushering in the data information age. Would IBM have created the personal computer, or Xerox the GUI in 1970? Would Apple and Steve Jobs have taken a foothold without capitalism?

It was capitalism through GE, Westinghouse, and Rockwell that gave all the components to NASA to put the first man on the moon. Kodak Films was invented with the backdrop of America's economic system that resulted in our lives and precious moments being visualized and captured in still and later in motion pictures. It was capitalism that created the middle-class of blue-collar workers in heavy industry, and it was capitalism that gave us Computer Numerically Controlled (CNC) in 1959 named the Milwaukee-Matic-II, the first fully automated machine that built tool parts (early form of nano technology, and a robot of sorts), and it was capitalism that created the first industrial robot "Unimate," which was installed in 1961 at the General Motors' New Jersey factory.

Without America's culture of capitalism, J.P. Morgan Chase, Goldman Sachs, and a host of investment banks would not have been there to give the nourishment of capital required to bring inventiveness to fruition. It is on the shoulders of America's culture of capitalism that rests Amazon, Facebook, Google, YouTube, Twitter, and their peripheral technologies. It is the free markets that have lifted so many out of poverty, not just as an idea but through reality. Does that make the free markets perfect? Not necessarily, but it gives the best chance to nourish and advance the human psyche.

The story of creativity and capitalism are inseparable bedfellows, one cannot live without the other. Regardless of how bad we may distort and flagellate capitalism with lesser forms of economic organization, our civilization's collective psyche mean reverts to its emotional, rational, seductive, and incomparable draw that resonates within our souls.

Central planning is built on an architecture of fragility and created by men of little achievement, yet demanding of power, but trembles at the possible renaissance of the ghost of the invisible hand, which is our eventual savour from frivolous idealogues.

The culture of bailouts in America did not come from nowhere. The roots of bailouts first started in the Great Depression with government's first immersions into managing the business cycle. It is here where the seeds were first planted in both the Hoover and FDR administrations, as they waded deeper into the natural economy with some unintended consequences. The Fed stuck to its knitting, which was to provide liquidity, and they failed even at that in the Great Depression. At a gala dinner, Bernanke formally admitted to Milton Friedman that the Fed erred in 1930 when they mistook deflation for inflation, and increased interest rates, and contracted the money supply, which exasperated the Depression.

Later, Nixon introduced wage and price controls, and in 1998 the Fed sheepishly bailed out Long-Term Capital, clearly working outside its mandate. But this was a dry run as it built enough nerve for 2008's Great Recession, for its bailout via the Treasury for just under a $1 trillion that had on its list GM, ING, Bank of America and a host of other corporations, with its mantra "Too Big to Fail!"

Fast forward to 2020, and the government starting to spend in the trillions, the Fed printing fiat money and buying the stock market through Wall Street, as well as directly buying commercial debt in the way of bonds, while certain firms are being lubricated with capital, many of which are zombies, and should be allowed to fail. And this story is continuing in 2022.

We have gone from a culture which understood risk that is met with boldness, to one that demands safety, and the mass psychosis that comes with it. We once understood that recessions are a natural part of the business cycle where weak firms perish, or downsize, and the sprouts of innovation are born out of new entrepreneurial organizations that deliver the future of tomorrow. Then this begs the following question: have governments taken on a new role of creating an electoral culture through behaviour modification where recessions are not tolerated? And has this retarded the natural buoyancy of capitalism? In fact, it seems that Keynesian thinking has set us up for even more severe recessions and a depression, because government and the Central Bank will not allow the rinsing of distortions in the economy.

Capitalism reinvents itself through creative destruction, and it is this element that allows new, more inventive, and nimble firms to germinate new green growth for the crop of tomorrow. By rescuing capitalism, are we inadvertently slaying a system that provides government and consumers the largest shoulders to stand on for their own very survival?

It is clear that with each rescue, may it be helicopter money for consumers or bailouts for firms, irresponsible money printing and unsustainable government debt has made financial systems even more fragile, and set the platform for even larger financial calamities. While, at the same time, government interference in the business cycle has not been able to show a history of success, resulted in perverted Keynesianism and left the toxic fumes of $30 trillion plus in the United States, and $16 trillion in the Eurozone with addictive entitlements, and in the case of Europe they sit parasitically on its only solid shoulders, namely Germany.

The United States had a capitalist system, if left alone, could always revive and reinvent itself, but now with a stock market pumped and propped up by the Fed with a sharp needle in the waiting to deflate, it is in a sad situation in need of training wheels as a fully grown adult on a perpetual basis, since it has morphed into an unsolvable puzzle of macroeconomic distortions. So distorted that the free markets cannot recognize the horror of the disfigured face they see in the mirror. It sits like an abusively beaten tragic hero into an addictive mirage of obfuscation, as the townspeople know that without capitalism, their dreams vanish into the barbaric hands of central control.

Young people come to America for entrepreneurship—it is this phycological promise as to one major reason why the U.S. dollar has stayed as the reserve currency of the world. By detesting the rich, specifically those in the $1 million to $50 million bracket, this mentality will drive out these seed planters, and instead by worshipping the multibillionaires like Jeff Bezos, Elon Musk, and Hollywood's high priests, it is this approach that will help displace the U.S. dollar's reserve currency status, along with recent developments in 2022, with sanctions that will eventually backfire.

When all we can offer Gen Z and the Millennials is a distorted form of capitalism that is a shell of itself, wounded, abused, and interfered with by the central planning illiterates of commerce in government, it is no wonder that many of the young fall into the toxic and stagnant arms of socialism. Much like modern day Romantics. With the Fed propping up the stock and housing markets with full blessings from government, it helps only 56 percent of those who own stocks, according to Gallup,[16] and the 65 percent that own homes, according to the U.S. Census Bureau,[17] hence, it is no wonder millennials and Gen Z are growing disenchanted with what is left of free markets. Homes are priced out of reach for many due to housing inflation, and stocks have no market driven price discovery where discounted cashflows, P/E earnings and enterprise value have made CFAs wonder why they went to school to study quants. Instead, all one has to do is watch the companies that the Fed is buying and pick those stocks just as key member of the Fed and Washington's elites do.

---

16   Lydia Saad and Jeffrey M. Jones, "What Percentage of Americans Own Stock?" Gallup, August 13, 2021, https://news.gallup.com/poll/266807/percentage-americans-owns-stock.aspx

17   "Quarterly Residential Vacancies and Homeownership, Fourth Quarter 2021," United States Census Bureau, February 2, 2022, https://www.census.gov/housing/hvs/files/currenthvspress.pdf

It is true that these inflated increases create even a larger wealth disparity, where Bezos' net worth is up $80 billion in one year. The rising culture of government dependency has addicted the poor to a perpetual diet of a behavioural reward system, while propping up assets of the well to do.

We now live in a culture that has little tolerance for recessions, and as a resulting tradable for this, we are participating in a pyramid scheme of insurmountable government debt, and distorted deployment of capital resources, and of course, there is a price to pay for this.

Zombie Companies

The story makes for dramatic theatre when we consider zombie companies. In the United States, they are on life support via the Fed or Treasury department, examples include Macy's, the four major airlines, Uber, and Carnival Cruise Line. Other techniques include companies such as WeWork, which is a zombie company kept alive by an ocean of private equity debt, which are transitioned to equity in the hope of materializing into a commercial success, or spinning them off as a SPAC to unsuspecting retail investors. Without these infusions of private equity and cash from capital markets, these companies are materially insolvent.

To better define zombie companies, for the most part, they are firms that have outlived their marketplace usefulness, to the point that they cannot usually make even their interest payment on debt at near 2 percent. But the debt is rolled over either by their bank, so the bank doesn't take the hit on their P&Ls, or the Fed simply buys their junk bonds. They basically are kept alive by infusing cash into their books, even though they burn through billions a year.

And perhaps the best example of a zombie company is the U.S. Treasury under its $ 30 trillion-plus debt load, which would lead to a sovereign state default without the Central Bank printing money out of thin air and lending it to them.

It seems we have taken a page out of Japan's Central Bank, where from the 1990s it has been purchasing a host of toxic assets including zombie companies, making Bank of Japan majority holder of the Nikkei index at near $500 billion, leaving an afterburn of monumental debt of nearly $15 trillion. Simply put, without the Bank of Japan propping zombie companies, the Japanese economy's house of cards would fall overnight.

The two graphs below show the inversed relationship between new start-ups decreasing since the 1990s, and the increase in zombie companies.

Figure 12.5 shows new start-ups decreasing, while zombie companies have increased.

Figure 12.5: New Start-ups decreasing vs Zombie companies increasing

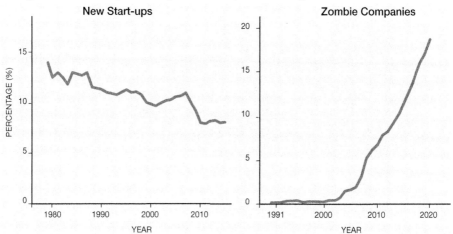

Source: Bookings Institution

In China, it is modus operandi to have zombie state-owned companies exists, since their write-down of debts would be catastrophic, exposing the banks' lending books, where the four major ones are owned by the CCP, and by 2017 there were a total of 69,000 state-owned firms losing 15 trillion Renminbi which equates to $2.2 trillion USD. It is this exposure the Chinese banks have and if they followed GAAP guidelines, the rot under their financial institutions would be painfully clear. This does not even consider their ghost cities.

Some of the zombie companies in the U.S. that created additional debt in 2020 include Carnival, which added $24.2 billion, Delta Airlines $24.2 billion, Boeing $32 billion, Macy's $1.2 billion, and the list goes on. The four major airlines combined account for $128 billion alone, while the entertainment business grabbed $28 billion, and when we add the grand total in 2020, according to Bloomberg, it comes up to $1.4 trillion.18

The government will use words like *strategic industry*, or *job programs* as part of their spin story, but in addition to burdening the taxpayer, they exclude numerous organisations from taking root to new ideas. And without creative destruction where old trees fall and new ones sprout, capitalism's very essence of perpetuity for 7,000 years comes to stagnation at the greater peril of socioeconomic welfare. Not allowing the new is the death nail of the entrepreneur, and without entrepreneurs, free markets become stagnant and fail, and the true victims are inventiveness and growth. And without growth, revenue diminishes for ever-growing governments, which might be the upside of the consequences!

By government interfering in the economy, obstruction occurs, which limits the expansional possibilities of healthy incumbent firms, while creating barriers and constraint to entry for newer, more nimble younger firms. It allows chronic monopiles such as the Lords of Silicon Valley, who also received Fed funding at the expense of the more inventive. It is inventiveness after all, that is the first child of capitalism!

It is very convenient for government to point to corporations or the wealthy as the villains, because it helps deflect from their own unmitigated failures, while ignoring the fact that government sits on the shoulders of capitalism, and without it, the emperor is naked. This being said, the business cycle downturns have unquestionably been exasperated by government with a plethora of empirical evidence presented in this book, the result being an

---

18   "America's Zombie Companies Have Racked Up $1.4 Trillion of Debt," Bloomberg Law, November 17, 2020, https://news.bloomberglaw.com/capital-markets/americas-zombie-companies-have-racked-up-1-4-trillion-of-debt

unrecognizable distorted form of capitalism that underperforms the historical societal contributions that this economic organisation has given civilization. No wonder the young are disillusioned with the free markets—they have never seen one, just capitalism's distorted shell of itself! In many ways, it looks like Ali in his last couple of fights!

With its best intentions, government has exasperated our economic downturns that, when all the facts are put together, the outcome is killing the goose that laid the golden egg of capitalism.

It was the best of times
and the worst of times,
it was the age of wisdom,
it was the age of foolishness, it
was the epoch of belief,
it was the epoch of incredulity,
it was the season of Light,
it was the season of Darkness,
it was the spring of hope,
it was the winter of despair…

—*Charles Dickens, A Tale of Two Cities*

13

A Tale of Two Economies

These are the best of times and the worst of times, depending what economy you are living in. One city received her inflated assets and the other, like a tragic lost romantic novel, hope was snuffed out of its last gasp of breath as it longs for what was once promised on a street called Main, where in a time gone by, the townspeople once gathered. One is a city of insatiable opulence, the other a place where hope for the future has been laid to rest in a slow foggy 25-year funeral procession.

It was the emergence of a stable middle-class in Ancient Greece that we first saw in her city-states. This promise gave common folk acquired titles to land and magistrate rights, giving them an equity much like nobility and the elites. It is perhaps here where hope was born.

The middle-class is paramount to a stable society, and they are being decimated by inflationary money printing and as a result of unsustainable low monetary policy, they cannot even find low hanging fruits, as we quickly see the unravelling of a country. Yes, we sold our inflation to China, to create higher standards of living, but this 20-year selling of inflation to China is coming to and end. Why? Because of higher wages in China, a weakening U.S. dollar against the RMB, money printing, 10 times increase in container transport prices, and an increase in the cost of raw materials, in what is more evidently looking like runaway inflation in 2022. Even in early 2021, it was apparent the era of low inflation was over, as the money printing scheme was coming home to roost with CPI inflation (the Fed bases its barometer on this) at the time approaching 5 percent.[1] The *Wall Street Journal* in some ways challenged the official 5 percent Consumer Price Index narrative, but did not challenge the Fed's transitory inflation lie, or that the cause of inflation is money printing, which would have been insightful and honest.[2] This just shows that the media, even the WSJ

1   "Alternate Inflation Charts," Shadow Government Statistics, accessed March 23, 2022, http://www.shadowstats.com/alternate_data/inflation-charts
2   Jon Hilsenrath, "Inflation Problems Depend on Where You Look at Them," Wall Street Journal, February 21, 2021, https://www.wsj.com/articles/inflation-depends-on-where-you-look-for-it-11613903414

is often joined at the hip with government where we are seeing no real separation. However, online media like Kitco News and the Max Keizer report were sounding the alarm bells of Tsunami inflation on the horizon, and to further challenge the official transitory narrative, effective inflation was closer to 10 percent, according to Shadow Government Statistics. There is a very credible argument to be made between official inflation numbers and effective inflation, meaning the one that the consumer feels on their skin.

Figure 13.1 shows Consumer Price Index from July 2017 to January 2022, and Figure 13.2 shows the official consumer inflation versus what Shadow Government Statistics believes it to be.

Figure 13.1: Consumer Price Index

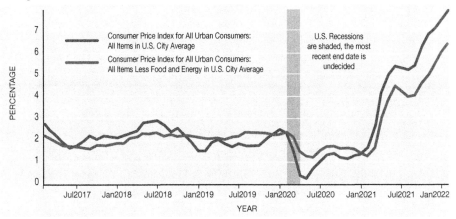

Source: *U.S. Bureau of Labor Statistics*   *fred.stlouisfed.org*

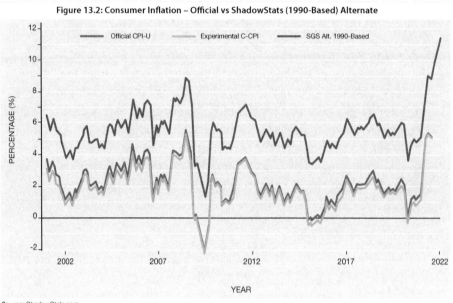

Figure 13.2: Consumer Inflation – Official vs ShadowStats (1990-Based) Alternate

Source: ShadowStats.com

With the development of the Russia-Ukraine war, the inflation narrative will be pushed in orchestration by government, the Fed and their willing lackeys, namely the MSM, as to blaming the war for inflation, which simply does not align with the facts. Why? Because energy and food were up substantially prior to the war, however the mainstream business news along with the MSM will spin a different narrative to gaslight the unsuspecting plebeians.

So, when we see higher prices everywhere against the CPI, we see the derivative of inflation's causation when we measure the rise in energy and agriculture prices from January 1, 2021, before the outbreak of the war on February 15, 2022, which is again caused by money printing and insolvent government, getting a lifeline from the Central Banks. Looking at inflationary numbers in a different scope, taking into consideration that between January 1, 2021, to February 1, 2022, well before the Ukraine war, oil was up 86 percent, natural gas up 240 percent, and according to the Rogers International Commodity Index that tracks agriculture including but not limited to wheat, soybeans, zinc, coffee, corn, cotton, and the list goes on was up 41 percent. The Russian-Ukrainian conflict will serve to exasperate inflation and shortages, especially in Europe, but is not the root cause.

The history of money printing is quite clear—Venezuela, the Weimar Republic, and Uganda come to mind—but many forget that the French Revolution, which was caused primarily by unsustainable government debt due to perpetual wars and squandering of the public purse, only to see the restless Romantics of Rousseau, stumble into the hands of Robespierre's tyranny of paranoia, and then cradle themselves into the genius, yet despotic emergence of Napoleon. These revolutions don't often work out as planned, since they end up replacing tyranny with a more in vogue strand of oppression. Currently, we are witnessing some social unrest, but if the dollar and asset prices fall, the revolution is game-on for all, including many in the entitled civil service who would lose their livelihood, which would be the tipping point—remember, taking a bone away from a dog has consequences.

The outcome is tragic, since this will ensure that a real power-hungry despotic ideologue waving the hand of benevolence and perceived justice will be put in place, as the mobs look for a culprit, imagined or not, psychotic ideologues like Trotsky, Lenin, Mao—all of which could not run the operations of a lemonade stand, started this way. So, we now have the classical thickening of the plot of the "haves" and the "have-nots" in the *Tale of Two Economies*.

The Great Divide

The effect of fiat money printing has devastated livelihoods of the middle-class, and the deplorables who have been misaligned by the deplorable media, when in fact, they are the primary victims of both the fiat system and, of course, inflation.

Wolf Richter wrote an October 2, 2021, article that provides the following insights:

> One percent of 126 million U.S. households—so 1.26 million households—are the prime beneficiaries of the Fed's actions.

At the end of Q1, 2021 their combined wealth was $41.5 trillion, for an average of $32.9 million per household. Over the past 12 months, their wealth increased by $7.9 million per household. The "next 9 percent" of the wealthiest households, with an average wealth of $4.3 million, gained on $708,000 per household in 12 months. The "next 40 percent," with an average wealth of $725,000 per household, gained $98,000 in wealth.[3]

The story of how the rich get richer is that they have appreciating assets like homes, bonds (they might regret this one), equities, precious arts, and the likes. Those who do not, get left out of asset class appreciation. The wealthy know that preserving wealth requires discipline, it is a full-time job, while anyone can squander it on opulence. This usually gets lost on the second generation, where 70 percent of them lose it, and by the third-generation, 90 percent lose it.

Figure 13.3 is a visualization of how this story plays out with the wealth effect of the top 50 percent.

3   Wolf Richter, "My 'Wealth Effect Monitor' for the Money-Printer Economy: Holy Moly, October Update," Wolf Street, October 2, 2021, https://wolfstreet. com/2021/10/02/my-wealth-effect-monitor-for-our-money-printer-economy- is-out-in-the-pandemic-the-fed-totally-blew-out-the-already-gigantic-wealth- disparity/

Figure 13.3: Wealth Effect Monitor: Per-Household Wealth, Top 50%

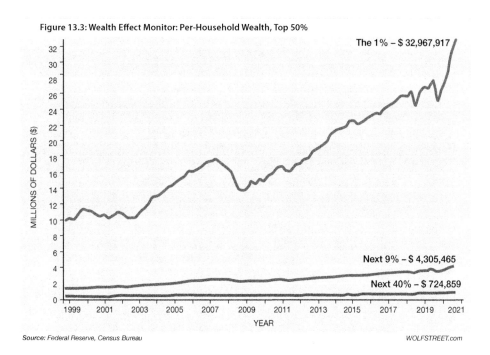

Source: Federal Reserve, Census Bureau   WOLFSTREET.com

A Look at the Bottom 50 Percent

The true victims of fiat money printing and its by-product, inflation, is the tragic place where hope has turned its back on these
groups. The list includes minorities, the youth, the deplorables,
the working poor, and people on intergenerational welfare who
will suffer at the hands of inflation where they will need additional
government subsidisation to buy more cancer inducing junk food
from Dollar Stores and elsewhere. By being depended on government, one eventually realizes they are looking for love in all the
wrong places, and back themselves into an addictive spiralling inertia that imprisons the psyche with invisible cages.

This is the true collateral damage that inflation and money
printing create, and the perpetrator of financial genocide on the
collective souls of these victims rests squarely on government with
its main accomplice the Fed.

The "wealth" of the bottom 50 percent is on average $122,500 in assets less $81,000 of debt. Traditional mortgage debt would constitute the majority, but this has changed. Mortgage debt used to be the largest portion of the debt, but consumer debt—credit card debts, auto loans, and student loans—overtook mortgage debt in 2018. What is more concerning is that much of the debt is not against appreciating assets, as people spent their helicopter stimulus on depreciating assets like cars and credit card indulgences. This can be seen with the bottom 50 percent who have $24,000 of assets in these durable goods categories, which really means they have no real assets. Sadly, the bottom 50 percent have only $1,356 per household in stocks, so the increase in the S&P, since the Fed's reinflated the stock market, does little for them.

Even though 65 percent of Americans own homes, the bottom 50 percent own fewer real estate assets, and if they do, their home equity is closer to $22,500 on average, with an average gain of $3,000 on home assets, since their homes are often worth less, while in real estate, location is everything. Hence, when the Fed took the unprecedented step of inflating the housing market, the lower 50 percent were nearly excluded from the wealth effect. The other factor to consider is that there is rent inflation in the market, again because of monetary policy, to the point of bidding wars for shelter. And this is no surprise with Blackrock buying swaths of new subdivision homes and renting them out.

Figure 13.4 is a chart from the Federal Census Bureau that helps tell the story.

Figure 13.4: Bottom 50%: Value of Major Assets per Household

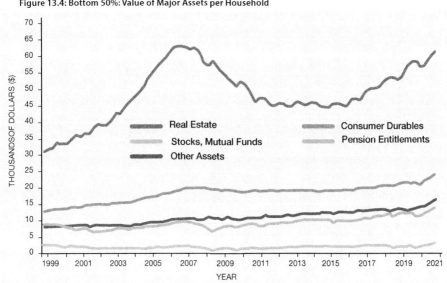

Source: Federal Reserve, Census Bureau

Renters and Landlords

Approximately 35 percent of American households are renters, and while it is understandable if someone is renting because they are young starting out their career in Manhattan, have been relocated, had a rough run, but in the long run, in the end, renting is a bad idea. According to Bloomberg, as of early 2021, approximately 20 percent of American renters are behind on their rent for a national for a total of $70 billion, affecting 11.4 million renters, while the U.S. government has created a moratorium on back rent, creating havoc on landlords, many of whom have mortgage obligations themselves, resulting in the weakening of property rights, which is a fundamental tenet of U.S. law that President Hoover first tampered with.[4]

4   Kriston Capps, "U.S. Renters Could Owe $70 Billion," Bloomberg, December 10, 2020, https://www.bloomberg.com/news/articles/2020-12-10/u-s-households-may-be-70-billion-behind-on-rent

Never to be outdone, California has used $5.2 billion taxpayer dollars from a congressional relief package in 2021 for the pandemic and bailed out landlords and tenants. Having the government fix a problem it created in the first place, is like a hit man being the emergency room doctor when the bullet-ridden patient arrives with weak vitals. It is these types of distortions in the rental and property markets where rent cannot be enforced that concerns lenders, with an outcome of tightening lending and rental rules.

These are all consequences of the moral dilemma.

We can turn around and say that government, business, and the Fed is the villain that is responsible for the tragedy of poverty and be done with it. Yes, we can dust-off old copies of Marx, prepare Molotov cocktails, dress as modern-day entitled proletarians, with more safety nets than circus high jumpers, listen to passages from what I'll call "Victims for Hire," as the high priests of Hollywood throw holly water on their cultish digital disciples in order to inoculate them from truth. However, before we finish deliberating for a villain, we might need to revisit the great divide and the wealth inequality gap.

The Wealth Inequality Gap

When people are in a spiral of poverty, poor choices are often a natural outcome, and much of the helicopter money is being spent on depreciating assets such as vehicles, and cellphones. It is this type of ineffectual and reckless spending that keeps people in poverty, and it takes discipline to say, "no to today, so you can discover the hope of tomorrow." Unfortunately, not everyone is in a healthy enough emotional state to do this, including the nouveau riche.

At this level, we cannot always blame government or the Fed's for poor choices, but there has to be a level of personal accountability. The wealthy are taught from childhood on how to handle money, to maintain and grow wealth—it is a resource, quite a skill that is sometimes passed on, since it takes incredible self-discipline and fiduciary resolve to keep wealth. If they cannot handle wealth, it is easy to lose a fortune, may it be the family business failing, fiat money being devalued, aggressive tax audits, confiscation, political unrest, land seizures, divorces, incompetence, opulence, or spending $250,000 in an afternoon on Rodeo Drive—the list of possibilities is endless. Remember, the top 10 percent are not stagnant, many join and many leave this percentile, but within it is the entrepreneurial class, and the job creators. Simply put, the top 10 percent is not a static phenomenon, meaning permanency—instead it is a dynamic percentile full of vertical movement.

Once we understand the high probabilities of the wealthy, and their offspring losing it all, we can then consider that about 70 percent of lotto winners lose or spend all that money in five years or less. Or take the case of the 78 percent of NFL players who, according to Kiplinger, go broke or are in financial straights within two years after their career ends. This story repeats itself in a wide array of sports including soccer, basketball, and hockey.[5]

Remember, if you put an ad on the job boards for prodigious money spenders, the response would crash the website, while this type of strategy might lead to zero percent unemployment. Well, so much for wealth redistribution!

Bringing us back to our main show about the two economies, once the bottom fell out of major markets in March 2020, the Fed went into action to reinflate the asset bubble to bring back the wealth effect. They used a combination of buying debt directly, in the case of the airlines and General Electric, and massive debt and stock purchases through Wall Street banks. The Fed is paying a premium on buying corporate bond ETFs to private banks on Wall Street, and without the Fed, these bonds would be worth much less, with the end result of inflating profits for the Wall Street banks.

5   Ron L. Brown, "How NFL Draftees Can Avoid Going Broke," Kiplinger, May 3, 2021, https://www.kiplinger.com/personal-finance/602725/how-nfl-draftees-can-avoid-going-broke

Main Street and the Fed

There are two economies on Main Street, where profits are paramount to survive, may it be one's own private tech start-up, or family business often running it with their own funds. The plight of the small business and the entrepreneurial class, which provides the sprouts of creativity, is often tenuous in the best of times. Loans are difficult to get without pledging personal assets and many being faced with lockdowns from the 2020-21 pandemic, are being put at peril for their very own survival. Further, when a private business in the start-up phases is losing money, it simply cannot drain working capital, unlike cowboys like WeWork founder Adam Neumann who soaked backers like PeopleSoft to the tune of over $1 billion while the company was hemorrhaging red ink.

To save the day, the Fed guaranteed $600 billion under the Main Street Lending Program in April of 2020 for small businesses, which has since been terminated; it guaranteed 95 percent of loans to help backstop the banks, and even with this guarantee, banks only approved 5 percent of the loans. Why? Because, when banks looked under the hood of these small businesses, the motor was running irreparably and was very shaky.

So how is it that the bank turns down loans of unsound companies, but investors buy up stocks like Uber that has never made a profit since its inception in 2009, and has bled over $18 billion since 2017? In both cases the position is unsound, yet in one the banks say no, and in the other investors clamour to. It is quite obvious that lending and borrowing rules were not in touch with reality, because it was created by the Treasury, meaning government.

The reality is that many small business owners put second and third mortgages on their homes during the pandemic, just to keep their baby alive. Remember, founders of a business consider the enterprise an extension of themselves, and the failure of that business is internalised unjustly as a failure of themselves, which is not fair because these are the types of people who have a passion to explore the unknowns of risk. Remember, what is worse in a lifetime, to try and fail or fail to try? Once business reverts to normal, whatever that new normal may be, many of their balance sheets will be decimated from the prolonged lockdowns. The result has been that many of these companies, when coming out the other end of the tunnel, they are barely hanging on by their teeth. Sadly, many of the larger businesses get taken over by private equity where their management creativity is suspect, or bankruptcy is the only alternative for many of these businesses, with key principles going down personally, because of all the personal guarantees they initially signed, which often includes their spouse, who is often put on the hook as well. Employees often become part of the family in these companies, and in many cases end up broken hearted, as they say goodbye to the family and drive away from the boulevard of tears, on their way to a street called pain!

Main Street creates 64 percent of new jobs and still employs most Americans, yet its plight as being the abused sibling remains.

When we contrast this to Wall Street, where public companies receive absurd valuations with little or no earnings, such as Uber, Netflix (that has since crashed), Ark, AMC, GameStop and even Tesla (which depends on government carbon credits and has reliability issues).6 Large public companies can always go to the markets and offer equity shares, commercial paper, or junk bonds that the Fed salivates at the chops to buy.

Better still, take a private company where it would be too expensive to go public, or it couldn't meet SEC and IPO requisites, wrap them up and repackage them into special purpose acquisition companies (SPAC), where they are loaded up with ugly ducklings, with high cash burn rates and sold as the homecoming queen—this is a reminder of the dot-com blow up! The SPACs then have a roadshow with talking heads helping them pump the balloon, while conveniently ignoring the lurking monsters in its toxic basket. This is the new mortgage-backed security (MBS) of

6   Tim Levin, "Tesla Makes Some of the Least Reliable Cars, Consumer Reports Says. See Which Brands Come Out on Top," Business Insider, November 20, 2021, https://www.businessinsider.com/tesla-reliability-model-s-3-x-y-consumer-reports-satisfaction-2021-11

the 2020s, but this time for highly unprofitable companies, which are often tech companies, as retail investors have been fleeced for their money with loses of up to 90 percent.

The Cabalatocracy

It seems that we have run into a marriage of twisted convenience between the oligarchs of Silicon Valley, Wall Street banks, government, the Central Bank, academia, corporations, Hollywood, and a supportive presstitute media that has abdicated critical reporting while happily providing obfuscation of truth, passing off as reason. This can only be called a Cabalatocracy.

I coin this term the Cabalatocracy, and their agenda is to sedate the plebeians, while Rome's treasures are sacked. In 1961, President Eisenhower during his farewell speech coined the term "the military industrial complex", which was relatively a simpler apparatus. It has now evolved into a Cabalatocracy, that when combined, acts as a coordinated kleptocracy of sorts.

Bertrand Russel wrote that in the Dark Ages, "The pope and emperor had an uneasy interdependence, since no one could be emperor unless crowned by the Pope in Rome; on the other hand... every strong emperor claimed the right to appoint or depose popes... They depended on each other to claim legitimate power, as it was galling to both."[7]

In the Cabalatocracy it is difficult to ascertain who ordains the emperor, as there are many king makers, but for now each seems willing to share power for the glory of drinking from the tyrannical cup of grandeur.

---

7   Bertrand Russell, *The History of Western Philosophy* (New York: Simon and Schuster, 1945), 393-394.

Figure 13.5 is a diagram and interlinking functions of the various honorary members of the Cabalatocracy.

Figure 13.5: The Cabalatocracy

THE CABALATOCRACY

Central Bank – AKA The Maestro

Fiat Money Printing • Easy Money • Asset Price Inflation • Protectorate of the Moral Hazard
• Creator of the Wealth Gap • Modus Operandi; Deny any Responsibility.

01

Media
"TRUTH NEED NOT APPLY"
Renaissance of Soviet Pravda. Daily Legacy & Social Media Propaganda. Abdication of critical thinking. A recycled fountain of misinformation. Emotion is welcomed, reason need not apply!

02

Corporations
A beacon of the self-proclaimed virtuous. Rewarded by the Central Bank for share buybacks. Purveyors of crony capitalism. Hotline to the Government.

03

Government "A CRISES MANUFACTURING CENTRE"
Tyranny. Oppressive taxation. Propaganda. Obfuscation. Abdication of Rousseau's Social Contract. Inefficiency. Overreaching. Untreated compulsive lying disorder. A well-rehearsed orchestra of lies and failures, passing off as good governance. Accountability need not apply! Survives, grows on Fed money printing and crises

04

Plebeians
Handouts in exchange for docility and votes. Addiction to Government, Social Media, Walmart, Amazon, and Netflix. Loitering in the Twittersphere.

05

Wall Street
Cronies and enlightened associates of all Primary Benefactors of Easy Money. Fictitious stock valuations. IPO valuations from the Twilight Zone.

06

Silicon Valley
Noted Members include YouTube/Google/Twitter/ Facebook. Censorship & compromised fact checkers disguised as free speech. Digital addiction leading to mass psychosis. Plebeians come to worship their digital Gods.

07

Three Letter Spook Agencies
"NOTED MEMBERS INCLUDE – CIA, FBI, NSA"
Acting as the 4th Branch of government. Ensuring everyone follows the script. Any rebels are brought into line with the assistance of other noted members of the Cabalatocracy. Heavily dependent of Silicon Valley's surveillance

08

Academia
Mind reformatting and Ideologue Factory. Delusions of Cosmic Vision. Student Loan Racketeering Centre.

09

Hollywood "HOME OF EMPTY VESSELS"
Hollywood high Priests posing as intellects wave their virtuous hands. False icons for the infatuated star-struck digital minions.

10

Medical Inc.
"A DIVISION OF PHARMACEUTICAL INC."
Untouchable Medical boards. Experimental Jab for Freedom. Politicized Science; empirical reasoning need not apply! Coordinated gaslighting with Silicon Valley's other prominent members of the Cabalatocracy, CDC, FDA.

A Look at the Actors of the Cabalatocracy

The Cabalatocracy has 10 major branches that work around the orchestration of Central Bank money printers, willing or unwilling, and together they help explain the current theatrical house that we reside in. They include:

The Central Bank: The Maestro

The Central Bank is the kingmaker of the Cabalatocracy, ordaining the emperor's reign with continuity, with money printing to facilitate the insolvent government Treasury as it is paramount to sustaining more fruitless government programs, and unsustainable debt. Through money printing out of thin air, the Ponzi scheme perpetuates by providing lubrication for the capital markets via Wall Street that uses accommodative monetary policy to distort asset prices in nearly every sector from equities, real estate, bonds, energy, food, and even Main Street.

This ruse perpetuates through purchasing toxic assets and throws small businesses under the bus. Asset price inflation creates the wealth gap with primary victims being mostly the middle-class, and the poor, as they do a slow-motion swan dive into obscurity.

The modus operandi is, print money out of thin air and deny any responsibility!

1. Media: "Truth Need Not Apply"

The legacy media, better known as the ministry of propaganda, the primary function is its never-ending "war on truth," as it is wrong on everything. An essential member of the Cabalatocracy as it does a renaissance of Soviet era Pravda and partake in intellectual fraud. Menu includes a daily à la carte of propaganda, gaslighting, alternative realities, and abdication of critical thinking. Studios are filled with overpaid, mostly unemployable talking heads suffering from circular logic as reporters espouse their well-rehearsed tapestry of obfuscation.

Emotion is welcomed in this recycled fountain of misinformation, reason need not apply, censorship in the name of defending freedom is the narrative, as truth has been thrown under the bus.

2. Corporations

Corporations are essential members of the Cabalatocracy, since without them what shoulders would government have to sit on? Even they have gotten into the game of defining the new moral fabric, as they now are a beacon of hope as self-proclaimed virtue signalers. Their Human Resource departments are preaching a woke sermon, as opposed to hiring for competitive advantage.

Crony capitalism is often the modus operandi, as share buy-backs for billions of dollars pump share prices to reward executive bonuses. When cash runs out as a result of such poor management decisions like not re-investing capital, that's not a problem as they atone for their sins and are rewarded with a lifeline by the Treasury via the Central Bank's money printing machine.

3. Government: A Crisis Manufacturing Center

Home of many swamp creatures, with taxpayer funded wet-suits auditioning for Stephen King's next house of the dead movie. Government is the command-and-control centre of the Cabalatocracy. Since antiquity, government's résumé has included tyranny, oppressive taxation, propaganda, a litany of lies, obfuscation, an abdication of Rousseau's Social Contract, inefficiency, unrelenting, overreaching, and incompetence, if left untreated bloating may occur.

Caution: if left in office too long members can suffer from untreated compulsive lying disorder where the presstitute media could join them for volume discount therapy sessions.

Warning: if left alone and unchecked, government is prone to creating a crisis where they can further coordinate with spook agencies, Big Pharma, Silicon Valley, and with another fruitless $5 trillion spending bill provided by their trusted drinking buddy, the Central Bank, where the intoxication of liquidity is celebrated till the wee hours of the morning.

4. Plebeians and Digital Minions

Like being locked in a theatre with no way out where the film repeats, the toxic cycle of media, crises, fear, government, and solution which, of course, only can be provided by government for the problem they first created. The plebeians and digital minions have little chance to come up for air as they get re-injected from the house of white with another dose of gaslighting and propaganda. Spending their days enforcing their chosen beliefs, any laggards of the groupthink will be whipped and feathered in the digital galleys of Silicon Valley.

Self-reliance is deemed to be barbaric, collective groupthink is the order of the decaying Rome. Much of their time is spent in an ideological lather to ensure their particular political party of favor wins, thereby ensuring that democracy is used to oppress the minority that did not vote for the ruling party. After all, isn't this the new face of Democracy where our elite rulers, unlike Marie Antoinette, don't even offer the paupers cake? The plebeians actually believe that government, in its present state, can be reformed with some regard for the citizenry and are even under the delusion that government works for them. If only their political party leader gets voted in; their messiah of hope will finally deliver them to the promised land!

5. Wall Street: Smoke and Mirrors

Cronies and enlightened associates of all primary benefactors of easy money in the magician's hands of smoke and mirrors—fictitious stock valuations, IPO valuations from The Twilight Zone. They are chief cronies of the Central Bank—they actually hang out in the same hood—as concepts like price discovery have gone the way of Michael Jackson's moonwalk. Too big to fail, Wall Street banks are the quintessential definition of the moral dilemma.

Analysts come up with fictitious stock valuations based on helium balloons and reruns from The Twilight Zone, as IPOs reside in steamy romance novels, all waiting for the pin to burst and leave 401(k) plans in the boulevard of tears. Wall Street banks fixing precious metal markets by shorting paper derivatives is met with only a fine, as the culprits do no time!

The modus operandi is *Pump & Dump* before the day of reckoning, as price discovery is thrown under the bus.

6. Silicon Valley: A Division of the Propaganda Ministry

First runners up for next year's gaslighting Oscars are none other than Silicon Valley's hired enforcers for the Cabalatocracy's war on truth. Distinguished members include the all-star dream team from the Valley include YouTube, Facebook, Google, and Twitter as the self-proclaimed high courts and arbitrators of veracity. Censorship is provided free of charge to those that have been deemed guilty of misinformation by ideologically driven financially compromised "fact checkers". The Silicon Valley branch of the Cabalatocracy has a hotline with the legacy media, government, and spook agencies to coordinate their war on truth and ensure their obfuscation of reality remains coordinated, reason or plausibility need not apply.

By chance, when truth confused for misinformation makes an unscheduled appearance, it is beaten back into the digital galleys like a fallen hero.

7. Three Letter Spook Agencies

Noted members include the CIA, FBI, NSA, DOD, and homeland security, as they act as the fourth branch of government, as distinguished members of the deep state. Being part of the swamp creatures, they can often be seen in wetsuits provided by an unsuspecting taxpayer. Always in a bromance with Silicon Valley's surveillance culture, they pass each other's dirty little digital secrets, resulting in stiff competition for the National Inquirer. Always on standby, the spook agencies with an all-star line up of script writers prepare narratives for the MSM teleprompter readers to recite as part of the 24/7 cycle of fear.

Occasionally James Bond can be spotted on the premises, just look for an Aston Martin!

8. Academia: Mind Reformatting

Early public education up to K-12, where math, science, literature, history, and grades are blasphemous, oppressive, outdated concepts, as only feelings are the important outcome of learning. Higher learning college programs include a four-year degree in mind reformatting with a major in "wokism", and a minor in victimology. Professors, with their cosmic vision evoke tenets of wealth redistribution, as long as it is not their own, and students get rewarded with an $80,000 debt as part of the racketeering scheme of higher education. Critical thinking, accountability and reason are blasphemous relics of intolerance, and need not apply.

9. Hollywood and Pop Culture Celebrities "Home of Empty Vessels"

Hollywood high priests, posing as authorities of reason, wave their virtuous hands from the hills of glitter as the infatuated star-struck digital minions lap it up like a Dairy Queen's milkshake and ask for more, with perhaps not realizing that they are worshiping an empty vessel. Hollywood infuses their warped sense of virtue by covertly infusing into films their new moral fiber of "wokism", a new religion desperately searching for a holy scripture. The plebeians go to the theatre, eat buttered popcorn, and become enamored with not only the plot, but their protagonist hero that desperately tries to rationalize the irrational.

For those that do not go along with the program of assembly line re-formatting of hard drives, the high priests of the entertainment industry can call on the Cabalatocracy, associates in the MSM, the Silicon Valley, and government to help them pass off gaslighting as truth. Surrendering the smoldering ashes of their souls into slavery, the digital minions and Plebians enamored at glitter give them a thunderous standing ovation.

10. Medical Inc. "A Division of Pharmaceutical Inc."

Medical Inc. is a key leading member of the Cabalatocracy. Distinguished members' primary qualifications include incompetence, unmitigated failures and corruption. Featuring untouchable medical boards, experimental jabs in exchange for freedom, politicized science. Empirical reasoning need not apply. The global division is under the WHO, who helps write the new tunes for their cabal to sing. Then, the other distinguished members of the Cabalatocracy namely the MSM and Silicon Valley take over, giving Medical Inc. their new hit single tune with 24-7 airtime, until it makes the top 40 hits for the minions to download on their Apple and Spotify playlists.

Scientists who subscribe to reason, scientific curiosity and empiricism not toeing the line are defamed as heretics, digitally cancelled as they are tarred and feathered by other members of the Cabalatocracy.

The Wealth inequality Gap—Is There a Way Out?

The current economic reality in the early 2020s is the quagmire that is suffocating dreams, while the middle-class is in a state of shock, and sadly has turned its back on hope. It is this coordinated Cabalatocracy that in many respects is a more participative kleptocracy of actors then its classical definition. Sadly, this is the hallmark of a declining power, while it bludgeons away at the tenets of fair play.

It is this wealth inequality gap that can only be closed by taking disciplined and decisive action; government programs will only increase this gap, and wealth redistribution, which amounts to confiscation, will eventually end up back in the hands of the well-to-do, as Andrew Carnegie once claimed. Further, confiscation would undermine the free market economy for the innovators and entrepreneurs, creating an underground economy, leading to a complete dystopian collapse. Listening to the upper bourgeois priests of Hollywood, unemployable Marxist professors, or equally mostly unemployable government bureaucrats, as they wave their wands of virtue, pointing at anything but themselves, will only leave one in the aftermath of emotional disillusionment. But there is a way out!

The haves own asset classes, namely homes and or stocks, and have learned how to build and manage wealth through discipline and emotional ability and the rationale of understanding the stock market. For those conditioned to be envious of the wealthy, so then, why do they give a pass to $20 million per year athletes that they support by spending $700 for front-row seats for a moment of ecstasy, as those athletes drive around town in their Ferraris flaunting, while their adoring fans get back in their Honda Civics to drive home? As mentioned prior, for those that have been born into wealth, they have the pressures of preserving it, and if they cannot, will lose it, and there are many examples of this.

Coming up for air from all the toxic fumes, consider this: if you create your own wealth, you have the advantage and the confidence of being self-made, or self-reliant, and no amount of money can buy such a solid psyche. Those born wealthy do not have this real privilege, a privilege that one can create with their own hands.

Hence, if you own stocks, scarce collectables, and homes, precious metals, with the low monetary policy and irresponsible printing of fiat money, you are the beneficiary of the inflating of the balloon. At the same time, you might consider exposure to agriculture, energy, physical gold, and Bitcoin.

As a side note, my parents never understood the stock market, they never invested and never appreciated monetary policy, and they signed a 22 percent mortgage in 1984, it does not mean I had to do the same, since one learns from this live example.

It shows that you like to learn by reading this book, or any other book that enhances your knowledge, since the genesis of knowledge is curiosity, and it is commendable you have taken the time to invest your time, whatever your circumstances.

So, if you are part of the 65 percent in the United States that own homes and 55 percent of those who own equities, you have solace in the wealth effect, which is inflationary in nature, further spreading the gaps between people with and without assets. It should be noted that the average return on real estate prices is closer to 4 percent per year, even though since March 2020 home prices are up nationally 29 percent, prices are stalling somewhat in early 2022. Comparatively, the stock market historically performs closer to 10 percent per year, according to Investopedia, even though the S&P is up almost 80 percent since the March 2020 pullback, making it a much better investment vehicle than real estate, especially when we consider the liquidity of stocks versus real estate.

This much is for sure, if you are part of stratus that does not own a combination of the following asset classes, including precious metals, energy, real estate, certain stocks and Bitcoin, you are either young or heading into, or are stuck in a spiral of poverty. We see some of the Robin Hood traders being inspired by Reddit, trying to accumulate quick wealth, but few in their exuberance of youth and blinded groupthink do not consider the vast majority as to how many got wiped out by GameStop, AMC, and the likes.

On a personal note, by not participating in these asset classes and others, financial outcomes will be challenging. Subsequently, moving financially forward takes discipline, sacrifices, and consistent contributions, while understanding that life is about trade-offs. Understandably, some descend into poverty out of no fault of their own, but by acting and turning off the excess noise in the world and taking their first step will rescue their future. As Warren Buffet once said, "The difference between successful people and really successful people is that really successful people say no to almost everything."[8] What he means by this is that one might need to give up some short-term creature comforts, and narcissistic material acquisitions, to say no to the present to participate in the future. The best piece of advice might have been from my mother when I was a newspaper boy, helping my parents save for their first home. She said, "If you are born poor it is not your fault, but if you die poor the fault lies with you."

This is not a book on stock advice, but by understanding the inner workings of economics, you can use this book to make meaningful gains, which become more apparent in the final chapters.

For those starting out, you can participate in the housing market through housing stocks, such as symbol Mid America Apartment Communities (MAA) contribute monthly, just like mortgage payments, with 10 to 25 percent down, and borrow at under 4 percent at Interactive Brokers to leverage an asset, and then flip this asset over as a down payment toward your first home. The idea here is that your savings will not get outpaced by house inflation. (This is appropriate in an ascending housing market, not descending).

Understandably, easy money has juiced up the value of stocks, bonds, and other financial assets, which benefits mainly the rich, inflaming social resentment over-growing inequalities in income and wealth. It should not be surprising that with this distorted form

8   Marcel Schwantes, "Warren Buffett Says What Separates Successful People From Everyone Else Really Comes Down to a Two-Letter Word," Inc., accessed April 7, 2022, https://www.inc.com/marcel-schwantes/warren-buffett-says-what-separates-successful-people-from-everyone-else-really-comes-down-to-a-2-letter-word.html

of capitalism, much of the youth say that they prefer socialism. The sad irony is that the rising culture of government dependence is, in fact, a form of socialism for the rich, the poor, and government because they all depend on the Ponzi scheme of money printing.

In *The Tale of Two Economies*, we can only guess at how tearful the ending of this story will be, as the victors and conquered will no longer recognize themselves or each other in the toxicity of the tragic ending. The magician's only enemy is truth if it is no longer being obfuscated in the vile hands of deception. The digital minions dance on cue and clap like seals in perfect unison at the will of their despotic masters draped in angelic righteous technological attire, as their next enslaving meme à-la-carte is served in its manifest destiny of finally slaying the remnants of truth.

So here we are in *The Tale of Two Economies*, where all streets lead to a market square called Broken. It is this boulevard the declining empire finds itself in denial from the pending horror that precludes them from visiting the library of what was once glorious.

Finally, we arrive at the doorsteps of the great divide, where government pits the poor against the wealthy, the poor against the poor, the middle-class against the middle-class, and the middle-class against the poor, only to inflate the assets of the well-heeled, and enslave the poor into dependency in exchange for votes.

Do we pillage off the very wealthy? Can the divide be closed by not only education in economics and finance, for the downtrodden without reverting to cultural discipline? Has discipline not built everything in our human history of progress, empire, and creativity? Is the gadget more important that could otherwise be invested in an appreciating asset like real estate or Bitcoin? Do the working poor only buy gadgets and fancy durables in a desperate leap to flirt with the American dream that is being dangled in materialism by the narcissistically opulent? Or does the purchase of materialism quench the desire for only a moment as to desperately uplift one from the depression of not having, and thereby spiralling them into poverty even more?

Government will not solve the poverty issues, it will only create more through people's dependence and enslavement to government, and in exchange for helicopter money or UBI they will receive votes to sedate truth. It is the integration of this toxic brew of the participative kleptocracy that is symbiotically engineered by the Cabalatocracy. What would the ghosts of the founding fathers say if for only a moment they could visit us to show their hands and clutch their hearts? What would Adam Smith or John Maynard Keynes think?

Back to Inflation

It is apparent that we are in the midst of a very fragile economy standing on pins where Wall Street is divorced from Main Street and the underlying economy. The questions become, will the depreciation on the fiat U.S. dollar bring in non-stop mass imported inflation, as signs are showing, since imports do cost more? Are the methods of inflation measurement academic in nature? For example, homes, and equities, and cars are not part of the Consumer Price Index, and low weights or the exclusion of price fluctuating foods, which constitutes natural flows of the consumers' economic purchasing function. Okay then— should we be calibrating inflation that reflects purchasing based on what we buy the most, or costs the most, such as homes and stock valuations? Has this carousel of low monetary policy not inflated our cost of living? Has this not excluded Gen Z and Millennials, regardless of their other shortcomings from the asset markets at some level?

According to the *Wall Street Journal*, we are already paying more for items we want more, and less for items that cost less.[9] But as of June 2021, the Fed admitted that inflation was at 5 percent, and 8 percent by 2022, but they claimed it was transitory. Quite simply, by 2022 the Fed-led inflation seems intentional, and they are going to print money until they can't, or other trading blocks use other

9   James Macintosh, "Inflation Is Already Here—For the Stuff You Actually Want to Buy," *Wall Street Journal*, September 26, 2020, https://www.wsj.com/articles/inflation-is-already-herefor-the-stuff-you-actually-want-to-buy-11601112630

mediums of exchange, which is becoming the case with India, Russia, and China. At the same time, we are experiencing substantial wage inflation that has been discussed prior, where companies simply cannot afford to lose their most skilled team members.

Put simply, we are seeing inflation on items in more demand, and deflation in categories with weaker demand. Figure 13.6 shows early 2021prices inflating on what we want more of and deflating on items we want less of.

Figure 13.6: Inflation in 2020

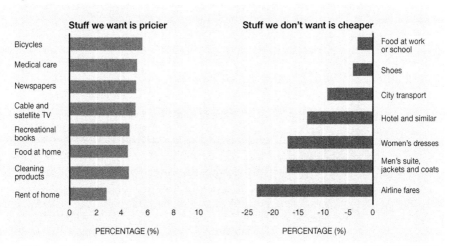

Source: U.S. Bureau of Labor Statistics

WALL STREET JOURNAL

It is imperative to understand what items help comprise the CPI, some of which include iPhones, ear buds, electronics, clothing, personal care items, transport, furnishings, tableware, footwear remain low in relatively cost escalation. In the past, in many cases, they dropped in price due to the Chinafication of manufacturing.

But this is changing now with inflation coming in from China, much of it being from raw material and container costs, so this means that slowly but surely, we can no longer live for today at the expense of tomorrow, as a tradable to maintain living standards.

What the West has done is export inflation overseas and import unemployment of the same, while diminishing its unparalleled inventiveness, with the loss of manufacturing. In fact, as mentioned prior the loss of manufacturing was perhaps the key reason the British Empire fell, while at the same time, the West's insatiable appetite for consumerism has ensured that its associated ecological mess is kept overseas as it waves its virtuous fingers at the rest of the world and lectures everyone on the environment. In essence, the West is acting as self-appointed narcissistic highbrows and treats the countries that are decimating their environment to facilitate the West's consumption as the culprits.

We can just say that inflation is a tax on the consumer, and then leave it like that, but dangers of violence can loom when pricing and shortages in life essentials can lead to inflation riots.

Inflation Riots

We are starting to see the instability caused by inflation. As of April 2022, Peru is experiencing violent inflation riots in Lima and throughout the country, and CNN in their never-ending war on truth is trying to spin the increased energy and fertilizer crises on Russia, when in fact prices were rising before the Ukrainian conflict. Further, Peru can always purchase oil from Venezuela, which has the second highest proven oil reserves in the world, as well as buy fertilizer from Canada and Mexico. The truth though is that the sanctions are exacerbating an already tight supply chain.

In Sri Lanka we are now seeing food and fuel prices spiking, mixed with shortages of the same. This is due to the rupee dropping in price against foreign currency reserves, meaning that fiat money and its eventual return to its intrinsic value of zero is creating societal instability, as well as some good old Sri Lankan corruption, which is an ample supply. However, if this country had hard money backed by gold and Bitcoin it would lead to corruption rinsing itself out with a new cat in town and the mice running out the door. When currency drops prices go up, and more than likely Sri Lanka will have their hand out to China and or the IMF. We are only seeing the tip of the ice of the devasting effects of fiat money.

In 2022 in the United States, we are already seeing some empty shelves starting with chicken due to a bird flu that is spreading. While at the same time, with higher fertilizer prices, agriculture prices will go through the roof during the fall harvest of 2022. The West has been a place of plenty, and not having is something that we do not have the temperament for. We are already seeing food hoarding in anticipation of food shortages which will be exasperated due to the container congestion, and lack of drivers at ports.

Inflation riots will more than likely follow in some parts of the West due to high prices and shortages, and the government in coordination with the Central Bank will print even more money to solve the crises, which was the root cause of the original problem. Of course, they will spin it off as someone else's fault, maybe Covid, maybe Russia, or find a new bogeyman to deflect the puck to, when the current crisis gets overwhipped and fades. Once the new crisis is established, it will be followed up with standard talking points prepared by the ministry of propaganda and sung like a church choir by the MSM and the Silicon Valley branches of the Cabalatocracy!

In today's world, manufacturing only accounts for 8.5 percent of the U.S. workforce and 11.9 percent of the GDP—it is this shrinking that is the perhaps the causation of the middle-class becoming its primary victim. True, manufacturing accounts for approximately $2.5 trillion of output in the U.S. and sounds impressive, but is pale in comparison to the U.S. capital markets which according to Siblis Research is worth $50 trillion.[10] And with the U.S. dollar being the reserve currency of the world, the agenda is to print as much non-hard-backed fiat money, have Wall Street and the aristocracy borrow it at 1 percent, and use it to purchase real assets ranging from Microsoft, Tesla, Apple, and the likes. While at the same time, the very wealthy are investing in luxury real estate, farmland, collectibles from art to classic cars, precious metals, and Bitcoin as a way of using unlimited fiat money as a vehicle to buy hard assets.

10   "Total Market Value of U.S. Stock Market," Siblis Research, accessed April 8, 2022, https://siblisresearch.com/data/us-stock-market-value/

The whole world accepts U.S. dollars and when they are flush with cash, they have little choice but to buy Treasury bills, hold cash, or buy goods and assets with U.S. dollars, although this is changing. And with the U.S. has gone from being the biggest creditor after the Second World War to biggest debtor, it simply uses this as leverage on its creditors. Because after all, with the circular flow of international cash, it is in the best interest of creditors sitting on U.S. cash to not allow the U.S. to default, since their fate is mutually intertwined with financial weapons of mass destruction.

This does not even consider the commodity and derivative markets, and it is this type of financial engineering with money printing that creates inflated wealth. In other words, the wealthy trade paper for hard assets. The notion of building an economy on manufacturing output and creativity is void, at least in America, because it cannot compete with financial engineering, relies on valuations based on inflated asset prices drawn from fiat money. These are the privileges of having the reserve currency—that is until the house of cards comes down.

This leaves the middle-class in a vulnerable position since few of them have resources of capital and knowhow of trading Ponzi fiat money for hard assets. This loss of the middle-class is exactly what happened in the Weimar Republic as they joined the poor.

However, with the flimsy ideology of MMT, the Feds will placate the deplorables and other working-class people with UBI, while the plunder continues by the aristocracy in this type of crony capitalism. After all, with plundering it becomes the accepted modus operandi, and the idea will be to feed some scraps to the ruined, make them believe they have a say in appointing the next emperor (in realty, chosen by the Cabalatocracy), to at least make them feel like they are cared for, and still believing in this defective form of democracy. Once this phenomenon sets in, the Stockholm syndrome of tyranny will be more sustainable. Going back to the CPI, the measurements of inflation, there is more to the equation; when we consider the technology that we use everyday, such as Apple, cable TV, Spotify, Instagram, Netflix, YouTube, and the internet, are all with minimal marginal cost of goods. Even by those standards, we are seeing inflation past the 5 percent range in the second quarter of 2021, well ahead of the Fed target of 2 percent, and as of 2022, it is easily exceeding 10 percent. Subsequently, we see lower inflation only by measuring processes used by academia, and, of course, the Fed. Hence, this is the conundrum we are in as to what is and is not effective inflation measurement, which is closer to 14 percent on an effective basis in early 2022, and this is just the beginning, because any meaningful increase in interest rates to tame inflation would bring the curtains down on the Ponzi scheme, meaning the U.S. dollar and Treasury.

The Inflation Trap

There is one more element to consider, and that is the fact that manufacturing employs less than 8.5 percent of the workforce in the United States, whereas in 1971 it was 25 percent. This is because the West and Japan are no longer the workshop of the World—we simply cannot find process efficiencies at home to help retard back inflation. Meaning, if we manufactured domestically, we would be our own masters of cost control.

This is especially manifesting itself with container traffic jams in China's major ports leading to container prices approaching $30,000 with congestion fees. It is almost impossible to re-shore much of this manufacturing, because of not only lost skills of the artisans of two generations ago, but also our cost structure, if we even tried to make electronics and the likes here, we would suffer overnight inflation of certain category of products of at least 50 percent, at the same time we do not have domestic supply chains and peripheral support industries in place. In the 1970s, much of this was in place.

Because our manufacturing is hollowed in the West, we are now in an even deeper *inflation trap* where we are taking it on the chin from multiple directions as we are unable to control production inflation. It is really five-fold.

1. Container costs and delays that will lead to shortages, which will eventually show up on P&Ls.

2. Lost knowhow and inventiveness to manufacture much of this in our domestic markets, as we would have trouble today putting a man on the Moon due to lost artisan skills from two generations ago.

3. Commodity prices for manufacturing inputs spiraling through the roof that includes industrial metals, and of course energy.

4. Exposure to China's own inflationary issues and associated geopolitical risks.

5. Fragility and tightness of supply chains.

This is the inflation trap we are in, and it will not be solved by some Harvard economist working in Washington or Ottawa who has never set foot in a factory floor. This is the effect of money printing and its accomplices, namely government and the Central Banks, who would be kept in check by a hard backed currency that would foster fiduciary responsibility. Covid-19 was and is a deflection for people too preoccupied to look under the hood at inflation's cause, effect and toxicity.

All we can do is watch the train approaching and can't seem to free us from the shackles that keeps us bound on the railroad tracks.

This is the inflation trap!

It is becoming apparent that technology as a trade-off for fiat money printing is no longer containing inflation, meaning we can no longer sell our inflation to China, since that gig seems to be up.

To break through all this jargon and get a visceral feel, all one has to do is look at the price of a car from last year to this year or look at the price of gas at the pump, laptops, and by keeping the grocery receipts just document the price of fruits and vegetables from a year ago. One might see 20 percent inflation in the practical purchasing behaviour of weekly basket of goods in 2022, especially when we include food and gasoline. Or consider how

Dollar Tree just moved its one-price sales strategy from $1.00 to $1.25, which in itself is a 25 percent tax on the people who can least afford it, namely the working poor, and those on assistance. CPI inflation measurements according to the St. Louis Fed is about 8 percent, this belongs in the fictional section of the library beside *Pinocchio*.

This is all from money printing, which the mainstream media (MSM) is desperately trying to hide in order to protect their fictitious narrative. If we are to believe the MSM tall tales, we would be under the impression that inflation is generic, and driven by natural demand and supply, which it is not. It is monetary in nature that Milton Friedman warned about in the 1970s, and the supply chain mess is caused by money printing, not the never-ending pandemic which is now a catalyst for government overreach, and abdication of the social contract. The blame squarely lies with the Fed and the Treasury, as they gaslight the truth hoping that the public is impervious to this.

Deflation and Automation

This brings us back to *The Tale of Two Economies* that potential deflation can underwrite. Consider the advent of numerical control (NC) in the 1950s, then the introduction of CNC technology with the Milwaukee-Matic-II in 1959, the first machine with a tool changer. Since I am a trained machinist, I'd like to elaborate on this technology; it is basically the automation of the machining of parts that can be used for brake rotors, to certain electronic parts with consistent accuracy that humans cannot replicate, while it increases human output by at least 20 times, it takes no sick days and doesn't strike for more pay, well, at least not so far. In other words, these machines are the driver that changed the tooling industry, as we knew it. We can see how something like this drives down costing, and these machines that were cost prohibitive 30 years ago at over $300,000, can now be bought in the $40,000 range, as this is a classical case of deflation.

Then, in 1962, the first industrial robot was employed in General Motor's New Jersey factory, which cost in today's dollars close to $1 million. Today, this same robot with cutting-edge technology for assembly, welding, painting, with seven directional axes and the likes, can be purchased from Rockwell Automation or Fanuc Robotics in the $35,000 range, and can create unmatched consistent assembly specs and produce exponentially higher rates of productivity when compared to humans producing the same. We can now see that industrial robots and CNC machines have driven down prices, especially in automobiles. If the opportunity arises, I highly recommend you visit a fully automated factory, where you'll witness the machines working in the dark and in cooler temperatures to save energy and associated costs, plus no labour strikes, while robots do not catch viruses. Now with an understanding of this, we are drilling to the core of deflation.

It is also worth noting that the quality and quantity of industrial robots and the technicians to maintain them helps define the competitive architecture of a nation, as Korea is number 1 in the world with 932 per 10,000 employees. (Please search the robot report).

Today, to add to the deflationary pressures, we are seeing the advent of artificial intelligence (AI), which was born in a workshop at Dartmouth College in 1956. AI, with ever increasing learning capabilities, are a destabilising, or at least changing professions, such as engineering, accounting, law, medicine, specifically surgery, defeating the world's best chess players, replacing stockbrokers, software coding and the list goes on. What all this technology has done and will do is, bring down pricing, as stated in Jeff Booth's book *The Price of Tomorrow*. So, does this mean that AI will increase consumer welfare in the way of low prices? Not necessarily and not in all categories, because AI still needs raw materials as a component of cost of goods, and the demand on commodities in an ever more overpopulated Earth will push up raw material prices, which are essential component in finished goods. Hence, in an automated factory, direct labour might constitute less than 10 percent of finished cost of goods, while the capitalization of AI and its upkeep might rival traditional factory overhead, meanwhile, other fixed costs such as rent do not change. The jury is out in respect to AI taming inflation and afford us long-term deflation.

Some final Thoughts

All this fiat money printing with no hard assets to back it, will more than likely put an end to paper fiat money as we know it, leading to hyperinflation and stagflation, remember inflation is another involuntary tax. At the same time, we could first go into a deflationary cycle, which would play havoc on company financial statements and asset prices, hence the wealth effect! What we are witnessing here is perhaps the demise of the U.S. dollar, that will print its way into hyperinflation, then currency debasement, and lose its privileged position as the reserve currency of the world as other countries trade in alternative currency that might be hard backed. At the same time the geopolitical implications of Russian and Chinese sanctions will accelerate the decline of the reserve currency status of the U.S. dollar, or at least give it parallel competition. This would not necessarily mean other currencies would do much better, since the Euro and its continent-wide legacy and entitlement costs from cradle to grave will come down like an anchor from the sky, and China with its shaky banks, insurance, real estate bubble, and state-owned zombie companies would capstone the tragedy of such an event. This is basically the scenario that James Rickards discusses in his book *The Death of Money: The Coming Collapse of the International Monetary System*, eloquently stated the following: "In the market today, the dead hands of the academic and the renter have replaced the invisible hands of the merchant or the entrepreneur."[11]

With the Central Banks recklessly expanding the money supply to meet the insatiable appetite for liquidity in markets and failed

11   James Rickards, *The Death of Money: The Coming Collapse of the International Monetary System* (New York: Portfolio/Penguin, 2014).

fiscal stimulus programs with no actual backing of hard assets, it is inevitable that other store of value will first challenge fiats, and then replace them. To consider other units of account, we need to keep our minds open to the fact that sovereign currency historically has a very checkered past, and then ask ourselves the question as to how responsibly has fiat money been managed by rogue Central Banks? The very real possibility of the end of government issued currency as we know it with its prodigious printing could come to an end, or at the very least, we will go back to a hard backed currency, that will replace the trust system with hard backed assets. To understand this better, we must come to terms with what we have built, namely a house of cards. But before we do, history begs us to consider the rich history of sovereign debt default, where it enamours and gifts us with perspective.

The tragic journey of fallen nations lies in the folly of her treasuries. The art of sovereign debt default is immersed in antiquity dating from Greek municipalities who defaulted on loans from the Delos Temple. In the quest for glory through expansion by war, the need to pacify its citizenry, kings in England, France, and Spain defaulted on loans ruining many Venetian lenders. Financial mysticism often employed in history in the way of debasement of coins was used to repay debt. Often the victims are commerce, citizenry, and the legacy of leaders. The great debasement of Henry VIII produced rampant inflation, as the penny fell 80 percent, and in these times the dynamic shifting relationship between price and value becomes evasive. In the 20th century, debasement and inflation wrote the barbaric tales of her wars.

In the end, the manifestation of sovereign debt default lies in the quest for glory, vengeance, and the denial of incompetence! It is this story we briefly visit.

CHAPTER

14

A Brief History of Sovereign Debt Default

Governments have a well-documented history of sovereign debt default—even the UK was bailed out by the IMF as recently as 1976. Over time, the house of cards was built on a foundation that Charles Ponzi could only romanticize about. So naturally, we step back into the past to understand the present so we can infer into the future.

The gargantuan debts that governments in the world are presently under is immersed in history that seems somewhat buried so far in the past and we have been ideologically obscured from its fertile lessons, namely the tragedy of governmental debt default.

The Romans did not have vehicles to print fiat money, so they financed government expenditures through either taxation or forced lending. When under duress, they would collect taxes on urinals, and when in desperation, they would debase gold and silver coins with cheaper coins in order to increase the money supply, which is an early form of printing money, using metal. As one can relate, oppressive taxation is nothing new, but unlike the Roman citizens who had enough vivacity and pride to create tax revolts, in the West, many are lulled into a permanent docile state and actually believe that large government is a societal force for good in its present elitist form. These are the consequences of a safe society versus an uncertain one that magnetically draws the bold, inventive and courageous!

Around the year 400 BC in Ancient Greece, where wars were financed through currency debasement—after all war seems to be an outcome of nation states—they moved from silver to bronze coins, but with an optic catch, namely, they created a bronze coin with silver coating. Subsequently, with debasement, asset prices go up, and currency value goes down in relative terms, a strategy employed in antiquity and beyond in lieu of not being able to issue bonds, like modern day governments do.

In the Far East during the Tang Dynasty, China found ways to finance itself by creating paper money as they debased their currency, eventually leading to devastating inflation, which forced them back into metal as a form of unit of account. So, in the case of the Tang Dynasty, they didn't necessarily default but drowned in inflation in lieu of debt default. Regardless, it is a devastating alternative poison.

Starting with the medieval period, and more specifically by the 11th century, wealthy merchants had accumulated enough wealth to be the lender of choice to European Princes. Later, the first commercial banks opened in Venice, Italy, and by 1157, the Bank of Venice had become a vehicle for raising public debt for the state of Venice. By 1397, Medici Bank was founded in Northern Italy along with many competitors that made it the epicentre of banking in Europe.

Before that advent of bonds being used as a vehicle to raise capital, the banks of Renaissance Italy were the lenders of choice for kings and princes. Subsequently, the 100-year war between the English and French was heavily financed by the banks of Venice and Florence, and the defaults of the French and English kings put some of the largest banks of the period into financial ruin. A notable defaulter was King Edward III of England during the 1330s, which fell hard on the Bardi and Peruzzi merchant-bankers of Florence.

Not to be outdone, the Spanish Crown had a host of defaults between 1557 to 1647, leading to the bankruptcy of the well-heeled, namely Fugger family of Augsburg, who were among the leading merchant-bankers of Europe, from the late 15th to the early 17th centuries. Royalty has it privileges, but has a history of financial shortcomings, and job hazards with the occasional beheading, as King Louis XVI discovered during the French revolution from the rage of Robespierre, and at the hands of his executioner, Charles-Henri Sanson.

Moving on to the modern age, the succession of debt default is rich in history, for example, it might come as a surprise to many, including President Obama who made claims to the contrary, that the U.S. government has indeed defaulted on debt payments. Once because of the War of 1812, when the White House laid in charred ruins and with an empty Treasury, the troops were not getting paid. In the ideology of war dating back to the Romans, savagery without remuneration is uncivilized.

The second time in 1979, was more of a technical default, when an administrative backlog led to bondholders having to wait up to a week to redeem $120 million dollars of their matured financial Treasury bills. However, the real cause was that Congress debated too long to raise the debt ceiling, (the eventual road to ruin), since having a bill pass as an amendment for responsible and sustainable balance sheets was going to lead to further debating, which was about government payment defaults, so the debt ceiling was raised in Congress to avert any loss of confidence in the U.S. dollar, as well as civil unrest when legacy and civil payments are not made. It is never politically prudent to reel in entitlements when there is the expediency of selling the future to sustain the present.

More Sovereign Defaults

Debt default history is deep in lessons that can perhaps point to the future of what is possible today. In older European history, most debt default was resolved through a combination of currency debasement and/or inflation, meaning if debtor nation owed the creditor in their currency and the currency the debt was owed in weakened against the borrower, by let's say 30 percent, then the borrowing country's debt would be reduced by the same amount. Thus, payments became manageable, and the compliance of debt repayment would follow.

In times of war, countries often abdicated their financial responsibilities to the enemy, after all, why make their payments when they could invest in a military to beat their creditors into submission? This was the case in World War I, when Turkey, Austria-Hungary, and Bulgaria suspended payments to enemy country creditors, and then in World War II, Turkey made an encore appearance as a chronic sovereign defaulter, along with their Allies, Japan and Italy.

As a side note, it is interesting to see that all three countries combined today have a total outstanding debt of approximately $19 trillion (not including legacy, local and provincial costs), with Italy being the new sick man of Europe's socialist utopia.

Other examples of sovereign debt default in the 20th century use revolutions and coup d'états as a pretext for not paying their debts. After all, what better reason can one have for stiffing creditors often in the form of bondholders than war? In the last century, it was by Russia taking cue from Karl Marx who had a personal reputation of not paying his bills, hence using the pretext of the 1917 Bolshevik Revolution, China in 1952 (Mao instead of paying creditors, was indoctrinating the masses on the virtues on utopian egalitarianism, except for the ruling government class, of course), Czechoslovakia in 1952, and Cuba in 1960 as Castro enlightened his people by overthrowing Batista and introduced the merits of communism. In the name of change, history is ripe with examples of replacing one strong man with another.

Of course, economics play a big role as a result of losing a war, as was the case for Austria in 1802, and again in 1868, and Russia in 1839. Civil wars led to defaults in Spain in 1831, and China in 1921. After a boom in the U.S. the collapse of cotton prices led to the economies of many southern states to be hit so hard that they defaulted on debt.

The rule of thumb is, under property rights, if debtor does not pay their creditors, certain assets can be seized such as homes and other portfolios, and in the same line of thought, the 19th and 20th centuries are abundant where some creditor counties seized or controlled sovereign assets.

Seizing Foreign Revenue Creation of Assets

In the case of creditors who lent to sovereign countries and debts were not repaid, the lenders had little solutions or debt recovery plans until 1868, when the British Corporation of Foreign

Bondholders (CFB) was created. CFB brought a battery of debt repayment remedies that changed the playing field for all. For example, as Federico Sturzenegger and Jeromin Zettelmeyer discuss in their book *Debt Defaults and Lessons from a Decade of Crises*, as part of their debt settlement in 1889, CFB negotiated with Peru to have their debt cancelled for $53 million in exchange for the right to operate their railways for 66 years and its associated profits.[1] Hence, the current Chinese debt traps have precedence in history.

In the 19th century, debt collection by sovereign defaulters involved more severe measures, as was the case of Peru. In 1889, $30 million in debt was cancelled and $23 million in interest was forgiven by creditors, but there was a catch—namely the right to operate Peru's railways and benefit from its associated revenue stream. As part of the package, Peru also gave the British two million tons of guano, which is a fertilizer very high in nitrogen.

Similar arrangements were made in other Latin American markets—Paraguay and Costa Rica in 1855, Colombia in 1861, the Dominican Republic 1893, Ecuador in 1895, and El Salvador in 1899. Between 1869 to 1931, the concept of confiscating sovereign nation revenue streams in exchange for debt relief was very much in vogue, as well as confiscating government revenue producing assets for the creditor nation. Other distinguished guests to the debtor hall of fame include Liberia, Tunisia, Egypt, Turkey, and Morocco.

This tactic could be construed as morally hard-nosed, but the question is, did these governments of the day efficiently and wisely spend their revenue resources, or did they squander much on bureaucracy, ineptness, inefficiency, or just plain self-serving corruption, in the lust of holding power? For example, if a consumer cannot pay the debts on their obligations, associated assets such as cars or homes can be replevied by lenders. Then, can this hold true for nation-states? The jury is still deliberating. In the case of Britain, much of this was happened during the time of their Empire, where they had the sterling Imperial Preference economic trading order,

---

1   Federico Sturzenegger and Jeromin Zettelmeyer, *Debt Defaults and Lessons from a Decade of Crises* (Cambridge: MIT Press, 2007).

reserve currency of the world, and a pretty good Navy to support these practices, all amounting to some enormous clout. However, all this changed after the Americans deposed the British pound over two wars in the 20th century, with the U.S. dollar becoming the world currency reserve after Bretton Woods in 1944.

Mexico has repudiated its debt on two occasions—in 1861 it resulted in France, Spain, and the UK invading Mexico, and France installing Emperor Maximilian. Sometimes emperors under the threat of the guillotine or firing squad get more done than democratically elected representatives, and in 1867, regardless of Maximilian's accomplishments and popularity, he was overthrown and unceremoniously executed by a firing squad. Being a dictator or emperor seems to be a position that comes with peril, since they don't have the same luxury as former democratically elected leaders do of making a mess, still having a pension, then claiming private citizen status when criticized, and going on the lucrative lecture circuit passing off policy failure for success.

Again, during the Mexican revolution in 1911, Mexico defaulted, because after all, the replacement of tyranny with even more cruel subjugation and disorder with the new leader, becomes a costly and barbaric business.

Erasing debt after a revolution is a true and tried approach as was the case of modern-day Turkey, who did not want to pay for the pre-war Ottoman debt after World War I, and how can we forget Russia, which wiped out its debts clean after the Bolshevik revolution in 1917? Remember these revolutionary types are almost always self-serving narcissists, lusting for power without accomplishment by agitating the classes, find division, work them into a frothing lather, and make things go from bad to worse, when they themselves create a permanent and concocted ruling class.

Sovereign debit default has happened to the British in 1976, when the UK pound sterling crisis was a balance of payments, or currency crisis, which forced James Callaghan's Labour Party government to borrow $3.9 billion ($17.7 billion in 2020 dollars) from the International Monetary Fund (IMF), at the time, this was the largest loan ever to have been requested from the IMF.

Defaults in the 1970s to 1980s and The Baker Plan

With the oil shocks of the 1970s and resulting higher oil prices, OPEC oil producers, specifically in the GCC region, were awash with cash and with high interest rates on deposits due to inflation, their money was deposited in Western banks. The excess liquidity on banks' balance sheets needed to be employed to not create a drag on their P&Ls, when the interest rates were upwards of 8 percent on deposits during this period—further, European banks were encroaching on U.S. lending market share in Latin American countries. Then the perfect storm occurred when banks that were desperate to lend, offered loans to riskier "less developed countries" in U.S. dollar denominations, and equally desperate government borrowers, primarily in Latin America, who obliged the lending overtures. And instead of using funds to export to create U.S. dollar liquidity, these debtor markets used the funds to balance their books, to finance significantly higher import bills, not to mention a fine *à-la-carte* of corruption. But what really exasperated the issue was that in local currencies, their values precipitously degraded against the U.S. dollar. The tumultuous outcome was that in debtor domestic dollar terms, when pegged against the U.S. dollar, these borrowing countries ended up owing more than what they originally borrowed.

In the 1980s, with a toxic brew that included restrictive monetary policy to combat inflation (higher interest rates past 20 percent) combined with much of the lending at floating interest rates, it was a perfect storm for a debt default. The story becomes even more tragic when severe recessions in the 1980s set the stage for what is now known as the international debt crises, with the regular cast of characters that included Mexico, Brazil, and Argentina, playing the leading roles, and doing a tango of sorts.

As a preventative remedy, if the debtors had currencies with the hard asset backing of gold, the crises would not have unfolded so acutely.

But the true pain was felt on the other side of the equation by the lenders, as their dubious loans came home to roost, since many had loans to least developed countries (LDC), equating to

290 percent of their equity. When the reality of default transpired, it became apparent that certain banks would default on the depositor liabilities. Subsequently, the Continental Illinois Bank was rescued by the FDIC via the U.S. Federal Reserve in 1984, to the tune of $4.5 billion. If a multitude of Western banks had the same fate, a contagion could transpire due to LDC exposure. Then it becomes difficult to see if a comprehensive plan could have been put forth at the time of lending.

In terms of remedies to the world debt crises of the era, many proposals were tabled including, Western banks insisting on debt repayment. Stemming from Bretton Woods, the IMF's original role was to protect the liquidity of the pegged exchange system, not to bail out countries who could not mange their economy. However, along with the World Bank, the IMF raised funds to lend more money to debt defaulter nations to help pay old debt, while at the same time, lenders were reluctantly forced to loan these same nations. This somewhat resembles the chronic alcoholic being given residence in a liquor store with the hope of redemption to be his ultimate goal.

Finally, to help ease the crises, U.S. Treasury Secretary James Baker in 1985, during the IMF/World Bank meetings proposed increases in new loans, with a view of providing a net inflow of funds to help create exports, which would then generate foreign currency earnings to help pay back the defaulted loans. This is often referred to as the Baker Plan—in the end, this plan could not provide enough credit facilities to enable this strategy, regardless of the Plaza Accord of 1985. Subsequently, the Baker Plan came up short and the crises continued until 1989, with the advent of the Nicholas Brady Plans, better known as Brady Bonds.

Brady Bonds are sovereign debt securities, an instrument denominated in U.S. dollars; however, these bonds were different because they were issued by developing countries and collateralized by U.S. Treasury bonds as well—they were convertible from Brady Bonds to U.S. Treasuries. And because they were tradable instruments, banks exchanged their nonperforming loans for Brady bonds, with the result being that they were exchanged for U.S. treasuries with the nonperforming loans being taken off the balance sheets of U.S. commercial banks. The IMF and World Bank also worked with lenders to restructure the debt as part of the Brady Plan.

In terms of Latin American countries such as Mexico, this plan resulted in timely payments of interest and principal.

The outcome of the Brady Plan was that it created a change of interchangeable assets to avert loan defaults of Latin American countries and avert a contagion on U.S. and European banks.

Much like a soap opera that can run indefinitely, later in the 1990s, a couple of other significant potential economic contagions appeared.

The Asian Financial Contagion

In 1997, the tiger economies of the Far East became overheated with GDP growth reaching almost 10 percent. The crisis in this region was due to overambitious asset values that included the stock market and real estate prices, which were further exasperated by direct foreign investment. It was a charming bubble of sorts, that is, until investors in Thailand realised the property values had flatlined and were no longer sustainable. The contagion of the loss of asset prices then spread to South Korea, Thailand, Philippines, Malaysia, Singapore, and Indonesia, where real estate prices tumbled. Even Japan was affected.

In the same year, the carnage became apparent when Thailand's property developer Somprasong Land defaulted, while Thailand's largest finance company, Finance One, went bankrupt. Greed turned to fear, euphoria subsided as foreign investment started to dry up, and regional currencies were hit hard by currency speculators that lead to runaway inflation. At one point, stock markets and currencies in the region lost up to 70 percent of their value.

Eventually the IMF, the international lender of last resort, with some help from the World Bank and Asian Development Fund (ADF) stepped in with a $118 billion packaged that economically stabilized the region. However, it came with IMF covenants that included some rigorous conditions, with higher taxes, a reduction of government spending, a reduction of the credit supply in the way of higher interest, and the closure of insolvent financial institutions. This tough medicine helped clean out the rot within the economy, by rinsing structural distortions, by not subscribing to the moral dilemma, which is politically prohibitive, not to mention heresy in the west!

In the end, the crisis was fueled by a familiar culprit, which is the expansion of credit hoisted on the tenets of fiat money printing that led to euphoria and its associated by-product of unsustainable distorted asset prices.

However, the crisis was not fully contained since it started to affect the largest country in the world, as we shall see.

The Russian Ruble Crisis 1998

The Russian economy was recovering from the fall of the Soviet Union and transitioning to a market economy, with debt inherited from the Soviet times. In 1993, Russia had created a market bond called the GKO, where they could issue bonds in rubles—five roubles were pegged to $1 USD. Providing a backdrop, inflation was as high as 135 percent in 1995, and fallen to 11 percent in 1997, while the GDP showed its first post-Soviet gain.

Against this more positive backdrop, there was still uncertainty in the marketplace from the Asian contagion, which showed up on a speculative attack on the ruble. The Central Bank of Russia (CBR) quickly moved to defend the ruble with its U.S. dollar reserves, which it had earned from selling oil. However, when oil dropped from $23 per barrel in 1997 to $11 in 1998, the perfect storm of a combined exogenous shock from oil, leading to speculator attacks on the ruble. Concomitantly, there was a lack of confidence with Russian Bonds leading to a liquidity crisis, and to defend it, in May of 1998 the CBR hiked interest rates from 30 percent to 50 percent, then a week later the CBR raised rates again to 150 percent, where interest rates put the brakes on the economy, while putting the

Russian treasury in a position where interest on bonds exceeded tax revenues by 40 percent.[2] Intuitively, this was an unsustainable dilemma, and a recipe for a collapse, after the fall of the Soviet Empire eight years earlier.

Then on August 13, 1998, Russian bonds, stocks, and currency collapsed, and in the case of the stock market, it declined 75 percent, coupled with 84 percent inflation in an economic tsunami, while state employees were not getting paid. Even with an IMF bailout, the crisis could not be averted because the country had no real plan to wade out of the water.

As a side note, it should also be noted that Boris Yeltsin, who was rarely sober, allowed oligarchs to ravage the natural wealth of the country while the Americans looked the other way. The ruble was not a hard backed currency, but as of 2020, Russia has the fifth highest gold reserves in the world at 2.3 million tons, as well as one of the lowest debts to GDP ratios in the 20 percent range. Further, its energy resource can be used at least psychologically to back the ruble.

If the global economy craters, those with hard backing of gold or Bitcoin or resources will be in a better position to avoid the tragedy of being enslaved in a state created fiat money, and especially to the U.S. dollar.

It is with this light sprinkling of economic history that warrants us with more insights, clarity, and intellectual inference, to venture off into the house of cards and discover the minute details of the largest Ponzi scheme created to date. So, with popcorn in hand, it is this thrilling ending that is now presented in the house of cards.

2 "Russia 3-Month Interbank Rate," Trading Economies, accessed April 8, 2022, https://tradingeconomics.com/russia/interbank-rate

From Liberty to Bondage

A democracy cannot exist as a permanent form of government. It can only exist until the voters discover that they can vote themselves largesse from the public treasury. From that moment on, the majority always votes for the candidates promising the most benefits from the public treasury with the result that a democracy always collapses over loose fiscal policy, always followed by a dictatorship. These nations have progressed through this sequence: From bondage to spiritual faith; From spiritual faith to great courage; From courage to liberty; From liberty to abundance; From abundance to selfishness; From selfishness to apathy; From apathy to dependence; From dependence back into bondage.

—*Alexander Fraser Tytler*

CHAPTER

15

House of Cards

Figure 15.1: The Cycle of Freedom to Bondage

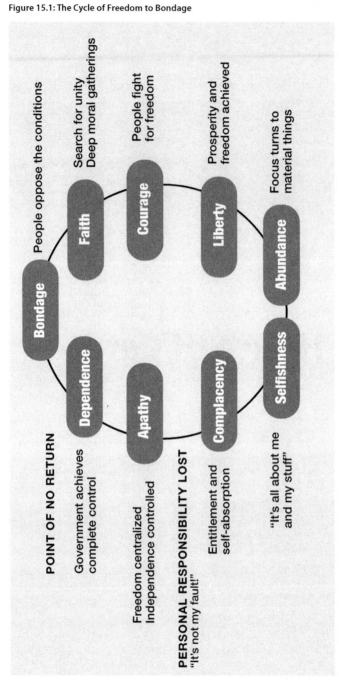

Source: Alexander Frase Tytler (1747-1813)

Building a house of cards is steeped in governmental history as Charles Ponzi and Bernie Madoc perhaps took their queues by studying sovereign debt defaults. Governments have a well-documented history of sovereign debt default—even the UK was bailed out by the IMF as recently as 1976, so now we leave the past to make sense of the present, so we can infer into the future, and it is here that we enter "the house of cards."

We are on cusp of an impending tragedy of the American and global economy. The U.S. economy has never recovered from 2008 Great Recession. Why? Unemployment—much of it demand deficient, some structural, stayed high ranging from 9.9 percent in 2010, and took until 2017 to return to 4 percent,[1] and this is not even the effective unemployment rate, which is much higher. In fact, unemployment was in the 22 percent range for 2017[2]—remember once you stop collecting benefits you fall off the official statistics. GDP stayed sluggish, mostly under 2 percent for the 2010s,[3] while government debt went from $10 trillion in 2008, and ballooned to nearly $30 trillion in 2021. And for all this debt there is nothing to show for it; no high-speed rail, no free education in science, technology, engineering, and math, which would greatly increase the competitive output of the labour force, no bridges and infrastructure to foster economic efficiency—all we have is just an assortment of wasted Keynesian wishing and hoping, lots of virtue signalling, and a more pronounced wealth gap.

If the economy had recovered, may it be in Europe or North America, interest rates would be normalized in the 5 to 7 percent range insuring there would not be distortions in asset prices, that

1   Kimberly Amadeo, "Unemployment Rate by Year Since 1929 Compared to Inflation and GDP," The Balance, updated April 3, 2022, https://www.thebalance.com/unemployment-rate-by-year-3305506

2   "Alternate Unemployment Rates," Shadow Government Statistics, accessed April 8, 2022, http://www.shadowstats.com/alternate_data/unemployment-charts

3   "Annual growth of the real Gross Domestic Product (GDP) of the United States from 1990 to 2021," Statista, accessed March 24, 2022, https://www.statista.com/statistics/188165/annual-gdp-growth-of-the-united-states-since-1990/

exclude the young and working poor from home ownership, while the stock markets would have price discovery based on empirical valuations. And finally, if the economy recovered from the great recession, it could stand on its own two feet without the never-ending fiscal stimulation and addiction of near zero interest rates. Put differently, when are the training wheels coming off?

The only result is that the 2008 mindset has created a large government with over $30 trillion of debt, and on the road to $40 trillion that will not get off the backs of the industrious, which is the government's go to villain, while creating a well rehearsed à la carte of propaganda to impose even more oppressive taxation to confiscate the fruits of one's labour.

In the magician's hands we have cosmetically masked the decay and toxicity of unsustainable debt through artificially keeping interest rates low.

The stark reality is that the outcomes of fiat money printing has resulted in consequences, some intended and some not, with the endgame being that we are in a house of cards propped up by a Ponzi scheme, with all options leading to bad conclusions. Let's first consider the wealth gap through distorted asset prices, in equities and real estate, where the train moves through the station so rapidly, the youth cannot get on board to catch their dreams. This is an unintended consequence of easy money, and to think government will fix it, when they have caused it, might qualify one as a candidate for the boulevard of fools.

The story continues: as of mid-2022 we are experiencing near 10 percent CPI inflation (this is what the Fed goes by), but the effective inflation rate, according to private market analysis from Shadow Government Statistics, it is closer to 15 percent. There are a number of consequences to inflation, as it will affect the working poor and those on fixed incomes, including on government support, where they will have to stretch their dollar even further. Yes, these are the people you see at local dollar stores, trying to make ends meet walking around like zombies trying to make sense of it all. And of course, it is inflation that could potentially knock the middle-class out of the game and hurl them into the working poor category, due to price increases on items we need to buy for the necessities of life. When prices rise and people's income doesn't, the consumer must cut back, which will contract the economy, or to take a Keynesian view, the marginal propensity to consume (MPC) will decrease, and in many respects, the MPC is a derivative of U.S. Index of Consumer Sentiment, which has dropped 34 percent from April 2021 to April 2022, which plays a huge role both on Wall Street and Main Street. Or better still, what if prices go up, demand diminishes and the economy contracts under a triple threat? This could easily play out with fiat money printing, especially as the U.S. dollar craters, and imports become dear. Or it is possible that we can have seesaw bouts of deflation, inflation, and stagflation.

This is all the Cantillon effect of too much money chasing too few goods leading to inflation, and this is essential criteria to be granted membership in the house of cards.

If only the problems were limited to this, we could find a way out through both fiscal and monetary policy. However, the U.S. government is insolvent, on life support from the Fed, and the rest of the world is not much better off. This makes for thrilling theatre, which brings us to Broadway shows, where since 2008, the sold-out production of *"As the Fed Prints, and the Treasury Borrows"* keeps the audience on the edge of their seats.

Socrates claimed that the best rulers are reluctant to rule but do so out of necessity—since they do not wish to be ruled by someone inferior,[4] and for questioning the competence of the aristocracy, his fate was sealed. This is where we take a deep dive into the anatomy of the Ponzi scheme that is built on a house of cards, and this time, with no tragic hero on the horizon to save it from itself. It is here where the plot thickens and as each character plays a vital role in delivering this Broadway debacle.

4   Plato, The Republic, trans. Desmond See (New York: Penguin, 1955), 347a-c.

A Peak into the Ponzi Scheme

The Ponzi scheme has been in the making for many years, going back to Woodrow Wilson, when he helped finance World War I by having the Fed purchase bonds. Just after the end of World War II in 1946, under FDR, the debt ballooned to 118 percent of GDP at $269 billion, where this core amount was never retired in subsequent years, as it was inflated away as a smaller percentage to GDP. It is true that total debt dropped as a percentage of GDP—by 1974 it was 31 percent of GDP, by the end of the Nixon era, however, had increased to $475 billion. Reagan had the honours of breaking the $1 trillion barrier with a deficit to $1.14 trillion by 1982, and by the end of the Clinton years, it went from $4.4 trillion, and reached $5.674 trillion, but in his defence, Clinton had a budget surplus in 2000, which has since been a blasphemous idea.[5]

By the time George W. Bush finished his presidency in 2008, it had ballooned to $10 trillion, as the baton was passed to Obama, and never to be outdone, gave us hope but no change (at least from the balanced budget perspective), when he doubled it in eight years to near $20 trillion, and Trump made "budget deficits great again" when he bumped it up to $28 trillion. And with Biden, the accumulated deficit will easily reach $40 trillion by the end of his first term—that is unless the debt market crashes from money printing, and the whole house comes down, earlier than anticipated. Hence, each time Congress increases the debt ceiling, we are now seeing this tragic story unfold, but there is more to this story.

From the 2008 financial meltdown, the key issues still linger, namely, risky lending, high taxation, household debt, sluggish GDP growth, and unsustainable government debt. The reason we are not seeing a robust recovery for the last 10 years is because the Great Recession was not cyclical, but structural, in nature. And the

---

5   "Annual Gross Domestic Product and Real GDP in the United States from 1930 to 2020," Statista, accessed March 24, 2022, https://www.statista.com/statistics/1031678/gdp-and-real-gdp-united-states-1930-2019/

structural issues in world economies have not been resolved, but only manipulated, masked, and exasperated to the point of no return through monetary policy and fiat money printing, resulting in perpetual systematic economic distortions. Much like the opening kick off, the ball is being punted down the field for a new generation to deal with it, assuming the house of cards can stand that long.

What's Under the Hood of That Car?

In another time it was a male ritual to ask what was under the hood of that car you're driving, in order to establish whether or not the engine could perform well enough to facilitate the flashy body, especially in a race, we still see this in stunt driving on streets. It was a passage of sorts from a time gone by, whereas today, cars are judged by connectivity to the internet of things! Either way under the hood, there are some horrible monsters that lie in wait, as our psyche denies the existence of the truth. Our Broadway play becomes even more intriguing as the protagonist desperately searches for the truth, but something in his psyche, deeply hidden in the layers of his soul, and knows that an unstoppable monster lurks in the shadows of deniability.

When we eventually look under the hood of the car, the U.S. is on track to have an accumulated deficit close to $34 trillion by year end 2022, which is a realistic inference since the Biden administration is proposing a $5.8 trillion budget with revenues in the $4 trillion range, as government spending programs are a tried and proven remedy for winning mid-terms (in anticipation that the treasury can spin a story and fictitiously find blame elsewhere). The White House is claiming that they are going to reduce the total deficit by $1 trillion dollars over 10 years, without any valid empirical forecast of budgets moving forward and contingency plans for an exogenous shock, which would keep the money printing press in high gear. However, what is not mentioned is that the deficit will reach a minimum of $40 trillion by the end of

2024.[6] So after racking up $40 trillion the administration is going to reduce the deficit by $1 trillion. What is not further considered is, the accumulated deficit could easily hit $55 trillion by 2032. This assertion is clearly a gaslighting attempt on people who confuse yearly deficits with accumulated. This type of spending is nothing short of financial abdication of duty, and a good reason to call in detective Colombo to ask some pointed questions.

To get a better idea of calculating the true debt in America, we draw from the site U.S. Debt Clock, where we start with $34 trillion in Federal debt, then add about $3.7 trillion for municipal debt and state debt (best estimate), giving us a total of $37.7 trillion, and then when we divide this number by total households, we are seeing that each household has a government liability indebtedness for $300,000 USD.[7] But it gets worse. To the disbelief of the protagonist, much like the tip of the iceberg, the horror story plays out more when we add unfunded liabilities such as pensions, excluding guarantees of foreign issued bonds, state and municipal pensions, (state government workers, teachers, police, fire, services, etc.), Fannie May, Freddie Mac, which are all underfunded. Not considered in this calculation is other municipal debt, in the way of underfunded state workers' legacy obligations. Drawing from a *Wall Street Journal* article, the combined debt of these obligations is the size of Japan's economy.[8]

Building on our calculation, when we add only unfunded liabilities of federal entitlements of Social Security, Medicare, federal workers' pensions, we have estimations of ranging from $55 trillion by the Government Accountability Office, to Cox & Archer estimating $87 trillion, to Kotlikoff's fiscal gap putting the number closer to $200

6   Sabrina Escobar, "What's in Biden's $5.8 Billion Budget? A Billionaire Tax and Boosts to Military and Social Spending," Barron's, March 28, 2022, https://www.barrons.com/articles/biden-budget-billionaire-tax-military-social-spending-51648473286

7   U.S. Debt Clock, accessed April 8, 2022, https://www.usdebtclock.org/

8   "The Pension Hole for U.S. Cities and States Is the Size of Germany's Economy," *Wall Street Journal*, July 30, 2018, https://www.wsj.com/articles/the-pension-hole-for-u-s-cities-and-states-is-the-size-of-japans-economy-1532972501

trillion. Let's say we infer that federal unfunded liabilities are $75 trillion (this is a conservative number), and add the accumulated deficit of $40 trillion by 2024, (excluding state and municipal unfunded obligations), we have a grand total of $115 trillion. Then using the number of households for dispersion of debt, which is approximately 123 million in the United States, we quickly see that each household in America is on the hook for $935,000, almost $1 million per American family of debt owed on behalf of government. Remember, this has nothing to do with personal consumer household debt.

This is the anatomy of the Ponzi scheme that will play out like an epic tsunami, as the patrons run out of the burning theatre before the play has ended.

If this was a private company, it would have collapsed long ago, with its directors put in jail for dereliction of duty, and all its employees laid off, but this is government, and this is the double standard we play by. This is perhaps the primary reason that government is a net negative on the economy, especially since the U.S. went off the gold standard 51 years ago.

To better visualize the carnage, if we stacked up $115 trillion in one-dollar bills, it would reach almost halfway to Venus.

It plays out like the exorcists as the villain of our participative creations, first in the name of liberty, takes us on the road leading to apathy, then we take a rest at the boulevard of dependence, before we venture to our final destination, a street named bondage. Understandably by now the reader might be heading for the fire exits but do please sit in your chair as the theatrical tragedy still has many more acts!

In much of the world, the stories play out the same way, take the case in Canada, when we combine federal accumulated debt of $2 trillion which is closer to 115 percent of GDP and total provincial debt of $1 trillion, which represents 57 percent of debt to GDP, we have a total 173 percent debt to GDP, or $3 trillion as a nation, by the end of 2021. This means each Canadian household is on the hook for $300,000 of combined provincial and federal government debt, making Canada's relative debt the fifth highest of industrialized nations. This, of course, does not include pensions, in the civil service, and other legacy costs, which are quite possibly underfunded. But Canadians are just as proud as Americans in showing gratitude to their captors in a dome called Stockholm syndrome, where many lie in docility!

Moving to Europe's total debt as a region is near 100 percent of GDP, which equates to $20 trillion, and again this number does not consider unfunded legacy obligations, provincial and municipal costs, as well as external debt to GDP. Europe has turned into a basket case for a region addicted to the culture of welfare and entitlement, and much like America's governmental spending, self-reliance is heresy to be tried in the public courts of the social media. Germany, in terms of GDP is its leader, but it is just not Greece, who owes 245 percent of GDP, and when we include external debt it rises to 310 percent of GDP, with a grand total of $500 billion, the list goes on—France, at 256 percent of GDP external debt, and 120 percent of GDP domestic debt, the UK is that $3.7 trillion of debt with public debt amounting to 112 percent of GDP, moving to Italy, their debt amounts to $3.2 trillion, or 168 percent of GDP, while their external debt is 154 percent of GDP, and when we turn our attention to Sweden, their external debt is 252 percent of GDP, while Germany is approaching 90 percent of GDP debt ratios.

As a result of this ocean of debt, the European Central Banks balance sheets have bloated to near $9 trillion as of 2021, including buying bond debts from the PIGS—Portugal, Italy, Greece, and Spain. Quite frankly, Europe sits on the shoulders of Germany, and the Euro currency is really the Deutsche Mark with updated artwork since January 1, 1999. The central banks should run a stress test on the toxic assets they purchased to see exactly what percentage of their accounts receivable is realizable. Better still, when the presstitute financial media comes out of their state of comatose, perhaps they can consider this question!

Surprisingly, the Eastern European countries having lived under the yoke of socialism and communism, for the most part, have their debt under 50 percent of GDP, including Lithuania, Czech Republic, and surprisingly Russia's is the lowest on the list with debt to GDP of under 20 percent or $245 billion. The primary reason Eastern Europe is under less debt is that with lower tax collection, and less able to issue bonds, government cannot grow—at least not yet—due to a lack of oppressive taxation. Hence, people expect less from government, and government works to deliver more for less, which might be a good idea after all. A good example is Hungary where the government has some regard for its citizenry, as opposed to Western elitists who are showing their tyrannical hands.

A Made in China Ponzi Scheme

No equation of the house of cards could be compete without its *protégé*, China, as it joins the dream team that includes, the United States, Canada, Japan and Western Europe. In China's case, its private sector, much of it unviable, owes money to the state apparatus that it simply cannot pay back, which makes for exquisite Chinese theatre with a history dating back to Shang Dynasty some 3,000 years ago.

As misery likes company, and never to be outdone, China makes good company, of being on the verge of its own meltdown.

In China's house of cards, the cracks are starting to show in a speculative residential real estate bubble with a host of shaky developers. Many of these developers have taken deposits including Evergrande who has defaulted on foreign investors' U.S. dollar bonds as part of their debt structure, which includes $300 billion in known liabilities and another $160 billion in off balance sheet obligations, according to Goldman Sachs. This story is more than likely the tip of the iceberg with a host of shaky Chinese property developers that are in debt to the tune of $5.2 trillion, according to the *Wall Street Journal*.[9]

Rumors are already circulating that Evergrande is dumping apartments at 50 percent off original price, and this is sure to upset retail investors who buy second properties as investments in

9   Stella Yifan Xie, "China's Economy Faces Risk of Yearslong Real-Estate Hangover," *Wall Street Journal*, November 8, 2021, https://www.wsj.com/articles/chinas-economy-faces-risk-of-yearslong-real-estate-hangover-11636372801

urban cities like Shanghai and keep them empty. It is one thing to default on bank loans where the top four Chinese banks are state-owned, but if the developers stiff the speculators on the deposit for these apartments, China will have a full-blown contagion crisis that will create social unrest leading to a double-edged sword.

To get an idea of the potential contagion, China's residential real estate market is worth $62 trillion versus America's $34 trillion and makes up 30 percent of their GDP. In other words, if the real estate market cracks in China, so follows the GDP growth, which is closer to 8.5 percent in 2021, if we are to believe official Chinese Communist Party (CCP) numbers.

With China's aging population, there just aren't enough buyers to go around, with 90 percent ownership in urban areas, and with approximately 108 million apartments being built.[10] Add to the equation that sales of the 100 top property developers are down almost 40 percent from September 2021, coupled by underpopulated ghost cities that were centrally planned, and the outcome is a perfect storm brewing. Eventually in the house of cards, demand and supply catch up to euphoria as the ghost of Adam Smith drops in for a malt.

Zombie Companies

China has other issues on the horizon, namely its zombie companies that are kept afloat by local governments leaning on lenders and a host of opaque accounting standards that do not write-off bad debt, as practiced in the West under GAAP conventions. Zombie companies, which do not have a viable business and that cannot deliver free cash flows, are mired in debt that would be considered severe Chapter 11 & 9 insolvency cases in the U.S. and elsewhere. These debts continue to be rolled over, and even though the Chinese government debt at just over 50 percent of GDP is man-

10   Wolf Richter, "How China's Model of Dictated Economic Growth Blew Up," Wolf Street, October 22, 2021, https://wolfstreet.com/2021/10/22/chinas-model-of-dictated-economic-growth-blew-up/

ageable, when we add household, corporations, government, and the financial sector, it amounts to over 300 percent of GDP, and it is this tenuous position China finds itself in. Figure 15.2 tells the story.

Figure 15.2: Chinese Debt 2019 (Percentage of GDP)

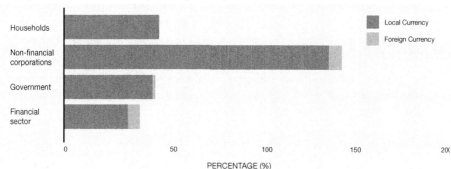

Source: *Institute of International Finance Bloomberg*

Traditionally, the government has stepped in as we are seeing now in the U.S. and implicitly signalled to the markets that it would backstop debt defaults by corporations, but it seems the CCP is backing off the gas pedal of saving debt-ridden and zombie companies. Of course, as for the art of saving zombie companies, the U.S. has learned from the CCP, which has drawbacks as this causes economic and competitive distortions. At the same time, it could be argued that the biggest zombie entity financially is the U.S. government and Central Bank.

This then brings us to China's other messy room in the house of cards, specifically China's mostly state-owned enterprises that are on the books of banks and state financial arms that it simply refuses to write-off and carry on. After all, China is a quasi-planned state-controlled economy, that lets companies have enough freedom so the state can live off them, much like the current West, where the modus operandi is as long as they toe the government line of their well rehearsed tapestry of obfuscation, the associated Cabalatocracy comes together to facilitate this symphony.

Local government financing vehicles (LGFV) that finance the Chinese zombie companies many of them state-owned, "Are in worst shape themselves, to the point where they could not pay interest, never mind principle, on their loans to government arms", said Larry Hu, chief China economist at Macquarie, in a June 25 note. LGFVs also like to keep the zombie companies running because they create tax revenue, because if they closed, the loss of jobs would stir up the locals into a political lather. To add to this distortion that amounts to a pyramid scheme, Dinny McMahon writes in his book *China's Great Wall of Debt* that, "Chinese zombies are kept alive by local governments, [which] provide subsidies and lean on banks to provide sufficient credit to ensure they remain viable."[11]

Take the case of Dongbei Special Steel Group's default on a bond payment in 2016; in the name of reform, the state sent a message that it would no longer coddle loser companies, but there was only problem, according to the *Wall Street Journal*, three months later, the result has been…nothing. "The ailing steel mill has missed five more payments on its $6 billion debt but has yet to formally file for the equivalent of bankruptcy protection, close unproductive units or start a restructuring of its operations."[12]

So then, who has the bad debt on their books, the LGFV, the bank, which could be state-owned, or the state? Put another way, someone has to hold the bag while the keystone cops come to investigate.

The road to clearing up these distortions in China's banking and debt system runs into challenges that includes a Chinese culture, where debt is not easily forgiven vs. the modernity of the world's financial system. The moral hazard is allowed to continue, which not only creates internal distortions in the economy, but other issues where these zombie companies desperate for cash dump products overseas, which then bring us back to anti-dumping WTO provisions. So, what many least developed countries (LDC) do is

---

11   Dinny McMahon, *China's Great Wall of Debt: Shadow Banks, Ghost Cities, Massive Loans and the End of the Chinese Miracle* (New York: Houghton Mifflin Harcourt, 2018).

12   Chuin-Wei Yap, "China's Sombie Companies Stay Alive Despite Defaults," *Wall Street Journal*, July 12, 2016, https://www.wsj.com/articles/chinas-zombie-companies-stay-alive-despite-defaults-1468303515

put a mountain of paperwork when dealing with new items as a way to protect against this type of dumping.

Even though China's government debt officially is near 50 percent of GDP it conveniently misses out on the corporations' debt, much of which is held by the government, which when combined, easily brings it over 300 percent to GDP. It is this house of cards that masks the underlying toxicity of its pending earthquake. Because of these distortions, much of China's miracle is built on the foundation of quicksand that it will have to deal with either writing-off debt by defaulting on bond payments or roll it over into equity. Either way, if the government swaps debt for equity, it is still dealing with companies with negative cash flows in unviable rustbelt industries, in many cases even after shedding its debt, it will reinflate the same crisis where equity masks debt with companies that are still bleeding red ink. In some ways, it can be compared to investing in horse and buggy companies in 2021.

As much of the world lectures China on its ecology from the high summit top of Western virtue, we have exported not only our inflation—up until recently, since this show is coming to an end because of money printing—to them that has raised living standards but have also exported our carbon footprints and dumped it in their backyard. This has come at an admitted cost of the decay of our own innovation, while China being lured by riches and aspirations of empire gets stuck with a bill that is closer to $2 trillion to clean up their environment. The consolation prize is that we can still wag our virtuous yet hypocritical finger at them in the politico of the new theology of environmentalism, which is eventually going to be a pretext to a tax grab.

So, when we lift the glitter of Shanghai's seductive skyline smoke and mirrors and blistering speed, there is much economic rot in the house called China, as it is sitting on a grand total of debt of approximately $50 trillion, opaquely interchanged between government, consumers and private enterprise (not including legacy costs such as pensions), within a $16 trillion economy. It is this tenuous dynamic that may very well fall like dominoes, making them an honorary member of the house of cards along with the

United States, Canada, Japan, and Western Europe. In the house of cards, currencies are not backed, as it does not occur to the guests to consider where the exit door is located before Mount Vesuvius engulfs Pompeii into an epic tragedy that will eventually play out in 4K at theatres near you.

More Debt for the Old Debt

Back in America, the U.S. Treasury cannot pay out its Treasury Bills when they come due, so it relies on the Central Bank to print fiat money to satisfy the maturity of bonds. Let's say that the U.S. federal revenue is $4.0 trillion, and $400 billion of bonds come due in any given year, and with $34 trillion in debt by the end of 2022, we can see a reduction of cash flows. But what about a year of $3 trillion of Treasury Bills coming due? How would the Treasury pay for it? Technically, this would make them acutely insolvent, but they will have the Fed print money out of thin air, lend it to the Treasury, which will expand the parameters of the Ponzi scheme. In essence, they are rolling over old debt with new debt, and then adding additional new debt with current deficits further ballooning the accumulated deficit.

Increasing the debt ceiling seems to make the news at least twice a year, both parties have a catfight about how much they can raise that ceiling, and it goes without saying that it has political connotations. What this really means is that Medicare, Medicaid, federal pensions, all of which are underfunded, have run out of money. Hence, the government increases the national deficit to continually pay for these obligations, and every year it is "soak, rinse and repeat", in exchange for votes. In the case of a tanking economy, a military war, augmented with a buffet of propaganda can be launched to deflect from the tragic play we are all living in. If this was taking place in a monarchy, which Socrates preferred over democracy, the emperor as his fate would have it, would be greeted by Charles-Henri Sanson's recycled guillotine from King Louis XVI.

True, some pundits will argue that the Social Security Trust Fund in the U.S. has $2.6 trillion of assets, which is accurate—the problem is that it has all been cashed out and pledged out as collateral. Congress has been raiding this fund since the 1940s, and if any private business handled both their free cash flows and especially their pension fund like this, on a sustained basis, they would collapse and be under a fraud investigation, with the directors wearing orange attire with embossed numbers and appearing in a new Netflix series. Thus, the only thing it holds is $2.6 trillion dollars of government Treasury Bills and not just any securities, these are "Special Issue" securities that can only be sold to the U.S. Treasury. Together, Social Security and healthcare account for about 60 percent of the U.S. budget, but if they were well managed, from tax contributions, and funds were invested into the future through equity vehicles, they could literally sustain themselves.

The Department of Treasury has no realistic hope of paying these funds back to the Social Security Trust Fund. The same with Medicare and Medicaid, where there is not a 5- or 10-year reserve to facilitate obligations.

So, it will pay for current pensions due through increased taxation, or better yet, they have to increase the debt ceiling to issue new bonds to pay for its current cash outflow obligations to pensions and other budgetary items. In 2016, the U.S. Treasury had a social security obligation of just over $1 trillion and the states combined have $400 billion, which means that even if the $2.6 trillion existed, which it does not, it would only cover just over two years of public pension obligations at the federal level. Put in perspective, the U.S. government revenue is $4 trillion, meaning social security takes up a third of revenues.

What if Interest Rates Went Up?

In 2021, the 10-year yield on treasuries was just under 1.7 percent, and in April 2022 has spiked to 2.95 percent since it has priced in Central Bank rate hikes, still this is not the natural rate of interest, since it is kept down but the Central Bank's bond purchasing program, meaning the Fed is intentionally flattening the yield curve. At 2.95 percent interest of let's say $34 trillion, the yearly interest is near $1 trillion, and at these rates as new bonds replace lower yield bonds, it will start representing about 20 percent of the 2022 budget. What if there was a run on the U.S. dollar where China says, "We are not going to accept U.S. greenbacks for goods," and then the Fed had to increase interest rates to defend the dollar? What if the Fed could no longer suppress the natural cost of interest, the U.S. 10-year Treasury Bond yield exploded and jumped to 7 percent, and the debt market exploded (bond market)? What if this so-called transitory inflation reached 12 percent CPI in 2022 and effective inflation goes to 20 percent, and we had a combination of runaway inflation, stagflation, and a bout of deflation to boot, and the Fed had to increase interest rates to defend credibility of international monetary systems? What if the Fed reads the economy wrong as it did in 1930, and made decisions based on lagging indicators? What if the Central Bank could not react to a seesaw of deflation, inflation, and stagflation?

This is a realistic possibility, and the result would be the most epic economic catastrophe one could imagine. Consider a combination of the interest on $34 trillion of debt of 10 percent which would spike to $3.4 trillion, accounting for near 90 percent of the U.S. federal revenue streams, although much of it would still be at lower rates until bonds became due and matured. The government could no longer maintain social security and healthcare since it could not afford to borrow fresh funds at 2 percent. Tax revenues would decline due to unemployment, the bond market would collapse, housing prices would precipitously decline at least 25 percent, leading to a loss of homeowner wealth of $9 trillion dollars. With the end of easy money, the stock market would decline by at least 35 percent, wiping out $29 trillion in wealth globally, this is a very conservative estimate. In fact, as of May 2022, the Nasdaq is already down 37% from all time highs and beats the shock of March 2020.

It gets worse—if the Fed tapered in any precipitous way, to defend the dollar, it would dry up the credit markets, then who would be buying all these junk bonds and B rated credit commercial paper? The contagion would implode since this would lead to bank failures, including Wall Street banks that have no capital holdback requirements and credit default swaps not being honoured—this almost happened to Goldman Sachs in 2008, as they had bought swaps as a hedge against the housing market from a failing ING that could not fulfill the financial insurance policy of a drop in the real estate sector it undertook. The contagion would spread like a California wildfire in July as the bottom would fall out from consumer demand. And this brings us back to the Fed trap, namely, if they increase interest rates, the economies will go into macroeconomic shock, leading to sovereign debt default with the U.S. being a prime candidate, and if they continue to print money, the U.S. dollar could collapse from overprinting, unleashing an epic bout of inflation.

This trap is clearly because of money printing and large government overstepping the boundaries of individual liberty. We are all in a trap, since government lives off the avails of the industrious, while many are captives of government, where the subjugated suffer from a Stockholm syndrome of sorts, where pacified hostages or the abused victims develop a bond with their captors. It is at this doorstep of the pending and undeniable tragedy we find ourselves, where just like the government and the Feds, we are trapped in this tragic interwoven dependency.

This brings us full circle back to the Scottish philosopher Alexander Fraser Tytler, purported to have said, "Liberty turns to apathy, leading to dependence, and of course the end game, bondage."

Looking for the Villain

In our quest to find a villain, which is an old age tradition, we emotionally absolve ourselves from the courage it would take to look in the mirror.

It is only natural that to find a villain of choosing, government propagandists will point us in the correct direction by using terms such as the wealthy and not so wealthy should pay their fair share of taxes. So then, this brings up the question, what do we mean by fair share of taxes, and then how do we quantify this? And of course, this quintessential definition of fair is not considered in state sponsored propaganda, and double speak, all paid for by the taxpayer of course.

To the credit of government, they are not accountable for their litany of failures, but proudly boast a monopoly on failed ideas masked as achievement!

In the quest to find the villain, qualify for redemption and to cure the woes, government enlightens its disciples that through oppressive taxation as being the solution to the crises to entice reaching the promised mountain top. Aha! It is here where we find 724 billionaires to pay for all this debt, that incidentally, they did not necessarily create, but did benefit from the money printing the most. With an acumen for finding villains at the direction of the virtuous, we go after the top one-tenth of 1 percent where often the terms envy, taxation, and confiscation interchangeably mean the same thing in Marxist double-speak folklore in the quest to build the elusive summit top of egalitarianism.

So now that we have identified the culprit, (well as least for now), U.S. billionaires accounting for total wealth of $4.7 trillion (mid-2021), up about 35 percent since the pandemic started, and let's guess they make combined $500 billion a year in income, which is unlikely, as their increase in wealth would be due to increased capital appreciation of assets. So then, let's hypothetically tax the $500 billion income at 80 percent and we still only get $400 billion dollars of taxation that will be squandered by the government anyway. Okay, that didn't work, how about we tax them 10 percent on their net worth yearly, which comes out to $470 billion?

Or better still, just plagiarize a page from Venezuela, Castro's Cuba, Mengistu in Ethiopia, Lenin, and Mao, and just confiscate what they wouldn't have the imagination to create. After all, the end game is wealth redistribution, with the only problem being that if it goes through government hands, they will not pay down the deficit, they'll waste much of it on a new perceived or real cri-ses, while feeding the remaining scraps to the plebeians for going along with the ruse. Think for a moment, are you really going to eradicate poverty through confiscation or handouts? Well then, how did the Great Society pan out?

The issue with free money that the recipients have not creat-ed—they will for the most part spend it, leaving them broke again in a year. In fact, Andrew Carnegie stated that business did a better job of redistributing wealth than government.

All these scenarios would result in a substantial deterioration of the equities and bond market, hurting anyone who owns stocks and have them run for the exit doors to greener pastures, while signal-ling to the world that the U.S. punishes wealth, which is antithetical to the American societal fabric. At the same time, it would suggest to the world that property rights have been thrown under the bus.

Put another way, it could perhaps wipe out half of the $48 tril-lion value of the U.S. equity markets, destroy anyone with a 401(k) plan and stocks, decimate pensions, while signal to the world that the U.S. dollar is no longer a safe haven, leading to a spike in the 10-year yield, while dethroning the U.S. dollar as the world reserve currency. This is not just mere conjecture, but a reasoned look at the economic dystopia that wealth confiscation would result in.

As a side note, this is actually happening slowly but surely, but in a different way. Just like Venezuela had their gold and foreign reserves confiscated, the Americans did the same with nearly $300 billion of Russian foreign reserves in February of 2022, as retribution for the Ukrainian war, which was not a prudent geo-economic strategy. Why? Because countries flush with U.S. Treasury bills such as China with $1 trillion with another $3.2 trillion in reserves, and Saudi Arabia with over $100 billion in Treasury notes and $415 billion in U.S. reserves might be looking at each other and thinking, "are we going to get stiffed as well if we don't toe the U.S. line?" In fact, this is what is happening with Russia demanding to be paid in rubles for gas and oil by hostile countries, while China, Russia, and India are considering trading outside the U.S. dollar and forming their own Club of Rome with their alternative SWIFT system, one called the SPFS. And by kicking Russia for the most part out of the SWIFT system, the U.S. no longer can see all their international transactions between Russia and its trading partners. In the end, America, by following these policies, is overextending the limitations of power, while self-inflicting the dollar's hegemony as the world reserve currency, inadvertently creating the groundwork for a competitive parallel monetary system to the U.S. dollar.

The cascading effect would signal to many entrepreneurs wanting to come to America that the grounds are hostile for business. Billionaires such as Bezos, Winfrey, Musk, and Kardashian have carefully crafted public images, and the digital plebeians who act as their disciples on Instagram are enamoured with them. In a sense they are a protected class—however, people in the $20 million to $100 million net worth category get the brunt of disdain from the public, as they are the freshly minted entrepreneurs, many that have only come to America a short time ago. Pick on them and confiscate their wealth instead of the billionaires. Pick on them, and it would kill the goose who laid the golden egg. Where than would entrepreneurs come from, and what would happen to innovation? Would inventiveness and arbitrage come from politicians?

All these proposals to tax the rich is a form of confiscation which will not even put a dent to pay for over $100 trillion of obligations that the U.S. government owes, and this does not even include the toxic assets approaching $10 trillion dollars that sit on the U.S. Central Bank balance sheets.

Even if we had a Karl Marx moment, on behalf of the proletarian 2.0 (aka the woke, led by the affluent), and confiscated 80 percent of billionaires' wealth, which would amount to $3.76 trillion, would be a drop in the bucket towards the debt of over $100 trillion. The result would be that all this confiscated wealth would only end up in the hands of their enlightened agitators, to create their new but this time a tyrannical ruling class. These revolution's almost always end up bad and are nothing more than a power grab by a group of narcissists, much like Robespierre who agitated the classes resulting in King Louis XVI being overthrown, only to be replaced by Napoleon.

The Russians discovered the same when the czar was deposed by the minority power-hungry Bolshevik communists. In Ethiopia students worked into an ideological froth, decided to overthrow King Haile Selassie in 1975, resulted in a disaster, as many students were sent to the deep countryside in the tribal areas to enlighten the masses, as Mengistu took power, and implemented a brew of a communism, confiscation, and elitism, which resulted in subjugation and disorder, as the governing class became the immovable ruling class with the convenience of a Swiss bank accounts, of course.

In history, revolution more often than not, has unintended consequences, namely that the most successful hero after attaining power forms the tyranny of which he wanted to escape from.

Taxation Reform and The Rich

Perhaps the solution is to make the rich pay their fair share of taxes, but conveniently omit the quantitative details as to what constitutes fair share. When all is said and done, if the word fair sounds fair there is no need to question it! After all, this is the grunt we hear in the media, and the rallying cry for the maestro after the completion of the concert for which a standing ovation is given. The only problem is, did the concert goers for Chopin really listen to the music and realize the violins, and horns were out of key? The conundrum with participative democracy is that, if enough people believe it, it must be true and just, or is it?

So, what do we mean by fair share?

This brings us to the top earners, as we need to go after the 1 percent, or better still, the top 10 percent. However, vilifying this income bracket is the stark reality that is not being discussed as to who pays taxes in America; here is where we look at the tax code and see some inconvenient facts to the fair share arguments, as we try to reconcile realities with visceral emotions.

In the United States, to be in the 1 percent you need to be earning $480,000 per year, and as strata group, they constitute 1.4 million taxpayers. Then, when we break the wealthiest top 10 percent of the top 1 percent, they pay 19 percent of taxes, and as a whole, the top 1 percent pay 39 percent of taxes, according to the IRS. In other words, if the U.S. revenue stream is $3.8 trillion, the 1 percent pay approximately $1.49 trillion of the U.S. budget amount. Then, if we combine the top 10 percent of earners in the United States, they pay 69 percent of taxes, which equates to approximately $2.62 trillion of a $3.8 trillion in taxes collected. Many of these people are employers, and are responsible for creating jobs, and not everyone can create a business from an idea, and create employment, because ideas, the tolerance of risk and realization are separate things.

Subsequently, the bottom 50 percent of earners as a whole pay 3 percent of the taxes. So then, what strata group is not paying their fair share of taxes? Then when the government exposed envy driven calls of "they should pay their fair share" of taxes, what do they mean by fair share, and fair to who? Do they mean fair to a large bureaucracy, entitlement, and welfare state that lives off the diminishing returns of the industrious, and their fruitions? Fair to the working poor, who are being ravaged by money printing and its favourite by-product, namely runaway inflation? Further, it might occur to them, that those on government assistance and physically able should be brought back into the workforce!

Should we be taking our marching orders as to who is the villain from the klepto-syndicate, aka the Cabalatocracy of Hollywood, media, Silicon Valley, universities, big pharma, government, banks, and self-virtuous corporations, as they sit in their palatial living rooms, in ensconced luxury, and wave their virtuous hands as they pit their disciples against each other in their quest to find a shifting villain? Should we salivate at the very prospect of the next word of the Cabalatocracy, as they first weave, then rehearse, then finally deliver this tapestry of fiction in the theatres of our minds? In fact, the toxic amalgamating of these institutions, I refer to as the klepto-syndicate, is straight from the playbook of Stalin, Hitler, Castro, Mao, and Chavez, where they controlled these institutions. The tragedy is not the wealth that is not only stolen, but more importantly, the mind through the blurring of empiricism, a bankruptcy of logic and intellectual reason.

Do we redistribute wealth? What if government was the broker of this, or some revolutionary idealogues with a modern four-year university degree passed off as education, running on the fuel of anger, who never ran a shoeshine stand, and then one asks, how much would be skimmed, wasted, and squandered, or a combination thereof. What would we do as the redistribution is squandered by Rome's plebeians, only see it squandered, back into the hands of the experienced wealthy industrialists and rentiers as the ghost of Andrew Carnegie looks on?

Do you think the wealthy would take it lying down and not transfer their wealth out of the country on the fast train, via Bitcoin or head for greener pastures, leading to a complete and unimaginable collapse of the asset markets? Who then becomes the job creators? Who then is left to confiscate from? Hence, all we will be left with is a would-be bastion of self-serving ideologues, creating an unimaginable dystopia. In fact, we do not have to look far as this line of thinking seems to be the next musical prescription in the declining West.

Who then runs the economy? Is it the naïve yet vicious left-wing professors and their cultish followers, who after four years in college have had their hard drives reformatted, and who have never considered the roots of deductive reasoning from Greek antiquity? Will these idealogues be speaking to the ghosts of their professors in later years, as they bitterly consider their outcome at 40 years old as barista makers at Starbucks? Or will robots be making our *café* lattes, while the feeble find purpose in circular debate?

When a system collectively punishes the creators with their special skills that can tinker with the imagination, vivaciously illuminate their dreams, flirt with their inventiveness that translates into industry, growth of capital, and employment, what then have we accomplished? Are we to live in a dystopia where idealogues with childish psyches replaces the essential risk taking and imagination of the entrepreneur? What happens when the entrepreneur leaves Dodge City and the final dagger is put into the heart of capitalism, the very same system that has lifted billions out of poverty and brought us unimaginable progress? Will envy be the litmus test of progress?

There are no easy answers to resolving this conundrum, but this much is for sure, government, and the Fed are stuck in a dystopian trap weaved into an ambiguous enigma. So then, this brings us to options available for the Feds and government.

The Fed is in a Trap

The Fed is really backed into a corner as a result of money printing, and the U.S. government is clearly insolvent, by any accounting standards. Both are in the same trap, as the economy can only continue on the fix of easy money until the inevitable implosion, hence, the Fed and government have five options, in respect to their over a $100 trillion obligation.

Government and Central Bank Options

Pay Back the Debt. This seems highly unlikely because there are no free cash flows from its near $4 billion revenue stream against its spending of $7 trillion in 2021. If they cut back Social Security, healthcare, civil service entitled pensions, it would be political job termination for the high priests of Washington, while the plebeians would rise up, doing their best imitation of Greece in 2010, when they could not handle unchaining themselves from the shackles of entitlement and took to the streets by not accepting austerity, meaning living within their means. This usually happens when a kleptocracy trickles into a culture as a way of life, where dependency on government clouds a nation-state's thinking.

In America, any significant cut to spending would lead to unimaginable social unrest and implosion. Even if they freed up $1 trillion a year, which is realistically impossible, it would take at least 100 years to pay back the debt, and this is assuming interest rates are low, the U.S. dollar survives as a reserve currency, and the 10-year yield can be controlled by the Fed. For how long can men with guns enforce the global stature of the U.S. dollar? In the case of long-term interest rates, if they spiked to 7 percent, where the fed lost control of the Treasury yield curve at $40 trillion in debt by 2024, it would result in $2.8 trillion of interest equating to 80 percent of the U.S. budget. In this scenario, it does not even take into account legacy obligations.

Figure 15.3 is a visual look at the budget below shows the architecture of the trap, where eventually some hard choices will have to be made.

Figure 15.3: Total U.S. Federal Spending vs. Total U.S. Federal Revenue for the year 2021

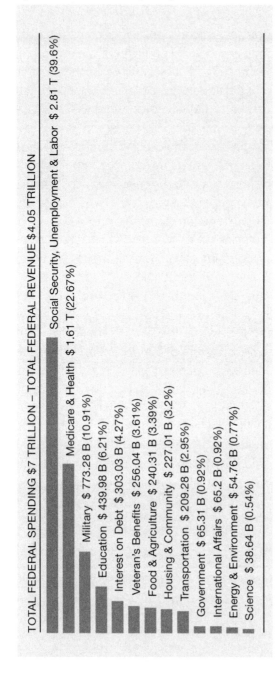

Source: OMB, National Priorities Project

Default on the Debt. If the U.S. government defaulted on its debt, it would signal to the world the end of the U.S. dollar as the reserve currency. U.S. Treasuries would no longer be considered a safe store of value, not that it is now, especially when involved in a political conflict that results in confiscation, as the Russians found out in early 2022. Equity and debt markets would crash, banks would fail, including the European Central Bank, which might well ahead of this scenario because of its own toxic nonperforming assets. It would affect the public who holds the debt personally and through investments in debt instruments, (especially Japanese citizens who own their public debt through bonds) insurance companies, mutual funds, pension funds, foreign governments, the list is endless. Put simply, the world economy would go through contractionary macroeconomic disequilibrium (a fancy term for a complete meltdown), which has never happened since the 1930s. In brief, it would signify the end of an empire and a collapse of global economies. Hence, there is a reason why foreign governments are not buying U.S. government debt, but instead they are unloading them. Much more prudent to stock up on energy, Bitcoin, farmland, and gold.

Restructure the Debt. This could be a very real possibility, but again, interest rates would go flying through the roof if the United States partly defaulted on its Treasury bills. Delving further would severely affect world equity, real estate, and bond markets, not to mention payment for international trade. An epic jolt like this to the monetary system would be cataclysmic and could lead to new instruments of settling accounts either in new fiats, Bitcoin, bartering, gold, regional monetary arrangements of emerging powers, or a combination thereof. Because after all, who wants to be paid in a shaky currency? Again, the outcome would not be much different then a complete default on debt, since a non-stop earthquake would shake out the financial world.

Much like the scenario of defaulting on the debt, a restructure would signal the end of an empire.

Inflate the Debt Away. Inflating the debt, in other words, weakening the currency, where the debt as a percentage of GDP becomes lower. There is a playbook for this as we look back at 1946, when debt to GDP was 118 percent, which amounted to $269 billion. This was never paid back since the GDP expanded and by 1960, $286 billion of debt amounted to 53 percent of the GDP. In other words, they did inflate the debt, but not quite, because the U.S. economy was going through its golden age of expansion with near 50 percent of world GDP.

By creating massive inflation in the double digits and with little real GDP growth comes with a host of problems that include a substantial weakening of the stock market, volatility in the bond market, severely punishing the middle-class and the poor because things would cost more, leading to massive unemployment and political instability. The credibility of the U.S. dollar as the reserve currency of the world would again command scrutiny, as no one wants to hold a debasing currency, and much like the restructure and default scenarios, the outcome would be dire, to say the least. Further, with massive inflation, business planning, forecasting, procurement in both goods and labour, and financial translation of foreign operations would create such adverse scenarios that the most competent CFOs could not even fathom. But the story would be more interesting if we could inflate away $34 trillion of official Treasury debt, while ignoring the over $75 trillion dollars of legacy debt. The idea in this scenario is that with an inflated economy, the debt to GDP would come down to let's say 60% of GDP compared to 130% of GDP, but this still does not eliminate the core $34 trillion of debt.

The theoretical hyperinflation required to lower the debt to GDP is a massive tax on its citizenry of at least 15% per year, which would lead to severe civil unrest and food riots, as we are seeing in Sri Lanka and elsewhere. Certainly, the rioting will be branded as domestic terrorism by branches of the Cabalatocracy. Even the military would cost more, to hire men with guns to quell the civil unrest in defence of the U.S. dollar. After all, why fight for ideology alone when fighting for money is more rewarding?

Raiding 401K, TFSA, and RRSP's. This is probably the ugliest scenario, where the government, in its desperation to maintain itself, will start dipping into people's 401(k) plans, and in the case of Canada, RRSPs and TFSAs. Do not think it is that farfetched because history will teach us that under Executive Order 6102 in 1933, FDR seized gold from the public in exchange for $20.67 per ounce, and then increased the price of gold to $35 an ounce. There is, of course, a moral pretext to this, where the national cause was of course to fight the Great Depression, which he and Hoover agitated, deepened, and prolonged in the first place.

And in Canada, we do not have to look far back, only to February of 2022, when the government ordered banks to freeze accounts of peaceful freedom protestors and their financial supporters who attempted to awaken the world out of their COVID-19 mandates. Imagine if the government ran out of money to sustain its bloated self, and in light of this, what radical actions would it take?

Realizing that many readers will think that the confiscation of investment accounts is an improbable scenario, we cannot be too sure...

Let us paint a picture as to how the story could spin, the narrative might read that the government has been there for you and now it is your time to do your part of your patriotic duty (sending your children to die in meaningless wars is not enough). In the background, they will reinforce this by constantly playing pre-rolls on YouTube, with the extended hands of compassionate actors, about a government being there for you, and now they need you. This will be spun as a temporary measure, (nothing is temporary with government and its greed) and will announce that they are going to borrow against your savings, stock accounts, and give you interest of 5 percent, which won't even cover inflation and the cost of capital.

They will use a combination of insatiable propaganda provided by the Cabalatocracy where those that are not pacified into the narrative will be depicted as selfish elitists and unpatriotic, as the punishment for this could include social credit score lashings, resembling modern day digital dungeons of torture. Remember, "everyone is in this together" slogan will be the battle cry, as the masses eventually enjoy the self-flagellation. In the background, a new revised version of Maurice Ravel's masterpiece "Vive La France" will be playing in surround-sound to romanticise the senses and to help people forget the stench of the propaganda in the air, while serving to serenade the deal in the making. To add to the road-show, the ruse might be passed off as wealth redistribution and the great cause for the ages, of course, as long as it's not govern-ment elected members getting their wealth and opulent pensions redistributed.

Then they will vilify these people who actually saved money for retirement through investments. In fact, Prime Minister Trudeau said this in his first election in Canada, that the annual contribution of $10,000 into the TFSA plans was only helping the wealthy, with-out a speck of evidence, while not considering that many seniors as well as the middle-class moved cash into this tax-free account. Remember, when gaslighting, the intent is to bypass reason and seduce emotion, as facts are mere blasphemy.

For the ones that resist and have not bought into the story, they will be vilified and punished for committing the horrific crime of sacrificing today for tomorrow, which was once known as plan-ning for a rainy day. The remedy for them will be a well-orchestrat-ed gaslighting as government will tap on the shoulders of their partners, the high priests of the klepto-syndicate better known as the Cabalatocracy, (Hollywood, Silicon Valley, media, academia, government, spook agencies, and the rest of the gang), as they will spin a toxic brew of propaganda from their palatial castles to criti-cize any remaining laggards who might still be flirting with reason or logic. With a final serving of an exquisite buffet of propaganda, the end game, of course, will be to ensure that all get aboard the train. And with a government central currency, it is so much easier to enforce tyranny.

The economy, and specifically currency that is in the hands of gov-ernment control leads to such unpleasant outcomes for a host of reasons demonstrated throughout this book, including the fact that all fiat money returns to its intrinsic value of zero. But what if there is a way to avert this, by considering a new paradigm shift that separates money from state and acts as the future of wealth storage? In the house of cards, we throw the future under the bus for the seduction of today!

This brings us to our second and final act of entertaining and stimulating theatre. And in this act, we visit a technology that separates money from the state, it is this place we eventually visit. But first, we look at some other hedges against inflation and political risk.

History is rife with confiscation. In times of upheaval and doubt, many wealthy and not so wealthy have lost their earthly belongings. This was the case of Jews in Nazi Germany, and in the 1910s of minority Christian Greeks, and Armenians in the Ottoman Empire during World War I, better known as modern day Turkey. In essence, FDR did the same thing by confiscating gold and then repositioning it to a higher price. When the lust of power and prescribed ideology is at peril it pushes the limits of tyranny, and the victims are often the industrious being depicted as villains. The kulaks in the 1920s, who were the most industrious peasant farmers of Russia, had their farmlands and homes raided, assets seized by the Communist Bolsheviks as many kulaks were killed, leading to starvation in the Soviet Union.

There is a deep history of the envious being led by an emotionally appealing tyrant riding in on a white horse pointing his benevolent hand at the perceived villain, who was actually the builder, and confiscating the fruits of his creations. The end game is not the attainment of the elusiveness of equitable economic justice, that is only a pretext for the true agenda, which is only for the pleasure of the power thirsty ideologue attaining "rule without accomplishment." For these reasons, it is always wise to seek shelter from the storm! Equipped with some brief strands of history, we take a look at some asset classes that could provide shelter from the storm.

CHAPTER

16

Shelter From the Storm

When the winds of change arrive, eventually we will have to reckon with the Ponzi scheme, as we discover that we built our nest in a house of cards. When the stock market corrects or melts down, there seems to be little safety in so-called blue-chip stocks that your money manager preaches, since they too join the sleigh ride down the hill, that might be just a little less steep. For example, in the March 2020 stock market meltdown Twitter declined 40 percent, Microsoft 8 percent, Google 23 percent, the Canadian banks about 23 percent, Bank of America 5 percent, NVIDIA gained, while the S&P was down 24 percent, and Nasdaq at near 20%.

When fear replaces greed, when the world you once knew slips through your hands like grains of sand, and when madness overwhelms reason, it becomes time to seek shelter from the storm. It is here where we consider other assets to find sanctuary from the storm and start by reacquainting ourselves with a timeless yellow glitter with a 5,000-year history.

Gold

In the case of cataclysmic shock, you can always trade gold for food and other necessities of life. While I realize that most people have never lived under shortages in the West, and perhaps cannot fathom the possibility, consider opening up your mind to such an outcome, because it is right around the corner as we are starting to see hoarding and empty shelves, while at the same time, we might see Sri Lankan food riots at a theatre near you. This reality is very possible with a scenario of shortages, supply chain breakdowns, and a government that will be there for themselves, and not there for you. In fact, government will only use such a crisis to further oppress or make one believe in the necessity of them in their current form. If you're not convinced, consider the pandemic, and see what type of mess they made with infective mandated coerced experimental drugs, and lockdowns, leaving people in a state of fear, where the lies are just starting to come to the surface, as they fight tooth and nail to keep their power over the unsuspecting and enforce their war on truth.

Historically, gold has been a sanctuary as a store of value for 5,000 years, and up until 1971 backed the U.S. dollar. Economists born since the early 1950s have not been trained on the monetary use of gold, since there was no need to after Nixon took the U.S. dollar off gold. However, gold was artificially suppressed at near $40 per ounce up to 1971 when the U.S. dollar went off the gold standard, and shot up to $664 by February of 1980, with a present price nearing $2,000 in 2022 according to the site goldprice.org. A major benefit of gold is that it would ensure governments would spend within their means while invoking the confidence of a hard backed currency. Naysayers will say that it could not meet monetary supply, but a higher price would be able to meet the M2 broader money supply that includes cash, checking deposits, and easily convertible near money. Further, gold prices in the past, when they were backing currency, were being manipulated by Central Banks to not reflect its natural price. Regardless, gold has a relatively limited supply, is a hard measurement of value, contains intrinsic qualities and is afforded historical reverence.

However, on the downside since March 2020, with almost every imaginable exogenous shock in the world economy, it has barely reached $2,000. Even with inflation appearing aggressively in 2022, it still is not acting as a store of value against inflation, well, at least not yet. True that many believe it is being manipulated by the paper derivative markets, with an underlying value of approximately $10 trillion, but still held by Central Banks, while it has to come to terms with its digital competitors. Regardless of one's views, physical gold should be held at some level in a safe location, (not in a bank), while think twice about buying gold certificates from banks that sells fractional banking certificates, which are not necessarily backed by gold, but only trust. Remember that these certificates of gold are worthless if governments seize them or if the bank becomes insolvent.

In a brief defence of gold, as well as silver, both of which are stores of value, it should be noted that gold held up well in March of 2020 during the stock market meltdown by dropping only for a few days and silver did drop more precipitously. At the same time, sliver is another store of value that one might want to consider and has commercial applications in industry.

Figure 16.1 is a two-year gold chart that visually tells the story, and as an exercise for the curious one might want to follow gold through various stock markets and financial shocks to see how it held up.

Figure 16.1: Gold Prices 2020-2021

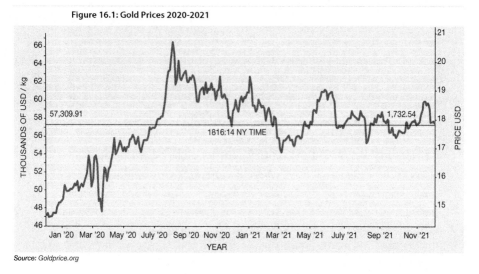

Source: Goldprice.org

The downside is that it is not easily transportable, somewhat confiscable and is facing headwinds of disruption in the way of a competing revolution of Bitcoin. So much so that many institutions are purchasing Bitcoin instead of gold as a hedge against inflation, so there is some evidence that Bitcoin is taking away gold's lunch money. If you want to buy actual gold that is physically backed in the Canadian mint, you can do this on the stock market through a Canadian company in Toronto called Sprott Capital. But still, it is wise to have physical gold or silver.

Oil

If companies want to hedge against inflation, oil has performed well, and what many people don't realize is that oil is integral to the manufacturing processes, from bearings to autos (about 80 barrels to build an EV or combustion engine), plastic, machinery, clothing, basketballs metals, construction, medical equipment, electronics, including TVs, and cell phones, and oil is even used in medical devices including heart valves, and yes the military industrial complex—the list is endless. Since its collapse in May 2020, when the price per barrel went to just under $18, it has roared back to over $100, with a five-fold return, outperforming the S&P in 2020-2021, and on its way higher according to Goldman Sachs, and would not be surprised if it slid past $160 a barrel. Then the question becomes, has owning oil stocks and ETFs a viable hedge against inflation? If we are to follow oil prices in the inflationary 1970s and 1980s, the answer is yes. It's true that fossil fuels are not favoured in respect to our current ecological-political environment, but the question of oil lies in a balancing act between a growing world population driving demand versus the time it will take to find economic and ecological substitutes that are viable. Simply vilifying it without a viable substitute for 97 million barrels of oil consumption a day will not take us on the road forward.

Even before the war in Ukraine, in early 2022 oil was approaching $100 per barrel, and the price is going up, not just from demand and supply, but also from speculators and fiat money depreciating due to money printing. When considering hedging, it might be a good exercise to ask what would be better to hold, $1 million of oil or cash as a safe haven, in an inflationary environment? In terms of currency, with Saudi Arabia having $28 trillion of oil reserves at $100 per barrel, which equates to about half the value of the U.S. stock market, is the Saudi RMB currency in some way hard backed with oil, making it a better option than the U.S. dollar, which is driven by paper contracts? Or consider Russia's oil reserves being worth near $8 trillion dollars, which in a sense backs the ruble, making it hard backed by this and other commodities. It seems that we are going into a super cycle of commodities with a growing population and insatiable consumption of the necessities of life including food, all driving scarcity of resources.

The strategy of owning oil as a hedge against inflation is applicable for company CFOs, entrepreneurs, and retail investors, and it is happening primarily because of money printing. Stop the money printing at the Central Bank and watch commodity prices fall in line, back into equilibrium. This of course will not happen, so buying oil and energy assets and related instruments is a good hedge against inflation, while taking in some excellent profits.

Semiconductors

We are currently in 2022 in a worldwide shortage of semiconductors, a $522 billion industry. They are needed for integrated circuit boards, to be able to build everything from household appliances, phones, computers, satellites, cars and basically the world we live in. The first carnage is the auto industry, where sales have dropped almost 10 percent year over year since June 2021, not because of demand, but because of chip shortages. According to Wolf Street, because of the shortage of chips, car production is almost at a halt as dealers concentrate on their premium models for grossing top dollar.[1] On the lot, the ritual of negotiating with the dealer on car price does not exist with the shortage of cars—as a result dealers are getting more than MSRP due to semiconductor shortages. Prices on wafers, which are essential for semiconductors are going up and affecting integrated circuit boards with price increases between 10 to 30 percent in 2021.[2] However, in early 2022 we are seeing prices stabilizing due to prices getting so high, the consumer has decided to keep their current ride. From a financial standpoint it could be argued that the semiconductor industry could be the new barometer of the global economy, or perhaps the commodity

1   Wolf Richter, "Average New-Vehicle Price Spikes 19% in 10 Months, to $44,000. Unit Sales Tick up, But Still Down 34% from March," Wolf Street, November 5, 2021, https://wolfstreet.com/2021/11/05/average-new-vehicle-price-spikes-19-in-10-months-to-44000-in-october-unit-sales-tick-up-still-down-34-from-march-amid-inventory-shortage/
2   Shawn Knight, "Copper Foil Shortage Could Force Motherboard and GPU Prices Higher," TechSpot, September 29, 2021, https://www.techspot.com/news/91489-copper-foil-shortage-could-force-motherboard-gpu-prices.html

that lubricates the current and the future. Taiwan produces 61 percent of the world's semiconductors, with Taiwan Semiconductor manufacturing 54 percent of the world's semiconductors, and then what would happen if China sabre-rattled or invaded the island nation? Of course, the talking heads in then media who are almost always wrong, and digital armchair experts would fan the flames. This would result in world markets going into a tailspin with an exogenous shock, with prices spiking uncontrollably, and many in the West nurtured on their misguided narrative of entitlements would be devastated and have to see therapists as to why they can't get an upgrade to the iPhone 13 Pro. Hence, with the possibility of Taiwan being invaded, it is not by accident that Taiwan Semiconductor is building a plant in Arizona, as China is still far behind in the high-end chip manufacturing.

Yes, we live in very tenuous times, economically and emotionally. If one wants to hedge with semiconductors, short of filling your garage with computer chips, there are ETFs including SOXX, which is the Philadelphia semiconductor index of a basket of companies. Strangely, even with the semiconductor shortages being felt in the auto industry and elsewhere, the index as of May 2022 has fallen 30% for the year. Regardless of where the market goes, there are numerous ETF derivatives based on leverage where the buyer can go long or short. Every CFO and entrepreneur should take a deep dive into this.

Agriculture Assets and Metals

Often in the middle of runaway inflation many companies become mesmerized like deer in front of headlights. After all, there are very few business executives today that have run companies in an inflationary environment of supply chain and wage price escalation. Their business strategy too often translates to one of a reactor or analyzer that can do anything but take action. Unfortunately, when it comes to cost increases due to rampant inflation, many companies take the position of passing it on through the supply chain and depending who your customer is and what your bargaining power is, you might or might not be able to pass on the price increase. If you can get price increases, your goods or services have strong bargaining power, but if you can't, you are eroding your profit margins and marginal contributions to the point of even putting your company on the financial ropes, where you are stuck in the middle, getting squeezed with no way out. Further, if you can get price increases you might face resistance with the end user, may it be a customer or B2B, and the slow down in sales will reduce your gross contribution dollars, even though you increased your gross profit per unit. Eventually the cure for higher prices is well…. Higher prices! Meaning, demand destruction!

With a population of nearly 8 billion in the world, we are starting to see a food sustainability issue, which will lead to shortages. When referring to agriculture we include wheat, corn, soybean, sugar, canola, orange juice, and the likes. All these ingredients are required to make sub-ingredients and of course finished food products that we consume every day. It should also be considered that against the backdrop of the Ukrainian war, China, India, and Russia together yield approximately 40 percent of the world's wheat production, and any sanctions will only bite back the West harder, especially Europe, who is on the brink with over-extended governments and entitlements it can no longer afford or sustain, and it would not take much to put them over the edge economically. Further, when we add fresh fruits and vegetables to the equation from the warmer climates, the supply demand equation becomes more tenuous.

The same story holds true when we look at metals such as aluminum, nickel, copper, palladium, zinc, rare earths, and the likes. All that we produce needs some of these metals to manufacture, and to have a remedy for inflation of your finished product, you have to go backwards in the supply chain and start hedging against the price increase you or your firm might be receiving because of raw material derivatives.

To paraphrase Milton Freidman, inflation is monetary (money printing) and is everywhere, so if you want to be a prospector and pioneer, as opposed to just watching all the inflation developing around you eroding your wealth, you can take some action.

More sophisticated investors might consider futures contracts, but a less volatile strategy is to buy leveraged ETFs. The idea is to purchase these commodities and offset the profits in your stock account against the price increases you receive, and the real savvy might not have to increase as much to customers, leading to higher market share. Here are the URLs for ETFs in both agricultural and industrial metals, and these can be used both for your company or your household to hedge against inflation:

https://etfdb.com/etfdb-category/agricultural-commodities/
https://etfdb.com/etfs/natural-resources/industrial-metals/

Real Estate

Real estate should be in everyone's portfolio, while certainly owning homes is preferable to renting, and it is a store of value, if backed by strong property laws, while it emotionally bonds with people because of its solid visuality and physicality. Historically, its return on investment is about 6 percent and has been discussed in the section on comparative asset inflation. At the same time, a home can be leveraged to buy other assets—unfortunately, some people use their home like ATMs to buy life's pleasures. The downside of real estate is that home prices are susceptible to higher interest rates, which many did not see in the red-hot housing market of the early 2020s. It lacks liquidity, especially in sluggish markets, and it can have liens placed on it, or in certain developing and developed countries, if the political winds change, confiscation can occur, which has a very real and brutal history.

I have some advice for budding entrepreneurs or small business owners: if you are running your company out of a commercial office space, it is highly preferable to purchase a house and rent it out to your company, especially if you outsource operations. This way in 10 years or so, you have an additional asset outside of your business since renting does not create value but sits on the expense side of your P&Ls.

What about someone who is in a financial disposition, and earning some income working for fiat money that depreciates quicker than they can save for their first home, as the price of real estate keeps climbing out of reach? Especially if they are young and inflation has distorted appreciating asset prices, and the dream of buying their first home is like a runaway train, meaning they save a bit, and the rate of savings cannot keep up with the rates of deposit required on a new home, due to an acute appreciation on home prices.

One way around this is to buy homebuilders stocks or REITs, which reflect the housing market, usually if those stocks are appreciating so are home prices, since there is a correlation. Examples include D.R. Horton, Toll Brothers, or ETFs that follow resale housing prices. Or you can invest in a rental company called Mid-America Apartment Communities Inc. (NYSE: MAA) and several home rental stocks, including Essex Property Trust (NYSE: ESS), AvalonBay Communities (NYSE: AVB), Equity Residential (NYSE: EQR), UDR (NYSE: UDR), Camden Property Trust (NYSE: CPT) and BRE Properties (NYSE: BRE).

What you do next is put down 15 percent on any of these stocks and pretend you are buying a $200,000 home for $30,000 down, as your broker (interactive brokers or some other) will lend you the rest (they are a lot less sticky than banks who are still in the industrial fiat age). Then you pay into it every month replicating a mortgage for $1,000 instead of putting it into savings, which is a losing proposition on currency deprecation of at least 10 percent per year. The idea is that you are increasing equity through both payments and appreciation, and idealistically if the stock goes to $300,000 in two and a half years, you can then sell it on the stock market in real time. The outcome is recouping your down payment, monthly payment, and appreciation providing you with $160,000 for a down payment for your physical home. Of course, you can play with these numbers on a spreadsheet. Please note that dividends have not been considered here.

Now if your REIT residential home stock is dropping, it reflects the prices on homes, where you might want to sell, and then take advantage of buying a home in a descending residential house price environment. Or if you still need to save for a down payment in a real estate market that is pulling back, you can short real estate stocks and dump the profits into your first home.

You can also purchase a second home using REITS without the hassles of being a landlord, and again if the home market goes south, you can sell your position in one second, as opposed to months or years, as can be the case with physical real estate. At the same time, you don't have to deal with upkeep, broken pipes, while enjoying the benefits of an appreciating asset that has liquidity at a touch of a button.

Remember, there is always a way to move forward if one is prepared to trade some of today for lots more in the future.

Although this is not a book of investment strategy, there are ways available to increase your lot in life. If you have little money, you can build it over a lifetime, if you prescribe into investing your time and money wisely.

The preceding are just some ideas and not investment advice.

Finally, Bitcoin is another option to buy and then trade it for another hard asset, namely real estate, which now brings us to the grand finale, which is either the potential revolution of our monetary system, namely Bitcoin, or a private money in the renaissance goldsmith era.

Bitcoin

Bitcoin is still a relatively new idea first brought to market in 2009 under the pseudonym Satoshi Nakamoto, but it is a fast-moving asset class, which is now front and center in the media where it can no longer be ignored, as institutions including pension funds are taking positions in Bitcoin as hedge against inflation, but the jury is out in the short term on this accretion at least in the short term. It is quite evident that the smart money has been in Bitcoin for some time now, as are early retail investors. With a host of dynamics in play where the asset class is starting to gain acceptance, and early critical mass including being an official legal tender in El Salvador, the central African Country of Car as other countries will follow. Yet, many are sitting on the sidelines trying to make sense of what is going on and might not have a deep understanding of what this asset class is, and why it's revolutionary and might be changing the way we view our monetary systems.

It usually takes most people about three years to get their minds wrapped around the Bitcoin space, with its blockchain technology where there is both a technical and emotional curve of sorts, because one cannot physically hold it in their hands which goes against 5,000 years of conditioning. Just as importantly, there is also the hurdle that most people have difficulty coming to terms with non-government issued monetary instruments, as this is an emotional curve of this new-to-the-world market technology as the psychology of technology acceptance has a history of being a late adopter in human history. Because, after all, we have been nurtured from childhood that only government fiat money can create a vehicle as a medium of exchange to ascertain value, subsequently, to be able to transition within a comfort level of a digital asset is the psychological divide that most people have trouble overcoming. Money has not always been in the hands of government, since private money in commerce existed in Britain during the time of the goldsmiths which was used as legal tender along with silver in America and in antiquity. Admittedly, Bitcoin has had a history of volatility of precipitous drops since 2009, but it definitely has passed childhood and is getting ready to leave adolescence, where the volatility is not as acute even though the price is down from 2021. Perhaps, the training wheels are coming off this asset class. Once one liberates themselves from the uncertainty and the declining asset of government fiat money that is not hard backed, and quite frankly managed recklessly, what one might see is the future of currency and store of value leaning toward Bitcoin, where at least people who live in relative liberty away from government have private money that cannot be confiscated. And this is a key tenet where our story begins as Bitcoin has two sides, one of volatility and uncertainty and the other of economic liberty.

The Case for Bitcoin

Decentralized finance is the same future that many experienced in 1995, with the early adoption of the internet. At the time, the old economy of classical industry did not understand the internet's core proposition and its ability to become an integral part of modern life, many thought it would just be a peripheral outlier of the economy. Even Microsoft and others like Netscape thought that the power lay in being in control of the browsers, until Google came along and showed that the turf war is the search engine dominance with its related algorithms and micro analytics.

Bitcoin's primary core proposition is that it is a digital asset, and separates money from state, and unlike fiat money, it has scarcity value at 21 million coins, of which no more can be created, because it is hardwired in the technology. But the fact that it is decentralized is the reason it is in the leader position of the emerging Web3, which might need some explanation.

Going back to the 1990s, the Web was to be the democratization of humanity being independent and that narrative seemed plausible until it became monopolized by the censoring cartel from Silicon Valley, the hope was that it would be decentralized, which is hardly the case today. So, in this respect Web 1.0 and especially Web 2.0 did not deliver the independent decentralized dream.

Today, the speak is all about Web3 that is finding ways to be decentralized and un-censorable, unlike Silicon Valley who is compromised by a combination that includes the spook agencies, ideology, and government, which altogether can lay a number of tricks from algorithmic shadow banning, censorship or straightout de-platforming, as part of the Cabalatocracy's agenda. This is where the story of Bitcoin comes in as it is truly the Web3 that is completely decentralized with bulletproof security, and it is the unique proposition it brings to the world.

Max Keizer, also known as the Godfather of Bitcoin says, "Bitcoin is the hardest money ever created in human history." Bitcoin is decentralized, meaning it cannot be controlled or manipulated by Central Banks and government.

True, there are other cryptocurrencies like Ethereum that runs off the Amazons AWS system, but have no finite qualities, where more can be dumped on the market by its founders and insiders like a stock—while it is not decentralized, meaning it is prone to manipulation. Ethereum is not really designed to act as a store of wealth and is more of a blockchain technology for smart contracts that banks and other institutions can use for transactions. I will not comment on other alt coins, since they do not hold the cache of Bitcoin, and their shortcomings include security and centralization, as many will not be around after the next shakeout or crypto winter!

Unlike fiat money, Bitcoin cannot be debased through infinite printing because it has scarcity value by being finite of only 21 million, no more can be produced. Bitcoin cannot be confiscated by government, which is essential to its core proposition, as this is an important attribute, as we found out when FDR seized gold. Bitcoin is quite possibly the greatest disruptor in finance in over a thousand years, to some, it is the last great hope of humanity. This is especially true of emerging countries that have been battered by their own fiat money, having to pay back IMF loans in U.S. dollars and being at the mercy of the U.S. dollar hegemony system that is now being challenged.

Individually, Bitcoin gives freedom from overreaching government, yes, many can choose the right to vote as the hallmark of freedom, and that's fine if you think it will give you freedom, but more are adopting Bitcoin as the true promise of freedom. Because it is perhaps the most perfect money ever created in human civilization.

From a technology perspective, all transactions are transparent and verifiable on the blockchain, and it is for this reason alone that it makes a terrible vehicle for illicit activity, as opposed to the U.S. dollar, where up to 6 percent is used for illicit activity. Janet Yellen, Treasury Secretary and former Fed Chair, conveniently ignores this in her attempt to slow down the DeFi revolution, while she does not appear to have a firm grasp on the Bitcoin technology. Of course, if it was up to Yellen, she would regulate it without considering that perhaps it is the Treasury and Fed who need to be regulated from uncontrollable fiat printing and spending respectively. For this alone, many kings, queens and despots in history would have been deposed by now or on the receiving end of the guillotine.

Bitcoin is the great disruptor—it is no longer an underground counterculture for IT libertarian types dreaming out the world in their basement quarters. To some, it is quite simply the digital gold. The sign of its emergence is everywhere—all you have to do is look around at its growing acceptance in our economic culture. When you look at the Times Square electronic ticker tape, you will see quotes for Bitcoin, and the same is true for Yahoo! Finance, where Bitcoin shows up besides the Nasdaq, gold, oil, 10-year yield and the likes. Prices are quoted now in the mainstream business news such as CNBC, Fox Business, and all business news channels which are almost always late to the party. Even *Barron's* put it on the cover of their October 23, 2021, edition and now tracks it in real time. If Bitcoin was a Brand name it is quite plausible that it is worth $1 trillion dollars alone, since it more than likely has name recognition that would rival Apple, Nike, Google, Coca Cola, Instagram, Tesla and the likes.

The developing story of Bitcoin is that of the essential fabric of the emerging monetary system. The adoption curve is turning into a tidal wave—the first notable name was Paul Tudor Jones II, billionaire hedge fund manager, and then, of course, Elon Musk came to party, even though he made a non-factual claim about Bitcoin mining ecological footprints, but still hung on to his 42,000 coins—he will more than likely start accepting Bitcoin as payment for Tesla cars again, as he might see the recent $20,000 low as a long-term investment on Tesla's balance sheets. Even Jack Dorsey, the former CEO of Twitter and one of the distinguished overlords of Silicon Valley, is onboard and is becoming an official Bitcoin evangelist with his new role as an angel investor in Foursquare, as he might have tired of dressing up as a Bohemian and censoring the New York Post and truth. Some think he was put up to this.

But it is Michael Saylor of MicroStrategy who become an official Bitcoiner in 2020, and who is holding 125,000 Bitcoins as of January 2022, argues that it is a much better store of value than fiat money in the long run but not in the short run, because of Bitcoin's price volatility against the U.S. dollar. He is now becoming the unofficial spokesman for this asset class. Building on the story, according to Buy Bitcoin Worldwide, several tech companies including DeFi companies like Block Inc. (formerly Square), exchanges such as Coinbase, insurance company Massachusetts Mutual, KPMG Canada, Tesla, and of course MicroStrategy, are also holding Bitcoin on its balance sheets.3 Countries that hold Bitcoin include Finland, Bulgaria, Georgia, and of course El Salvador, as well as host of ETFs that have exposure to Bitcoin. Also, in Canada it can be traded in RRSP's and ETFs with Bitcoin funds from 3 IQ and Purpose Investments that are 100 percent hard backed by actual Bitcoin in their custodial possession.

So why are these companies buying Bitcoin, and why are more public and privately held companies buying Bitcoin? The reason is that many of these companies that have substantial cash on their balance sheets are concerned that the currency will debase, as it certainly is in our current hyperinflationary environment in 2022. Hence, a prudent company might want to consider having Bitcoin on their balance sheets, while also accepting it as payment, as a long-term appreciation play. Put differently, the market is coming to terms with the fact that cash is a depreciating asset, while Bitcoin, in the long run, is said to be an appreciating asset class if one can climatize to the volatility. Since 2011 to mid-2021, Bitcoin has returned 35,000 percent making it the best performing asset class in history, outperforming bonds, Nasdaq, Amazon, the S&P, gold, silver, and oil. Put differently, especially in an inflationary environment that comes with currency debasement, there is systematic risk in having too much cash on the books, and many COO and CFO types are deliberating on carrying Bitcoin as a hedge of sorts. Much like the goldsmiths of England, Bitcoin is private money that is separated from state, and this alone gives it allure.

3   "Bitcoin Treasuries," Buy Bitcoin Worldwide, accessed May 8, 2022, https://www.buybitcoinworldwide.com/treasuries/

The story of its rapid adoption goes deeper, the oldest bank in America, Mellon, started accepting Bitcoin deposits in 2021, Goldman Sachs, and J.P. Morgan Chase now have investment vehicles for clients that want Bitcoin, and even Mexican billionaire Ricardo Salinas Pliego, and owner of Banco Azteca, is working on accepting Bitcoin deposits, and personally has 10 percent of his liquid portfolio in Bitcoin. Of course, the Mexican government, with a well-documented history of crashing the peso, is reluctant to get on board, since they would have hard asset competition, and must enjoy being at the mercy of the U.S. monetary system that can turn the taps off at will if sovereign companies do not toe the line. Blackrock Capital, the largest portfolio manager in the world at $10 trillion in assets under management, holds Bitcoin, as does billionaire investor Ray Dalio. The story continues where even though Warren Buffet, and especially his partner Charlie Munger, a pronounced hisser of Bitcoin has invested $500 million into Nubank, a South American Digital Bank, which in turn owns Easynvest, which, as of 2022 is offering QR Bitcoin ETF (QBTC11). This is the same Warren Buffet that has consistently underperformed the S&P, largely ignored the tech boom with the exception of Apple, which he acquired much later in the game. But this time, he did not want to miss the train, much like Ed Sullivan who was frustrated by not booking Elvis Presley on his show first, then when he was in England in 1963 and saw commotion about the Beatles, he asked his manager to book them. The list gets deeper: even George Soros, (who should have played a villain on the original Batman series of the 1960's) the Rothschilds, and Kevin O'Leary now own Bitcoin.

The story gets more interesting when Bitcoin banks such as Mogo will now pay you interest on your Bitcoin, while approve fiat money loans with Bitcoin pledged as collateral without the lending rituals of the bank, which often resembles being questioned in front of the Grand Jury before getting loan approval.

Let's consider again the big story of El Salvador's young visionary President Nayib Bukele, now making Bitcoin along with the U.S. dollar legal tender, meaning it is freeing its citizens from the tragedy of fiat money, the IMF and the U.S. dollar hegemony and the friction costs of the diaspora sending money back home. Bitcoin fixes many things, and the first one is that almost overnight the perception of El Salvador as a headquarters for MS-13 is starting to diminish, maybe since they might be going to the U.S.

Bukele is offering landed immigrant status for Bitcoin investors and is drawing in the high-tech sector to his country for Bitcoin mining that requires some advanced skills and equipment, which will lead to a Bitcoin culture being adopted. As well in the big picture it will perhaps help make El Salvador a technology hub of Central America, while creating clustered knowhow in this region of peripheral skills in programing, AI, mathematics and so much more in intensifying the region's competitive architecture.

To make it in compliance with environmental concerns (ESG), Bitcoin mining in El Salvador is using natural energy harnessed from its Volcanoes that produce electricity through its geothermal wells. Bitcoin is changing the perception of El Salvador almost overnight because all of a sudden, the ambitious are pulling up stakes because opportunity draws knowledge and ambition to be with a pioneering country that welcomes the future with open arms. Bukele and his cabinet are emancipating their country from the spiraling debt trap of the IMF, but not without a fight, as the U.S. spook agencies are trying to disrupt things by turning loose the MS-13 on his plans with a renaissance of violence.

Subsequently, the El Salvador government is giving out $30 of Bitcoin to all citizens, ensuring that their population has an appreciating asset that can help them escape poverty and hardship. Remember, there are still governments that administrate with some regard for their citizenry. Currently, Paraguay and Honduras seem like the next countries considering Bitcoin as an official tender, and it is inevitable that the dominoes will fall as other nation-states adopt Bitcoin as legal tender at some level.

Eventually, the Luddite banks will follow suit screaming and kicking, and if they don't, they might resemble someone today that does not have basic IT literacy. Further, it is not unreasonable that after or even before the next economic meltdown, Central

Banks will hold some Bitcoin in their balance sheets, assuming they already do not. Going back to Bitcoin mining, it requires powerful computer equipment, energy, and a mathematically intensive system where miners are rewarded with Bitcoin upon successful verification of a block once proof of work is shown. This process will go on until the year 2140 when all 21 million coins have been mined, and then the owners have additional reward systems.

Bitcoin frees countries from fiat slavery to the point that it is being used in Venezuela, and Nigeria, both cesspools of corruption, with government issued currency having creditability issues. Take the case of Lebanon, with a worthless currency, inept and corrupt government, and monthly limitations on bank withdrawals since they are insolvent, where depositors have been stiffed for their money. Remember once your money is in the bank, it is no longer yours as the depositor, is not a secured creditor, which economist Murry Rothbard noted in his book "The Great Depression" so it might be better to buy a Sealy mattress and stuff some money there. Governments cannot solve these types of crises like Lebanon because they caused it—they are the problem, not the solution. "Depending on government to fix the problem is like calling the axe murderer to the scene of his bludgeoning and simultaneously asking him to act as the emergency room doctor"!

Conversely, if Lebanon had been on a Bitcoin and or a gold standard, government officials would not have been able to either manipulate, squander, or confiscate a nation's wealth. If Lebanon had been on the Bitcoin standard, it might have regained its status it once had in the 1950s and 1960s as the Switzerland of the Middle East. A Bitcoin backed currency would ensure governments spend within their means, without any excess funds to either bribe voters, create wars or squander. Bitcoin's separation of state from money would have saved people not only in Lebanon and other countries from holding worthless fiat money, as the fiat Ponzi scheme will slowly unravel itself for the empty shell that it is.

Bitcoin is the ultimate democratization of opportunity and helps narrow the gap of rich from poor. Bitcoin is at some level the future, and it is not going away.

The War on Bitcoin or the case against Bitcoin?

There is very little doubt that Central Banks and governments in general are concerned about the competition from Bitcoin for a host of reasons already mentioned. But the most important reason is that it is a substitutional threat to the house that the Ponzi scheme built via fiat money. But at the same time, it can live as a benevolent sheriff besides fiat and leading by example.

One has to watch the news from a very perceptual sense of consciousness when Bitcoin comes under fire to put all the dots together as the Fiat Inc. unleashes their propaganda machine. Jamie Dimon, J.P. Morgan Chase CEO, says that Bitcoin is not a legitimate asset class, yet when the price dropped, they bought it for clients. It's the same story with Warren Buffet, where his partner Charlie Munger stated that Bitcoin is antithetical to civilization, yet Berkshire Hathaway buys into Nubank, a digital Brazilian bank that deals in crypto digital assets, including Bitcoin. At the end of the day, why let feelings get in the way of making money?

The attacks on Bitcoin continued in the late spring of 2021, and of course, Janet Yellen, a chronic money-printer, waded into the orchestration when she stated that Bitcoin is an "extremely inefficient" way to conduct monetary transactions, without considering the antiquity of the SWIFT system that allows the U.S. to monitor all U.S. dollar transactions. Later, she called for regulation without taking into account that being a former Feds Chair is a conflict of interest in her role as Treasury Secretary, especially in light of the fact that she received millions from Wall Street for speaking engagements. One could also argue that running $4 trillion yearly deficits might be a little on the inefficient side as a Treasury Secretary.

Then comes the story of Elon Musk, who did a turnabout on Tesla accepting Bitcoin in early 2021, and then claimed that the mining operation was not ecologically sound environment social governance (ESG). The fact of the matter is that Bitcoin mining uses only 1/10 of 1 percent of the world's energy, and most of that is already going to go to waste in terms of excesses not used. Michael Saylor, an MIT trained engineer and founder of MicroStrategy, states that banks and their operations use a higher percentage, while much of the energy running EV cars leaves carbon footprints including its manufacturing carbon processes in addition to lithium mining.

Now we visit other things that drove FUD (fear, uncertainty, doubt) about Bitcoin, specifically, that Bitcoin miners were kicked out of China in the spring of 2021, and that this would affect hash rates, meaning mining. The real reason that China kicked out the Bitcoin miners was they were a threat to their pending digital RMB that is not backed by anything. But at least China has the backing of actually producing technology and products as opposed to the Americans who buy and sell monetary instruments based on what is a diminishing fragile trust system. Further, when you do a deep dive into the story, China did not ban Bitcoin, it only banned the deposit of Bitcoin into its banks, since it is by far a much harder currency then the RMB, either in paper or digital format. After the China mining FUD fiasco, it seems that China in the way of the CCP is having second thoughts on Bitcoin, since they are now sending out survey's about allowing Bitcoin being accepted again, as they might be realizing that their digital RMB will have to take on Bitcoin on a global scale, while realizing that they might have given away the goose that laid the golden egg.

The media, led by Yahoo! Finance, really pumped this story without first realizing that the Bitcoin miners leaving China, who were mining over 50 percent worldwide, is a plus. Why? Because, now mining is becoming less centralized, as miners have moved to friendly quarters such as El Salvador, Kazakhstan, Texas and so on, resulting in even cleaner energy. Further, by the miners leaving China, which at one time produced 50 percent of the new Bitcoin, the asset becomes even more democratized.

Coming full circle, Elon Musk in late 2021 indicated that soon, Tesla will again start accepting Bitcoin.

Creating FUD (fear, uncertainty, doubt) was perhaps a very well coordinated attack on Bitcoin that drove its price down about 50 percent from its May 2021 high, while large institutions were gathering Bitcoin as well as Ethereum on both the spot and OTC markets. When asset prices drop, it is just normal human psychology to start reading multiple news sources, comment boards, case in point Yahoo! Finance, Reddit, the *Wall Street Journal*, and the likes and go through a full-blown psychological state of Bitcoin derangement syndrome, according to Simon Dixon, especially when rumours are spread through trolls, and people who have just missed the boat insist that the digital asset will be cratering. Simon Dixon who is a Bitcoiner Evangelist wrote the first book in 2011 that included Bitcoin called "Bank to the Future." People who want to buy and hold this asset need to be in a strong psychological state to dollar cost average and not sell their position. There is another advantage of Bitcoin and gold for that matter, namely becoming your own central bank.

Become Your Own Central Bank

We have all been brought up with paper money as a store of value, and it is hard for most to emancipate from fiat thinking. Fiat thinking is different from Bitcoin, or even gold thinking, especially where cash is no longer a store of value, a depreciating asset but a medium of exchange. We have become slaves of the artificial construct of working for paper currency, strangely, people work all week for depreciating government issuance that when undressed, is nothing more than decorated paper backed by nothing, and without printing limitations. One must free themselves from the fiat world that is controlled by the Central Banks, government, and crony capitalism.

When you become your own Central Banker, you no longer have to go through the bank's approval process that is arduous, with the undressing of your personal info with degrading applications for funding, often resembling a cross-examination before the Grand Jury. Because Bitcoin is not your daddy's currency, and if you own Bitcoin, you can go to a lender such as YouHodler and get up to 90 percent of your crypto in an instant loan by pledging your Bitcoin. You will then be paying the loan back in fiat money, which is a depreciating asset, and once you pay off your loan and get back custody of Bitcoin, you will have an appreciating asset. In essence, if your fiat depreciates against Bitcoin during the lifetime of the loan due to relative inflation, you might end up paying 70 cents on the dollar for the loan.

Conversely, if you want to deposit your Bitcoin, you can receive anywhere from 4 percent to 12 percent on your deposit, depending if it is stable coin or not, you have two profit centres. The first, during the length of the crypto term deposit, one at let's say 10 percent return, and the second on an appreciating asset, which might give you a 20 percent return (being conservative) for a total return of 30 percent in the Bitcoin space.

The Bitcoin space is very fast-moving, where now a Toronto-based crypto lending firm Ledn has announced that with $70 million of raised capital and is offering Bitcoin-backed mortgages.

In many respects, the inventiveness of decentralized finance is like the beginning of the internet in the late 1990s, and much like the internet, it is not going away, and even with regulation, it is truly a democratized space and asset class, unlike the current big-tech internet giants of Silicon Valley who have suffocated the initial dreams of the internet through centralized control. It is for this reason that even the bohemian Jack Dorsey calls it blockchain Web 3.0, because of its true independent not central nature.

When we have a collapse of the fiat system and/or the equity and Treasury markets, there is still the refuge of gold. Gold and silver still have a hold on the history of the human psyche dating back 5,000 years, and it must be included in your "morning after" plans. Its advantage over Bitcoin and Ethereum is that you can hold the precious metals in your hands, hence, the 50- to 70-somethings will more than likely not as easily accept cryptos, and instead rely on the physicality of gold to soothe their deeper inner psyches, and this is quite understandable. To prepare for the financial Armageddon that will further wipe out the middle-class, you should own physical gold or silver. But do not buy gold certificates from banks because they are not backed by physical, and in a bank failure scenario, they are worthless pieces of paper based on an antiquated fractional swift based banking fiat system. Hence, it would be wise to hold physical gold and silver, or purchase from Sprott Capital, whose equity fund is backed by physical gold and silver in the Canadian Mint.

In a worst-case scenario, you can exchange your physical gold and silver with bullion dealers into cash, or if fiat money is not accepted, gold is probably the easiest thing to barter for food, goods, and services, as entrepreneurs will take advantage of any arbitrage opportunities in an underground economy. People who have lived in tough times in developing counties are naturally climatized to this and will be proficient in bartering and underground economies. True, precious metals are cumbersome, but there is still a strong case to make for the solidity of gold and silver in times of upheaval. Especially if there is a collapse of government and lawlessness takes hold, but then again, with current government with its overreaching and greedy hands, a case could be made that we are already living in law by press conference or decree.

Some Closing Thoughts on Bitcoin

We are seeing now the merging of the U.S. Treasury and Central Bank, where they no longer operate independently, as they should, under legal mandate. This, of course leads to more currency debasement. Simon Dixon, CEO and cofounder BnkToTheFuture.com, said the following about Bitcoin:

> *Fiat money has attributed value because a government declares it legal tender—it has no intrinsic value! Bitcoin has intrinsic value beyond the trust of its community! Bitcoin doesn't lean on a system of debts; its value is how effective it is as a medium of exchange!*[4]

4   Simon Dixon, "What Is the Great Reset?" YouTube video, accessed April 8, 2022, https://www.youtube.com/watch?v=PSAskMp96wl

China currently has the social credit score system where if you associate with the wrong people, it could affect your status within the society, and exclude you from buying train and plane tickets, as well as a host of other things. Much of the technology and surveillance systems for this was developed by Silicon Valley, as well as UK firms. It is apparent now that it is only a matter of time that the United States will adopt a centralized digital U.S. dollar. This will increase government surveillance, and even your passports can be linked to your bank accounts, vaccine status, tax collections, unruly social media comments, summary judgments, making it a very convenient seizure target for overreaching government, where they can put your complete life on hold at a switch of a button.

Just like an episode from the series called *Startup*, you can have all your liquid assets frozen, and with the elimination of cash, you would not be able to buy a sandwich or groceries with a government issued digital money. This is not a far-fetched conspiracy; it is a very real possibility.

It's true that Bitcoin is volatile in the short term, and this makes it an asset that is not for everyone. However, it doesn't have the manipulative trading curves that Wall Street has in terms of regulating the stock market, where the end game is computer trading curves that obliterate price discovery. Comparing this to Bitcoin, it trades 24/7, has no trading curves, and does not have its hands out to the Central Bank for bailouts, and cannot be lobbied or censured. It is this element of pure price discovery that it brings to the market. When Bitcoin climbs up to $250,000, it will be a near $5 trillion market cap, halfway to matching gold, and worth near two times more than any company in the world based on capitalization value.

Bitcoin is the counterculture—it is a vehicle to detach governmental control over one's personal life. With its unbreakable fiduciary commitment, it could possibly act as an oversight of government economic monetary follies. It is no wonder that it's being accepted by a host of companies from Domino's to Microsoft, Home Depot, Starbucks, Whole Foods, PayPal, Red Cross, Virgin Galactic, Subway, AMC, and the list goes on. Even property taxes in Richmond Hill and Innisfil, Ontario, can be paid in Bitcoin, the mayor of New York is now being paid in Bitcoin, and Bitcoin is being accepted by tax collectors in Florida for payments associated with driver licenses and ID cards, automobile tags and titles and property tax.5 This does not mean that Bitcoin will displace government currency per say, but its best gift to humanity is that value will be exchanged between two parties without the overlord of government. And this might be the key proposition to humanity by emancipating from their feckless masters via Bitcoin!

When one's mind becomes liberated from mismanaged sovereign currencies and considers a private asset class that cannot be confiscated by overreaching governments, then one thinks in a different paradigm and starts seeing the future of tomorrow with acute clarity! Admittedly, this acceptance takes time for most of us, as this is because most people think in a fiat world in respect to valuations, and units of account, as they are quick to trade Bitcoin when it goes either up or down. Though the prudent will accumulate during a crypto winter. When stuck in the fiat world for weekly wages one is working a 50-hour week for a depreciating instrument controlled and manipulated by Central Banks and government, as opposed to a long-term appreciating Bitcoin asset.

Again, Bitcoin is a long-term play, and should be treated as art and other collectables.

Bitcoin is part of the future, according to Michael Saylor, it is the most revolutionary monetary development in 5,000 years, and no wonder it is being called digital gold. In many ways, Bitcoin is the currency of resistance!

5   Annaliese Milano, "Florida Tax Collector to Accept Bitcoin, Bitcoin Cash Payments," CoinDesk, May 14, 2018, updated September 13, 2021, https://www.coindesk.com/markets/2018/05/14/florida-tax-collector-to-accept-bitcoin-bitcoin-cash-payments/

CHAPTER

17

The Future of Tomorrow

The future of tomorrow holds both hazard for those borne by safety and incredible opportunities for the bold. The reason is that disruption has always created our future from the Industrial Revolution that brought us the cotton gin and the steam engine, which eventually led to Stevenson and the railroad that was the catalyst for urbanization, and its associated economic organisation. It was Karl Benz's first practical prototype of the gasoline internal combustion engine that allowed Henry Ford to develop industrial and efficiency engineering that ushered in mass economic affordability of the automobile, and other goods. Or consider the effects of still film, and then motion picture by Eastman Kodak, as the world had a chance to see itself.

Technology has undeniably changed not only our psyches but our economics. Consider the works of the most prolific inventor of the 19th century, Thomas Edison, with breakthroughs like the first long-lasting practical incandescent light bulb, the phonograph, the alkaline battery that was originally used in electric cars in the earlier 20th century, as well as being the founder of General Electric. The story goes on with the Wright Brothers' first flight, or Nikola Tesla demonstrating a radio-controlled boat in 1898 at Madison Square Garden. Alexander Graham Bell then entered the equation with the advent of the telephone where he ran into much resistance at the time.

As we move deeper into the 20th century, John Vincent Atanasoff and Clifford Berry delivered the first computer, namely the Atanasoff-Berry Computer (ABC) in 1937, and then the IBM mainframes in the late 1940s that was originally not warmly received by IBM's president at the time, Thomas Watson. We then in the 1950s invented industrial robotics, put a man on the moon in 1969, and by the 1970s we had the first PCs from Microsoft and Apple, which evolved with GUI, email, and by the 1990s, were delivered into the arms of the internet, social media, AI, electric cars, digitization, and now Bitcoin, Web3 and the metaverse. Historically, all disrupters have in some way met with resistance from the old guard way of thinking, as the innovators are bold, and are addicted to the adrenaline of danger, the laggards have an affection for safety, and this is the story of not only economics but the human moment!

So perhaps now is a good time to peek into the looking glass and consider the future of tomorrow.

Wage Inflation

All these disruptions changed the world economic order. For example, consider that by people staying home during the never-ending pandemic, it has created a culture of remote working. Then employers might do an efficiency study of working at home versus in-office and see that although there are some benefits, for instance, travel time and ability to focus on efficiencies, there are also drawbacks, such as loss of belongingness that physical presence brings, nuances of physicality, mentoring newer staff, and the amount of time spent on household distractions, including the use of social media, all of which can break down the discipline of an organisation.

Without a supervisor on sight, we already see the inexperienced people being exposed to customers calling, as they rely on putting the call on hold while messaging for assistance. In a physical environment, people share knowhow in real time and exponentially move the organization and excellence up the learning curve. So yes, there are caveats to remote working and as K-12 kids were dupped for 2 years of Zoom teaching, passing off as education.

With wage inflation, firms might then become enlightened and outsource work overseas to lower cost centres. Do not think that a faceless woke corporation has your best interest at heart when the real role of the human resources department is to avert litigation. Hence, what we could see is overseas cost centres going up the migration scales and start eating up traditional white-collar jobs. This, of course, is already happening, since you can hire a PhD in mathematics, stock analyst, engineer, coder, accountant, tech support, accounting, law, and even a virtual assistant at a fraction of the price.

Domestically, we are seeing higher wages due to money printing and helicopter money, and this will be a driving force in the way of cost-push inflation, meaning wages in certain sectors will go up in the West to the point then, as where possible, it is outsourced to developing countries, resulting in driving up wages in foreign labour pools.

In the United States, for relatively low-skilled labour requirements, Amazon is taking a playbook from multinational corporations who operate overseas, and end up driving wage prices overseas, by poaching the best from local firms in foreign markets. According to the *Wall Street Journal*, "Within a few months, a handful of the employees at his company, mattress manufacturer Serta Inc., had decamped to Amazon. 'We had no choice but to compete,' he said. 'The company raised its starting pay by roughly $2 to about $15 an hour and has since raised it about another dollar,' he said."[1]

In September 2021, Amazon announced that its starting wage now averages $18.32 an hour, compared to the federal minimum wage of $7.25 an hour, which shows that the marketplace has a better handle on wage price discovery than bureaucrats in government who have never run a lemonade stand, never mind a company. The labour market is so tight that Amazon is offering a $3,000 signing bonus, resulting in poaching employees left and right from local competitors.

It seems that labour requiring physical presence such as trades, warehousing, manufacturing, and, of course, medicine, will benefit. However, the future employee in cases that does not require physicality, might really be selling their skills in a global marketplace, where they can be contracted by the day, week, month, or year. And they can use venues like LinkedIn, Upwork, Fiverr and the likes. This will, of course, on a global level increase wages in developing countries, while in the West, it will put pressure on long-term

1   Sebastian Herrera, "Amazon Emerges as the Wage-and-Benefits Setter for Low-Skilled Workers Across Industries, Wall Street Journal, December 7, 2021, https://www.wsj.com/articles/amazon-emerges-as-the-wage-and-benefits-setter-for-low-skilled-workers-across-industries-11638910694

wages. People will have to come to terms with the new era of job security which comes to terms with the certainty of uncertainty, and embrace risk, just like entrepreneurs; safety need not apply!

Put differently, there is a case to be made that because of disruptive technologies, classical model of employment has been disrupted by labour that will offer their skillset in the global platform. So, the days of the safety, pat on the back, and a gold watch after a lifelong career at a corporation has really come to an end, unless you are in the C-suite as part of the king of the castle. So, the future might very well result in employees taking a page out of the entrepreneur's playbook, by selling their skills in the strange new global world marketplace!

A benefit is that if you offer contracted services to a host of companies, they can pay your company directly as a subcontractor freelance arrangement which give you a host of tax reduction benefits, hence, if you are demanding higher wages, you must compete and differentiate with a global labour pool that just might take your lunch money.

And finally, in respect to reshoring manufacturing, it will be facing headwinds against wage inflation leading to, quite possibly, another step backwards, this in addition to structural skillsets missing. Again, the winner of this fight will be the one who has the finest industrial robots, technicians, efficiency engineers, and low tax jurisdictions.

The Middle-class Need Not Apply

A key tenet of stability for democracies is to have a stable middle-class, which keeps reaching for that higher ladder that is a reminder of 1950s America and beyond. Once you lose your middle-class, you start to lose societal stability, because the middle-class creates content, prosperity, and for the highly industrious members, an opportunity to increase one's financial lot in life. The middle-class is a litmus test and proof that it as a propagative vehicle and springboard to attain upward mobility in the quest to reach the high summit, once you eliminate this, the institutions of Western societies start to crumble, as the plausibility of the American dream comes under intellectual assault.

But in the new world order, the middle-class are quite expendable as they will become the most tragic victims of the Central Bank money printing that is leading to sustained inflation, which might go on for a decade, as it did from the mid 1960s to early 1980s, as they do not have enough appreciating assets like the wealthy, such as art collections, physical gold and silver, large stock portfolios, real estate portfolios, and Bitcoin, they are being set up for the big takedown.

Table 17.1 shows a snapshot on consumer debt.

Table 17.1: Personal Consumer Debt

Type of debt	Average debt in 2020	Type of debt	Average debt in 2020
Credit card	$5,315	Student loan	$38,792
Personal loan	$16,458	HELOC	$41,954
Auto loan	$19,703	Mortgage	$208,185

Source: BankRate.com

When we go into a catastrophic economic collapse, these people will be the hardest hit, as they have not planned for such a shock, because of a collapsing fiat money and its associated money printing and insolvent Treasury. The middle-class and the working poor often do not have the sophistication of having appreciating assets, or at least not ones that can weather a storm, because they are too busy chasing weekly fiat money and trying to make ends meet. In other words, many are in a vicious cycle that exhausts their psyche and have trouble coming up for air. Even the more disciplined ones that have saved money for a rainy day, will see the value of their savings be decimated by debasement of non-backed fiat money.

Few will have gold or Bitcoin to pay for life's essentials in the case that it allows them to buy essentials in the event of a societal breakdown that would include ATM's running out of money, and banks limiting withdrawals. The house of cards will especially hit the middle-class and working poor, where their home could be underwater, where debt exceeds home value, just like government.

Much of this happens because getting through the trials and tribulations of daily life leaves little time to plan, as the refuge of Netflix, and pop culture provides a precarious sanctuary against the coming tsunami.

The middle-class will join the poor and will be gaslighted by the media narrative that the free markets caused this when we have not had a free market since President Warren Harding. Government will get a Teflon coating and get protection like a mafia Don by the media with the full support from the Cabalatocracy, in ensuring that truth will be considered heresy even more so now, and will get lost in the quagmire of the matrix, never to be seen again, as it lies in the ashes of obscurity.

Distinguished members of the Cabalatocracy including the high priests of Hollywood, and media talking heads from their palatial castles of opulence will administer another injection of hyper-propaganda, as they will point to capitalism as the true culprit. Yes, the same capitalism that shoulders their privileged way of life, and the same capitalism that government parasitically lives off.

Crisis after Crisis

We're living in an age of crisis after crisis, where nonstop we are being exposed to fear and anxiety as a way of being controlled. When one crisis fades a new one emerges just as sure as the sun will rise in the East.

In 2020 we were exposed to the COVID-19 pandemic, which seems like it's never ending, but has subsided at some level. What the media needs for their talking heads is to espouse a renaissance of anxiety, to better insert people back into their cycle of fear.

So just when things were starting to look more normal, sadly a tragic war has erupted between Ukraine and Russia. Hence, I will not comment on the war, however I will comment on the economic implications, namely the sanctions.

Firstly, after the ruble dropped to near 133 versus the U.S. dollar in February 2022, it has rebounded to 60 as of May, it is stronger than before the outbreak of the war. The sanctions have not had the effects the West would like, and exactly the opposite effects because Europe is dependent, especially Germany's industrial engine, on Russian energy. In an environment that was already inflationary, the strategy of sanctions has poured gasoline on the inflation fire that certainly was there before the war. But now, by going along with these sanctions Germany is putting itself at peril, and this is hardly strategic, but a form of the West's vengeance on Russia coming back to bite them with unintended consequences.

We need to consider that Russia has the largest proven reserves of natural gas in the world, of 1.688 billion MMcf in the ground, and with natural gas near $7 per NYM $/mmbtu, up from $5 in April, it opens up a huge headache for Germany's manufacturing economy, since if Germany catches a cold, Europe will get pneumonia. Further, at current prices Russia has reserves of natural gas worth approximately $12 trillion and compare this to the U.S. gold reserves worth $573 billion. So then, one might reasonably think that natural gas reserves are an asset much as gold. Moving to oil, Russia has 80 billion barrels of proven reserves, and at $100 per barrel this equates to $8 trillion, while holding the fifth largest gold reserves in the world, and a debt to GDP of 20 percent.

Looking at agriculture, Russia commands 24 percent of the wheat exports of the world, and is the fourth largest producer of fertilizer, where we are currently seeing higher prices as of April of 2022 and shortages in both sectors. It goes then that Russia with $20 trillion in energy reserves, along with its agricultural assets, fosters the ruble's stability. Hence, for practical purposes, the ruble is a hard resource backed currency. It is this paradox that perhaps many in the political class of the West did not consider when imposing sanctions in their "what if scenarios" when strategic planning.

The inflation genie is becoming a raging fire, and a Frankenstein monster of sorts as it becomes apparent that the U.S. unleashed its weapons of mass financial destruction, without considering the full extent of its ramifications both to itself and its European allies. And finally, by confiscating Russian foreign currency reserves, it has in fact sent a signal to friends and foes alike of the ramifications for not politically complying with America's will. Except for one problem, which is that countries like India, China, and Russia are taking note, using their own currencies to trade with each other and building their own 21st century Club of Rome. All the while, losing comfort with 10-year Treasuries, and U.S. dollar foreign reserves sitting in New York or London that are in essence monetary instruments living in a house of cards. Germany, and much of Europe, because of dependence in Russian energy and agriculture simply cannot comply with sanctions, since it would be economic suicide that might take decades to recover from, if ever.

Politically, as well as economically, this has turned into a blowback for the United States not only with inflation, but a self-inflicted wound resulting in a diminishment of U.S. monetary hegemony as the reserve currency of the world, which results in weakening America's global bargaining power.

Since the COVID-19 crisis is running out of gas, the financial talking heads will sing the Central Bank's timeless classic hit single "Money Printing" as the only solution to revive the sluggish world economies. Because, it has worked so well since the 2009 Great Recession of money printing that has been passed off as an economic recovery. Now they have great reason to blame inflation on the war, hence absolving themselves from accountability, and carte blanche to keep printing.

When this schtick is up, another crisis will mysteriously appear on the horizon, maybe climate change, leaving the citizens of Rome in state of perpetual anxiety and mass psychosis. The important thing is to find a pretext or a smoke screen, if you will, to keep the money presses going.[2]

2   "Gold Reserves," Trading Economics, accessed May 8, 2022, https://tradingeconomics.com/country-list/gold-reserves; Rob Cook, "Top 20 Largest Wheat Exporters in the World," Beef2Live, May 7, 2022, https://beef2live.com/story-top-20-largest-wheat-exporters-world-0-206491; "Natural Gas Reserves by Country," Worldometer, accessed May 8, 2022, https://www.worldometers.info/gas/gas-reserves-by-country/; "Production Volume of Nitrogen Fertilizer Worldwide in 2018, by Country," Statista, November 24, 2021, https://www.statista.com/statistics/1252656/nitrogen-fertilizer-production-by-country/

Like the spin cycle of a washing machine, plebeians and the digital minions (mostly found in the Twittersphere, Instagram, Reddit, Telegram, TV etc.) will go into another hopeless cycle of fear.

The cycle of fear starts with media in orchestration with government, until a crisis is established then moves into a state of societal fear, much like the virus, then the calls come out for more government which always ends in tyranny with no exceptions. Then government will deliberate, find an erroneous solution dressed in seductive optics for the plebians to buy into, then spend money it doesn't have by calling in the Central Bank money printers and creating a mess, while employing the propaganda ministry so no one could remember what the crises was in the first place. Then its "Soak Rinse and Repeat" just add some laundry liquid softener to make the next cycle of fear more tolerable!

This is diagramed in Figure 17.1

Figure 17.1: The Cycle of Fear

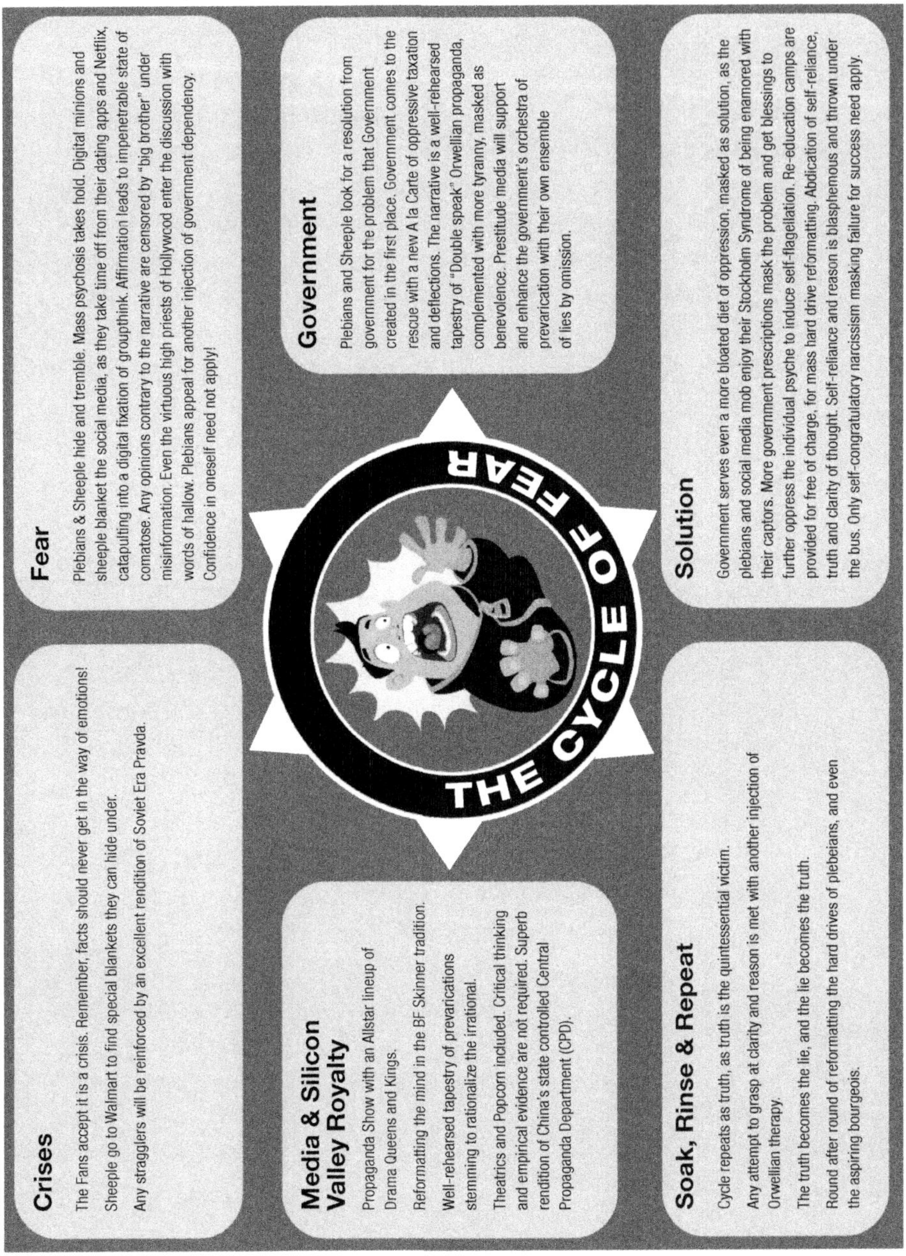

Crises

The Fans accept it is a crisis. Remember, facts should never get in the way of emotions! Sheeple go to Walmart to find special blankets they can hide under.

Any stragglers will be reinforced by an excellent rendition of Soviet Era Pravda.

Fear

Plebians & Sheeple hide and tremble. Mass psychosis takes hold. Digital minions and sheeple blanket the social media, as they take time off from their dating apps and Netflix, catapulting into a digital fixation of groupthink. Affirmation leads to impenetrable state of comatose. Any opinions contrary to the narrative are censored by "big brother" under misinformation. Even the virtuous high priests of Hollywood enter the discussion with words of hallow. Plebians appeal for another injection of government dependency. Confidence in oneself need not apply!

Media & Silicon Valley Royalty

Propaganda Show with an Allstar lineup of Drama Queens and Kings.

Reformatting the mind in the BF Skinner tradition.

Well-rehearsed tapestry of prevarications stemming to rationalize the irrational.

Theatrics and Popcorn included. Critical thinking and empirical evidence are not required. Superb rendition of China's state controlled Central Propaganda Department (CPD).

Government

Plebians and Sheeple look for a resolution from government for the problem that Government created in the first place. Government comes to the rescue with a new A la Carte of oppressive taxation and deflections. The narrative is a well-rehearsed tapestry of "Double speak" Orwellian propaganda, complemented with more tyranny, masked as benevolence. Prestitute media will support and enhance the government's orchestra of prevarication with their own ensemble of lies by omission.

Soak, Rinse & Repeat

Cycle repeats as truth, as truth is the quintessential victim.

Any attempt to grasp at clarity and reason is met with another injection of Orwellian therapy.

The truth becomes the lie, and the lie becomes the truth.

Round after round of reformatting the hard drives of plebeians, and even the aspiring bourgeois.

Solution

Government serves even a more bloated diet of oppression, masked as solution, as the plebians and social media mob enjoy their Stockholm Syndrome of being enamored with their captors. More government prescriptions mask the problem and get blessings to further oppress the individual psyche to induce self-flagellation. Re-education camps are provided for free of charge, for mass hard drive reformatting. Abdication of self-reliance, truth and clarity of thought. Self-reliance and reason is blasphemous and thrown under the bus. Only self-congratulatory narcissism masking failure for success need apply.

As the culprit—the free market—has been convicted without evidence in the public square by an evening of insatiable emotion, the full gaslighting effect takes place as to behaviour modification of the former middle-class as they join the poor, who might feel the coup d'état less, because they have become desensitized to their tragic fate of government assistance as a way of life. Together, they will plead, and vote for more government, believing they will attain safety in numbers at the expense of abdicating self-reliance and individualism.

This will be a tragic trade-off, because with each soak rinse and repeat cycle, they will be hurled deeper into the Stockholm syndrome as slaves that boastfully relish their invisible shackles. Socialism and communist strands will take hold in the midst of the night as a centrally planned economy and way of life demands that its subjects rationalize the irrational.

Noted members of the Cabalatocracy—the bankers, the high priests of Hollywood, the media, the government—will get off scot-free and walk the streets like un-convicted mafia Dons being praised for providing soup lines. And the bourgeoisie and the very rich will espouse wealth redistribution, as long as it is not their money being taken away. This will be relatively easy, since without a middle-class, there is no opposition to tyranny. Because the middle-class still believes in ideals and its manifestation.

To offer wisdom for the coming funeral procession of the middle-class and hope, I must rely on the eloquent words of 18th century philosopher Jean-Jacques Rousseau, who stated:

> *Man was born free, and everywhere he is in chains. Many a one believes himself the master of others, and yet he is a greater slave than they. How has this change come about?*[3]

3   Jean-Jacques Rousseau, *The Social Contract, trans. Maurice Cranston* (New York: Penguin, 1968).

Hard Backed Currency, Central Banks, and Sovereign Debt Default

Historically, the story of fiat money always ends in tears as it returns to its true value of zero. Paul Krugman, the U.S. economist and New York Times columnist said, "If you like, fiat currencies have underlying value because men with guns say they do."[4] Its not an impossible assertion, because the British pound lasted 300 years in various forms, because of Great Britain's military might, especially on the high seas and is the rare exception to the rule. Eventually it was replaced by the U.S. dollar as the reserve currency.

The history of the steady procession of non-hard-backed money printing has been sprinkled throughout the book, and its toxicity ranges anywhere from inflation, stagflation, creating wealth gaps, the loss of real savings. Government debt is allowed to grow at astronomical numbers because of the nature of fiat money, and Central Banks have incomparable control of manipulating the economy, power over the markets and government. Or put differently, the Treasury and Central Bank must operate under law as separate, now operate as one.

To see Central Bank Chairman Jerome Powell read scripted lines and questions while not take responsibility for inflation is an abdication of truth. The Central Bank policy in conjunction with the U.S. Treasury has caused this unsustainable mess, and for all intents and purposes, they are merged, and to think that Janet Yellen is not the fusion for this is naïve. Much like the Holy Roman Empire, where for centuries since 800 AD, where the Pope coronated the Emperor, in turn the Emperor would claim the right to depose or appoint the Pope, which was galling to both. The symbiotic relationship is the same, with the executive branch coronating the Fed Chair, while the Chair, through continued money printing, coronates the President by lending to the insolvent Treasury. If the

---

4   Paul Krugman, "Transaction Costs and Tethers: Why I'm a Crypto Skeptic," *New York Times*, July 31, 2018, https://www.nytimes.com/2018/07/31/opinion/transaction-costs-and-tethers-why-im-a-crypto-skeptic.html

money printing presses slowed down or stopped, the President would unleash the dogs of the media and other noted members of the Cabalatocracy, in order to save his crown—in the end, both are reluctantly tolerant of each other, as their mutual fate lies in each others' hands.

Subsequently, the U.S. dollar is doing a theatrical slow-motion swan dive off the Empire State Building, where the decline is barely perceptive to the naked eye. Government and the Fed, of course, will never blame themselves for inflation and have shameless public inquiries to look under every stub and tree for the culprit, except the fraudulent and shaky foundations of the Ponzi scheme of money printing. They even push the narrative that the uptick in inflation is due to a surge of natural demand again. The narrative is, "are you going to believe what you see or what I am tell you"?

The Central Bank via Wall Street and direct are buying many assets, much like the Bank of Japan, and when the bubble they and government created bursts, it will be dystopian and tragic. What will be the pin to burst the bubble and create a black swan event is open for debate. But to the prudent, my advice is to keep an eye on the debt market, the U.S. dollar index, and especially the 10-year Treasury bond, and if rates spike, and the Central Bank cannot keep it suppressed, there will be few places to hide. Currently, the war in Ukraine will help deflect away from the pending tsunami, as the pandemic mysteriously disappears under the fog of war and propaganda, as each new crisis is fueled by the Cabalatocracy finding even a higher elevation of euphoric fix to occupy the collective conscious of the digital minions. Sadly, these wars are fought for economic interests and arms sales, at the expense of human life.

In high school I had a very inspiring history teacher, Mr. Neumsch, who happened to like teaching the virtues of communism, and was a member of the Canadian communist party, and it is where I first learned about this ideology. He always looked at things from an unorthodox perspective, and over time we became friends as many classmates and I would go to his apartment and make conversation with him and his wife at his parties, as I glossed over Mr. Neumsch's book collection that included Das Kapital by Karl Marx. Back then, high school was quite academically rigorous, went up to grade 13 in Canada as a stream for advanced topics in preparation for university. It was at this time that I unknowingly learned how to write and look at things from a more critical perspective. But the one thing he once said in class has never left me was when he exclaimed in respect to war, *"When you go fight a war, and hopefully come back alive, what do you personally gain, and who really gains?"* It was my awakening moment that I even understood back then and let me think more clearly of the tragedy of war to this day!

When we study the classical economists mentioned in the book, we come to the realisation that we stand on the shoulders of giants, while we humbly peak into the future.

It is quite possible that a large Central Bank could potentially collapse, and a prime suspect is the EU, where it has lent money out of thin air to some noted deadbeats that are very sick, insolvent patients, including the PIGS (Portugal, Italy, Greece, Spain) that owe almost $6 trillion, while the European Central Bank's known balance sheets show almost $9 trillion, much like the U.S. Fed there is a non-disclosed balance sheet that does not show up. The EU balance sheets are full of toxic assets, and if a chartered bank held assets like this, namely insolvent European countries, they would default on depositor obligations and be called in by regulators for running a quasi circus, and this would not pass a stress test. This is all a result of reckless government spending on unsustainable and addictive social entitlements, in exchange for power and the status quo.

Any one of these countries can go into sovereign debt default—or China, where the banks are full of toxic assets posing as stability, or the UK, but especially the Bank of Japan, who makes Bernie Madoff look like a prudent custodian of fiduciary discipline.

The collapse of the Ponzi scheme, which is, of course, international in nature, will more than likely include a combination of sovereign debt default and the eventual collapse of one of the major Central Banks as the ECU seems to be a top candidate. To keep things in perspective, if any of these insolvent countries were an individual or a corporation, they would not qualify for a loan to open up a hotdog stand!

It is here where we will see the new world order and the great reset!

The New World Order and The Great Reset

The great reset of the 20th century was Bretton Woods in 1944 whose offspring included the IMF, World Bank, GATT, and the gold window, and the U.S. dollar being the reserve currency of the world. Reset 2.0 was when Nixon took the U.S. dollar off gold.

"In the great reset 3.0, you will own nothing but will be happy," according to Klaus Schwab,[5] a noted member of the ultra elitist Davos club, World Economic Forum (WEF), an international branch of the Cabalatocracy. We might be happy at first, that is, of course, until we find out that much like the communist party of the former USSR, and the current thugs running the CCP and so-called Western democracies, the elite members of the Cabalatocracy will live in palatial and opulent luxury, in their castles of virtue. And, of course, there will be a daily diet of egalitarian "doublespeak" propaganda to help the plebeians (including the former middle-class), to live in their perceived egalitarian utopia. After all, as a form of self-flagellation, they will plead for this as a perverted form of compassion and re-affirming their convictions.

5   Klaus Schwab, *COVID-19: The Great Reset* (Geneva: Forum Publishing, 2020).

Because money is losing its value in an inflationary environment, savers are punished, and the people will borrow to buy things. The imprudent will spend it away on short-term emotional lifts like restaurants and grown-up toys, while the more prudent will leverage the easy money on buying assets, like homes, driving up the real estate bubble, knowing that the debt they pay back will be in lesser inflated dollars.

Once the Ponzi scheme collapses, the corrupt Central Banks and government will orchestrate a cycle of fear, by tapping their presstitute propaganda arm, namely the media, and of course, the highly censored Silicon Valley. Any rebels that dare posit intellectual sobriety and accountability, will be publicly displayed, tarred and feathered in the modern digital galleys and town squares, which is, of course, much more civilized than the fate of King Charles I of England. Once the rebels are made examples of, the minions will hide under their blankets and go into their cycle of fear, as shown in Figure 17.1.

During the collapse of the house of cards, the macroeconomic cataclysmic exogenous shock will destabilize nearly all financial institutions. Many chartered banks will become insolvent, there will be an abundance of worthless fiat-based Treasury bills, some Wall Street banks will collapse, the derivatives markets will be toxic, the equities market will meltdown, with spikes in interest rates, real estate will take a big hit, bank deposits could perish, and our systems of trade and settlement would come to a near grinding halt.

Even if some of this played out, it would be a dystopian nightmare, because people in the West, in the allegiance of safety, do not have the same strong bones of the greatest generation that were built during the Great Depression. Our abundance from success has led to selfishness then apathy, dependence, and then tyranny, which of course, can only be delivered by government, as quite simply, history supports this. The collapse, which will be caused by government and the Fed will come up with a solution, but not without caveats! Because once the fraudulent fiat money collapses the reset will begin, as all the actors of the Cabalatocracy will take their places before the opening curtain is lifted for the show to begin.

Central Bank-Issued Digital Currency

With banks and the U.S. dollar imploding, leading to the loss of the world reserve currency status, affecting bank depositors, a solution will come about with some caveats, of course.

According to Simon Dixon, author of *Bank of The Future*, we will see the formal merger of the U.S. Central Bank and the U.S. Treasury as one. The Central Bank along with the Treasury will issue a new U.S. digital currency to pay depositors and help stabilize the new digital U.S. dollar, and the U.S. digital currency will be used to support U.S. Treasury bills. It will be hailed as a technological marvel, as the narcissistic authorities will be paraded and formally coronated as the savers of the world economic system, yes, the same ones who destroyed it. To add some icing on the cake, with the new digital currency, the Central Bank will now say that it could be used to digitally eradicate wealth inequality. Of course, this is nothing more than doublespeak propaganda, since they are the architects of wealth inequality, as they are in bed with other noted and essential members of the Cabalatocracy, namely the Wall Street banks that they will bail out, to ensure they have comfortable weekends with the aristocracy in the Hamptons, where their real estate assets will continue to escalate unabated.

But there is a digital noose to this, that some may not have considered, because if one thinks the amount of surveillance that YouTube, Instagram, Facebook, and the likes has on people is concerning, it will be a walk in the park, compared to what the government issued digital currency will do.

Your digital currency can be downloaded into a wallet on your phone, and everywhere you spend and everything you purchase will be on a central database, controlled by the Central Bank and the government. This will be the beginning of a social credit system, much like they have in China, which incidentally Silicon Valley helped build. For example, the government might give fiscal stimulus to give segregated demand by increasing the sales of laptops or cars, and if they are not used in 30 day or 60 days of its issuance, they can be removed from your digital wallet.

Everything can be tied into your digital wallet, consider the never-ending pandemic based on contentious science, where this digital wallet is connected to your vaccination records. If you decide to espouse anything that is in contravention of the official narrative, it could lead to strikes on your social credit score. And if global taxation is implemented, it will be collected at the source, and if you fall behind on taxes, it can be collected digitally. At the same time, IRS audits, which is a form of thuggery, they can come to tax audit summary finding, without evidence and have your money seized. When Central Bank digital currencies (CBDC) are first introduced, it will come to bear free gifts of digital money into your digital wallet and will be embraced as the coming of the Messiah as finally the calls of wealth distribution are answered after a 7,000 year wait. This will of course be the hook and once everyone is wired in with seat belts fastened, it will be accepted as part of our socioeconomic new normalcy, it will be at that point when the long knives come out for the plebeians who do not toe the line with government initiatives, their wallets will be frozen, with no paper money as an alternative to conduct business. Just imagine that you can't even buy groceries, as a result of not complying with this Orwellian dystopia, your family could go hungry. Plebians will turn on those that don't comply with the program as they will be accused of being self-centred and selfish at the expense of the greater good, as the orchestra of the Cabalatocracy plays their latest album in the background, namely "That was then this is now", as part of their behaviour modification therapy.

Of course, this will all be under the guise of wealth redistribution, as government will advise God that they are now in charge, and He should take a well-earned vacation. For those rebels who do not comply with this scheme of wealth distribution being the deflection, this will be considered heresy and not willing to sacrifice for the greater good, will lead to being digitally tarred, feathered, and displayed in the town hall of Twitter, Instagram and other platforms of the Silicon Valley Cabalatocracy as the digital minions clap in appreciation of compliance of being moral, without realising of their own enslavement, will hiss at anyone who joins the resistance. This can be easily accomplished, since conformists look down upon individual thinkers as somehow being immoral, and often put them in the camp of the selfish. No need to look far—with the pandemic, the conformists took a drug on EUA with no legal recourse against injury, and in the beginning stages, accused the non-jabbed of being spreaders, that is until the truth contradicted this. For entertainment and theatre, Hollywood will do a remake of the 1955 classic "Rebel Without a Cause" with a new cast of woke actors that will throw credibility under the bus.

Hence, you can see how easy it is to divide and conquer, and the pandemic is just a dry run before the heavy lifting starts, to make sure that individual liberty is sitting on shaky foundations.

This loss of privacy will start gradually like the first few minutes of anesthesia—it will feel pleasant as one enjoys the relaxed sleep, not realizing in their dreamy state that by giving government incremental power they will never relinquish it without a French Revolution or American Civil War type event. What we see here is communism, and it never appears without its essential bedfellow, tyranny, but this will be a new type of communism, still built on the tenets of Karl Marx's central control of the economy. More than likely, it will start as democratic socialism, which is an oxymoron, because the word "democratic" is the seduction part to sign one up into the intellectual anesthesiology of socialism. A backdrop is in order, so we can infer America's state-run form of capitalism that seems to be on the horizon.

The Former USSR and Mao's China

Once the great reset sets in, it will be the more powerful form of communism that not even Lenin, Mao or Stalin ever commanded. Why? In the case of the former Soviet Union, they made the mistake of taking over all means of production, and confiscating all remanence of free enterprise, as the Soviet communist government was inept at creating affordable, timely products and services that free market could deliver more efficiently. This was due to the

Bolsheviks who were inept at enterprise while drinking a potion of ideology. The same story with Mao's China in 1949, by destroying free enterprise, much like the Soviet Union did. The government did not have the financial means to impose its largeness, and subsequent finances required for sustained tyranny.

In both cases, tyranny needs to sit on the shoulders of enterprise, as well as the industrious, and of course, in the case of China, it did just that. First Chinese Li Yuanpeng Peng, and then Premier Zhu Rongji, in the late 1990s, liberalized the economy from its double-digit inflation, where 60 percent of the people lived on less than $1.90 a day, streets were jammed with bicycles not cars. Today, it is a leading economy, the workshop of the world, powered by some of the foremost technologies.

As much as Clinton and his advisors thought that with trade liberalization would come freedom, they were greatly mistaken. The end game of the China's Communist Party was to grab even more power by letting free enterprise flourish via the WTO. As a concession for China opening its markets, the U.S. just had to surrender its annual rite of deciding whether to grant China most-favoured-nation status as a trading partner, ensuring full access to the American market unconditionally.

Now, with the economic might to impose more sustainable tyranny in China, and global intimidation such as caustic ambassadors, insisting that Huawei 5G be accepted (technology stolen from Canada's Nortel), the new game is in play. Because now, the CCP can comfortably sit on the shoulders of state-managed capitalism to financially augment themselves. After all, why let a thing like capitalism within a communist state get in the way of tyranny? Perhaps it is the best form of financial despotism. Of course, the communist party is skilled at dividing and conquering, keeping everyone in check by pointing at the wealth disparity as being caused by the free enterprise within a central state. Sound familiar?

State-Run Capitalism

Now that we come full circle to 2021, China's iron-fisted ruler, Xi Jinping and his apparatus of propaganda, has turned his claim to fame to address wealth inequality in China, since even he has to appear as having some regard for his subjects.

According to the *Wall Street Journal*, "China minted more than half the world's new billionaires last year, surpassing the U.S. as the first country with more than 1,000, according to Shanghai-based research firm Hurun Report. Yet more than 600 million Chinese people—more than 40 percent of the population—subsist on average monthly incomes of less than $157, Premier Li Keqiang said last year. That was about $40 below the average amount spent each month by those living in rural China in 2020."[6]

In 2020, the top 1 percent of individuals owned about 30 percent of China's wealth, up 10 percentage points from 2000.[7] In the U.S., the share of wealth controlled by the top 1 percent increased only 2.5 percentage points to 35 percent during the same period, according to Credit Suisse Group AG."

Even if you have a good education as a quality control technician and live in Beijing or Ningbo, small two-bedroom condos are in the $900,000 USD range, and with a salary of $1,080 per month, it is out of range for many, especially, when interest rates are in the 5.5 percent range.[8] Add this to the fact that Chinese banks demand large down payments, it is no surprise that Zhang Hang, a 25-year-old, says that even with considerable help from his parents, he

6   Stella Yifan Xie, "What's Driving Xi Jinping's Economic Revamp? China's Social Mobility Has Stalled," Wall Street Journal, November 14, 2021, https://www.wsj.com/articles/xi-jinping-china-economy-growth-poverty-tech-beijing-11636915358

7   Ibid.

8   Frank Tang, "China GDP: 2022 Economic Growth Target Is Within Reach, 'But It Will Come at a Cost,'" South China Morning Post, March 11, 2022, https://www.scmp.com/economy/china-economy/article/3170010/china-gdp-2022-economic-growth-target-within-reach-it-will

hasn't earned enough to buy a place of his own in Beijing.[9] In contrast, the wealthy buy multiple properties, and what we are seeing is China's own wealth gap.

But who created this in the first place? Was this type of crony capitalism not a by-product of the CCP, its financial support for builders, and loose monetary policy with a history of bailing out the incompetent sectors at the expense of creating macroeconomic distortions in the economy? Further, no one in China accumulates great wealth without friends in the Communist party getting a piece. Is this starting to sound like America and the West?

And now Xi Jinping, the supreme leader of China's Communist Party is riding on his white horse to diminish China's wealth inequality gap. Yes, the same Xi Jinping and CCP that created these pricing distortions in various asset classes, from real estate to equities, and building ghost cities, while subsidizing property developers, including Evergrande, which has defaulted on bonds. If you are an associate with the Communist Party, you live well, and prosperity does not occur without their ordained blessings as their officials' line-up to take bribes from the private sector. And it you fall out of favour, you are silenced and put in their doghouse, just ask Jack Ma, the founder of Alibaba, who was reeled into line after doing his imitation of Elon Musk, and James Dean.

Xi Jinping's true agenda is to pit the unwealthy against the wealthy to consolidate power, while absolving the CCP from its shortcomings. This way with the support of a complacent peasants' class, who make up much of the military, the party has a well-gaslighted audience to enforce rule.

It is nothing more than a classical ruse, and it is here that government in America and the West is extracting its new Chinese based model, where it gets many of its cues of tyranny, as it ushers in its very own Cabalatocracy. Chinese culture historically is more

9   Stella Yifan Xie, "What's Driving Xi Jinping's Economic Revamp? China's Social Mobility Has Stalled," Wall Street Journal, November 14, 2021, https:// www.wsj.com/articles/xi-jinping-china-economy-growth-poverty-tech-beijing-11636915358

agreeable to authority, and is less prone to questioning it, whereas in Western culture we were taught to question authority, which is perhaps the genesis of democracy that first sprouted in the West for this reason. However, unfortunately now we are sitting back and not questioning authority, because the government gods will unleash on us three distinguished members of the Cabalatocracy establishment, namely Academia, Mainstream Media, and the overlords of Silicon Valley. After the digital minions deliberate in the social media forums, the victim that threatened groupthink with intellectual clarity will have a fate that will reside under the finality of the digital guillotine.

America's State-Run Capitalism and the Cabalatocracy

In the *Brave New World* of dystopia that Aldous Huxley wrote about in 1932 he states, "...most men and women will grow up to love their servitude and will never dream of revolution."[10]

The agenda is control—John Locke, Rousseau, Jefferson, Madison, and the American Constitution are just ghosts in the night that must sail away into the romanticism of history. The new type of central control will not affect the means of production as in classical socialism. After all, as stated earlier, Soviet communism and Mao's China were both economic disasters, and if they were not, we would have a successful example of central planning with a stranglehold on means of production. In fact, both regimes would still be intact.

However, the West should never be underestimated for its unparalleled inventiveness. America has learned from China's Communist Party, who holds citizens on a short leash, because in this new type of tyranny, the West will keep its subjects on a longer leash as it has figured out how to build a more sustainable tyranny. The new Communism will not be Nikita Khrushchev debating

10   Aldous Huxley, Brave New World (London: Chatto & Windus, 1932).

Nixon in the 1959 Kitchen Debate, the red scare and Joe McCarthy looking under every rock for a communist.

In defence of communism, it just needed to be tweaked a fair bit so it can be more plausible and durable. The first thing one needs to understand in the Great Reset is that you cannot simply crush capitalism; why kill the goose that lays the golden egg? After all, what would all the mostly parasites in government, the bureaucracy, and civil service live off the avails of? In other words, sustainable tyranny needs economic fuel from its host, and must not be too heavy as to crush its food dependency chain.

The new communism is going to be more formidable, and sustainable in the West than anything prior, because of its more complex "plug and play" organisation. This state-run capitalism will put China to shame when it comes to coercion and gaslighting, because it has a more refined and proven establishment. After all, America has the Cabalatocracy of Empire, and why crush it when by working in cohesion, it creates the 800-pound gorilla that not even Mao and Lenin could fathom or had the inventiveness to create.

By outsourcing the various branches of state control, much like a business, the whole will be greater than the sum of the parts. It is here where we finally meet face to face with the Cabalatocracy starting with the official mouthpiece of the government, namely the presstitute legacy media that is uploaded on YouTube for double the propaganda effect. After all, some high-end media production of the news is more visually indelible than an amateur YouTuber that might have a larger audience. And with YouTube placing the legacy media at the top of their streams, they still have weight as a propaganda arm, as they protect the dismal outcomes of the failed pandemic response that have us running on the same stationary treadmill for two years. Gone are the days of a fair and balanced free press, as they do their finest rendition of the former USSR Pravda, and the South China Morning Post.

In the Great Reset, the ruling class weaned on crony capitalism will have their members, profess their cosmic vision, and to promote left-wing policies of confiscation, under the guise of wealth redistribution as long as it is not their own money, eventually the high priests of Hollywood enter the picture. When not waving virtuous accolades or rubbish on Twitter, they succumb to lobby groups that infuse their particular bent, under Social Impact Entertainment, meaning having enough woke characters in film and television series to rationalize the irrational as part of ongoing behaviour modification. Hence, after having their hard-drives reformatted by the legacy media, the plebeians and the aspiring bourgeoisie dole out $25, including popcorn, attend the movie theatre to get another fix of propaganda and "wokism" infused into a film. All this is included in the price of admission.

Moving to Silicon Valley, according to Professor Shoshana Zuboff, author of The Age of Surveillance Capitalism, Google has surveillance strength on nearly every aspect of our lives; and the data they hold basically can incriminate us at their will, since all our activities and preferences are kept on their databases. Google is highly skilled at lobbying Washington, where most lawmakers are clueless about their algorithms and advanced data science. The trail leads all the way to the White House, especially when we consider the case that in the Obama years, 197 individuals had migrated from working for government to Google, and 61 went from Google to government, including 22 White House officials. In other words, the spook agencies, Silicon Valley and the Executive branch are firmly imbedded in each other at some level. This is the smoking gun of censorship and its agenda.

Naturally, when truth or empirical reasoning veers its villainous head, the Cabalatocracy calls 911 and Silicon Valley shows up, commissioning its dogs and censors, which is compromised of fact checkers funded by dark money as is the case of Center for Countering Digital Hate (CCDH) and PolitiFact. The minions cannot believe their eyes or their reformatted minds, for that matter, when their all-star lineup shows up in their superhero outfits at the stadium of glory, with fans cheering hysterically as the greatest dream team ever assembled appears, which includes the most noted members of Silicon Valley's Cabalatocracy, YouTube, Instagram, Wikipedia's idealogue editors, Google's algorithms, Facebook, and Twitter to put the horror of truth back in its shoe box!

The idea is to protect their party who, with its fragile ego, gets rattled at the sight of truth and reason. Then the digital minions get an equitable distribution of gaslighting as they tap their phones in a feeding frenzy for their favourite party and perceived causes, while being further induced into digital Stockholm syndrome. With a prescribed injection of censorship, any detractors of the narrative are tried in Silicon Valley's kangaroo court, found guilty as spreaders of misinformation, and dumped into the pile of the Salem witches. The war on truth has many willing and unpaid soldiers armed with smart phones and apps as the only required military training.

Then there are corporations, including banks that misconstrue their products and services as virtue, as they too come out with corporate commercials played in the legacy media and pre-rolls on YouTube, further guiding the minions, plebeians, and aspiring bourgeoisie on how to think. When corporations are not busy contributing to their chosen party, or lobbying government and corrupt politicians, and affecting elections, while they promote Lockheed Martin, a company that is always looking for a good war to juice their financials, or promote unproven drugs like Pfizer, or in the case of Coca-Cola's constant promotion, which effectively is causing type 2 diabetes in the Black community and elsewhere.

Of course, other members of the Cabalatocracy approve with polite applause as their work is a complement to the overall agenda. And this brings us to Wall Street that along with the Central Bank and government are causing the greatest wealth divide, unprecedented, sustained inflation including a 9.6 percent jump in wholesale prices, asset price bubbles, and macroeconomic distortions that is clobbering the middle-class, and the deplorables both of which are expendable in the brave new world of the Cabalatocracy's great reset.

Government, of course, is key and central to the great reset. In this more centralized environment and as mentioned, it will not take over the means of production, but will live off its avails. But as part of the new reset, the plebeians and digital minions will ask for more government and vote for the same, which brings me to a quote from Elon Musk when he was perplexed on why the youth had a thing for large government, and a disdain for corporations: *"The government is simply the biggest corporation with a monopoly on violence. And where you have no recourse."*[11]

Yet the youth blames corporations and gives government a pass. Realizing that many spears have been thrown at government, I posit that large government and individual freedom cannot coexist, as large government always leads to tyranny, there is no exception in recorded history.

Of course, it goes without saying that the Central Bank, after they merge with the Treasury, will work to further deflect the ineptitude of their actions, as they display the Frankenstein's monster they created, better known as inflation, the demise of the middle-class, which they will deny they engineered, as it is always someone else's fault. And by holding the distribution of the U.S. dollar now in digital Central Bank-controlled format, they will put the final invisible collar around the neck of their citizens, who will be begging for their next fix. Whoever does not toe the line in the brave new world called the Great Reset, could see their money disappear. Of course, this will all be assisted by other noted members of the Cabalatocracy, including the spook agencies.

Then in the backdrop much like Phil Spector who provided the "wall of sound" recordings for artists in the 1960s, academia will provide their own wall of sound, as they dis on corporations, even though they live off them, or any elements that flirt with reason or consider academic discourse, or the marketplace of ideas. Remember, academia is never accountable for their failed ideologies. Still, academia is competent at waving their virtuous wand of egalitarianism and wealth distribution, where professors who earn more than the plebeians and minions, conveniently ignore their own hypocrisy as they live off the vestiges of capitalism and its endowment funds.

11   "Elon Musk on EV Subsidies, Corporate Titles, and China: The Full Transcript," Wall Street Journal, December 8, 2021, https://www.wsj.com/articles/elon-musk-on-ev-subsidies-corporate-titles-and-china-the-full-transcript-11639012832

Government who pretty well has a monopoly on K-12 education and propaganda, children are being taught to confess their family's private matters to teachers, as the educational system becomes the self-appointed arbitrators of virtue, replacing the churches confession box or the tightness of family and community that once held the society together.

This is how the foundations of state tyranny is gradually introduced in a society under the anesthesia of ideological virtue. Once all is in place, the show can begin as young impressionable hard drives will be reformatted for those that enter through the dark galleys of public education, where brainwashing is passed off as education.

The Cabalatocracy being perceived as a compassionate organisation, they will tap the shoulders of big pharma, as pandemics mysteriously appear and disappear, which they only have the answers for, only to be alleviated with their benevolent hands. Then those who do not graduate with the prescribed behavioural modification outcomes from the oasis of propaganda being administered by other members of the Cabalatocracy, will be put in medical gulags, re-education camps, be given behaviour remodeling serum, as big pharma and others will help enforce the war on truth and reason! So why bother with truth or reason, since after all it is an antiquated idea from the Greek philosophers and the romantics? In this brave new world, truth is so yesterday!

A More Durable Communism Dressed as Equity

The America, the West we once knew, will no longer be recognizable in this dystopian inference, while voting for one's preferred political party, especially in Canada, is like playing musical chairs on the Titanic.

In the name of equity and wealth redistribution, people will get eased into the new reset, first with softer terms like "democratic socialism," meaning that at least they get the right to choose who is going to hang them. For occasional reinforcement as part of the behaviour modification program, the Central Bank will fill up digital wallets, which will make them more loyal to their master. Later the true agenda will come into play, which is more and more like communism, but this will not be the communism of Brezhnev's Soviet Union or Mao's legacy, on the contrary, in this scenario, it will be more modern and sustainable, with willful, and compliant oppression.

This might need some explanation, consider the fact that Mao and Lenin never had the infrastructure of the free market or established press, because much of this had to be created; may it be the five-year plans, the KGB, politburo, Academy of Sciences, Pravda, or a modern military. It was after the fall of Czar Nicholas that the Bolshevik Revolution took place, and after Mao's ouster of Chiang Kai-shek and the Nationals from the mainland to Formosa, better known today as Taiwan. Still in these two new communist states, institutions had to be built at the expense of much human carnage.

Put simply, both these communist states did not have the societal infrastructure to hit the pavement running, in relative and absolute terms when compared to the United States. They never had the spook agencies like the CIA, NSA, FBI, Homeland Security in place that uses Silicon Valley technology. They did not have Hollywood that seduces and enamours; they never had established government institutions, and a legal system; they did not have the financial capital of the world, namely Wall Street—there was no Central Bank, and no perceived system of voting. Neither did they have the surveillance state of Silicon Valley, where its addicted captives come into their digital hive willingly to confess as the public hears more about their personal life then the world's oldest Catholic confessional boxes. Mao or Lenin did not have the legacy media both domestically and internationally to orchestrate unrelenting propaganda. They never had the finest educational institutes that America and the UK enjoy that would be immediately complicit in their Orwellian dystopia, where they could churn out a generation riding high on romantic egalitarianism and the cult of "woke", masked as virtue.

And no, these communist states did not have a pharmaceutical industry that gaslights through the compromised media, questionably funded fact checkers with a clear mandate to obscure reason and truth, and medical boards that are a political albatross. Currently, doctors and other medical professionals that do not follow the narrative of a life on prescription dependency as opposed to healthy lifestyle choices, and one solution only to a pandemic, are censored, slandered with their livelihood at peril by the enforcement arms of the medical boards, like old school Chicago-style gangsters.

In fact, it took aver 60 years to create some of what America and the West have, in terms of the institutions of the Cabalatocracy, all of which have been discussed. (For diagram refer to Figure 13.5.)

In the great reset, America will lead at some level, as they create a new never-before-seen form of communism. In this model they have learned well from modern China and will allow a capitalist system to sustain the centralized control of government and be intertwined with them. In fact, I dare to say that America has a more sophisticated form of capitalism, especially in financial engineering, as well as the luxury of having the reserve currency of the world, at least for now. In this model, everything from the media, Silicon Valley, Wall Street, corporations, and the balance of the Cabalatocracy will further amalgamate, if you will, to create the most formidable ruling class in human history. The occupiers of these institutions will constitute America's aristocracy, and they will pretend to deplore free markets, but will protect and keep the larger corporations alive and vibrant to feed off them like parasites, to fulfill their insatiable lust for power. Because they know that the goose who laid the golden egg is essential in this model, and any attempt by a new sheriff in a white hat to come into Dodge City to be a hero and institute reason and bring back freedom will be met by gunslingers that the townsfolk will mostly stand behind, as they rather enjoy the enticement of their safety and slavery, as opposed to a new dawn of liberty that will surely bring uncertainty.

Unlike Mao's China and the Soviet Union governments, this new model has the advantage of the capitalist system that government not only lives off of, but with complicit institutions in commerce that prop it up. It is, in essence, a complicit arrangement and monopolies in contravention of anti-trust laws, and runaway crony capitalism. It is naïve to not consider that these institutions are not already working together, both overtly and complicitly to help cover the mountains of prevarications and lies with an end game agenda of obfuscating truth. Anyone who has lived under totalitarianism will immediately recognize the game, for example, people from Eastern Europe, and Mao's cultural revolution.

Unfortunately, in the West, there is nearly no one alive that has had to fight for freedom from tyranny, hence, their safety beleaguers weakness, which evolves to dependency and then slavery. In this strange dystopia of 1984 George Orwell wrote, "*The past was erased, the erasure was forgotten, the lie became the truth.*"

A parliament of the elite will form a permanent ruling party of the new aristocracy, much like the Soviet Politburo with complicit institutions both public and private that play their essential roles, as they will share power and live off the fruitions of capitalism in a neo-communist totalitarian state. President Eisenhower in 1961, during his farewell address, prophetically warned about the military industrial complex, as today, the manifestation of all these more complex and complicit institutions makes it more powerful. Together, they should make for thrilling theatre on Broadway of the real-life story of the Cabalatocracy, as it will be a sold-out show for years to come with people lining up in the rain to buy tickets!

The plebeians, the deplorables, middle-class, the digital minions, and the likes will all get their fix of egalitarianism, equity, and wealth redistribution with consistent gifts of digital money via universal basic income in their accounts in exchange for docility and votes. When questioned, they will defend and point with billowing chests to their democratic right to vote, as they choose their next oppressive master, which will sadly obscure their self-inflicted slavery. Perhaps Socrates was wise to have concerns about democracy, since he felt that people needed to be educated on voting, as he much preferred a monarchy. In the books of the Republic, Plato insinuates that democracy is actually one of the later phases during the decline of an ideal state.

Most will own nothing and be happy, according to Klaus Schwab (he and his elite WEF cultists should practice the same), while the Central Banks will continue to print fiat money to acquire hard assets and equities for themselves as well as their crony capitalist cohorts, just before the fiat system collapses and they eagerly switch to Central Bank digital currency, which will be sold as the second coming of the Messiah. The last vestiges of self-reliance, individuality will be stabbed and culturally slayed in the town square and sold off as an antiquated relic of self-serving greed that had to be reckoned with. And with a new government issued digital currency, it will be easy to rule over these willing participants of slavery, through behaviour modification of giving and taking, kissing and slapping, until they will be happy in their state of abuse, and only ask for more in their Stockholm syndrome.

The aristocracy that is an essential branch of the Cabalatocracy will have enamoured fans, much like groupies in a rock band, or followers on Instagram, and Twitter since everyone wants to join the anointed with their cosmic vision. The most promising of the enamoured will be indoctrinated into the lower echelons of the Cabalatocracy, where they will be rewarded with privilege, rank and opulence, much like those associated with the communist party in the former Soviet Union and today's China. Toe the line, and privileges as well as upward mobility exists for a few, and they will be held up as a glowing success stories of this new dystopia.

Of course, this toxic oasis of corruption will be built on a combination of crony capitalism and communism, where truth will lie in a sad tragic rubble of unrecognition.

Many smaller and medium sized companies will be thrown under the bus, that is, unless, of course, they are needed by the Cabalatocracy.

This scenario described could easily manifest itself, as America and the West will school China on how to create the finest model of a capitalist state within a communist infrastructure.

Much like the lead up to World War II, there is going to be disruption and upheaval, and it is imperative that one protects themselves and their assets in the brave new world.

To participate in the future of tomorrow comes with risk and disruption, to ignore it will put one at peril.

In the *Practical MBA for Economics*, together we have met many of the great economists from Adam Smith to Keynes, we have visited economic peril in the way of depressions, we have seen how the free markets, after President Harding, have had piece by piece distorted and bludgeoned. Bretton Woods was visited and the great reset of the mid-20th century, and the advent of the U.S. dollar, as we considered the perils of inflation and unemployment, while reflecting on technology. Somewhere we considered both the benefits and caveats of trade, while deliberating the powers of government and the Central Banks. This trip, at the expense of affecting our queasy stomachs, took us on the roller coaster rides of booms and busts, financial crises, their cause and effects. We have considered the case of capitalism, sometimes loathed yet essential, while propelling the world it has built even in its distorted version. We then opened the history vaults, visited sovereign debt defaults, and eventually we found the courage to stand up to emotional denialism by coming to terms with the horrors and orchestrators that reside in the house of cards. Finally, to find solace and peace, we sought "shelter from the storm" to realize that the individual is not an idea, it is our sense of self, always in conflict with the failure of collectivism, it is this moment where we first consider the existence of the Cabalatocracy.

The Western cultures gifted the world with the first functioning examples of the coexistence of freedom and order, but have now transgressed to subjection and disorder, on the way to what might be the final tragic destination of subjugation and order. To derail this will require men and women with bold resolve, but in a safe society candidates and a free will are in short supply.

With the lessons, as well as insights of the past and present, it is here where I trust with some clarity, I leave you hopefully fuller, in that uncertain, opaque, and often enigmatic dimension. A place where the human psyche meets the horror, yet glory of what will come, as to only give us a moment to ascertain, ponder, and infer upon the future of tomorrow!

It is this doorstep of the unknown where we all reside.

Printed in Great Britain
by Amazon

86286223R10298